PRECISION AND SOUL

ROBERT MUSIL

PRECISION AND SOUL

Essays and Addresses

Edited and Translated by

BURTON PIKE *and* DAVID S. LUFT

THE UNIVERSITY OF CHICAGO PRESS

Chicago and London

BURTON PIKE is professor of comparative literature and German at the Graduate School of the City University of New York.

DAVID S. LUFT is associate professor of history at the University of California at San Diego.

The University of Chicago Press gratefully acknowledges the contribution of Inter Nationes toward the publication of this book.

Originally published in volumes 8 and 9 of Musil's *Gesammelte Werke* edited by Adolf Frisé. Copyright © 1978 by Rowohlt Verlag Gmbh Reinbek bei Hamburg.

The University of Chicago Press, Chicago 60637
The University of Chicago Press, Ltd., London
© 1990 by The University of Chicago
All rights reserved. Published 1990
Printed in the United States of America
99 98 97 96 95 94 93 92 91 90   54321

Library of Congress Cataloging-in-Publication Data

Musil, Robert, 1880–1942.
    [Selections. English. 1990]
    Precision and soul : essays and addresses / Robert Musil ;
edited and translated by Burton Pike and David S. Luft.
        p. cm.
    Translation of selections from v. 8-9 of Gesammelte Werke in neun
Bänden.
    ISBN 0-226-55408-2 (alk. paper)
    1. Musil, Robert, 1880–1942—Translations, English. I. Pike,
Burton. II. Luft, David S. III. Title.
PT2625.U8A25 1990
833'.912—dc20   90-10828
                                                                      CIP

[There is] an abiding miscommunication between the intellect and the soul. We do not have too much intellect and too little soul, but too little intellect in matters of the soul.

Musil, "Helpless Europe"

CONTENTS

ESSAYS 1918–1933

ADDRESSES 1927–1937

FOREWORD

Musil, who was born in 1880 and died in 1942, achieved his initial success in 1906 with the publication of his first novel, *The Confusions of Young Tör-less*. It was not until 1911 that his next works of fiction, two novellas, were published as *Unions*; this coincided with the start of his activity as an essayist. After the First World War he published two plays (*The Visionaries*, 1921, and the farce *Vinzenz or the Girl-Friend of Important Men*, 1924) and three novellas (*Three Women*, 1924). From about 1924 until his death in 1942 he chiefly devoted himself to his great unfinished novel *The Man without Qualities* (parts of which were published in 1930, 1931, and 1943). For much of his career Musil was a working journalist of an intellectual kind, writing serious articles on culture, contributing to the literary feuilletons of newspapers, and reviewing books and plays for various newspapers and periodicals.

In his essays as in his fiction, Musil kept insisting that life is not a sequential narrative of packaged actions or ideas but a fluid network, changing from one minute to the next, in which actions and ideas are inseparable from sensations and emotions. He sought to reconcile this view of the way the mind functions with an appropriate ethical framework for living, or working toward, the right life. Language, broadly defined, plays a central role in this process; it is primarily referential, although in some mysterious fashion it also points beyond the empirical world. Musil's goal in language as in thought, running through these essays and all his writing, was, as he put it in *The Man without Qualities*, a union of "precision and soul," with the aim of getting people to change so that their ideas and values reflect the dynamic, problematic reality of the modern world and not the outworn values of a hundred and fifty years ago.

The essays in this volume are drawn from volumes 8 and 9 of the *Gesammelte Werke in neun Bänden*, edited by Adolf Frisé (Reinbek: Rowohlt, 1978). The German edition is a sound reading edition but not a critical one. It was the result of a compromise between the incomplete three-volume edition of the 1950s and a critical edition, which would be premature: Musil's manuscripts are extremely difficult to decipher, and some are still in the process of being transcribed. Our selection is extensive and includes all the major essays (and all Musil's addresses) contained in the 1978 German edition.

Since Musil's purpose was to engage his readers' thoughts and feelings directly with the problems of modern culture, we decided to make this an edition for the general reader rather than overburden it with scholarly apparatus. In making our selection, we chose those essays that we judged would be of greatest interest to a wider English-speaking audience, which would not have access to the originals. To let these eloquent essays and addresses speak for themselves, as far as our translations will allow, we have kept explanatory notes to a minimum, relying on information at the head of the texts where the reader might need some orientation, and supplying occasional notes to identify unfamiliar figures or references. We have made a deliberate decision not to include an index to this volume. Musil's essays tend to be associative and were meant to be read as wholes; ideas and names that might ordinarily be indexable are almost invariably allusive rather than substantive.

There is a distinctive break in tone and subject matter between the essays Musil wrote before the First World War and those he wrote after: the language of the prewar essays is, like his fiction of the period, syncretic and impressionistic (Musil, who mocked literary and cultural movements for their oversimplifications, would have called it "pressionistic"); the postwar essays, while retaining the passion, are written in a clear, incisive, and more public style.

This book has been a truly collaborative effort. We had originally planned to work as a troika, with Philip H. Beard as our third partner, but it proved impracticable to synchronize three busy schedules at different universities. In recognition of our initial intention we are pleased to include Professor Beard's translation of "Helpless Europe." David Luft and I each translated half the remaining pieces, he doing the more philosophical, political, and cultural essays, I the more literary ones and the addresses. We have gone over each other's work as well as our own many times; we can only hope that any remaining errors have been held to a minimum. The responsibility for the stylistic unity of the volume as a whole rests with me as general editor.

All the ellipses, fragmentary sentences and paragraphs, and notes in the text are Musil's unless otherwise identified (many of these essays are fragmentary drafts). Material between slashes is Musil's variants; material in square brackets (mostly supplying punctuation and filling out abbreviations, and occasionally completing names) is the translator's or editor's (mine), unless otherwise specified. Titles in brackets indicate that the original was untitled. The dates following the titles are those of composition; dates of first publication can be found in Appendix B.

. .

Walter Benjamin wrote that "there is no muse for philosophy, and there is no muse for translation, either." Translators can only sigh at this conspicuous oversight. Musil's subtle, idiosyncratic, and somewhat elliptical style in these essays is one of passionate abstraction that poses formidable problems for the translator. The abstraction is in the ideas, the passion in the cadences and rhythms: a throbbing intensity infuses every line, while every line is also the product of an incisive analytical mind trained and well versed in such fields as psychology, philosophy, mathematics, and engineering. The typical Musil essay is a mix of feelings, ideas, and observations that finds its inner logic not in the linearity of narrative sequence but in a dynamic process of thinking. In this mix concepts operate as functional relationships within changing contexts, not as fixed entities. As a result these essays are not, typically, polished wholes with a beginning, a middle, and an end. For Musil the essay is a chain whose meaning consists rather in the sequence of its links than in the chain as a whole. As he himself puts it,

The thoughts of the essay lie firmly and immovably fixed in a basalt consisting of feelings, will, and personal experience, in such combinations of idea-complexes that only in the spiritual atmosphere of a unique inner situation do they give off and receive bright light. Essays make no claim to universal validity, but have the effect of people who captivate us and slip away without our being able to fix them rationally, and who prick us with something intellectually that cannot be demonstrated. Essays may also contain contradictions; for what in the essay has the form of a judgment is only a snapshot of what is not capturable except in a snapshot. Essays are subject to a more flexible, but no less strict logic. [From a 1913 review, not included here, of a number of collections of essays by various writers.]

Musil was, of course, consciously basing his open conception of the essay on Emerson and Nietzsche, for whom the essay was also a passionate, assertive, and challenging call to change one's life.

Insofar as one can pin down national characteristics in a summary way, Musil's use of language to represent the world in his essays is peculiarly Austrian: he perceives the world neither empirically, as is generally the case with the English essay, nor as a systematized abstraction, as often happens with the German essay, but rather in elaborate sentences that are the expression of an Austrian temperament for which multiplicity and multivalence are the measure of reality.

A thorny problem for the translator is that in all these selections there is an openness of conceptual terminology and a remarkable subtlety in using words for their nuances, so that the same word needs to be translated differently in different contexts. *Geist*, the most notorious of these, comes out variously as "mind," "spirit," or "intellect," depending on which element is felt to predominate; but frequently Musil relies on the harmonics of the other meanings, which English cannot do. English, as a highly concrete language with an enormous vocabulary, uses specific terms for specific situations, so resonances in English tend to be the resonances of individual words. German, like Greek and Latin, uses a much smaller vocabulary to cover many diverse categories, so that words, especially conceptual and abstract ones, will often have a "cross-field resonance" in which, while one connotation is clearly indicated, the others clearly echo, as in the case of *Geist*. Musil was a master at conjuring these resonances. This is why, in a few cases where he uses the same material twice, we felt that the differing context called for a slightly different translation. In the absence of a corresponding vehicle in English (to say nothing of the different cultural context), we decided to stay as close as possible to Musil's considerable idiosyncrasies of thought and language.

We have also translated *man* as the impersonal "one" for the most part, although it is usually rendered in English as "you" or "we," or as a passive construction. This is because usually Musil uses *man* not as a pronoun of personalization or generalization of the personal, but as referring to a detached intermediary agent between subject and reader. This "observer" may be partial or impartial, but he stands apart from the "action"; yet he is still, from that vantage point, an active agent; hence the passive is rarely appropriate.

In keeping with its challenging nature, Musil's style in these essays also demands that the reader participate in their ongoing thought rather than simply observe it from the outside: the reader is expected to catch and be caught up in the emotional nimbus of ideas. While some of the historical references might be difficult for us to catch now, Musil's larger concerns strike the reader of our time as extraordinarily vivid descriptions of our own dilemmas and feelings, as Professor Luft makes clear in his introduction.

The addresses Musil gave present additional problems. To mention just one, in translating the memorial speech on Rilke we were faced with two questions in, or properly speaking, *before* translating: who was Rilke, and

what did Rilke represent for Musil? We could count on some general acquaintance with Rilke on the part of our readers, but it is not easy to make
clear through the translation itself what Musil's attitude to Rilke was. Aside
from admiring his poetry, Musil identifies himself with Rilke as a writer
whose true greatness has been misunderstood by his time, and when he attacks the philistine age it is on his own behalf as well as Rilke's. The key to
making this evident, insofar as it can be done through the translation itself,
lies in capturing the cadence, the rhythm of Musil's writing: partly polemi-
cal and heated, partly personal and sensitive, it is a charged rhythm. In this
instance, Rilke is serving as a surrogate model for Musil as well as the subject Musil is depicting. Here, capturing the tone helps the translator capture
the meaning.

Historically, these essays open a window on what it *felt* like to be a committed intellectual in Germany and Austria between the Teens and Thirties
of this century—not a partisan, but a passionate outside observer. Approaching our task from two directions—David Luft is an intellectual historian,
my fields are comparative literature·and German—has been of enormous
help in deciding exactly what, in these wonderful and complex essays, had to
be translated, and how it might be done.

Burton Pike

INTRODUCTION

Aside from the one great attempt by Nietzsche, we Germans have no books about people, no systematizers and organizers of life. With us artistic and scientific thinking do no yet come into contact with each other. The problems of a middle zone between the two remain unsolved.

"Commentary on a Metapsychics"

These essays, written between 1911 and 1937, offer a perspective on modern society and intellectual life that still speaks quite directly to the situation of the late twentieth century. Robert Musil looked out on the world from Vienna and Berlin during the most catastrophic period of Europe's transition to contemporary society. His essays address science and mathematics, capitalism and nationalism, the changing roles of women and writers. And yet these immediate and tangible problems often dissolve into even more complex social and intellectual relationships, so that the reader begins to see the world and the possibilities of thinking and feeling in new ways.

Musil was one of the great essayists of the twentieth century, part of an extraordinary generation of essayists writing in German that included Thomas Mann, Hermann Broch, Walter Benjamin, and Georg Lukács. But among the novelists and philosophers of his generation, no other made the mode of the essay more central to his way of thinking. In this Musil belonged as well to a broader tradition of essayists: skeptics and explorers of

I want to thank my editor and cotranslator, Burton Pike, and also Peter John and Elaine O'Brien, for their readings and suggestions. My thanks as well to the Academic Senate Research Committee of the University of California, San Diego, for supporting my work on this project.

inwardness with whom he consciously identified himself, notably Montaigne, Emerson, and Nietzsche. Musil is best known for his novel *The Man without Qualities,* itself largely essayistic in form and intention, but he still does not have a clear identity in the English-speaking world. And Musil is not yet, as he should be, a full participant in the intellectual exchange of our culture along with Hegel, Marx, Nietzsche, Freud, Wittgenstein, phenomenology and existentialism, and the arguments of structuralism and poststructuralism.

1

Unlike Thomas Mann or Brecht or Einstein, Musil did not become a part of intellectual culture in the Anglo-Saxon world during his lifetime, and he was still unknown to most Americans when he died in exile in Switzerland in 1942. Born in Austria in 1880, Musil belonged to the generation of writers in German who reached creative maturity in the decade before the First World War. This was the most important generation for the German novel: Thomas Mann, Broch, Kafka, Hesse, Döblin, and Musil himself.* Musil grew up in the late imperial society of Habsburg Austria, and it was Brno, a city of Germans and Czechs in Moravia, that played the largest role in his youth. His father was professor of mechanical engineering at the Technical Institute there, and Musil's own early training and education were strongly shaped by the positivistic scientific atmosphere of late nineteenth-century Austria, an intellectual world that was relatively untouched by the historicist, idealist traditions of the German Empire. As an Austrian who was trained in engineering and experimental psychology he shared in the sophisticated scientific culture we associate with Kafka and Wittgenstein; like them he was influenced not only by Darwin and Mach, but also by Nietzsche and Schopenhauer. Musil's positivist background was much like Freud's, and it shared a good deal with the perspectives of Franz Brentano, who was a major philosophical influence on Freud, Husserl, and Musil's mentor in Berlin, Carl Stumpf, and who set the tone for the positive treatment of science and empiricism in Austrian universities.

As a young man Musil went to Germany to study; for a few months at the Technical Institute in Stuttgart and then from 1903 to 1910 in Berlin, where he studied philosophy and psychology and pursued a literary career. After his marriage to Martha Marcovaldi in 1911 he became an archivist at the Technical Institute in Vienna. Just before the war broke out in 1914 he

---

*On Musil's relationship to this generation of intellectuals, see my *Robert Musil and the Crisis of European Culture, 1880–1942* (Berkeley: University of California Press, 1980).

returned to Berlin as an editor of *Die neue Rundschau*, Germany's most important literary journal. Thus in the decade before the war he developed his characteristic position between the intellectual worlds of Vienna and Berlin, although with stronger connections to Berlin and to Paul Cassirer, Alfred Kerr, and Franz Blei, as well as to a variety of literary periodicals, many of them part of the Expressionist movement which dominated literature and the arts in Germany after 1910.

During the prewar years Musil described himself as a conservative anarchist in the process of turning into a democrat, who would vote Liberal or Social Democratic until something appeared that could actually work. He was contemptuous of political life, especially in Austria and Germany, in part because of its preservation of "outworn ideologies such as Christianity, monarchism, Liberalism, and Social Democracy. . . . Since these ideas are never actually put into practice, the parties give these ideologies the illusion of meaning and sacredness, which in addition to everything else is also a sin against the spirit" ("Political Confessions of a Young Man"). And he came to believe that this rigidification of political ideologies was itself one cause of the First World War and of the form it took.

The war drew Musil back into Austrian life—as an officer on the Italian front, as the editor of a military newspaper, and as a bureaucrat in the Republican Defense Ministry after the collapse of the Austro-Hungarian Empire in 1918. In the 1920s Germany became the real center of intellectual life for Musil (although he lived in Vienna), but his empiricism and his sympathy for modern science made him unusual in the intellectual world of Weimar culture, where both left and right were strongly influenced by German idealism and critical of liberal rationalism. These were years of intense politicization and polarization in German history, and like all writers of his generation Musil was deeply affected by the war itself and by the series of political, social, and economic crises in Germany and Austria, which began at least by 1917 and continued into the 1920s at various levels of intensity, thanks to war, revolution, inflation, hunger, and general social disorder. After the First World War, many of Musil's essays addressed major political themes, such as the Treaty of Versailles or *Anschluss* with Germany, but the overriding concern of these postwar essays was the larger catastrophe of European culture and ideology that found expression in the war. He believed that his generation's attempt to confront the formlessness of morality and civilized life had been foreclosed by the outbreak of the First World War and that the generation born after the Second World War would have to begin again where his own generation had begun before 1914.

The essays Musil wrote between 1911 and 1914 are a blend of youth and great intelligence. What makes the prewar essays important is the application of an original mind to the most individual realms of feeling. In these essays he begins to craft a way of thinking that encompasses order and disorder, the elasticity of humanity and culture, and the enormous complexity of modern life. Already apparent in the prewar essays is Musil's devotion to a specific intellectual form that orders what we know (or nearly know) about the history and possibilities of the soul's movement in a nonmetaphysical, nonreligious sense. What is most valuable in essays such as his reflection on Catholic modernism, "The Religious Spirit, Modernism, and Metaphysics," is that Musil saw what was essential or potentially valid in decaying institutions, and he had ideas about what living meaningfully in the modern world could be like. He was resistant to the side of liberalism that simply expressed the rationalism and bureaucratization of the modern state, and there was something in the religious atmosphere of prewar intellectual culture that he valued in a purely human way. Musil shared Nietzsche's interest in the value of a truth, and he proposed the intellectual goal of discovering and organizing truths that would give "new and bold directions to the feelings, even if these distinctions were to remain only mere plausibilities; a rationality, in other words, for which thinking would exist only to give an intellectual armature to some still problematic way of being human: such a rationality is incomprehensible today even as a need" ("The Religious Spirit, Modernism, and Metaphysics").

The postwar essays are distinguished above all by the much greater role of politics, of practical considerations and issues. Many of these essays will be important for historians because of the substantive themes addressed: the state, nation, race, and culture, in the historical context of central Europe during the fascist era; but Musil's views extend beyond this to a way of thinking about politics in the modern world. The addresses of the 1930s in particular were written with the politics of Hitler and Stalin in mind, but there, as elsewhere, his views were expressed not as a statement of fixed dogmatic positions but as part of the ongoing process of opinion, response, and thought in which they are embedded. There is also an important change of scale in the later essays and addresses: the early essays are for the most part tentative explorations of states of individual and cultural consciousness that sometimes have the feel of fiction, whereas the later essays ordinarily address more general issues, often in a more systematic way. The postwar essays also display a more crystalline prose and a clearer structure.

Musil felt strong affinities with German classical humanism (with Goethe, Schiller, and the late eighteenth century) and with a conception of the education of mankind that rests ultimately on individuals, and he often emphasized the distance Europeans had travelled in passing from this vision to the collectivist social forms of the 1930s. But he also looked forward to a second beginning for this tradition after the defeats of the 1930s. Even without the extreme political forms of the 1930s, modern society had diminished the importance of individuals in favor of larger economic and professional structures. This was most dramatically apparent in the mass experiences people had in the war and the feelings of impotence in those individuals who did not support Hitler. All this pointed to the vulnerability of the "free spirit," which depends on individuals rather than collectivities such as religious and political associations. Musil believed that the size of the social body had increased without a comparable increase in the number and kinds of bonds holding people together in common activity. And yet Musil himself was an instance of Wilhelm von Humboldt's notion of "significant individuality as a power of the spirit that springs up without reference to the course of events and begins a new series. He saw nodal points and points of origin in creative people who absorb past things and release them in a new form that can no longer be traced back past their point of origin" ("The Serious Writer in Our Time"). At the heart of Musil's intellectual mission was a defense of the writer's intellect against the German academic model of the mind, a defense of the creative individual:

As the sensitive person who is never given his due; whose emotions react more to imponderable reasons than to compelling ones; who despises people of strong character with the anxious superiority a child has over an adult who will die half a lifetime before he will; who feels even in friendship and love that breath of antipathy that keeps every being distant from others and constitutes the painful, nihilistic secret of individuality; who is even able to hate his own ideals because they appear to him not as goals but as the products of the decay of his idealism. ("Sketch of What the Writer Knows")

2

Musil had an impious view of his own literary heritage. He knew where its peaks were—Goethe and Rilke—and how much triviality was served up to *Gymnasium* students in the name of national pieties. His view of literature was more international and cosmopolitan, and he understood that in his generation most of the valuable impulses had come to German literature from the outside—from France, Russia, and Scandinavia. Moreover, he argued in favor of a concept of literature that would take into account film as well as the essay. Philosophy had an important place in Musil's concept of literature, but he would also have understood why few people today read philosophy. He distanced himself from anti-intellectualism, but he believed that most of the inherited fund of philosophical argument was locked into words and concepts that hardly touch the life and feelings of the average person in our civilization. He believed, indeed, that the proper philosophy of our time is to have no philosophy.

Musil resisted conventional philosophical discourse. He had little to say about Hegel, although he is more interesting when he writes about Kant, as readers of *Young Törless* will recall. Musil admired the Vienna Circle in principle, but we do not know for certain that he even read Wittgenstein. Although he took some note of the emergence of existentialism in his own generation, he mistrusted what he regarded as the unnecessarily idiosyncratic language of Heidegger. He refers from time to time to Plato or Aquinas as great minds, and he believed that the philosophers around the School of Chartres had come close to his own understanding of science and mysticism. But the philosophers who engaged him in earnest were mainly modern, mainly empirical, and at the experiential edge of academic philosophy, such as Mach, Nietzsche, and Emerson, the three minds who shaped Musil's thinking as a young man. Musil's remarks about Freud are recurrent and stimulating but rarely developed in earnest. In his approach to the problems of the human sciences Musil was closer to psychology than to linguistics, but his own training and research were in experimental and Gestalt psychology rather than psychoanalysis or other clinical approaches. Much of his writing in the 1920s was sociological and strongly recalls Weber's analyses of ideologies and developments in modern anthropology. But Musil's real devotion was to literature.

Musil wrote during the first third of the twentieth century—in a culture somewhat different from ours. But it is perhaps helpful to imagine him addressing three characteristic intellectual types who continue to play important roles in our culture. The first of these is the type of the scientific or empirical mind in the broadest sense, including not only the natural sciences but the attempts to address the human sciences (and human values) in the same spirit. At the opposite pole is a literary type who responds to the problems of modern culture by bemoaning the loss of some earlier culture or value (whether Christian or classical or German) and the threat that scientific intellect poses to feelings and traditional values. Since the scientist ordinarily received less appreciation in Musil's culture than in ours, Musil often came aggressively to the defense of science and intellect. And since Musil's generation was shaped by a powerful neoromantic and anti-intellectual resurgence, Musil's role within literary culture was often to criticize emotionalism and irrationalism. A third type is distinct from the scientific positivist and the literary intellectual, but related to both. This type might be characterized as rationalist in the broadest sense. Here Musil had in mind most of the systematic side of the history of Western philosophy, but he was also thinking of most attempts in morality and ideology to order the material of human feeling and action. In the attempt to extend the search for laws and regularity into the realm of ethics, this type is related to the scientist; and he is related to the more emotional, literary type in his effort to provide a firm order for the feelings in order to cope with the chaos and formlessness of modern life.

Although Musil had affinities with each of these types, he believed that the problems which the individual confronts in modern society require a new way of thinking and feeling that is unlike any of them. This new way combines the scientists' passion for facts and precision with the creative person's understanding that the striving for mundane lawfulness can kill. What he called "essayism" is Musil's attempt to shape the inner life, to order the realm of the feelings and find a middle zone between science and art. He wanted to achieve a balance of thinking and feeling that is neither science nor ideology nor premature philosophical totality, to shape the inwardness that was left unformed by the collapse of traditional ideologies in the early twentieth century.

Musil was attracted not to arguments or doctrines, let alone to a systematic philosophy, but rather to ideas and thinking as they are embedded in a process of lived experience—and this is the kind of thinking he had in mind under the heading of the essay. His indifference to the reassurance of dogma is a suspension of belief that not all readers find attractive. His essays assault the needless ideological rigidity of intellectuals, while appreciating the role that irrationality plays in human experience and motivation. Instead of despairing about a lost worldview, Musil was constantly absorbing the world as we actually *live* it and trying to understand its possibilities on the assumption that we barely understand a civilization that is just now coming into being. Musil offers little that is programmatic or prescriptive; instead his essays display a consistent will, an intuition of what it might be possible for human beings to *be*, whether in thinking or feeling, in sexuality or political organization. But always, what he knows must be understood in relative, functional terms, in a context, in a world of other possible intentions and values.

Musil believed that the authentic sources of ethical motivation are partly nonrational or suprarational, and that there is no fixed body of morality on which to depend. But essential to his conception of the motivated person and the ethical imagination is a respect for objectivity, reality, and what is impersonal. He wanted to understand and form the feelings without distorting what can be known of the factuality and lawfulness of the world, and he regarded the question of how to balance unrestrained subjectivity with completely objective behavior as one of the major difficulties facing his culture. "A person is not only intellect, but also will, feeling, lack of awareness, and often mere actuality, like the drifting of clouds in the sky. But those who see in people only what is not achieved by reason would finally have to seek the ideal in an anthill or beehive state, against whose mythos, harmony, and intuitive certainty of rhythm everything human presumably amounts to nothing" ("Mind and Experience"). Musil wanted to mediate between objectivity and subjectivity, between the complexity and uncertainty of reality and the needs of the feelings. He wanted to apply the values of freedom, truth, and objectivity (the values that the West had applied to intellect and to physical reality) to the feelings and the inner life. And this began with the rejection of the great ideological superstructures of modern idealism in order to begin the search for new ways of being human—in literature and life. "If I want to have a worldview, then I must view the world. That is, I must establish the facts. The smallest fact from the connection between the soul and hormonal balance gives me more perspectives than an idealistic system" ("The German as Symptom").

3

I also believe that few people remain completely untouched by the thought that instead of the life they lead there might also be another, where all actions proceed from a very personal state of excitement. Where actions have meaning, not just causes. And where a person, to use a trivial word, is happy, and not just nervously tormenting himself.

To allow people to find this attitude—to approach it, after which each person could adjust it for his individual case—is the task of ideology. Guiding the soul. Informing the soul. ("The German as Symptom")

Musil's essayism was aimed at "a *possible* person" and "a *possible* image of the world" (his sketch for an introduction [Appendix A]). This essayistic way of thinking tended to fall between the subjectivity of the self and the impersonality of objective truth. Musil's passionate commitment to individuality and the recovery of an immediate relation to experience was directed against nineteenth-century liberalism's illusions of individualism and accomplishment, but he was also opposed to all fixed ideologies, whether religious or political or professional, and to all other encapsulations of self and experience. Musil's importance lies not so much in any specific view as in his way of thinking about modernity: both about the tremendous quantity of information made available to us daily and about the confusion of moral and aesthetic values that Western culture has experienced since the turn of the century.

What characterizes and defines our intellectual situation is precisely the wealth of contents that can no longer be mastered, the swollen facticity of knowledge (including moral facts), the spilling out of experience over the surfaces of nature, the impossibility of achieving an overview, the chaos of things that cannot be denied. We will perish from this, or overcome it by becoming a spiritually stronger type of human being. But then it makes no sense from a human point of view to try to wish away this enormous danger and hope by stealing from the facts, through a false skepticism, the weight of their facticity. ("Mind and Experience")

Musil was preoccupied by the attempt of Europeans to come to terms ideologically, morally, and culturally with the transformation of their world in the late nineteenth century. He believed that the task of intellect was to build up the ethical and emotional life of the individual in modern civilization, and that this could be done only by coming to terms with one's real life. Giving up on intellect in the name of "intuition," "soul," and "feeling" could only lead to 1914 or 1933. He believed that we feel the way we think, but that our ideas fail to keep up with reality. The important feelings always remain the same, but they can be locked into ideologies that prevent us from understanding our experience. He believed that something like this happened in 1914, when all of the traditional ideologies—Marxism, Christianity, and Liberalism—failed or broke down. These and other ideologies had failed either to give sense to the peace or to resist the enthusiasm for war because they no longer informed the inwardness of most Europeans or described the reality they were actually living. What was needed was a new and more patient way of thinking that overcame rigidity—in thought as well as feeling. He wanted to ground the possibility of the absolutely motivated life, to create a spirituality commensurate with the conditions of life in modern civilization.

Musil's essays (even before 1914 and still more consciously in the 1920s) emphasized the transformations of modern life that make it difficult for individuals to find sense in their experience, to feel themselves part of a meaningful community, to balance their thinking and feeling, and to adjust to constant changes in ways of living. He believed that the sheer scale of modern life had transformed the individual's relationship to culture, and he certainly recognized that science and technology created new conditions for human experience. But he did not believe that this situation represented a desperate loss of old cultures and values but rather, simply a new situation. He wanted to develop a new way of thinking about life in modern civilization that would maximize the human being's capacity to be open to experience and respond to it in a flexible way.

We strive to conform the incalculable curve of being to the rigid polygon that passes through our moral fixed points by breaking the rectitude of our principles into ever new angles, but still without ever achieving the curve. It may be that the inner life has the same need for fixed connecting points that thought does; but as ideals these have led us to a point where things can hardly go any further, since—as everyone knows—in order to approximate it to reality we must burden each ideal with so many limitations and disclaimers that hardly anything is left. ("'Nation' as Ideal and as Reality")

For Musil, an ideology was concerned not with the systematic organization of knowledge but with the feelings, with the ordering of the inner life. "Ideology is: intellectual ordering of the feelings; an objective connection among them that makes the subjective connection easier" ("The German as Symptom").

From Weber's generation Musil inherited a world divided between relativism and the commitment to the ethical without objective justification, between a meaningless civilization and the lost individual. As Musil put it before the war, in describing the individual's absorption in his profession or narrow interest: "Today the individual as a person stands in the midst of a community of incomprehensible size . . . . Of all the unheard-of experiences that, as a child, he believed were waiting for him, he experiences nothing . . . . he feels the need to make the unknown distances smaller, . . . and everything in him that is idealistic becomes localized" ("Literary Chronicle"). At the same time Musil remained skeptical throughout his life about the capacity of political elites to understand this situation and come to terms with it; he believed, indeed, that modern societies were run by "powerful, specialized brains in the souls of children," who continue, "in ignorance of any other culture," to lead "the life of the spiritual hamlet from which they happen to have come" ("Political Confessions of a Young Man").

In Musil's generation nationalism became the nearly universal vice of political life, and his critique of it illuminated his understanding of the emotional structure of the individual and the fragments of emotion that never find order or sense or integration into the self: "Wherever the national ideal becomes the goal of a struggle of a passionate yearning it degenerates into an inhibition, the way a hysterical knot forms in people; an inhibition that is always demanding to be, finally, entirely itself instead of constantly having to be able to dissolve and redefine itself in the normal course of everyday tasks" ("*Anschluss* with Germany"). Here Musil displays his Austrian distaste for nationalism but also demonstrates his acute awareness that an ideal can be a dreamlike demand that fails to respect the actual contours of reality; yet he was determined to shape experience and institutions toward the future. "Therefore, when life does not live up to a system of ideals, I am not able to see much idealism in them. One should finally realize that it is not that life fails to conform to ideals out of disobedience, as in school, but rather that the mistake must lie with the ideals" ("'Nation' as Ideal and as Reality"). But it is important to see that there is an enormous amount of idealism hidden in Musil's assumptions about the unity and universality of human nature, in his emphasis on its malleability, as much for good as for evil, in his trust in empiricism and intellect, and in his belief that the emotions can outgrow their attachments to rigid preconceptions and habits.

Musil's view of what the nation represents set the tone for his treatment of modernity and ideology, although his definition of the nation is utterly removed from anything a nationalist might have recognized: it is perhaps more nearly a description of the emergence of modernity as a common European experience—but with an empirical sharpness and metaphoric brilliance that carry well beyond the period when he wrote it.

In the course of an extraordinarily confusing historical period, millions of individuals have stuck their heads into a world that they understand to very different degrees and in very different ways, from which they want completely different things, of which they see little more than the thread of their own livelihood and hear some great general noise, in which here and there something echoes that makes them prick up their ears. This enormous, heterogeneous mass, on which nothing can quite make an impression, which cannot quite express itself, whose composition changes every day as much as the stimuli that act upon it, this mass, nonmass, that oscillates between solid and fluid, this nothing without firm feelings, ideas, or resolution, is, if not itself the nation, at least the really sustaining substance of the nation's life. ("'Nation' as Ideal and as Reality")

Musil's strength was in his capacity for complex perceptions and powerful intellectual concentration and in his gift for compressed formulation and simile. But he repeatedly confessed his failure to give his ideas systematic form, and it is difficult to get a clear overview of his central themes and arguments. Musil resists reduction, and his mind is wide enough to take in more varieties of experience than most ideologies and philosophies care to admit. But certain themes and arguments persisted throughout his productive life, and he did have an overall view, which was most directly developed in his essays of the mid-1920s, especially in "The German as Symptom" and "Toward a New Aesthetic." Two fundamental distinctions run through the whole of Musil's essayistic production, even in the early essays where his characteristic formulas have not yet appeared. One is a distinction between kinds of knowledge: the firm, dependable knowledge of science, which Musil called "ratioid," and the individual experiences that concern the writer and the essayist, which Musil characterized as "nonratioid." A second distinction parallels the first; however, it concerns not experience as knowledge but the human being's relationship to experience—experience not as it becomes knowledge, but as it becomes experience. Here Musil distinguished between the ordinary condition of everyday life and what he called the "other condition," between the normal relationship to experience—the attitude that lies at the basis of science and the practical mastery of the world—and the relationship to the world that characterizes ecstatic and contemplative states. These two concepts—the nonratioid and the "other condition"—are fundamental to all of Musil's essays and require some clarification.

4

Musil argued throughout his essays that "the pointless battle in contemporary civilization between scientific thinking and the claims of the soul can be solved only by adding something, a plan, a direction to work in, a different valuing of science as well as literature!" ("Mind and Experience"). He wanted to find a way of thinking that balanced an understanding of the continuities and conceptual linkages among experiences with a respect for what is individual in experience, and he formulated this problem in terms of "the distinction between ratioid and nonratioid, which I did not invent, but have simply named so poorly" ("Mind and Experience"). This distinction is similar to Wilhelm Dilthey's distinction between *Erfahrung* and *Erlebnis*, that is, between the communicable, repeatable experiences of science and the unique experiences portrayed by the writer. For Musil, the writer represented "a specific attitude toward and experience of knowledge, as well as of the material world that goes with it." The ordinary attitude toward knowledge Musil called *ratioid*, by which he meant not rational, but simply knowledge "that science can systematize, everything that can be summarized in laws and rules; primarily, in other words, physical nature" ("Sketch of What the Writer Knows"). This "monotony of facts" is what characterizes scientific knowledge. What is a great virtue in science, the ability to tuck new facts into the old order, to subsume things under categories, and to label them unambiguously, turns out not to be the right way to proceed in the realms of art and ethics. Despite his great respect for scientific knowledge and his complex view of how such knowledge is formed, Musil's own interest in knowledge was aimed primarily at the realm of ethics and aesthetics.

Musil believed that the distinction between ratioid and nonratioid helped to explain the poet's resistance to secular rationalism—since the temptation of the kind of rationalism Musil criticized was to formulate human experience in a way that leaves out everything that "does *not* come under the laws of the rational mode of understanding" ("Literati and Literature"). Musil emphasized the connection between science and civilized morality, and he satirized the ways in which science and rationalism had been applied to inwardness. Like Nietzsche, Musil wanted to move the life of the mind away from academic philosophy in the direction of art and literature, but he wished to do so in a way that was not antagonistic to intellect and science. Musil disliked the appeal, popular in his day, to special faculties of intuition or feeling or to the personality and genius of the writer. The operative distinction, he asserted, concerned the nature of the facts under consideration and not the subjectivity of the poet, who was not required to be a visionary, a madman, or a child. "The significant person is the one who commands the greatest factual knowledge *and* the greatest degree of rationality in connecting the facts: in the one area as in the other. But one person finds the facts outside himself and another within himself; one meets with coherent sequences of experience and another doesn't" ("Sketch of What the Writer Knows"). Musil's intent in arguing the case for the nonratioid was to envision an age when both methods would be recognized in their proper domains.

Just as Musil emphasized the special tasks of the writer's intellect in the realm of the nonratioid, he also distinguished between the normal relation to experience and the heightened relation to experience that is common to art, religion, and erotic excitement, which he called the "other condition." This intensification of experience—whether contemplative or Dionysian—is characterized by a weakening of the role of ego in the social sense; it expressed Musil's interest in "a deeper embedding of thought in the emotional sphere, a more personal relation to the experiencing subject." Common to all experiences of the other condition is that "the border between self and nonself is less sharp then usual . . . . Whereas normally the self masters the world, in the other condition the world flows into the self, or mingles with it or bears it, and the like (passively instead of actively)" ("The German as Symptom").

Musil's distinction between the ordinary relation to experience in everyday life and science and a second relation to things that he called the other condition refers not to objects of experience but rather to different ways of experiencing these same objects. He wanted to relate the routine of everyday life to heightened conditions of the ethical-aesthetic self. He regarded moralities and ideologies not only as remainders of outmoded systems of ethical energy, but also as traces of a heightened relation to the world, which he believed could be equally apparent at a concert or a church service, falling in love or meeting a boxer in the ring. But he believed that his own generation was only beginning to understand this other condition, which had grown confused and corrupt in modern culture and expressed itself socially in pathological forms, such as August 1914.

What interested Musil was not a particular version of goodness, whether in politics or business, but rather conditions related to love and poetry, which "rise above the transactions of the world," that element in secular life that he regarded as "religious in the most important sense." Musil re-

minded his irrationalist contemporaries that the fall from grace into calculation did not occur with modern science. Instead, science and capitalism are
simply the most successful recent forms of the normal relation to experience. The manipulative relation to experience is always the principal one,
because the tasks of survival have always come first; instrumental, calculating thinking and the readiness to use force must always have been in the
forefront, while inner immersion in experience and an indifference to ego
and mastery must always have been exceptions, always jeopardized by the
danger of annihilation.

Immediacy of experience is much of what people seek in sexuality, religion, or music: the predominance of feeling over the abstractness and dead-
ness of so much of our everyday experience. But Musil thought it was a
mistake to blame intellect and thinking for the abstract, lifeless quality of
everyday experience. The mistake is not thinking, but rather the entrap-
ment of either thinking or feeling in the formulaic or the practical. Musil
believed that the tendency toward rigid formulation was "the enemy of the
saint as well as the artist, of the scholar as well as the legislator" ("Toward a
New Aesthetic"). The limitations in the way we organize ordinary experience are justified by pragmatic considerations of mastery, but they eventually empty experience of value, and the narrowing of the mind to fixed
preconceptions is as much a danger for the feelings as for the intellect.

Musil believed that every art is called both to give faithful account of
reality and to liberate its audience from the formulaic, but literature (especially the novel) is relatively better equipped to describe reality, while the
nonverbal arts often move more quickly to the other relation to experience,
to an unconceptualized experience, a world without words. Among writers
of his own generation, Musil believed that Rilke had come closest to expressing this unconceptualized experience. He identified Rilke with a kind of poetry that "cannot forget the restlessness, inconstancy, and fragmentation
that is concealed in the whole of life; one could say that here it is a matter,
even if only partially, of that feeling as a totality on which the world rests
like an island." Musil admired Rilke's poetry because his thoughts and similes did not unfold "by leaning up against the wall of some ideology, humanity, or world opinion," but arose "with no support or hold from any
side as something left over, free and hovering, from intellectual movement"
("Address at the Memorial Service for Rilke"). Whether in the novel, the
essay, or the lyric poem, the task of literature for Musil was the recovery of
the motivated life.

David S. Luft

ESSAYS 1911–1914

The Obscene and Pathological in Art
1911

This essay appeared in the journal Pan *as part of an ongoing controversy over censorship. The influential critic Alfred Kerr had attacked the head of the Berlin police, Herr von Jagow, who had confiscated an earlier issue of the magazine for having published Flaubert's diary of his travels to Italy and Egypt (1844–51). Musil is also lashing out at the restrictions placed on a lecture by the Danish author and educator Karin Michaëlis. Still close to the inward world of his two novellas published as* Unions *the same year, this essay shows Musil's conception of art as the manifestation of an inner world more complex and disturbing than most strict moralists can imagine.*

The writer of this essay is the author of that psychologically absorbing book that appeared as his first several years ago and was praised to the skies by serious critics. It was called *The Confusions of Young Törless* and has up to the present not reached the printing of the "dangerous age" of puberty.

There is something undeniably boring about ordering thoughts long familiar to reasonably clever people for the sake of some external purpose. But in certain circumstances there is nothing that might seem to one well-known enough not to bear frequent public repetition. Flaubert has been forbidden in Berlin. Alfred Kerr has already irrefutably demonstrated in a few words in these pages that this was done in violation of the law, which specifies that

3

sexual arousal in a representation is allowed if it is connected with an artistic purpose. But in Frankfurt a lecture by Karin Michaëlis on the critical age in women has also been forbidden and could be delivered in Munich only before an audience of a single sex—either one. And consider the unanimity of the authorities and German public opinion in the following cases:

A dealer and promoter might exhibit works of Japanese wood-carvers in which several couples tangle in monstrous embraces like clusters of grapes, with limbs groping like feelers across the ground or winding back into themselves like corkscrews in the unutterable loneliness of the subsequent letdown, eyes hanging like trembling, whirling bubbles over vacantly staring breasts. Or an artist might represent the basically still barely conventional, middle-class procedure that Frenchmen, Félicien Rops in his letters for example, ecstatically call "kissing the sacred mount," we suppose on account of the man's back being bent in canine lust, and the woman's distant, vaguely searching indifference. Or a writer might depict how someone looks at his mother's trembling hands and lies, lies, and lies again that they are trembling more and more and getting more and more tired, something that is absolutely not true but has been invented to hurt her. Or he might depict a close relative naked on the operating table, already gnawed at by the knife; or he might have felt how one grabs a woman in an accident, like an object, and in doing so undresses her: hasty resolves of one's constricted horizon of consciousness. Felt, too, without thinking about regions one has never entered.

But someone, anyone, speaks—objectively, minimally, medically—someone in charge, a gentleman, and something lies proffered, motionless, a wound, half-strange here, flowerlike, some half-bleeding sliminess, opening up amid the stretched white skin of a side like a mouth . . . an automatic association . . . kissing it, pressing on it the defenseless skin of the lips. Why? Who knows? An external similarity? Melancholy? . . . For a split second horror at the idea, and then again words of command and quick manipulations. And suddenly an unforeseen reckoning, quick as lightning, with one's own life, lying in wait for who knows how long for this accidental moment of weakness: commands, manipulations internally as well, even in being alone with oneself this idiocy of the straight line, the laid-out path crumpling up the soul with roaring emptiness around what is most solid, most dependable.—This is an inhibition (felt perhaps as resistance against the learned professor and the tense impartiality of his colleagues, or perhaps with fright as a soft bumping into oneself in the darkness deep inside), a scattering; leaves of a disintegrating tangle, "I," flutter slowly, oscillating. Distant, pale irrelevance, otherwise suppressed and temporally hectic half-actions, pieces of arousals, never brought to climax yet still sexual, still not permitted here, still Promethean, are palpable for the first time. They become—sometimes sharpened for a while just by the sharp, patient step-by-step of scientific language—bright as day, horrible, called upon to defend their existence, hostile and already filled with the torments that, living harmlessly close beside each other, will gently suffocate them. And a writer would insist on it: naked, even a mother or a sister is a naked woman, and is stripped in one's consciousness perhaps precisely under conditions that make it appear most reprehensible. Something like this, but better written.

Herr von Jagow has, in a transparent case revolving around actions no one would be seriously reproached with for carrying out, merely overlooked the artistic aim associated with representation. This artistic purpose was not stuck on didactically, but lay in the value of the humanity with which it was endowed, which hovered light and trembling around the way things were stated. But there are cases where for all the human value of what is depicted, and for all the artistic means with which it is depicted, and in spite of all respect which need not be denied them, the artistic purpose sufficient to justify the representation is either denied or subordinated to another purpose. To exclude these cases from being considered as artistic representation is the agenda not only of police chiefs and district attorneys, but also, today, of magazines trying to climb on the bandwagon of art. I have pointed out such cases and will speak about them: there are things about which one does not speak in the German cultural community. I am not the only one this fact fills with shame and anger, and to counter it I will argue for the viewpoint that art ought to be permitted not only to depict the immoral and the completely reprehensible, but also to love them.

In saying this, I am assuming that—and in general it will not reasonably be denied—from the standpoint of society some things are quite properly considered immoral, reprehensible, and pathological. But in that case there are only three possibilities for the assertion being made: Either the obscene and pathological, as depicted by an artist, is no longer really at all itself. Or one would have to assume (aside from those cases where it is presented only for contrastive effect, in order to be attacked and such—cases that, moreover, do not exist) that an artist's preference for these things is something different from what one reasonably demands of "real" seriousness (that is—in order not for a second to admit an artsy confusion with the artist's roguery and exuberance—an artistic seriousness). Or, even in life, the obscene and pathological have their good aspects.

All three assertions are in a certain sense true.

Art may well choose the obscene and pathological as its starting point, but what is then depicted—not the depiction itself but what is represented as obscene and pathological—is no longer either obscene or pathological.

Leaving aside all the folderol about the mission of the artist, this is an axiom that already follows from sober observation of the specific functions that give rise to the work of art. If one has other than artistic desires, one does not gratify them through art; it is much simpler to gratify them without distraction in the real world, and they can be sufficiently gratified only in the real world. To experience the need for (artistic) representation means— even if desires in real life should provide the impulse—*not* to have a pressing need to gratify them directly. It means to depict something: to represent its connections to a hundred other things; because objectively nothing else is possible, because only in this way can one make something comprehensible and tangible, . . . as even scientific understanding can only arise through comparisons and connections, and as this is the only way human understanding can arise at all. And even if these hundred other things were to be obscene or pathological: their connections are not, and the tracing of these connections, never.

It is no different in science. One finds all sorts of things in scientific books, harmless anatomical indecencies and perversities whose inner picture one can hardly even reconstruct out of the elements of a healthy soul. But one should not let oneself be deceived by disguises such as empathy, social obligation, or the glittering savior's mask that doctors wear; one's interest in these processes is direct, it seeks knowledge. Art too seeks knowledge; it represents the obscene and pathological by means of their relation to the decent and healthy, which is to say: art expands its knowledge of the decent and the healthy.

An artist receives the impression that something he has avoided, some vague feeling, a sensation, a stirring of his will, is dissolving in him, and its elements, released from the connections in which habit had frozen them, suddenly acquire unexpected connections to often quite different objects, whose dissolution spontaneously resonates in the process. In this way pathways are created and connections exploded, and consciousness drills new accesses for itself. The result is at best mostly an imprecise notion of the process to be depicted, but surrounding it is a dim resonance of spiritual affinities, a slow undulation of further networks of emotions, will, and ideas.

This is what really happens, and this is what a sick, ugly, incomprehensible, or merely conventionally despised process looks like in the artist's brain. But so too—linked in a chain of associations, seized by an emotion that lifts him up, draws him along, and removes the pressure of his weight— must it appear in the brain of him who understands the representation. This totality is the object that is depicted, and on this rests—and on nothing else, not on any lyre-twanging morality—a purifying, automatically desensualizing effect of art. What in reality remains fused together like a molten drop is here dissolved, untangled, interwoven—made divine, made human. It is enough to have once held the work of a pathological person in one's hands in order to understand the difference in the product.

To be sure, art represents not conceptually but imagistically, not in generalities but in individual cases within whose complex sound the generalities dimly resonate; given the same case, a doctor is interested in the generally valid causal connections, the artist in an individual web of feeling, the scientist in a summary schema of the empirical data. The artist is further concerned with expanding the range of what is inwardly still possible, and therefore art's sagacity is not the sagacity of the law, but—a different one. It sets forth the people, impulses, events it creates not in a many-sided way, but one-sidedly. To love something as an artist, therefore, means to be shaken not by its ultimate value or lack of value, but by a side of it that suddenly opens up. Where art has value it shows things that few have seen. It is conquering, not pacifying.

It therefore sees valuable sides and connections in events that horrify others. In most collisions between art and public opinion either these values are not recognized, or (the typical case) even the attempt to recognize them is rejected out of horror at the circumstances in which they have been acquired. The artist is advised that in a healthy person the impressions he is dissecting have no constituent elements, but are disgusting through and through. And against this there remains just one thing better than modestly recalling the evidence that for quite some time clung to the sun's revolving around the earth: taking up the fight on the most fundamental level of these contradictions and standing up for the theory that—in this age which has so much anxiety about health and decadence—the boundary between mental health and illness, morality and immorality, is sought in a much too coarse, geometric way, like a line that is to be defined and respected (every action having to be on one side of it or the other), instead of our recognizing that there is no such thing as simple spiritual poison, but only the poisonous effect of a preponderance of one or another element of the spiritual mix. One can be no less sickened with disgust about this by an excess of popular ideas than by unpopular ones, but one must realize that every action, every feeling, every intention, every area of interest, or however one might tote up what is usually trotted out to accuse a writer and his characters of spiritual inferiority, can just as easily be healthy as sick; that in every healthy soul there are places identical to those in sick ones, and that deciding which is which depends only on the totality—on a relation of number, surface, weight, tension, value, or any other complicated relationship—of those details that today are divided into the healthy and the sick. This significance ought not to be bestowed on these details for all time, but only according to what they produce in a specific case in a specific soul.

In fact there is no perversity or immorality that would not have, as it were, a correlative health and morality. This assumes that all the elements of which perversity or immorality is composed have their analogy in the healthy soul that is fit for social life. And this assumption is correct and will not be difficult for any writer to prove, whatever examples one might set before him. Any perversity can be depicted; the way it is constructed out of normal elements can be depicted, since otherwise the depiction would not be understood. If the desensualization of the depiction rests on this activity of construction, then the humanizing of the model rests on its possibility. But if, furthermore, the process of constructing can contain, in a decisive passage, worthwhile elements, so can the assessment of value. This is the key to that combining of elements that makes understanding and the artist's love for the immoral and perverse possible.

This process aims at an intellectualized, as a chemist would say "enriched," representation. But in life this can also be joined by an exact primary model. So that while it is not to be denied that the sick and immoral exist, what needs to be brought into the focus of thought is that the boundaries must be drawn differently. To give an example: one must admit that a sex-murderer can be sick, that he can be healthy and immoral, or that he can be healthy and moral; in the case of murderers these distinctions are indeed made.

As soon as values gain maturity by means of an art that does not avoid such matters, it is unworthy and fainthearted to rail against them. This is not an area one will get into unless enticed by certain values, but the chubby-cheeked standpoint of "healthy-at-any-price" German art is narrow-minded. Dangers need not be denied. There are half desires that do not reach as far as daring to be realized in life yet attempt this in art, and there can be people who use life as well as art for this purpose. But in doing so they either suffer this energy-transforming effect (and then it does not matter in the least whether the people involved incidentally happen to be sick as well), or there really can be no talk of art. Still, all this might not be enough to exclude every side effect; it might also be true that among the public people gladly absorb only the raw material, true that art achieves its effect in more dynamic, less disciplined inwardnesses than science does and is therefore more dangerous; but these are all difficulties, and not objections. Science too has its train of spiritual marauders, but it still will not be proscribed when, as is beginning to happen, it will have penetrated further among ordinary people than it has today. What is done for science must also be done for art: accepting undesirable side effects for the sake of the main goal, and moreover diminishing their importance by making this main goal more magnificent. For one should reform forward, not backward: social illnesses, revolutions, are evolutions inhibited by a conserving stupidity.

In everyday life too people will have to learn to think differently in order to understand art. Let us define as morality some common goal, but with a greater measure of permitted side paths, and agree that the movement in that direction should be based on a strong, forward-directed will, in order not to suffer the danger of plopping into the smallest quibble on the road.

Novellas
1911

This is one of a number of sketches for a foreword to Unions, *two novellas* (The Perfecting of a Love *and* The Temptation of Quiet Veronica) *that constitute Musil's most extreme experiments in representing minutely shifting states of feeling and consciousness as the axis of living in the world. Musil elsewhere calls this difficult fictional technique "the maximally charged path, the path of the smallest steps."*

Right on the surface are characters, temperaments. A little deeper, honest people have specks of rascality, rascals specks of honesty, the great have moments of stupidity, etc. This is the sphere of the great epics, and of the depiction of great people in the drama. Here the masters are Tols[toy], Dost[oevsky], Haupt[mann], Thackeray. A little deeper still, and people dissolve in futility. It is the sphere in which one breaks off in the midst of a passionate outburst. One has the feeling that here nothing is left of oneself; there are only ideas, general relations that do not have the inclination or the capacity to form an individual. This is the sphere in which these novellas take place, and it is from this sphere, from its existence, that they derive their conflict. From this deeper sphere taken seriously; not from the futility, but from the tragic enthusiasm it engenders.

All love tragedies contain the same superficiality: the accidental entry of the third. Rilke said it, and demanded an adultery that only takes place between two people. Adultery between two persons (carried out with any third person who happens to come along, a representative of the first sphere) because of the awareness of the existence of that innermost sphere in which lovers dissolve in futility, in things that are as much themselves as they are others, and in which the individual is only the transitory point of reflections, all of which are valid applied to someone struggling to get still closer to the beloved than in the consummation of love.

Or in the words of the poet: " . . . is not every brain . . . a high-noon solitude" " . . . on this loneliness . . . could be made together." That is before. Then an accident, an urgent trip, a strange man in the utter clarity of his ridiculous existence.

The technique: in the writer, nothing stands between novel and story except weightiness. Those means by which people have always tried to distinguish drama, novel, and story are secondary characteristics. In particular, what makes the difference between novel and story is the degree of empathy, the degree to which one puts oneself in it (least in the drama). One could try to determine that these stories were formed by disgust with storytelling.

Profile of a Program
1912

In these two heavily corrected drafts Musil is tentatively probing for a way to broaden his fictional technique beyond the encapsulated hermeticism of The Perfecting of a Love *and* The Temptation of Quiet Veronica. *He stands back and asks larger questions about the function of the writer, about how the writer can be "empathetic and thoughtful"—and modern and accurate—rather than "decorative, exaggerated, pathetic," yet still reach a public more at home with the latter kind of fiction.*

Soul is a complex interpenetration of feeling and intellect. What sort of interpenetration is a question that belongs to psychology. But no one should mistake the fact that the element of growth in this coupling lies in the intellect. To talk about the wealth, breadth, depth, greatness, charm, or humanity of feeling is misleading; notice from what primitive spheres these metaphors are still borrowed. It is intellect that brings these quarter-tone gradations upwards into feeling.

Strong emotional experiences are for the most part impersonal. Anyone who has hated another person so much that only chance stands between that person and death knows this, as does whoever has fallen into the catastrophe of a deep depression, anyone who has loved a woman to the dregs, anyone who has beaten others bloody or ever come up behind another person with muscles trembling. "Losing one's head," language calls it.

Emotional experience is, in itself, poor in qualities; qualities are brought to it by the person who has the experiences. Nuance, however, is nothing but making a presumably simple experience the mediator between two or more experiences. Nuance is feeling, its entire intellect[ual]-emot[ional] vicinity and the connecting pathways.

The feeling of the dying person . . . is not to be distinguished by any other means from that of an insignificant suicide; the ultimate melancholy surrounding the resolve. The greatness of two loves cannot be measured against one another. Then too, through all hist[orical] time the supply of feeling has been limited. The same thing happens over and over; a few perversities are missing or added, they appear and are instantly assimilated, that is all.

Our time is irritated and successful. Warlike and brutal like almost no other, ingenious and teemingly overenergized in a newly unique way. It runs over the individual, sucks him dry: Anabaptists, Protestants of feeling, romantic poets, are stuck in small ridiculous benevolent communities in the same cell with liberal leftist pastors, dancers to Beethoven, and health nuts. No one can deny that every small sinuosity of this monstrous body of the time would be a great epic in itself. But to reproach someone with passing this raw material by is terribly one-sided.

Our time rages on. We are still awaiting its poet.

The recreational aesthetes are still spooking around.

We must be clear: Are we speaking of an art that has the masses as its subject, or of an art that takes the masses as its goal? This is, as always, a cluster of fine reproaches, but only a cluster, and all this talk of "healthy," "strong," "manly" art, what does it lead to? An art for individuals as a mass, or *one* mass as an individual?

And the answer is that all world history knows only two types of artistic effects. One type makes one empathetic and thoughtful; in a theater it makes a hundred people seized by the same thing lonely in respect to one another; it means not loving a book, but coming back to certain pages from time to time. The other is the decorative, the exaggerated, the pathetic that can stampede a hall full of people who are otherwise indifferent or offensive to each other into a dervish dance of applause, or produce by means of a book an epidemic of enthusiasm which is followed a year later by a yawn.

The effects of this second type are the effects of suggestion: a certain mediocre quality in the work is its precondition, as also in life people who have great personal influence are not presumed to be any too intelligent. (Intellectual and artistic, content and medium, mind and magic.)

(And the books that please both high and low? Either the former is not true, or they contain incidental qualities that make it possible for the "low" to get excited.)

And one thing must be noted: books of great vitality, books that are feats, are surrogates or—they are concealed meditations. To be God and to write a theodicy are two things that cannot be compared with each other in any way, and one might prefer the latter. (But whoever can write a theodicy renounces the former.)

But why, then, do we write art? To say things yet again? Once was justified, but we aren't rhapsodes. Why don't we occupy ourselves with the relativity principle in physics, with Couturat's logical-mathematical paradoxes, with . . . ?

Because there are things that cannot be exhausted scientifically, and that cannot be captured in the hybrid charms of the essay either; because it is destiny to love these things, the destiny of the writer. Ideas and feelings are impersonal and inartistic: how they are interwoven is personality and art.

The artist's thinking is not goal-oriented, if by goal one understands judgment with a claim to truth. For in his province there is no truth. There is too much talk of psychological truth, and of ethical truth not even that. Drill possibilities into souls!

This is not the program of art, but it is the program of *an* art—and one must know where one intends to stand.

This art can appropriate any object; the heroic epic, vice, virtue—it is characterized by how it does so—unenthusiastically, critically, pensively, building on previously heterogeneous elements.

It is not the only kind of art. The concept "classical art" was not exhausted by Goethe; Goethe is: a few experiments in that direction. The concept of naturalistic art has not been hurriedly buried like a dog; it is the experiment, not yet even undertaken, of the wandering point of fixation, the *dis*unity in disparate phenomena, the concept of pathetic art; [and it] will demand the study of pathologic effects on the audience—these are incredibly promising fields, and they demand only one thing: that we make all things new, break with all traditional demands, investigate the always foreign body of the subject, and, according to one's imaginative powers, strike off a piece of it.

But all intellectual daring today lies in the natural sciences. We shall not learn from Goethe, Hebbel, or Hölderlin, but from Mach, Lorentz, Einstein, Minkowski, from Couturat, Russell, Peano . . .[1]

And within the program of this art the program of an individual work of art might be this:

Mathematical daring, dissolving souls into their elements and unlimited permutation of these elements; here everything is related to everything else and can be built up from these elements. But this construction demonstrates not "this is what it is made of," but "this is how its pieces fit together." For this reason, in the representation too it is only a question of sequential ordering. What is taken as psychology is freer ethical thinking—people will say this is an immoral art, and yet it alone is a moral art. Let us stay with this for a while. The need for an *être suprême* and masochism are not without material connection: frigidity and absolute, impersonal sensuality, absolute sensuality and the intimidating, growling, potentialized masculine, but above all inhuman—frigidity and inhumanity are not without their connections.

These are significant connections of meaning, not just psychological connections. They are of three kinds: the causal scientific; the individual-psychological, where one establishes it in an individual, nonbinding case, constantly concealing it behind the singularity of the case; and the third, where one does not show the occurrence but the meanings themselves, and where one shows them (for the sake of brevity) not in the individual case but in the abstract generality.

In both the second and third cases, novella and novel part company; peacefully, technically. The second is the method of the novella. One thing that is certain is that the novella cannot be an abbreviated novel. Otherwise one would be wandering about on the plain of the flesh, and the meanings would lie on the distant horizon; here, wandering on the plain of meanings on whose horizon only a thin, distant haze of this alien flesh is lurking. If one were to make a scene out of every paragraph—everything would be so comprehensible. But must one always explain? Perhaps. But no one can take it amiss if, for once, one does not explain. That is un-unholy art.

It becomes unidimensional, not cubic, art.

The one case is less tenable than the other; I will choose from it haze and mist, "people who have manifested themselves." This can't be demonstrated, only suggested.—

To put it differently, it is a matter of "obligatory motivation." An art out of disgust at what has always been done, which plays at sitting in aesthetic moral judgment, which is not to be dignified and, even in the individual case, not to be excused.

One can undertake the experiment of rolling up every paragraph, every sentence, and reconstituting them as scenes: they will be good scenes; one can test their ideational content, it will be within the limits it wants to be within, and will not allow itself to be expressed abstractly. Or will people really not understand this? See fogginess instead of microscopic detail? Confuse bold strokes with vapidities? An expectation that is to be endured. And one optimistically imagines the fate of such a book in Ger[many].

Love and self-destruction wanting to step over boundaries.

It is a dangerous art, it will overlook what lies nearest at hand, and also the whole for the parts.

Beginning? Put yourself in the following mood:

Profile of a Program

A person dallies with the woman he loves, and in a flash has a vision that she will deceive him. Only a fraction of this interval will be occupied by the idea of the causal connection—combined fragments of a chain of possibility, such as can quickly be found anywhere—the experience is not this insignificance, but something difficult to characterize. I am trying to say: This man I am speaking of will not be shocked that his beloved could be unfaithful to him, but rather that while being unfaithful she nevertheless still remained his beloved; it is the imagining of a strange network of emotions within himself. It is not understanding and forgiving, not considering it as possible or probable, but it is *inner* understanding: a being confounded, a sympathy and an empathy. More precisely: not the act of "understanding inwardly," but the product [that confuses him—*Musil's note*]. I presuppose this: whoever understands it will understand the type I am speaking about in what follows.

Without my trying to specify a closer conceptual analysis of this construct, it can (yet still) be noted how much it constitutes what is crucial for the artistic representation of mental [*seelische*] processes as well. For here too one can—at least within the vagueness in which the writer's psychology moves—derive pretty much any final state from any beginning; but what one gains, and the connections one is striving for, do not lie in this appearance of forced sequentiality. I mean, the pathways that lead in a person from, say, love to unfaithfulness are also aesthetically speaking uninteresting (do not provide any *complete* art[istic] interest) to the extent that each single step along these pathways does not have, aside from its psychological probability, the value of an empathy, an enticement—in short, a value. The causal connection shows itself in art, too, as only the pretext for spreading this network of connections of concomitant values step by step. (Here too the essential is only the network of connections of concomitant values; the causal connection reveals itself as merely the pretext for extending it.)

If I therefore assume that a story is to be written in order to contain one of these strange networks of emotions, this story may not be (in its innermost essence) causal either, that is—separated into its two subcategories—it will not rely on external events, nor will it be psychological. For the external events as well as the psychological processes are really only the impersonal part of fate. (Psychology is the nonindividual component of the personality.) More precisely: since the story cannot dispense with either of these things, it will have to express some way or other that it is not *privileging* them.

The theory of a work of art, insofar as every work of art has its own unique style, is necessarily paradoxical, that is, it does not entirely fit any other case aside from this one. In general, causality—even if it has the subordinate role of merely mediating the essential—is by no means to be neglected, and even contains components of the essential.

If I place myself on the ground of my everyday rational thinking in order to connect the two poles with each other—here the secured happiness of a blissful hour, there the misfortune opposed to it, unfaithfulness—I see immediately that there are countless such connections: egoism, which leaves traces of polygamy in every love; everything one understands by female psychology (a sweet feeling of each other experienced through the fog in the lush haze of a dinner hour—is rather experience, content); the entire bundle of possibilities for good and bad writers—and I too would proceed causally here, would say more or less: the manifestation of emotion is, according to the state of our knowledge of the soul, not accidental. It is the disguised expression of conditions that are already present, and I would allow these to develop one after another as the story unfolds.

And I do not in any way deny that this manner of presentation has advantages that cannot be gained any other way; but there is something missing in all these mediating bridges (something that bends them back again into my love at every step, or if they have it, then all these bridges are no longer just causal). It is still a question of this further determinant, and is nothing more than the more profound degree of "empathy" that makes unfaithfulness a palpably coexisting element even in love.

In contrast to causality, one could also speak of motivation (at the point where I emphasized the value of empathetic feeling), and divide the aesthetic phenomenon of "empathy"—without claiming theoretical completeness in doing so—into three components, which interact to produce it.

First, there are suggestive effects present. You will excuse me for employing this concept, which is widely used in a vague sense but is probably the right one to use here; for precisely the effect of the "plot" rests on it. Because an action is narrated as if it were real, or because facts are narrated, it not only has a stronger impact, but also produces quite specific effects.—

The second part of this empathy consists in understanding [*Verstehen*]. Here the chains of feeling associated with what is read by the hearer are often composed of quite different experiences of his own; one understands with their help, but the way one understands something foreign or alien. While the third component of empathizing—apparently only a higher degree of understanding—approbation, being shaken up, and the like, rest precisely on one's feeling that one is experiencing what is being narrated as a new experience of one's own.

The determinant mentioned previously is nothing but this. Motivation must reach down to the deepest values and connections I can attain.

Consider for a moment—to understand this—how many good books are written in Germany, and how few of them furrow the soul so deeply that after a few days the surface is not smooth again. The motivation is insufficient.

Now one will of course not want to play at metaphysics or world history (as Hebbel thought); the *tertium separationis* is the condition that one cannot express what ought to be said directly as pure conceptualizing; otherwise everything except precise exposition would be inferior. It is not a question of a different method, but of a different sphere. Such a sphere is that zone between emotions and rational understanding in which the real blossoming of the soul takes place. An interweaving of the intellectual and the emotional. And this is the proof that the manner of which I am speaking here is an artistic one.

This is the main point, and several technical restrictions can be derived from it. The backgrounding of the causal has already been mentioned. Connected with it is the foregrounding of the imagistic. It need not be this way at all. As mentioned, this could all be spread out quite well in a novel and given flesh, but the ideas that I developed, be- [*sic*]

In other words, understanding a person means constituting him out of elements of one's own experience.

It is far more important that one learn to follow the traces of intentions than whether a work is good or bad.

Instead of constituting a valuable experience of a val[uable] person out of merely suitable elements, one can also take the opposite position of constituting any random, merely suitable experience out of valuable elements. From a ma[ximum] of such elements.

Not from the barely sufficient grounds of causality, but from motives. Nothing happens accidentally, but every thought, which is also of course a psychological event, is first and foremost an objective necessity.

But exactly this is also the innermost strand in causal representation. For here one can . . . derive, but what one gains, the connective element, lies . . . propagating works [*sic*]. But if one knows this, is it not more direct, more objective, truer in a "manly" sense, to renounce it entirely, and *only* give this connection? Doing so will meet with resistance.

In doing this one gives up an important resource: suggestion!

Politics in Austria
1912

This irreverent essay will interest students of Austrian history and culture, but its real significance lies in what it has to say about modern art and culture generally. Before 1867 the multinational empire of the Habsburgs was ruled from Vienna by German-speaking aristocrats and bureaucrats. In 1867 the Ausgleich, *or compromise, divided the empire into a dual monarchy: Austria-Hungary. Diplomatically and militarily a unity, the two parts went their separate ways in domestic politics. This essay foreshadows Musil's satiric vision of Austria ("Kakania") in* The Man without Qualities *as a metaphor of modernity.*

People think too one-sidedly in this context about the difficulties of the nationalities problem. Although this is a genuine problem, it has long since become a matter of convenience; it is no longer a serious subject, but has turned into an unacknowledged evasion and malingering. Like shallow lovers, who are constantly overcoming separations and obstacles because they sense that the moment these obstacles are overcome they will have no idea what to do with one another. Like passion, simply a pretext for not having feelings. When the day of reckoning arrives, it will be a blessing that the bad manners people have acquired in the meantime will still know how to produce even from trivial occasions the appearance of neglected idealism. But behind this appearance the emptiness of the inner life will reel like the emptiness in an alcoholic's stomach.

There are few countries in which politics is pursued so passionately as here, and none in which politics, accompanied by comparable passion, remains such an indifferent affair: passion as pretext. On the surface, everything is so very parliamentary that more people are shot dead here than elsewhere, and all the wheels stop every few moments for the less-than-perfect juggling of parties; one is allowed to insult high officials, generals, and advisers to the crown; with threats in parliament one can make important people tremble; people make money with the aid of politics, and box each other's ears. But this is all half convention, a game by agreement. The fear one arouses, the power one exercises, the honor one gathers to oneself, despite the fact that in all relationships that are genuine and commonly regarded as important they are entirely authentic, remain insincere in one's soul, wraithlike; believed and respected, but not felt. One takes them seriously to the extent of impoverishing oneself for them, yet it seems that arranging one's entire life this way to such an extent does not signify the ultimate. One *could* see great idealism in this, even if, at first, a negative idealism. Action never quite defines these Austrians on its level. Their religiosity is not credible, nor their childlike loyalty to the Emperor, nor their anxieties; they wait somewhere behind these. They have the passive fantasy of spaces left unfilled, and jealously grant a person everything except his claims, which are so prejudicial spiritually, for the seriousness of his work. The German, on the other hand, stands in relation to his ideals like those unbearably devoted wives who are glued to their husbands like a wet bathing suit.

Under present conditions, of course, meaninglessness predominates in any case, and Austrians while away the waiting period with noisy bustle. Their energetic gestures are a mark of weakness, whereas elsewhere even the appearance of impotence depends on dammed-up masses of energy. And so German parliamentarism is like a field-happy nag protesting against a lashing by earnestly and soberly brushing the spot with its tail, while here in Austria there are passions in public life behind which one yawns with unruffled mind. One does not know what it is one is letting oneself be dominated by: now and then a hurricane comes along and all the ministers immediately fall like practiced gymnasts, but the storm is calmed, and their successors arrange themselves in precisely the same positions, with minor changes that might satisfy the experts but must remain incomprehensible to outsiders. Nonetheless, outsiders too immediately declare themselves satisfied. There is something uncanny in this obstinate rhythm that has no melody, no words, no feeling. Somewhere in this country a secret must be hidden, an idea, but no one knows where. It is not the idea of the state, not the dynastic principle, not the idea of a cultural symbiosis of different peoples (Austria could be a world experiment): apparently the whole thing is really only motion in the absence of a driving idea, like the weaving of a bicyclist who isn't going forward.

Unfortunate political situations of this kind always have their basis in cultural conditions. Politics in Austria still has no human purpose, only Austrian ones. It does not make one a self, although with its aid one can become anything else, and in politics no single self is able to get anywhere. The instrument of social democracy is not yet solid enough in this country, and other powerful contradictions are missing, such as that between the intellectual drive of a few disquieting people who live like magnificent vermin on the refuse of the German merchant state and the righteousness of a Junker class with two legs rooted in the Bible and two in the soil. Our social structure in Austria is, almost all the way to the top, a homogeneous mixture of bourgeois and cavalier styles. In one's natural state one is high-strung and blooming with health. A hairdresser's assistant, who shared his ideals with the ladies of the aristocracy while he was waving their hair, would have had a career here as a German poet not long ago if he had not, after a party, inadvertently put on a fur coat that did not yet belong to him. At that time he was already frequenting the most aristocratic houses and reciting his poems at teas, and the bourgeois press would certainly not have been able to resist this light-fingered hair-calligrapher for long, for being high-strung is the press's weakness as well.

In Austria we lack the great ideal antithesis between bourgeoisie and aristocracy. Even elsewhere this antithesis has only expressed itself in a very preliminary and distorted way—in the intellectual circle of liberalism—and is temporarily concealed by the economic antithesis "proletariat-property," although this latter is only a smoothing of the road for the march. But meanwhile, in large states that have a backdrop of world trade and world-wide connections, something new has developed, a paradox: a nonintellectual but cracked soil in whose fissures, despite its barren inauspiciousness, culture is now settling better than ever on what are, for it, barely suitable surfaces. Today culture no longer realizes its goals through the state, as it once did in Athens and Rome, but utilizes instead of the perfection of the whole (which does not permit much enhancement) its imperfections, its gaps, its inability to encompass each and every individual. Dissolving in the incalculable number is what constitutes the fundamental cultural difference between this and any other age, the loneliness and anonymity of the individual in an ever-increasing crowd, and this brings with it a new intellectual disposition whose consequences are still unfathomable. The clearest example we can already see today is the small amount of serious art we have. Its inability to both be good and please many at the same time is actually unprecedented, and apparently indicates, far beyond being a kind of aesthetic quarrel, the beginning of a new function for art.

The real precondition of this culture, however, is the bourgeoisie. For it is characteristic of the bourgeoisie not to create any families that do not quickly decline, no tradition, no inherited ideals, and no enduring morality: such things as are necessary in learning to walk, but interfere with running. Because of its commercial interests, the bourgeoisie does not concern itself with culture directly, but tosses out lump sums *for* it. The bourgeoisie produces no fascinating people, no prototypes, and thus does not produce either the temptation that has always emanated from such people, which is to form an ideal type from the narrow and always-dated realm of the humanly real instead of, with unfettered imagination, from the realm of human possibilities. The creative person remains unknown aside from his accomplishment: more thought and feeling than human being, he creates forms of the soul in an ideal laboratory, without at the same time having to guarantee their general usefulness the way a regular manufacturer would. And even the lack of comprehension with which his creations are met turns to their advantage, for today's injudiciousness is tomorrow's open-mindedness.

This kind of bourgeoisie does not exist in Austria. Destiny still makes one an Austrian only on some personal recommendation, and it is hard to dishonor one's recommender. And so one treasures catastrophes because they take the responsibility upon themselves, and misfortune is needed because it generates violent gestures behind which everyone disappears and becomes conventional. Since heroism is the most impersonal form of action, one lives one's political life like a Serbian heroic epic. Little Joan from Domrémy was a farm maid in men's trousers; the penitent gets lice from being an ascetic; when the hero acts, he is fenced in like an animal in the experience of his heroism; blood, sweat, and dust make his clothes stick together like boards: he can't bathe, they rub him raw, hang stiffly on him; he rattles like a mad kernel in his shell; his field of vision is constricted to the *fovea centralis*, his glances remain firmly stuck to objects. Necessity and the hero go together like sickness and fever. And so every violent act has something pathological about it, a restricted consciousness, a final, progressive, vortexlike ascent. But, even without this ascent, the political hero in Austria is the refined technique of a restricted consciousness. A bad habit, acquired through frequent illness. Quite properly one does not take it entirely seriously, but will not let go of it so long as the substance required for the entire spectrum of consciousness is lacking.

The Religious Spirit, Modernism, and Metaphysics
1912

Modernism here refers not to literary but to Catholic modernism, especially in the decades after Pope Leo XIII's 1891 proclamation in Rerum novarum *of the church's intentions of coming to terms with modern society. Musil was not Catholic himself, although baptized one, and like many Austrian intellectuals he disliked much about Roman Catholicism. This essay displays the intense antistatism, even anarchism, of the young Musil (which he shared with many of his generation), but also his conviction that the Catholic church had failed to comprehend "the enormous, still-unlived value of its own unreason."*

Modernism is the attempt to permeate religion with middle-class reason—and in this, and not just the way it manifests itself in individual instances, it is a form of Protestantism. It is directed against reason as much as against religiousness, and something of the spiritual odor that arises from the enthusiastic playacting of the bourgeois amateur clings to the suffering as well as to the raptures of its martyrs: a mixture of the breath of passion and the breath of bad teeth.

Historically, however, modernism is enormously significant as the final outcome of the fateful struggle of Catholicism against the state, a struggle that began with the church allowing itself to be misled into wanting to rule the state in the state's way, and ended with the church being dominated by the state in the church's way, that of invisible spiritual penetration. Out of the church-state there emerged the state-church, and modernism is not an accident that happened to the church, but an organic disease. Indeed, it is impossible to enumerate how thoroughly Catholicism today is saturated by middle-class reasonableness; one need only recall how even baptism—once the most powerful expression of the church's opposition to the state, a symbol of entry into a spiritual countercommunity, a mystical adoption, less the bearing of a name than being led by means of a name on the first steps of one's inner way—is today bound up with middle-class record-keeping: with the identity card, the need for an enduring characterization resting on the firm distinctions of compelling reason; which means that being a person is made impossible by the "individual," that incalculable spiritual and intellectual destiny that tears away the protective covering of the soul's anonymity and drives it to mindlessly repetitious, merely defensive expenditures of energy and renders inaccessible to it everything it might do if it did not always first have to look after a person. Everything points to the person as if with fingers and, like an unprotected line of retreat, paralyzes all intellectual initiative. It is, therefore, no less characteristic that the kind of reason modernism appeals to for all its demands is of the same kind that led to the greatness of the contemporary state than it is natural that in this situation the church, while holding fast to a spirituality opposed to this sort of rationality, must do so in senile fashion, merely spelling out dogmas by rote; but for the longest time it has had no understanding of the enormous, still-unlived value of its own unreason.

The rationality of middle-class society that has been appropriated by the state—and which is far too much, unfortunately, the rationality of the church as well—is in its manifestations a simple, sober rationality, or in its own words economic rationality, which leaves the safe ground of ordinary experience only with reluctance and, even in the boldest of its valid hypotheses, only goes as far as is absolutely necessary to achieve a comprehensive overview. It is a cautious and, might one not object, cowardly rationality; what it values most highly is its own security. It asks only whether what it asserts is true, never whether this truth is also beneficial; indeed, one can say that the concept of the *value* of a truth has degenerated and become almost incomprehensible because of the insistence on giving it a uniform value. The type of reason that would renounce the ripening of completely verified knowledge—the kind of knowledge that allows us to roll iron, fly in the air, and gain nourishment—but that would strive to discover and systematize truths giving new and bold directions to the feelings, even if these distinctions were to remain only mere plausibilities; a rationality, in other words, for which thinking would exist only to give an intellectual armature to some still problematic way of being human: such a rationality is incomprehensible today even as a need.

The result of this (no less than that much-lamented incapacity of our time to feel that makes Europe in its leisure hours an amusement park) is a formless excess of feelings, from whose stored energy modernism draws nourishment along with all the other forms of praying and dancing oneself to health and uncorseted human dignity. Nothing, therefore, is more pernicious than to demand more feeling from our rational age, for this would involve feelings that have long been left undeveloped and unarticulated; and there is nothing more deplorable than those skeptics and reformers, liberal priests and humanistically oriented scholars, who moan about "soullessness," "barren materialism," what is "unsatisfying in mere science," and the "cold play of atoms," and renounce intellectual precision, which is for them only a slight temptation. Then, with the help of some alleged "emotional knowledge" to satisfy the feelings, and with the "necessary" harmony and rounding-out of the world picture, all they invent is some universal spirit: a world-soul, or a God, who is nothing more than the world of the academic petite bourgeoisie which gives rise to him; at best, an oversoul who reads the newspaper and demonstrates a certain appreciation of social questions.

It is certainly only the intensity of understanding woven into them that distinguishes the feelings of a Saint Francis from those of some shoemaker who castrates himself out of religious enthusiasm and nails himself to a cross. But there is no emotional *knowledge* or other, second kind of knowledge that could exist in opposition to science. Within a prescribed framework, this excludes all other possibilities; only the framework itself—the choice of questions according to the needs of a purely rational, pragmatic intellect which is limited to what is knowable as certain and real—can be transcended or, if one prefers, subscended. There is only *one* knowledge, but to esteem in the gathering of knowledge only the achievements of reason is merely a historical convention. In fact, the first of the men who established this new direction—Galileo, Copernicus, Newton, and their intellectual and spiritual comrades—were still altogether religious; their methods were not intended to inspire a defection from the church, but rather meant to flow back, someday, into reinforcing orthodox belief. But just as, in a column of marching soldiers, one soldier buckles and the whole column begins to deflect imperceptibly until it suddenly gives way somewhere, this too constituted something none of them intended, a causal sequence; and the restricting of intellectual and spiritual needs to the mania of progress gradually arose from a whole carpet of questions being unrolled, a process that can no longer stop because the material world gives way before it. The real proof—not of the truth but of the importance of science—is never arrived at this way, unless it were to lie in this progress itself and its consequences: the mastery of nature, technology, and material comforts: this whole ingeniously inventive manner of never managing to finish the preparations for living, in whose energetic maneuvers there lies, at bottom, the fear of a synthesis.

In the giant ashlars of this uninhabitable house of knowledge one can find a lost corner here or there, and be unscientific without becoming an idiot: with last and first aporias: with the ends of causal chains, the limits of validity of laws, the influence that practical requirements still have on the form of theory; with the difficulties of completing the system without contradictions—or with simple everyday things, for science has eyes only for events that recur in changing situations, and not for unique, isolated events that happen just once; even a stone falling from a particular roof remains for science a mere fact, an accident, whose structure science can investigate no further; the law—the law by which it falls—plays only a small role in this, and everything else remains: perhaps that rain fell, or that the sun then came out, or that the wind blew; . . . facts, accidents, or should we want to explain them according to meteorological laws as well, we would still only deduce from *another* set of facts by means of these laws that the sun shone or the rain fell somewhere else, and that the air pressure was one thing here and another there, . . . the enormous loneliness of mere facts, shoved into the middle of our picture of the world by a race of knowledge-happy scientists who simply do not notice the accidental, something that is *only* an event, opening outwards just a few steps off the path, while the saint of knowledge gazes into the uncircumscribed visionary desert.

But however one goes about it, as soon as one goes beyond the boundaries science has drawn for itself, not much in the way of knowledge will be produced; and all metaphysics is bad because it applies its intellect in the wrong way. It stakes its ambition on a task that violates the nature of reason: proving the reality of the hereafter, instead of (for a more discriminating taste) making such a thing "possible" in the first place. In this fashion metaphysics builds a bridge, but the land to which it is supposed to lead is tiresome. In Kantian terms: metaphysics is transcendental, and the transcendent is pure boredom. If metaphysics were, let us say, confronted with the task of thinking through hardness, weight, spatial extension, temporal persistence, and the electrical, optical, magnetic, and thermal constants of things as qualities of a *soul*—would it not set all its ambition to proving that this could be done, and could be done in these swarming monisms, spiritualisms, idealisms, and so on, instead of first working out what kind of strange new souls these would be, with their silent tic of always expressing themselves in the same gesture, with their stubbornness congealed into law, with their nurses' equanimity, which shows equal concern for the falling of stars and the vagabond's nosebleed, and not least with their bad taste in only revealing themselves to scholars. And conversely: to pursue the sort of spiritual formation of the human being that would be required for it to feel itself living within the circle of the person like a free-floating, loose, somewhat uncertain eccentric among strange pedants, refusing nothing so much as being as firm and solid as they; not, like these pedants, always the same, an "individual," but preferring to outsmart them through their weaknesses, like a little man going at the uterus of a gigantic woman and, in the fateful moment when they suddenly reach climax with ridiculous manic gestures, enjoying her with the superior defenselessness of his brain.

Only once did the church demonstrate, in Scholasticism, that it could construct an intellectual system of this sort—the kind that makes man the goal of metaphysics—whatever else this system may be. That this system later collapsed was entirely understandable, and occurred only because of an oversight that might easily have been corrected. For even the paradoxical requires a truth at its foundation from which it can branch out, and it is only that this truth, at the time the edifice for the teachings of Aristotle, had developed dry rot after two thousand years of service. It might easily have been replaced by the new one. But the church was not under any compulsion to do this; it long ago closed the book of essays on its life, and has since successfully steered this book towards mass recognition, with ever-repeated astigmatic reprintings.

On Robert Musil's Books
1913

By means of an imaginary scene in the landscape of his brain, Musil wittily defends his experimental attempts to enlarge the boundaries of fictional technique against journalistic and uncomprehending critics.

This writer's brain: I hastily slid down the fifth turn in the vicinity of the third mound. Time was pressing. The mass of the cerebral cortex arched over me gray and unfathomable, like strange mountains at dusk. Night was already falling over the region of the medulla; colors of precious stones, hummingbird colors, shining flowers, scattered perfumes, disconnected sounds. I confessed to myself that I would soon have to leave this head in order not to commit an indiscretion.

So I sat down just once more in order to summarize my impressions. On my right was the site of *The Confusions of Young Törless*; it had already fallen in and was overgrown with a gray crust. On my other side I had the small, strangely inlaid double pyramid of *Unions*.[2] Obstinately bald in outline it resembled, covered as it was with dense hieroglyphic inscriptions, the monument of an unknown godhead in which an incomprehensible people had brought together and piled up tokens of remembrance of incomprehensible feelings. European art it isn't, I admitted, but so what.—

A belated geologist of literature then sat down beside me, a not uncongenial young man of the modern school who—overcome by the fatigue of the disappointed tourist—fanned his face with his handkerchief and began a conversation. "Unpleasant region," he ventured; I hesitated to respond. But hardly had he resumed talking when we were interrupted by one of our host's writer colleagues in shirt-sleeves, who noisily threw himself down beside us. I could only make out a cheerful smile shining in a face supported by a fist, as this person, the picture of ink-fresh health and energy, picked up our conversation at the very point at which he had interrupted it. From time to time he spat into a small, tender fold of the Musilian cortex and rubbed it in with his foot. "Disappointed?" he shouted at us, and his words jumped down the mound. "What did you really expect? It couldn't disappoint me! In that thing over there"—he jerked his thumb in the direction of *Törless*—"there's a lot that shows talent. But even there all Musil did was descend into the hardly earth-shaking problems of a sixteen-year-old and show an incomprehensible degree of respect for an episode that has very little connection with grownups. But in *Unions* there is this joy in boring into the psychological. . . ."

It seemed to me I was already familiar with this objection from someplace, perhaps I had read it somewhere; an answer as from an earlier time urged itself upon me, and I interrupted him. "The sixteen-year-old," I said, "is a stratagem. Relatively simple material, and therefore easy to manipulate in depicting spiritual relationships, which in the adult are complicated by too many other things that can here be excluded. A state of weakly inhibited reactivity. But the representation of an immature person, tempted and groping, is of course not itself the problem but merely a means to give form to or indicate just what it is in this immature person that *is* immature. The depiction, and all psychology in art, is only the car in which one is riding; if you notice only the psychology in the author's intention, you've been looking for the landscape inside the car."

"Oh," the literary geologist said, while with his little hammer he broke off a piece of brain, ground it in his hand, looked at it earnestly, and then blew it away. "Sometimes this writer has too little power of description." "No," I smiled, angered, "he doesn't much want to describe!" "Well honestly," the geologist replied, "I know so many writers."

I wanted to shut up. One cannot correct in an individual case the confirmed prejudices the age has about writing. If, with stern discipline, Musil fulfills needs even before they have been aroused, it's his business to come to terms with it himself. But just then I had a strange experience. This brain on which we were sitting seemed to have become interested in our conversation. I suddenly heard it whispering something into my sacrum, softly and with jaggedly pulsating sounds, which must have been caused by the passage through my spinal column. It fought its way up my back and I had to get it out. "The reality one depicts," I repeated, thus impelled, "is always just a pretext. At some time in the past storytelling might simply have been the reactive touching once again, on the part of a strong person who didn't have many concepts, of those good and bad spirits of experiences the remembering of which made his memory cringe. The magic of speaking, repeating, and discussing them was a way of defusing them. But since the rise of the novel we hold to a view of storytelling that derives from the novel. And this development leads to the depiction of reality finally becoming a subservient tool of the person who is conceptually strong, who uses it to slink up on recognition of feelings and upheavals of thought. These are not to be grasped in the abstract and in concepts, but only—perhaps—in the flickering of the individual case. They cannot be encompassed in the completely rational middle-class business-minded person, but through less consolidated units that transcend him. I maintain that Musil understands these —and does not just point them out or intimate them—but one has to know what a work of literature means for one before one starts arguing about whether it is well done." "Good," whispered the brain, "good."

But the geologist had his answer ready. "The decisive quality in a writer is not speculation but vitality. Just think of our truly great storytellers: they depict. An artful optic alone forms the response; the artist's thought and opinion never intervene in the happening itself; they do not lie, so to speak, in the picture plane, but are only palpable as its perspectival vanishing point." The brain under me grumbled that vitality, with all due respect, is ultimately only a means and not the end of art. "One can," I acknowledged further, "at some point feel the need to say more and say it more precisely than is possible by such means. Then one puts together a new means. Art is something halfway between the conceptual and the concrete. Ordinarily one narrates in actions, while the meanings lie mistily on the horizon. Or the meanings lie exposed, in which case they were already more than half-known. Would it not sometime be possible, out of impatience, to broaden out more the objective relationship between feelings and thoughts, which is what it's all about, and only indicate by means of that vibrating haze of strange bodies that hovers over an action what can no longer be stated in words alone? It seems to me that in doing this one is merely inverting the proportions of a technical formula, and one should regard the process the way an engineer would. But you, who call this speculation, overestimate the difficulty of depicting people—a few little touches suffice, the more familiar the better. Those writers who place such great importance on the complete verisimilitude of their characters are like the somewhat fussy God of the theologians, who bestows free will on mankind so it will perform *His* will for *Him*. For the characters in a book are created only so that feelings, thoughts, and other human values may be placed in them, which are drawn out of them again by means of the action."

But here the word slipped away from me and went over to my colleague the healthy writer. "Be that as it may," he decided, "it's theory, and such a theoretically ingenious techniques may well be suited to this particular writer. But practically speaking it is as I said before, that these books simply do not have the slightest connection with the true forces of our age. They appeal to a small circle of hypersensitive people who no longer have any feeling for reality, not even perverse feeling, but only literary conceptions of it. It's a matter of an artificially nourished art, which becomes barren and obscure out of weakness and plays that out as pretension. Indeed," he suddenly shouted, as if he had to show one idea special respect, although we were both waiting for him to finish, "the twentieth century is raining events like cats and dogs, and this person has nothing decisive to report about either what's going on in life or the life of what's going on! The soul of his poetry is mere supposition." And he flexed his biceps.

The geologist took advantage of this momentary distraction to successfully seize the word. "What is the content of his most recent stories?" he asked with conviction. "There is none," the wordsmith answered, calmly happy. "What happens?" "Nothing!" the writer replied with an expression that said: Why mince words. "There's this one woman who's unfaithful to her husband because of some sort of contrived idea or other that this must signify the fulfillment of her love, and there's this other who weaves neuropathically between a man, a priest, and the memory of a dog that appears to her as now the one, now the other. What happens is already decided from the beginning and is repulsive and insignificant. It's an intellectual and emotional thicket in which not even the characters in the action make any forward progress." "It's about life itself that he no longer has any ideas," the colleague concluded, appeased to the point of benevolence.

I thought I had to keep silent. Even Robert Mayer's treatise on energy[3] had seemed overingenious and empty to his professional colleagues. But then my earlier experience came back to me more strongly. Individual words and short sentences boiled up in me with some force, but longer insinuations were covered as though by a gentle, tough mass. They were occasionally interrupted, and only broke through again directly in a subsequent place. "Don't let them get away with it," the brain begged sharply, to which I replied, "It's not a question of my books, which might be ephemeral, but of preparing the way for a greater insatiability in matters human and emancipating storytelling from being a profession for nannies!" I felt as if my brain had duplicated itself, and while one was moving up and down my *musc. longissimus dorsi,* the other was swimming around in a weakened state and shadowy as the moon inside my skull. At times they approached and seemed to flow into each other. Then I lost my body in a peculiar feeling halfway between self and nonself. I spoke, and the words came out furrily, like unripe fruit; it was only after the last letter emerged that they seemed, in this strange atmosphere, to become what they said.

"The question," I slowly began, "whether a work of art is obscure because of the weakness of its creator or only appears obscure to the reader because of his own weakness, is one that bears looking into. One would have to dissolve out the mental elements of which the work is constituted. The decisive elements among them are—despite a comfortable prejudice on the part of the writer—ideas." My colleague jumped up. "Of course, they can never be presented purely as such," I was still able to get in. "I'm not advocating rationalism, and I know that works of art can never be completely reduced to supposed meanings. One can only describe their content through new combinations of the rational with the devices of telling, with depictions of the situation and other irrational forces. But ultimately writing means first of all thinking about life, and then representing it. And understanding the human content of a work of art means to fill in the infinitely broken polygon of a chain of feeling and ideas with not only the brilliant play of ideas, but also with the absolute and indefinable plain insights of the diction, the shimmer of the characters, the silence, and all those things that cannot be reproduced. This asymptotic devolution, by means of which alone we constantly absorb spiritual fuel in our minds, is the human purpose of the work of art; its possibility is the artwork's criterion. If this succeeds, then one would achieve a result that you have already anticipated: that what you're attacking is not the impotence of the synthesis, but that even before you judge the synthesis you aren't able to understand the individual feelings and ideas about whose crystallization into destinies so much fuss is being made here."

The writer remained sarcastically silent, and I continued, "Strong, pure experiences of feeling are almost as impersonal as sensations; feeling itself is poor in qualities, and it is only the person who experiences it who brings particularities to it. The few differences there are in the manner and course of feelings are insignificant: what the writer creates by way of great feelings is an interpenetration of feeling and understanding, the original experience becoming inwardly the mediary among several others; it is feeling, its intellectual-emotional vicinity, and the connecting paths between them. There is no other means by which the feeling of Francis of Assisi—that polyplike, pusillanimous fellow who powerfully twisted the world's image with a thousand feeding stations (oh, you little birds my brothers!)—can be distinguished from the feeling of some enraptured little pastor; or the final melancholy, regarded in and of itself, that surrounded the resolve of Heinrich von Kleist [to commit suicide—ed.] would be none other than that of some anonymous suicide.

"If one keeps this straight, one won't fall for the legend of the reputedly great feelings in life, whose source-springs the writer need only find and hold his little bucket under. But this legend governs our art. One could say that wherever a decision might be looked for, our literature offers only a hypothesis. Where a person moves and influences us, it happens because groups of ideas open themselves up for us, among which he summarizes his experiences and his feelings as they acquire a surprising significance in this complicated reciprocal synthesis. This is what should be depicted when it's a matter of giving shape to a human being, whether he be good or repulsive, for our benefit; but instead one always finds that its presence is only naively assumed, and the act of working it out is begun only around this assumption, which is stuck inside the person like an inner armature. One portrays the way one thinks such people will conduct themselves inwardly and outwardly in the course of the action; but this psychological inwardness is really only a second degree of externality imposed from the outside in comparison to that central work of personality, which only begins underneath all the surfaces of pain, confusion, weakness, and passion, and often only later. In this way one gives—and this is true for depicting the soul as well as actions—only the consequences of what the essential thing in people is, but not the thing itself, which remains underdetermined, like everything where all one need do is draw consequences from causes. This art does not get close to either the kernel of the personality or a balanced impression of its destinies. This art, which lays such great value on these things, has strictly speaking neither action nor spiritual stringency and stands, regarded as a whole, for all its new twists and turns, uncreatively still."

I awoke. My companions were sleeping. The brain beneath me yawned. "Don't get mad at me," it whispered in the depths, "but I can't keep my eyes open any longer." At these words I shouted in order to shake the others awake: "In *Unions* destinies crystallize from the center outwards. But the fact that art that has a goal in mind does *not* choose the fashionable is—you must see this—not a characteristic of art, but a characteristic of the fashion, which would never have become fashionable if it could not seize and be seized by preartistic means. The conjectural is the conjecture—." But I no longer saw my companions, and was speaking uncannily into emptiness. The sentence I had begun slipped cold and shivering with darkness back into my throat. I hastily made a few necessary preparations and, pursued by the silence, slid down the nearest fissure. I caught myself by the threads of the eye, slid along them, let go, and skidding glided through, as I had hoped, beneath the sclera; felt in the same moment a rush of air and, hygroscopically swollen to my full humanity, went home contented, if also somewhat benumbed and thoughtful.

Political Confessions of a Young Man
A Fragment
1913

Musil was sensitive to the inner disorder of Europe as its old values and institutions unravelled, and he sought a kind of thinking that would be even bolder than the contradictions characterizing the conflicts between tradition and modernity. He believed Europe to be on the verge of apocalyptic change because of the rigidity and failure of the existing political parties and leaders, but he also thought it possible to "overcome with a single leap the reverses that have so slowed development from cavemen to the present, and arrive at a new epoch for the world."

I recall a saying of Goethe's that made an odd impression on me some years ago. It runs: one can only write about those questions one does not know too much about. Few people will understand the profound happiness and sadness of this admission. It expresses a simple spiritual fact: that the imagination works only in twilight. There is a kind of thinking that creates truth as clearly as a sewing machine, stitch by stitch. And there is a kind of thinking that makes us happy. It gets into you so impatiently that your knees shake; it piles up insights before you in flight and storm, believing in which will absorb the life of your soul for years to come, and—you will never know if they are true. Let's be honest: you are suddenly transported up a mountain from which you can see your inner future with blissful breadth and certainty, like—let's be honest, like a periodic madman, a manic-depressive in the early stages of mania. You don't cry out or do anything foolish, but your thinking is unencumbered and gigantic as if with clouds, while the healthy mind fits thoughts together snugly like bricks and has the overriding need to test every single step again and again against the facts. The healthy way of thinking impoverishes you, solitary one, because it never allows you to get beyond the answers to a few questions, which your soul obviously cannot live on. It makes you unfruitful. But from time to time you must repeatedly force your intuitive way of thinking back to this healthy thinking, must test it against it, must submit to it, must not allow yourself to wander too far from it if you don't want to fall into extravagance, which is the same as meaninglessness. Anyone who does not avoid precise knowledge with a secret shame and yet with burning resolve does not understand Goethe's confession. May this excuse me for what I shall try to write down during these weeks.

I never used to be interested in politics. The politician, whether a deputy in parliament or a cabinet minister, seemed to me like a servant in my house, whose job is to attend to the indifferent matters of life: that the dust does not get too deep and meals are ready on time. Of course he carries out his responsibilities badly, like all servants, but as long as it is done passably I do not interfere. If from time to time I happened to read the program of a political party or parliamentary speeches, I merely felt confirmed in my view that this was a quite subordinate human activity that should not in any way be allowed to move us inwardly. But at the bottom of all this lay an old prejudice of mine. I don't know when I acquired it, or what I should call it. I was pleased by our world. The poor suffer; they constitute in a thousand shadows a chain descending from me to the animals. And really on down past the animals, for no species of animal lives under brutish conditions the way many humans live inhumanly. And the rich pleased me on account of their inability to make use of their wealth in a spiritually meaningful way, which makes them as droll as those insects that glow in the air, which have, when observed more closely, a hairy, silly little sack of a body containing a thin, pathetic little stem of nerves. And the kings pleased me in their majesty as good-natured people with a little idiosyncrasy that everyone accepts with a wink. And religion pleased me, because we have long since stopped believing, and yet we live on quite earnestly in Christian states. And much else of this kind.

It was not only joy in the variety of phenomena, and not only the almost philosophical shock at the extraordinarily tenacious, flexible, uncrushable nature of man that helped these undignified monkeys dominate the earth, but above all the appreciation of the great inner disorder itself, which lies in our mistreating our neighbor but feeling sorry for him, subordinating ourselves to him without taking it seriously, or speaking about one murder with aversion and about thousands with perfect calm. For, so it seemed to me, such an illogical disorder of life, such an unravelling of once-binding energies and ideals, would have to be fertile soil for a great logician of spiritual values. Since this kind of existence is extraordinarily bold in its coupling of contradictory elements, even if only from inconsistency and cowardice, only one step remains: to consciously become even bolder. And here, where every feeling peeks furtively in two directions, everything drifts, nothing is held to and everything loses its ability to enter into combinations, we would have to be able to examine all the inner possibilities once again, invent them anew, and finally transfer the virtues of an unbiased laboratory technique from natural science to morality. And I still believe today that we could overcome with a single leap the reverses that have so slowed development from cavemen to the present, and arrive at a new epoch for the world. To give this a name: I was a conservative anarchist.

Perhaps the idea that changed this for me will be thought ridiculous. It is short and simple: You are already—it said to me—in what you desire a creature of democracy, and the future is to be attained only through an intensified and purer democracy.

I had always regarded the view that all people are fundamentally equal and brothers as a sentimental exaggeration, and I still do, for my feelings have always been more repelled than attracted by the feelings of others. But I believe I see clearly that science is a product of democracy. Not only that the great scientist works alongside the ordinary one, and that the greatest barely surpasses the average of the next generation: what is decisive is that through the democratization of society that has taken place over the last two hundred years a greater number of people than ever before have come to collaborate, and that among this greater number—contrary to aristocratic prejudice—the harvest of talent has proved to be greater. I am not overlooking the flattening that sometimes becomes a danger through making scientific industry too much of an anthill, but I believe that the number of great achievements is in proportion to the number of ordinary ones; for the genius never makes anything new, but always something that is just different, and the average talents provide him the possibility within which his genius condenses into achievements. The violent upswing that has characterized the knowledge and mastery of nature during this period can be explained only in this way. It is ungrateful to always object that these achievements of the intellect have been of no use whatsoever for the soul, indeed that since their time the spiritual has undergone a process of atrophy. All of them, even the good ones, have, certainly, destroyed simple happiness by creating a basis for a more complicated kind, but it was not their task to bring about this more complicated kind of happiness themselves. That is our task. Scientific reason, with its strict conscience, its lack of prejudice, and its determination to question every result again the moment it might lead to the least intellectual advantage, does in an area of secondary interest what we ought to be doing with the basic questions of life.

But even the bad effects we have suffered from science may be traced back to its democratic origins. It is the impoverishment of the inner whole to the advantage of individual parts, the existence of powerful, specialized brains in the souls of children. Not only is it usually depressing to listen to men of science pass judgment on other than scientific questions, but the mathematician also does not understand cultural historians, and the economist does not understand the life of the botanist. This divergence of taste is not simply a consequence of the unintelligibility, and therefore the greatness, of science. For were scholars sons and members of a unified society, science would then be a many-sided, balanced articulation of the mind, circumscribed by good taste, a social exercise, and it would be to our education what the athletic prowess of the Renaissance *gentiluomo* is to the record-setting achievements of modern sports. But instead they come as young people from the most disparate areas of human society, equipped with the most diverse customs, demands, and aspirations in life, and bore in with their heads at the place in science where they have landed; continuing frugally, differently from one another, and in ignorance of any other culture, the life of the spiritual hamlet from which they happen to have come.

And not only in science, in art too we find the same gain and the same complaint. For what is more precious in art today, I ask myself, than that freedom of movement of the feelings, which we owe to a loosening of moral prohibitions and aesthetic uniformity, in the last analysis here also to the too-great number of human beings? This makes possible that extraordinary flexibility of perspective that allows us to recognize good in evil and the ugly in the beautiful. The rigid appraisals (which we have inherited) dissolve, and their elements create new formations of our moral and artistic imagination. But the fact that we have not been able to make these accomplishments prevail also comes from this, as do the artistic fragmentation, the impotent multiplicity of tiny communities, and the lack of inhibition in destroying the old and inventing the new with which the arts are full to overflowing because they are not burdened with a public. The mistrust with which everything new is felt to be folly and, not least, that there nonetheless remains this senseless, deceptive, universal hunger for artistic redemption, for a Homeric simplicity in which we could, with all our differences, someday subside once again into unity. Still, there is no question in my mind that we will never give up such hard-won advantages, or that we can overcome the damage they do. Or that we will win out if we exaggerate even more the developments that have led us to this point.

Thus—sketchily—my thinking. And my conviction has since driven me to something my feelings don't want to know anything about. I am undertaking preliminary theoretical studies that should make it possible for me to involve my will. I am looking for an economic program that would ensure the implementation of a pure, energizing democracy, one that would raise up even greater masses. Of course, until then I will vote Social Democratic or Liberal, as circumstances require, but it is clear that we need something that will lead us beyond the shallowness of our present parties; and any such idea requires an economic program as a prescription for its realization. And I ask myself quite naively: Who will shine my shoes, haul away my excrement, crawl into a mine for me at night? My Fellow Man? Who will do those tasks whose execution requires that one stand at the same machine for a lifetime doing the same thing? I can think of many things that are despised today and yet that have charm the moment one does them voluntarily. But who will submit to those many other tasks imposed only by necessity? And I want to travel more comfortably than I do today, and have my mail delivered more quickly. I want better judges and better apartments. I want to eat better. I don't want to have to complain about the police. Damn it, I, a human being, inhabit the earth and shouldn't I be able to have more comfort in my own house than these wretched conditions of today?

In the meantime we engage in politics because we don't know anything. This is clearly revealed in the way we go about it. Our parties exist from a fear of theory. The voter fears that one idea can always be contradicted by another. Therefore the parties reciprocally defend themselves against the few old ideas they have inherited. They don't live from what they promise, but from frustrating the promises of the others. This is their silent community of interest. They call this mutual interference, which permits the realization of only small practical goals, *Realpolitik*. None of them really knows where it would lead if people actually took the agrarians seriously, or the demands of the big industrialists or those of the Social Democrats. The parties really don't want to engage in politics at all, but simply to represent classes and have the ear of the government for modest requests. I would not be opposed if for this reason they wished to leave politics to others, but as it is they still conserve outworn ideologies such as Christianity, monarchism, Liberalism, and Social Democracy by tying themselves to immediate economic advantage. But, since these ideas are never actually put into practice, the parties give these ideologies the illusion of meaning and sacredness, which in addition to everything else is also a sin against the spirit.

I am convinced that none of these parties has a feasible economic program, and that one should not even bother thinking about improving any of them. They will be blown away as soon as the wind comes up, like all kinds of trash that has piled up on the still ground. They will be falsely posed questions, to which there will no longer be a "yes" or "no" as soon as a longing passes through the world. I cannot prove this, but I know that, like me, a lot of people are waiting.

But still it is quiet, and we sit as if in a glass cage and are afraid even to try to break out, because if we did the whole thing could immediately shatter to pieces. We are trapped along with those things we value most in the money economy, with art, inventions . . . indeed we love money like a kind of God, a kind of accident, an irresponsible decision-making mechanism. Do we really trust any sort of social organization to promote good artists and suppress bad ones? To recognize the value of inventions or other ideas that will be apparent only years later? We are profoundly convinced that the state is the most terrible blockhead. Even money is not parceled out in accordance with justice, but it is at least parceled out according to luck and accident, and it is not the stabilized hopelessness that the all-powerful state would be.

And so I have these depressing days. An hour ago I visited a Roman madhouse and then a church. So that it doesn't look as if I'm setting up a point, I will say right away: Everything looked to me like the situation we're in. Seven men—the physician, five big guards, and I—walked through each room of the ward for disturbed patients. In a cell by himself a naked man was raging; we could hear his screams from far off. He was blond and muscular, and his beard was covered with viscous saliva. He constantly repeated the same motion, throwing his upper body around with a single jerk of his muscles, and at the same time always making the same gesture with one hand as if he were trying to explain something to someone. Screaming something no one understood, always the same thing. For him it was probably the important point he had to make clear, had to hammer into the ear of the world; for us it was a pulverized, formless shouting. Afterwards I sat in on the singing of Franciscan nuns. A tiny voice passed by timorously; one did not know whether it was an old or a young voice, and the voices of the sisters caught up with it and warmed it in the cold uncertainty of outer space. And a few steps from me someone sang along blissfully and destroyed everything. It was one of those old men who can't hold back their prayer-stool urge three times a day and who allegedly love the God of the Catholics so much. The peasantlike old-maidishness that is poorly ventilated in Catholicism sank mustily over me. Are such awful detours necessary in order to arrive at this moment of song? Are detours necessary? Jolts, spasms, aimlessness, different ideas? Is it nonsense to take part of this and try to cut a path through? Will everything happen by itself, some time or other, inadvertently? And never through knowledge and straightforward intention? I recalled the *giardino zoologico* not far from the church; everything seemed like this to me. There an animal paces back and forth, back and forth. Imprisoned without a fence. I saw it yesterday. Isn't this really the way it is: man, an animal from outer space entangled here? Imprisoned without a fence. Back and forth. Back and forth. Not understanding why he can't get out? Without sentimentality and completely cool: it is he. Still, I am annoyed at this literary idea. I felt the weight of the old desire to declare everything useless. I have relapsed. But I have the will!

Moral Fruitfulness
1913

In the spirit of Nietzsche's Beyond Good and Evil, *Musil here argues for a way of thinking about ethics that would do justice to the complexity of emotional relationships and the solitary realities of moral life.*

Egoism is a fiction of moral theoreticians; to want only one's own well-being is by no means merely a matter of one's personal feelings. Only complete emotional deafness, an automatism without accompanying consciousness, would be purely egoistic: the short circuit between sensory stimulation and will, without interposing an emotional connection to the world. The libertine, the significant criminal, and the cold-blooded person are varieties of altruism too, just as Don Juanism has been recognized as a form of love.

It has been demonstrated that every altruistic impulse originates in acts of selfishness; one could just as easily demonstrate that altruistic motives are hidden in every egoistic action, without which it would be inconceivable. Both are equally comical when advocated in such an extreme way: conceptual dignity in a rickety pot on the one hand, on the other an intellectual game into which one is forced because the emotional ground beneath it is so shaky.

What always turns up in practice when we investigate instances of egoism is an emotional relation to the environment, a relation between "I" and "Thou" that is difficult at both ends. But it is just as true that there has never been a pure altruism. There have only been people who had to make use of others because they loved them, and those they had to harm because they loved them and had no other way to express it. Or who did both because they hated. But hate and love too are only deceptive forms of appearance, accidental symptoms of a driving force that occurs in many people and that one can only characterize as moral aggressiveness, as the utterly fantastic compulsion to react to one's fellow human beings in some vehement way, flowing into them, annihilating them, or creating constellations with them that are rich in inner inventiveness. Altruism and egoism both are possibilities for expressing this moral imagination, but taken together they are nothing more than two of its many forms, which have never been counted.

Similarly, evil is not the opposite of good, or its absence; evil and good are parallel phenomena. They are not fundamental or ultimate moral antitheses, as has always been assumed, probably not even particularly important concepts for moral theory, but rather practical and impure summations. Diametrical opposition between good and evil corresponds to an earlier stage of thought that expected everything from the dichotomy; in any case this opposition is not very scientific. What gives all these moral bifurcations the illusion of importance is the confusion with the dichotomy: worth opposing/worth supporting. In fact this genuine antithesis, which plays a role in all problems, contains an important element of morality, and any theory that wanted to smooth over or obscure this opposition in some way would be a bad theory. But "to understand all is to forgive all" is no greater a misunderstanding than deciding that the excusability or inexcusability of a moral phenomenon exhausts its meaning. Two things are confused here that must be kept entirely separate. What we should oppose or support is determined by practical considerations and factual circumstances, and, if one allows enough room for historical contingencies, can be explained completely. To punish a thief I do not require an ultimate justification but only an immediate one, but this involves no trace of moral reflection and imagination. If, on the other hand, a person feels paralyzed the moment he is about to punish someone, if he sees his right to lay hands on another person suddenly disintegrate, or if he begins to do penance or carouse to death in bars, then what has moved him no longer has anything to do with good or evil; and yet he still finds himself in a state of the most vehement moral reaction.

The extent to which morality is basically experienced as something adventurous and experimental demonstrates that even its theoreticians have left the solid ground of utilitarianism, and have often attempted to elevate "Thou shalt!" to a unique experience in order to allow feeling—elaborately disguised as duty in the looming form of a stranger—to knock from the outside. The categorical imperative, and what has counted since as specifically moral experience, is at bottom nothing but a grumpily dignified scheme to return once again to feeling. But this forces into the foreground something entirely secondary and dependent, which assumes moral laws instead of creating them; an auxiliary experience of morality, and by no means its central experience.

Of all the moral propositions ever enunciated, the strongest altruistic atmosphere belongs not to "Love thy neighbor as thyself," or "Do good," but rather to the proposition that virtue can be taught. Every rational activity needs other people, and can develop only through an exchange of shared experiences. But morality actually begins only in the solitude that separates each person from every other. That which is incommunicable, the encapsulation in the self, is what makes people need good and evil. Good and evil, duty and violation of duty, are forms in which the individual establishes an emotional balance between himself and the world. What is most important is not only to establish a typology of these forms, but even more to comprehend the pressure that creates them or the distress on which they rest, and these are infinitely various. The act is only a stammering language for expressing whether we are dealing with a hero, a saint, or a criminal. Even a sex-murderer is, in some cranny of his soul, full of inner hurt and hidden appeals; somehow the world is wronging him like a child, and he does not have the capacity to express this in any other way than the way he has found works for him. In the criminal there is both a vulnerability and a resistance against the world, and both are present in every person who has a powerful moral destiny. Before we destroy such a person—however despicable he may be—we ought to accept and preserve what was resistance in him and was degraded by his vulnerability. And no one does morality more harm than those saints and scamps who, in tepid horror over the form of a phenomenon, refuse to touch it.

The Mathematical Man
1913

Musil here announces a theme that continues throughout his essays: his respect for reason and the Enlightenment and his conviction that writers must do in their field what mathematicians do in theirs. Musil was at home with mathematics and physics, and he was able to see what could be valu-

able in the imagination of the mathematician for understanding human experience.

One of the many absurdities about mathematics that has gained currency from ignorance of its nature is that people refer to important generals as mathematicians of the battlefield. Actually, the logical calculations of these generals ought not go beyond the dependable simplicity of the four arithmetic maneuvers if they are to avoid responsibility for a catastrophe. The urgent necessity of pursuing the process of deduction involved in even such a moderately complex and obscure matter as solving a differential equation would in the meantime abandon helpless thousands to their death.

This says nothing against the genius of generals, but something for the peculiar nature of mathematics. People say mathematics is an extreme economy of thought, and this is also true. But thinking itself is a vast and undependable affair. Thinking, even if it began as simple biological economy, has long since become a complicated passion for thrift, which is no more concerned with the dilatory process of utilitarian application than is the miser with his paradoxical, voluptuously drawn-out poverty.

Mathematics makes it possible under favorable circumstances to perform in a few moments an operation that one could in principle never complete, like the enumeration of an infinite series. Complicated logarithmic calculations and even integrations can already be performed by machines; mathematical calculation today is as simple as entering the numbers of a problem and turning a crank or the like. A professor's administrative assistant can in this way dispose of problems whose solution two hundred years ago would have required his professor to travel to Herr Newton in London or Herr Leibniz in Hanover. And even in those problems (whose number is of course a thousand times greater) that still cannot be solved by machines, one may call mathematics an ideal intellectual apparatus whose task and accomplishment are to anticipate in principle every possible case.

This is a triumph of intellectual organization. It is the old intellectual highway, with its perils of weather and highwaymen replaced by Pullman cars. This is what economy looks like from an epistemological point of view.

People have asked themselves how many of these possible cases can actually also be applied. They have considered how many human lives and creative hours, how much money and ambition have been consumed in the history of this enormous system of savings, are still invested in it today, and are necessary just so we don't forget again what has already been gained; and people have tried to measure this in terms of the practical use to which it is put. But there too this difficult and decidedly complicated apparatus shows itself to be economical, indeed strictly speaking incomparable. For our entire civilization has arisen with its assistance; we know no other way; the needs it serves are completely satisfied by it, and its aimless abundance is of the uncriticizable kind of irreducible facts.

It is only when one looks not toward the outside at their utility, but within mathematics itself at the relationships among the unused parts, that one sees the other, real face of this science. It is not goal-oriented, but uneconomical and passionate.—The average person doesn't need much more mathematics than he learns in elementary school; the engineer only enough to find his way around in the collection of tabulations in his technical handbook, which isn't a lot; even the physicist ordinarily works with quite simple mathematical tools. If they should need something different, they are mostly left to figure it out for themselves, since the mathematician has very little interest in such applied tasks. And this is why specialists in many practically important branches of mathematics are not mathematicians. But not far away are immeasurable realms that exist only for the mathematician: an enormous nerve center has coalesced around the point of origin of a few lesser muscles. Somewhere inside, the individual mathematician is working, and his windows do not open to the outside, but into adjoining rooms. He is a specialist because no genius is any longer in a position to master the whole of mathematics. He believes that what he is doing will probably eventually lead to some practical cash value, but this is not what spurs him on; he serves the truth, which is to say *his* destiny, and not *its* purpose. The result may be economical a thousand times over; what is immanent is a total surrender and a passionate devotion.

Mathematics is the bold luxury of pure reason, one of the few that remain today. Even many philologists pursue interests whose practical value they themselves probably don't see, and this is even more true of the collector of stamps or ties. But these are harmless whims, which play themselves out far from the serious business of our lives, whereas it is precisely here that mathematics encompasses some of the most entertaining and intense adventures of human existence. Let me offer a small example: We may say that we live almost entirely from the results of mathematics, although these themselves have become a matter of indifference to mathematics. Thanks to mathematics we bake our bread, build our houses, and drive our vehicles. With the exception of a few handmade pieces of furniture, of clothing, shoes, and children, everything comes to us through the intervention of mathematical calculations. All the life that whirls about us, runs, and stops is not only dependent on mathematics for its comprehensibility, but has effectively come into being through it and depends on it for its existence, defined in such and such a way. For the pioneers of mathematics formulated usable notions of certain principles that yielded conclusions, methods of calculation, and results, and these were applied by the physicists to obtain new results; and finally came the technicians, who often took only the results and added new calculations to them, and thus the machines arose. And suddenly, after everything had been brought into the most beautiful kind of existence, the mathematicians—the ones who brood entirely within themselves—came upon something wrong in the fundamentals of the whole thing that absolutely could not be put right. They actually looked all the way to the bottom and found that the whole building was standing in midair. But the machines worked! We must assume from this that our existence is a pale ghost; we live it, but actually only on the basis of an error without which it would not have arisen. Today there is no other possibility of having such fantastic, visionary feelings as mathematicians do.

The mathematician endures this intellectual scandal in exemplary fashion, that is with confidence and pride in the devilish riskiness of his intellect. I could adduce still other examples, for instance when mathematical physicists were suddenly wildly bent on denying the existence of space and time. But they did not do this in a dreamy haze, the way philosophers sometimes do (which everyone then immediately excuses by saying: Look at their profession), but with reasons that rose up before us quite suddenly as palpably as an automobile, and became terribly credible. This is enough to show what sort of fellows these are.

After the Enlightenment the rest of us lost our courage. A minor failure was enough to turn us away from reason, and we allow every barren enthusiast to inveigh against the intentions of a d'Alembert or a Diderot as mere rationalism. We beat the drums for feeling against intellect and forget that without intellect—apart from exceptional cases—feeling is as dense as a blockhead. In this way we have ruined our imaginative literature to such an extent that, whenever one reads two German novels in a row, one must solve an integral equation to grow lean again.

Let no one object that outside their field mathematicians have banal or silly minds, or that they themselves are the ones who have left their logic in the lurch. Here it is none of their business, but in their field they do what we ought to be doing in ours. Therein lies the significant lesson and model of their existence; they are an analogy for the intellectual of the future.

If something of this seriousness shines through the playfulness I have been directing at the nature of mathematics, I hope these concluding remarks will not seem unexpected. People bewail our age's lack of culture. This means many things, but basically culture has always been unified, whether through religion, social convention, or art. For social convention we are too many. For religion there are also too many of us, although this can only be asserted here and not proven. And as far as art is concerned, ours is the first age that cannot love its writers. And yet, not only are there spiritual and intellectual energies at work in our time as never before, but also a unity of mind and spirit as never before. It is foolish to maintain that this is all a matter of mere knowledge, for thinking has long been the goal. With its claims to profundity, boldness, and originality, thinking still limits itself provisionally to the exclusively rational and scientific. But this intellect gobbles up everything around it, and as soon as it lays hold of the feelings, it becomes spirit. Taking this step is the task of writers. To do this they don't need to learn some sort of method—God forbid, psychology or the like—but only aspirations. Yet they are helpless in the face of their situation and console themselves with calumny; but even if our contemporaries have no idea how to transfer their intellectual level to the level on which they live, they still have some idea of what is beneath their notice.

[On Criticism]
presumably before 1914

In this essay Musil returns, as he frequently does, to the problems of stan-dards in criticism and reviewing, activities in which he was heavily engaged. As a practical critic with an intellectual program, he struggles with the question of how one can best do justice in newspaper reviews to the com-plexities of an experimental kind of literature, while genuinely informing the reading public without simply pandering to its ignorance.

Only in the most unusual cases is it useful to determine whether a book is good or bad; for it is just as rare for it to be one or the other. It is usually both. It makes sense to intercede for a great artist who is not yet recognized, and it makes sense to tear apart pretentiousness. It makes sense to write about a book if one can demonstrate something about it or if the critic feels an outburst of temper or enthusiasm rising up within him. It really makes no sense to take books one after the other, as publishers throw them on the market, and describe and evaluate them with the aid of at most fifty conven-tional standards. But that is just what the average critic does. In his socio-logical contingency he is a journalist, in his getup an eternist.

One of the most important tasks of a prize competition would be to moti-vate someone who was discriminating and precise to initiate an inventory of the concepts with which our criticism operates. The complete lack of content of these concepts would, presumably, already emerge from the fact that their various nuances cancel each other out to the point of nullity, which a comprehensive comparison would reveal. This cannot be proven as long as the data have not been systematized, but let someone try to read through all the reviews published on a single day by a given group of journalists, which can extend from *Die Aktion* to *Die neue Rundschau* to *Die n[eue] f[reie] P[resse]*,[4] and on most days he will laugh at their unanimity. It is a unanimity of words, of vagueness, and not of concept.

Such experiences move me to attempt to single out just one critical concept and, if not to investigate it in the manner indicated, at least to observe the main ways in which it manifests itself. I choose the concept of the psychologist, in its two different senses of "depth" psychologist, or psychoanalyst, and experimental psychologist.

. .

There was a time when the label "psychologist" was hung on every writer (who halfway tolerated it); psychology was in fashion. Today one can say that the label is mostly a term of invective. A depth psychologist was a demonic kenner of souls; an experimental psychologist is someone who finds his satisfaction in the *petits faits* of the soul. This expresses a change in attitude towards causality, and to this extent the change is time conditioned and justified by the time. But it also contains a complete misunderstanding of the significance of the psychological for art, and its extremely vague application stems from lack of understanding.

1. Is the psychological event an event like any other, part of the fullness of the world. It is interesting in itself. It is reality. Emphasizing it is connected with the question of naturalism in art, a question that is by no means exhausted by false experiments. All due respect to Expressionism's zooming upwards into the vacuum: strong intellectual achievements demand a broad basis and multifarious rootedness in reality.

2. Can this event, which really must be called eidetic (is a phenomenon), be accounted for psychologically. And here one must ask, What is psychology? Of course a science with a distinctive methodology that orders inner events not predominantly in terms of causality, but still according to a specific methodology, and that brings things into mutual relation. This has nothing at all in common with the way a work of art orders things. Above all: psychology strives for truth and factualness. Psychoanalysis is to be distinguished from psychology. But in principle the same.

3. Let us examine a so-called psycholog[ical] novel that really is a work of art. Strictly speaking, its psychology is always false, must consciously be

understood as somewhat false. This psychology must not place itself in contradiction to experience, at least not without foundation. But it is imprecise.

Call to mind the sense of the two sentences:
    Know yourself in order to know the world
              and
    To understand all is to forgive all
Psychology in the literary work has the same meanings contained in these sentences, knowing oneself and understanding someone else. Accepting this assertion settles the entire discussion, which has gone on for more than ten years, about the value or uselessness of psychology for the literary work. I know the world (here meaning the human, moral world) by knowing myself. Not by knowing what a reaction time means or an experience of phantom movement, things that interest psychology. Not by spreading over it the schema of the conceptual net developed by psychiatrists for psychiatric use, or the schematic framework of psychoanalysis. But by reconstructing the experience from its motivating elements.
    What is psych[ology]
    Psychol[ogy] and motivation [*Motiv*]
      Motivation [*Motiv*], *movere, movens*. Anything that moves something.
    Opposition to causal[ity]
        "   " reality
    Incarnation and motivation
      (Problem of Express[ionism])

At any rate p[sychology] in the hands of German critics is something entirely different from what people professionally involved with it understand by it/

Express[ionist] criticism too works with the means of Impressionism, with the impression that is reported.

[Franz] Blei is the only nonimpress[ionistic] critic, K[arl Kraus] the impressionist with an inner sense of lawfulness.[5]

Contribution to the formation of crit[ical] ideas
Stock-exchange atmosphere, which does not produce any finished goods but needs a rise with a reciprocal fall every few years
pedantic as well as unfinished

The object of psychol[ogy] is the general case.
"   "   " literature the personal case
Task of literature: *movere;* one part of that is: signify, augur.

The Goals of Literature

What the Goal of Literature Is Not

presumably before 1914

Musil is here concerned with one of his favorite themes, the disjunction be-tween the quality of a work and its relative popular success, a concern that obsessed him. On the one hand, he regarded popular success as a sign that the serious writer had sold out to popular taste (Musil called this kind of writer, with Thomas Mann in mind, the "big-time writer"—"Grossschrift-steller"); on the other hand, he longed for public recognition for his own uncompromising brand of writing.

In discussing this question two facts should be chosen as a point of depar-ture: 1. Many writers achieve in exemplary fashion goals that criticism posits as worthy. 2. Although this is the case, one remains on the whole dissatisfied.

. .
It would be worthwhile if someone who has the time would collect and order all the German reviews of German literary works of the last ten years according to both these viewpoints. I don't have this statistically ordered ma-terial available, and it would in any event be overwhelming; I can only pro-ceed from memory and call upon the memory of anyone who reads the literary reviews, newspapers, and chiefly jacket blurbs with *their* collection of reviews. One comes to the . . . conclusion that every year in Germany so-and-so many books are created in "a new language full of poetic beauty." So-and-so many are "profound," so-and-so many people "advance to the first rank among contemporary authors." Not to speak of the "abysses of passion," the "ordered spheres of sovereign magnificence," etc., which we find by the dozen. The reactivity is too great.

It is to be noted that by no means everyone, and by no means the same voices, attest to this; it is only the same thing that is attested to. (This is part of understanding the phenomenon.) In general, every good book (and for the most part these are good books) reaches only a small group, and it reaches each such group in a limited variety of ways (which is part of the comedy of it). One must rely on the witness of ten to twenty reviews, and this is possible because few books receive more. The success that goes beyond this is, I believe, a matter in itself, with special (psychological, pathological) motives.

Concerning great success right at this moment . . . it's like this: The book has for the most part some kind of artistic qualities, although these are not always predominant. It pleases too many people uncritically. Who don't discriminate. The process is similar in kind to mental epidemics. Even the better kind of people are carried away retroactively by the works that follow. Then even without opposition from criticism there comes a reaction, a slackening (this, too, similar to pathic processes). I would maintain that it is rare that one of an artist's books turns out better or worse than his others. Most people, of course, believe this to be the explanation. Rarely. Varying production on the part of an artist assumes a constitution far out of the ordinary. One can say that most good works take two or three years, and that in this time the smaller periodic perturbations cancel each other out. But artists who have great periodic perturbations in ability are rare, nor is the other case too frequent either, that of not finishing (for which Eulenberg[6] interceded). Aside from these two dangers the complete artist is usually present in every one of his works, with of course the greatest divergence in their degree of success, but there can hardly be any error in judging the personality that stands behind them:

Therefore neither great critical mass enthusiasms nor the extravagant dispensation of praise in small things is to be excused.

If one seeks the reasons for this—except that for a long time they were not to be found. Naturally they go back to critical talent being as rare today as artistic talent (not all that rare, but vanishing). It is impossible to complain about this. One symptom to be investigated, however, is that the reviews are mostly finer than the works; that is, they express things that the works themselves do not succeed in realizing. Things, however, which in the reviews too are mere words, lacking the fullness of representation. I single out a random handful.

Therefore one can allow that many people demand apparently worthwhile goals but do not have the standard to achieve them because they lack a real notion of the goal.

[On the Essay]
1914?

*This is probably Musil's most important statement of his conception of the
nature of the essay as an intermediate and mediating form of discourse between morality and life and between science and art. Musil's approach to
this problem is unusual in that he was a writer who was also highly trained
as a mathematician and scientist and deeply read in philosophy, and the
form of the essay offered a congenial place in which he could bring these
areas and problems together and confront them.*

For me, ethics and aesthetics are associated with the word *essay.*

It is said to come from "weighing," and is mostly used by scholars only
to characterize the smaller excrescences, those not written with full commitment, of their life's work; it is also called "attempt." I can also make use
of it in this latter sense, to which, however, I would like to give a different
content.

Is the essay something left over in an area where one can work precisely. . . . Or: the strictest form attainable in an area where one can*not*
work precisely.

I will seek to demonstrate the second case.

Description of the field: on one side lies the domain of epistemology, the
science of knowledge. On the other side, the domain of life and art. At the
outset it cannot be put any more exactly; for this reason we must ask how
the domain of knowledge is circumscribed. For our purposes it is *not* best to
say that it excludes subjectivity completely; "completely" goes too far. For
a certain cold, rational subjectivity *is* preserved, but there are spontaneous
and accidental factors as well. We might better say: Its results are objective.
It is dominated by the criterion of truth. This is an objective criterion; it lies
in the nature of the field. There are mathematical and logical truths. There
are facts and a combining of facts that are generally valid. That are systematic or in accord with laws. In both cases—and at the same time this is the
least of the claims we make for them—they admit a far-reaching spiritual
order.

And there are areas that do not admit of such an order. Try detaching
from writers' books the characters they have charmed into them, and applying to this fictional society the moral laws of human society. One will find
that every book-person consists of several people, that he is simultaneously
good and reprehensible, that he has no character, is not consistent, does not
act causally; in short, that there is no way one can order and classify the

moral forces that move him. One can indicate for this person no other path than the accidental path determined by the action of the book. The question whether Törless was right or wrong to torture Basini, whether, further, his indifference to this question is to be taken as a sign of right or wrong, simply cannot be answered. The question why it does not even arise could be answered only in a genuine essay.—As people belonging to a moral circle, with duties, obligations, and intentions, we read a poem and, as we read, all this changes a little in a fashion that can be pinned down almost only by feelings, which quickly dissipate.—Something similar may be said of those experiences we undergo in unusual moments such as those of love, of an anger out of the ordinary, or of any unaccustomed relation to people and things.

The essay lies between these two areas. It takes its form and method from science, its matter from art. (The expression "from life" is not correct, because it encompasses the matter of laws as well. What in life is analogous to art is what was meant above by the "area of life.") The essay seeks to establish an order. It presents not characters but a connection of thoughts, that is, a logical connection, and it proceeds from facts, like the natural sciences, to which the essay imparts an order. Except that these facts are not generally observable, and also their connections are in many cases only a singularity. There is no total solution, but only a series of particular ones. But the essay does present evidence, and investigates.

Maet[erlinck][7] once said: Instead of a truth the essay gives three good probabilities. We will later raise the question when such a probability is to be called "good." But for the moment we would like to ask once again how there can be areas in which it is not truth that dominates, and in which probability is something more than an approach to truth.

It must lie in the nature of the objects. That which is logical in an extended sense remains the same. Heretofore, to be sure, the distinction had been sought in such an extended sense of the function. Intuitive knowing was placed in opposition to the ordinary kind, and the attempt was made to derive from intuitive knowing the dignity of mystical knowledge. There is also intuition in the purely rational sphere. Beyond this, this conception is applied scientifically to. . . . But the mystical function is not this intuition, but a far more encompassing and conceptually less pure one. Man not only thinks, he feels, desires, senses, acts. Just as there are purely automatic actions without the participation of thought, so there are also purely rational ideas without the participation of the feelings or the will. And there are others as well. When a thought seizes us, bowls us over, etc., it does in the area of feelings what a revolutionary insight does in the purely rational area. The depth of its effect is a sign of how great masses of feeling are empathetically involved. Masses: for here it is not a question of feelings in the narrower sense of the term, but of basic feelings, dispositions of feeling, out of which individuality is composed. This is still a largely uninvestigated area. But one can assume that one factor here is the general emotional makeup of the individual, what has been called temperament, reactivity, stimulatability, etc.; a relatively stable state. Another factor is the personal experiences, including mental ones. These are preserved in a series of complexes interwoven with trains of thought. Depression is a so-called emotional disorder, but it consolidates its dominance with the aid of connected ideas which it colors. Philosophical pessimism, stoicism, Epicurean wisdom, are by no means simply rational structures, but also experiences. Now a rational course of thought can be true or false, as can an affective one, but aside from that it "speaks to us" or doesn't speak to us. And there are trains of thought that really work only through the mode of feelings. For a person who has no ear for them they are completely confusing and incomprehensible. But here it is nevertheless visibly a matter of an entirely legitimate means of understanding, even if it is not of binding general validity. The number of such ways of reaching understanding among people is moreover greater than assumed (chimpanzee couples, effect of a leader through charisma, etc.). Even the individual person has the experience that the same thought can be dead for him at one time, a mere series of words, alive at another.

This sudden coming alive of an idea, this lightninglike reforging of a great complex of feeling (most penetratingly imaged in Saul's becoming Paul) by means of the idea, so that one suddenly understands the world and oneself differently: this is intuitive knowledge in the mystical sense.

On a smaller scale it is the constant movement of essayistic thought. Feelings, ideas, complexes of will are involved in it. These are not exceptional functions, but on the contrary normal ones. But the thread of an idea tears the other functions out of their situation, and their rearrangement—even if it is only virtual—conditions the understanding, the resonance, the second dimension of the idea.

Since the difference does not lie in the function, it can only be grounded in the nature of the field. We know how much more limited the circle of our knowledge is than that of our interests.

We now exclude mystical interests because their object is metaphysical and because they claim superior knowledge, while we claim for the essay only the reshaping of what is human.

Maeterlinck, Emerson, Nietzsche, in part Epicurus, the Stoics: leaving aside the transcendental, the mystics, but also Dilthey, Taine, and nomothetic historical research, all belong in the circle of the essay. Here lies the human branch of religion.

We are confronting a new division of intellectual activity. That which is directed at knowledge, and that which is directed at a transformation of man. Complexes of feeling struggle for dominance. Leading ideas of centuries or generations. New kinds of relationships among people are showing up.

Now of course a rational reworking of the various results is valuable. At least a systematic ordering. It is simply that it must struggle with difficulties that can never be entirely overcome because of the ambiguity of expression. History of the spiritual movement.

Postscripts: Here Hegel's triple scheme of the rise of the concept is determinant.

Rathenau is the example of the degeneration of an essayist into a philos[ophical] dilettante.

A further boundary area of essayism is political writing in the daily press. It is exploitative without increasing the resources. Schleiermacher, Schelling, Hegel, Lassalle.[8]

The lack of systematic thinking determines that people write poetry and live like swine. Determines Romanticism, Expressionism, eccentricity. Speaking past one another.

Literary Chronicle
1914?

Musil shows himself bemused at the impulse to write; as always in these essays, his ironic rumination is directed at himself as well as others. Underlying it is his serious concern with establishing a proper relationship between the difficult problems of aesthetics and specialization on the one hand, and people's everyday lives on the other.

People who write. If one were to express in miles of line lengths or pounds of paper everything published every year just in Germany, one would immediately see that one was dealing with one of the most peculiar of social forms. For something must be wrong with the living of life if its migration onto paper is so extensive. This could not be said if the printed word were merely a form of communication, like the spoken word but with an extended reach; in that case it would serve to exchange experiences, and would match them in number. But in truth the printed word has today become much more a vehicle, not exactly of loneliness, but certainly of encapsulation within a group. Even leafing through bibliographies of scientific writings—whose only aim we would most expect to be communication—one is quickly astonished, no longer at the degree of specialization, but at how every little twig spreads out into a microcosm whose literature can hardly any longer be encompassed, and that closes like an impenetrable globe around those installed inside it. Indeed, there are people who, having devoted their lives to gathering the literature of stamp collecting or dog breeding, must recognize with dismay in the twilight of their lives that they had underestimated their task, and would have done better to have dedicated themselves just to European stamps, or to the breeding of setters. There are periodicals for metal-lathe turners, for watchmakers, shoemakers, hatmakers, and firemen.

What is remarkable is not the factual specialization, which is of course given, but the closed human sphere you enter, as if by mistake, whenever you open such a magazine. Suddenly a Mr. What's-His-Name comes out at you big as life, a man who is said to have paved the way in truly brilliant fashion for the American shoe in Europe, or a Mr. Different, who for twenty years has served the extinguishers of fires, not only with the rich hoard of his experience, but also with the outspoken manliness of his idealistic attitude and his constantly alert class consciousness. There is also a technical journal that only publishes serious literary contributions from the engineering profession.

In science this writing mania of the soul is less comical, but basically the same. Does one not require an upstanding fellow to be completely absorbed by his profession? Once, a European was a Christian or a Jew; today he is either a Frisian, an economic geographer, or a dye chemist, even with his soul. The large clouds have been atomized, and from every direction small spherical drops condense from the exploded mass of feeling. Today the individual as a person stands in the midst of a community of incomprehensible size, to which he is bound by relations such as national sentiment, racial equality, and humanity; but except in odd hours, in spite of all well-meaning protestations, these remain quiescent. He feels himself reluctantly dissolving into something of enormous size from which, except for a few comforts towards which he rapidly becomes dulled, he only receives by way of tangible counteraccomplishment the guarantee that things can continue as they are without disturbance. Of all the unheard-of experiences that, as a child, he believed were waiting for him, he experiences nothing, or something trivial that by chance happens to drift by the place in life where he is standing. He is in a forest, can't stir, and does not see the forest for the trees. So he feels the need to make the unknown distances smaller, to move into the center of a modest overview, and everything idealistic in him becomes localized.

Writing too must somehow concern itself with this matter of feeling. Writing attracts allegiance and demonstrates affinity; somewhere a person is being listened to with attention. This feeling clings to the officially objective activity of research along with research's tendency to seek the universal, as firmly as evenings over beer cling to scientific congresses.—But it is especially in serious philosophy and literature, the two areas in which one ostensibly needs to be only a human being, that that which is too constricted and too narrow in life expands without resistance. It is not to be assumed that people really have as much to talk about and tell as people do in literature, and if one examines the content of what is imparted, it is mostly not by any means so original as to explain the compulsion to express it. Looking at the matter this way one recognizes, rather, in general little else than a constantly stirred-up subjective rearrangement of an old inventory. The imagination does not fly or rove (an idea of long ago!), but writing appears, as when a minor religious functionary comes home and is the head of a family: power, capricious order, subjection of the world in effigy. *My book is my castle* [in English in original—trans.]; the writer is always right! This explains why there is really no longer any audience for this literature, but only authors, who move toward or away from one another. The reader is not looking for the leader, but the person who shares his point of view; he is himself the author of a weltanschauung and an anonymous aesthetics, and—based on the error that every judgment about art is, after all, merely subjective—he sees in the other only a kind of executive authority, someone who displays the arrangement of his mind. The consequence of this is the extraordinary lack of influence of this literature on the society and its debasement to an empty self-affirmation on the part of authors. If one sees this self-affirmation practiced daily by innumerable otherwise amiable Europeans as a harmless habit, painlessly and among their daily tasks, the idea burgeons to that of an ugly mania, a belated schoolboy vice practiced by bearded men.

Aesthetics as activity concerned with life.
    Usual: aesthete = dandy
    aesthetics full of activity concerned with life.

Commentary on a Metapsychics
1914

The term metapsychics sets a satirical tone for this review of Walther Rathenau's Zur Mechanik des Geistes (On the mechanics of the spirit).[9] *But Musil also saw the common ground between himself and Rathenau: although Musil criticizes Rathenau's narrow views on ethics, he appreciates his attempts to describe the condition of mystical awakening that Musil would later refer to as the "other condition."*

The notion that good works in this world somehow constitute our existence in the next—this pet idea of contemporary spiritualist philosophy, which no longer has enough confidence to guarantee personal immortality—has about it something of the child's need to take his toy to bed with him at night and into the dark hole of sleep. When combined with inappropriate didacticism there is something devastatingly comical about it, as in the case of Eucken [10] and sometimes even in Bergson. In Novalis—who never forgets that the thoughts that are in him were once in the body of his little beloved (whose brain they haltingly imitate)—it has suprasensuousness, a touching intensity; a pollenlike floating through the world of ideas as through a cloud of rose-dark fish eggs. Or it contains—this notion of the eternity of an encompassing totality of spirit which includes the personal—an ethic for the world here below, a song in a column marching with locked arms, a hymn to the brotherhood of man, the Marseillaise of a throng excited by its fear and marching from darkness into darkness. As it is in a small way in Emerson. I cite these instances in order to show something of the range of feelings that resides in these questions, and to recall the responsibility that the otherworldly owes to the profane. From among such possibilities I sense in Rathenau's book that of confessing to the others; I suspect that many of the book's dominant notions came to him in hours *before* the actual conceptualization and writing, and that they flowed from inspiration; but I don't see enough attention to other human possibilities.

When Rathenau says that the right sort of person—he calls him soulful—inclines toward love, renunciation, thought, intuition, and fearless honesty; that his character is loyalty, magnanimity, and independence; his comportment assured, serenely calm, and steady; that he is more likely to be strong than smart, self-confident than experienced; that he has a serene freedom of life, an inclination to transcendental exaltation, an intuitive religiosity: one can recognize in this the *program* of a human type that—if set out in a work of art or described with the same ultimate, inner resource in an essay—*can* be valuable, depending on how its qualities are defined more narrowly in relation to each other and to other people. But if, instead of painting an individual from this palette, authority is claimed simply for the palette itself, exclusively for this assortment of moral colors, then this is a different matter, and memories crowd in: that Dostoevsky was an epileptic, that Flaubert was one too, and that at profound moments in their lives their conduct could not have been an "assured and serene freedom of life." Horace ran from battle. Schopenhauer spewed venom. Nietzsche and Hölderlin went insane. Wilde was a convict. Verlaine an alcoholic. Van Gogh put a bullet in his gut. If those are exceptions, one would like to see the rule. But the early Greeks, to whom Rathenau appeals for the rule, loved Odysseus as well as Achilles; Nietzsche taught us to distinguish between the Apollonian and the Dionysian types, and even the tradition of the supposedly greatest of all Apollonian types, Goethe, is—as Bahr[11] showed in a good, older work —a legend. The exceptions seem somehow to be tangled up with the rule.

And if it is claimed that Egyptians and Asians produced only soulless art, although one thinks of the strange souls that came to us from there in etchings and stone; if it is said of spiritual peoples that their spirit hovers above the world of appearance and raises itself to the sovereign perspective of humor, which "apparently lightheartedly and detached, and yet full of the highest understanding, espouses the cause of all creatures," although one recalls that Dante, Goethe, Beethoven, and Dostoevsky had very little sense of humor as opposed to the lovable Thackeray, who had a lot of it; if it is mentioned that France has not produced a single poem, that great art is always simple and reflects the absolute, whereas one knows that these questions of art, when looked at more closely, turn out to be less simple; if it is said that what dominated among spiritual peoples were faith, loyalty, war, and positive ideals, while they were far removed from materialism, peace, erudition, and analysis, whereas one feels today along with many others that there can also be warlike virtues in erudition, knows that peace and faith usually constitute a unity, and fights for the view that ideals should not be posited prior to analysis but allowed to spring up behind it—then one recognizes that, despite all the modernity, the world is here being carved up once again into heaven and hell, whereas it is *between* both, made up of some kind of mixture; and it is precisely from such a mixture (which still needs much more study) of good and evil, sick and healthy, egoistic and self-sacrificing, that the questions of the earth blossom forth.

. .

Rathenau's book has a worthy excuse for this: that group of human conditions called experiences [*Erlebnisse*] of the soul or love, to use an expression that has become customary among essayists. His description in this book is beautiful, even if substantively.it can hardly offer anything new. It is the fundamental experience of mysticism.

This experience arises—Rathenau's description is masterful at this point—from a striving analogous to the power of love, a nameless power of concentration, an inner gathering and union of the intuitive powers. What must be overcome is neither a power nor an indolence nor a suffering, but paralysis and rigidification. This love submerges itself in nature without vanishing; it rests, so to speak, over the world of phenomena with out-stretched wings. Intentionality dissolves; we are not ourselves, and yet for the first time *are* ourselves. The soul, which awakens in this moment, wants nothing and promises nothing, but nevertheless remains active. It requires no law; its ethical principle is awakening and ascent. There is no ethical ac-tion but only an ethical condition, within which an immoral activity or way of being is no longer possible. The distinction between what we value and what we disparage, between what we love and hate, or cherish and despise, is very slight, and tells us only one thing: whether the growth of the soul is inhibited or fostered. In these sentences there is no cranny that is not im-pregnated with experience. This condition cannot be described to someone who does not already know it. Whoever knows it knows that emotional rec-ognitions, great inner transformations, and life decisions often appear in such moments to the person experiencing them as if they had risen up out of nothingness. In those moments one realizes that everything one had pre-viously thought with untouched understanding is completely irrelevant. One is in that condition of awakening that all mystics have prized as enter-ing into a new existence. Central factors always contribute to the sensory picture that we receive from the world; in this altered condition a strange emotional tone hovers over the world; the world itself seems changed. But one feels this miraculous movement already beginning to rigidify as soon as the intellect tries to grasp it in words.

If we transpose ourselves empathetically into the spell of such moods, we can understand the distaste for reason and analysis, the supposed simplicity, the lay piety, the ideals wide-eyed as children, the disdain for everything argumentative. These things do not necessarily belong to this experience, but they are understandable, and even the Greeks referred to such condi-tions with a word of love as the great "simple-ness" [*Ein-Falt*].[12] One recog-nizes the range of these assertions all the way down to the completely evanescent as it flickers up in such moments of inspiration, sometimes clearly, sometimes dimly and fleetingly marked out.

. .

The task Rathenau set for himself was to write a philosophy out of this condition. The condition is humanly important.

There are three possibilities. We may regard the experience as a rare and fragile one (which it is), whose preconditions one studies, whose content one tests against other of life's contents, and for which one searches for the fitting place in oneself. In this, despite all the corners of the soul we can sneak up on, the normal zones of inwardness remain the guiding centers. Or one tries to extend the condition of inner contemplation to the condition of all of life, and sacrifices normalcy to it. The religious mystics had the convention of God for this. They sank into God and were expelled out of him again, but God remained as a permanent possibility, as a sometimes achieved reality, and by being connected to his existence this condition gained breadth and stability. This is not possible today, but there remains a third way: since in exalted moments one recognizes the efforts of reason as worthless, to draw the consequences, which means attempting to construct out of the experience the spirit of the person who belongs to it and then thinking the world by means of this spirit rather than through reason. To attempt this is the purpose of the book; probably a hopeless task, but venturing such a task is still a more than ordinary service.

Nonetheless, what is missing in the execution is the experience, and a rational mysticism replaces a mysticism of feeling. This displacement is absolutely typical for all systematic attempts in this field. All that remains of contact with the spiritual is the strained holding on to a few concepts fashioned in the most intimate moments, among which everything else is interpolated with a spirit that is by nature outside the trance, and that is distinguished from scientific understanding [*Verstand*] only by renouncing its virtues of method and precision. The evidence of intuition slips away into the noncommital aperçu. What first presents itself as an aphorism, a clever insight, becomes a few lines later solidified material for new and further construction, and what emerges is a very peculiar pseudosystem, a kind of exasperated game of ordering in which the goal is to form preconceived figures from a number of specific stones. If, in addition, a difficult inner condition is maintained by force, as is repeatedly necessary to provide a locus for these insights, a certain vacuum of feeling arises behind the concentration of attention, and the spiritual content is dispersed. But at these points of inner loss external aids to the feelings always appear; metaphysics as ennoblement and heraldic speculation, which hangs the flayed skin of experience on the stars.

Even Rathenau's book is no exception to this fate; this can't be demonstrated in the details because it is the fatal flaw underlying the whole. The misfortune is that people who are concerned with such questions today have little understanding of the virtues of clear thinking, and will hardly feel that here everything is being lost again; while others, who would have such understanding, have for the most part no intimation that there is something here that has been grasped at a great depth but been lost again on the way back to the surface. Aside from the one great attempt by Nietzsche, we Germans have no books about people, no systematizers and organizers of life. With us artistic and scientific thinking do not yet come into contact with each other. The problems of a middle zone between the two remain unsolved.

ESSAYS 1918–1933

ON LITERATURE

Sketch of What the Writer Knows
1918

Musil was steadily working toward a statement of the function of the writer in modern society, at a time when the serious writer was being devalued as a cultural leader. This essay also contains what is perhaps the clearest of a number of definitions in Musil writings of two opposing kinds of knowledge, which he characterizes as the "ratioid" and "nonratioid," that play such an important role in his thinking, especially in The Man without Qualities. *In later essays Musil refers back to this definition several times.*

To the degree that respect for professors, damaged in the period of the 1848 Frankfurt Parliament and of Bismarck, has risen in our society, respect for writers has fallen. Today the professorial intellect has achieved its highest public standing since the world began, while writers have come to be called "men of letters," by which is meant people who are prevented by some obscure infirmity from becoming competent journalists. The social importance of this phenomenon is not to be underestimated, and is worth investigating. This investigation is limited to a consideration of intellectuality, and turns out to be, on a small scale, an attempt at a theoretical examination in cognition in that it observes the writer only as one who perceives in a certain way and in certain areas. This is a deliberate limitation that can, of course, only be justified by the result. But however much the talk here will be of the writer as a particular species of human being, it should be noted in advance that this species includes not only those who write; many also belong to it who avoid this activity. They form the reactive counterpart to the active portion of the type.

One can describe this type as the person in whom the irredeemable solitude of the self in the world and among people comes most forcefully to mind: as the sensitive person who is never given his due; whose emotions react more to imponderable reasons than to compelling ones; who despises people of strong character with the anxious superiority a child has over an adult who will die half a lifetime before he will; who feels even in friendship and love that breath of antipathy that keeps every being distant from others and constitutes the painful, nihilistic secret of individuality; who is even able to hate his own ideals because they appear to him not as goals but as the products of the decay of his idealism. These are only isolated and individual instances, but corresponding to all of them, or rather underlying them, is a specific attitude toward and experience of knowledge, as well as of the material world that corresponds to it.

The best way to understand the writer's grasp of the world is to proceed from his opposite. This is the person starting from fixed point *a*, the rational person on ratioid territory. (I ask to be forgiven the execrable neologism, as well as the historical mistake behind it, for nature has not oriented itself toward rationality, but rather rationality toward nature. However, I cannot find a term that adequately expresses not only the method but also its success, not merely the subjection of facts but also their submissiveness, this undeserved obligingness on the part of nature in specific instances which it would, of course, be tactless of man to require in all cases.) Roughly delineated, this ratioid territory embraces everything that science can systematize, everything that can be summarized in laws and rules; primarily, in other words, physical nature. It succeeds with moral nature, however, in only a few cases. The ratioid area is characterized by a certain monotony of facts, by the predominance of repetition, by a relative independence of facts from one another, so that they can usually also be joined to previously formed groups of laws, rules, and concepts in whatever sequence they may have been discovered; but above all the chief characteristic of this area is that in it facts can be unambiguously described and communicated. Number, brightness, color, weight, speed: these are concepts whose subjective aspect does not diminish their objective, universally communicable significance. (On the other hand, in the nonratioid area one can never have a sufficiently concrete conception of a fact such as the content of the simple sentence, "He wanted it," without having to add to it endlessly.) One can say that the ratioid area is dominated by the concept of the fixed and solid, and by the deviation that it excludes from consideration; a concept of the fixed as a *fic-*

tio cum fundamento in re [fiction with a basis in fact]. Here too, at the lowest level, the ground is shaky; the most basic principles of mathematics are logically unsecured; the laws of physics have only an approximate validity, and the constellations move in a system of coordinates that nowhere has a locus. But still one hopes, not without reason, to bring order to all this, and Archimedes' statement of over two thousand years ago, "Give me *a fixed place to stand* and I will move the world!" is even today the expression for our hopeful behavior.

It was from this kind of activity that the spiritual solidarity of mankind arose, and it flourished more than ever under the influence of a single faith and a single church. So nothing is more comprehensible than that people attempt to hold on to the same process even in (in the broadest sense) moral relationships, although this gets harder every day. Today even in the moral realm one proceeds on the principle of pile driving, and the solidifying caissons of concepts are lowered into the indefinite with a grid of laws, rules, and formulas stretching between them. Character, law, the norm, goodness, and the imperative, things that are solid in every respect, are such piles, to whose petrification one holds fast in order to attach to it the network of the hundred individual moral decisions every day demands. The ethic still dominant today is, in its method, static, with the fixed as its basic principle. But since on the way from nature to spirit we have stepped, as it were, from a motionless collection of minerals into a greenhouse filled with unexpressed movement, the application of this ethic demands a really comic technique of limitation and retraction, whose very complexity allows our morality to appear ripe for decline. Think of the popular example of the variation of the commandment "Thou shalt not kill," from murder through manslaughter, killing an adulterer, duel, and execution, all the way to war; and if one seeks the unifying rational formula for all this, one will find that it resembles a sieve, in using which the holes are no less important than the solid mesh.

Here one has long since entered nonratioid territory, for which morality merely serves as a leading example, as the natural sciences are for the other area. If the ratioid is the area of the domination of the "rule with exceptions," the nonratioid area is that of the dominance of the exceptions over the rule. There is perhaps a gradual shading from one into the other, but the distinction is such a polar one that it calls for a complete reversal of attitude in him who recognizes it. In this region facts do not submit, laws are sieves, events do not repeat themselves but are infinitely variable and individual. There is no better way to characterize this region than to point out that it is the area of the individual's reactivity to the world and other individuals, the realm of values and valuations, of ethical and aesthetic relationships; the realm of the idea. A concept, a judgment, are largely independent of the manner of their application and of the person. An idea is in its significance largely dependent on both; it always has a meaning that is only occasionally definite, and that dies if removed from its context. I take at random an ethical proposition: "There is no opinion for which one should sacrifice oneself and expose oneself to the temptation of death." Anyone who is shaped or even breathed upon by traces of ethical experience will realize that one can just as easily maintain the opposite, and that it would require a long treatise merely to show in what sense one meant it, merely to string experiences together to point in a particular direction, which then nevertheless branches out somewhere into a boundless thicket, although not without somehow fulfilling its purpose. In this realm the comprehension of every judgment, the meaning of every concept, is surrounded by a delicate envelope of experience as by an ether, by a personal free choice and, alternating with it every few seconds, a personal determinism. The facts in this area, and therefore their relationships, are infinite and incalculable.

This is the territory of the writer, the realm in which his reason reigns. While his counterpart seeks the solid and fixed, and is content when he can establish for his computations as many equations as he finds unknowns, there is in the writer's territory from the start no end of unknowns, of equations, and of possible solutions. The task is to discover ever new solutions, connections, constellations, variables, to set up prototypes of an order of events, appealing models of how one can be human, to *invent* the inner person. I hope these examples are clear enough to exclude any thought of "psychological" understanding, comprehension, and the like. Psychology belongs to the ratioid area, and the multiplicity of its facts is by no means infinite, as the possibility of psychology existing as a science of experience teaches. What is incalculably multiple are only the soul's ways of working, and with these psychology has nothing to do.

The failure to recognize that this is a question of two essentially different realms lies with the middle-class attitude that the writer is an outsider (from which it is not far to seeing him as unsound of mind). But in truth the writer is an outsider only insofar as he is the person who pays attention to exceptions. He is neither "madman" nor "visionary," neither "the child" nor any other deformation of reason. Nor does he apply any different kind or capacity of perception than the rational person. The significant person is the one who commands the greatest factual knowledge *and* the greatest degree of rationality in connecting the facts: in the one area as in the other. But one person finds the facts outside himself and another within himself; one meets with coherent sequences of experience and another doesn't.

Of course it might only be pedantry to analyze in such detail what is perhaps only a platitude, and I would like to add by way of apology what I have left unstated, although it is just as important: the differentiation of literature from the so-called cultural and historical sciences, which is not a simple one, but confirms what I have said above. But whether such investigations are to be judged as pedantry or as indispensable will be determined in the last analysis only by the importance one accords the demonstration that it is the structure *of the world*, and not of the writer's disposition, that assigns him his task: that he has a *mission!*

The writer has often been allotted the task of being the singer, the glorifier of his time, of ecstasizing it as it is into the superluminescent sphere of language; he has been charged with providing triumphal portals for the "good" person and the glorification of ideals, with providing "feeling" (meaning, of course, only certain feelings) and renunciation of the critical faculty that diminishes the world by taking away its form, as the collapsed pile of stones that was a house is smaller than the house had been. Finally, it was demanded of him (in the practice of Expressionism, which has this in common with the old Neo-idealism) that he confuse the infinitude of the object with the infinitude of the object's relations, and this gave rise to a completely false metaphysical pathos: these are all concessions to the "static," and the demand made by them contradicts the powers of the moral realm and is inimical to reality. It will be objected that everything I have said reflects only a purely intellectual point of view. Some creative works, of course, have few of the characteristics here considered central, and yet are shattering works of art; they have their lovely envelope of flesh, and that of the Homeric epics still shines down to us through millennia. This is basically the result of certain mental attitudes that have either remained constant or that recur, while the movement of humanity that has taken place in between has come from the variations. The only remaining question is whether the writer should be a child of his time or a begetter of ages.

[Psychology and Literature]
around 1920

In this sketch Musil objects to the loose and faddish use critics make of concepts—in this case, psychology—instead of developing rigorous analytical tools that would lead the public to a greater understanding of literature.

For more than twenty years the word "psychology" has belonged to the instrumentarium of the German critic. At first, to be a psychologist was the highest praise, but in the latter part of this period it has frequently been used—and in this lies, as we shall see, a certain progress—as a term of censure. Clear notions are as seldom associated with this idea as with any of the terms of criticism. That critics as well as writers suffer from these obscurities might justify the beginnings of a systematic investigation, in spite of the awareness that the methodology will be pedantic and the results incomplete and. . . .

Except for the most recent period, one will find few reviews of plays and novels in which an attestation of the author's psychology is not presented as well. This psychology is mostly to be regarded—naturally reflecting less the work than a weakness of the contemporary evaluator—as profound, probing, precipitous, knowledgeable, or the like. Even that in more recent times the word has faded and wandered off into the lower spheres of criticism proves—since this repression is of a piece with new principles [of psychology]—its still undiminished importance. To be psychological is today almost as much a gravamen as it was earlier. Nevertheless, it is exceedingly seldom that one will find clear ideas associated with the word.

It shares this fate with all the frequently applied terms of criticism, as everyone honestly concerned with criticism will admit. The "subjectivity" of criticism, which arose from rejection of a completely useless aesthetic pseudolearnedness—a "subjectivity" that even under the sign of Expressionism still operates with the impressionistic means of personal expression—has not been very favorable for the development of reliable concepts. The assumption that this bears a large part of the blame for the regrettable chaos of judgments in which our literature must develop is not far off the mark.

The unpleasant lack of consistency in our literary judgment, which never flows freely but is always clumpy in a deadening middle-class way or

That today criticism demands of a work of literature that it not be psychological, while fifteen years ago it demanded the opposite, encourages me to bring up the fact that there is no such thing as "psychological literature." This would have to be literature whose aim it was to give psychological explanations: didactic poems. The impossibility of this genre is evident even from the psychological side: there is a philosophical and speculative psychology, an experimental psychology, a psychiatric, and a psychoanalytic psychology. In their methods and, in part, in their goals they are all different, but one thing they have in common: they are aiming for knowledge. They systematically trace phenomena back to other phenomena, they seek the relatively general in the individual case. There has never been a literary psychology—which is to say a psycho-logy—with this goal. To be sure, during the period of Naturalism something like this *was* striven for, more clearly by the French than the Germans. There was the ambition (side effect of Marxism) to be scientifically precise in literature. This attitude, with its ideal of an antipathetic disillusionment and cynicism, was much more valuable than one can comprehend today. Of course the results were not great, or (if one can place Flaubert here) they were unfaithful to the theory. Psychology was regarded as a means. But what was this "psychology" of writers! From the standpoint of explanation: pseudoexplanation; tracing of phenomena back to other complexes of phenomena that had been personally selected as useful. The only necessity in this: that after a certain number of steps the explanation necessarily got bogged down. As literature, as we shall see, completely adequate; but it was not psychology.—Even Dostoevsky—and what derived from him—was no psychologist. His psychology too was false, but because he was a great writer he twisted it around for his purpose.—However, the reverse case exists: psychological works that are like works of literature. These are depictions of pathological processes of the soul that are marvelously penetrating, and so strongly metaphorical (for the "normal" reader) that the addition of interpretation that would make them into great literature is hardly missed.

There is a big difference whether one—see above: side effect of Marxism—as a half-scientific person whose imagination is gripped by the pleasures of science writes a pseudoscientific novel (cf. many pages in Zille, Elise,[13] Balzac, Zola), or whether one really goes all the way to the end of the trampoline of science and only then jumps. This psychological novel has not yet been written. It would perhaps start a new trend (could even be a metaphysical one: respect for law).

Analyze as an example of antipsychological literature a story by Kasimir Edschmid.[14] Show what the absence of psychology destroys in the content. (But don't overlook his aims!)

The psychological novel is not to be defended, but rather the rejection of psychology attacked.

Cinema or Theater
1926

From 1913 to about 1930, Musil was active as a drama reviewer for various newspapers. As is most evident in the essay "Toward a New Aesthetic," he was one of the pioneers in taking film seriously as an art form that introduced new concerns into aesthetics. In this response to a question circulated by the Magdeburgische Zeitung, *December 25, 1926, he objects to the failure of theater in the nineteenth century to contribute to intellectual progress because it was too concerned with success and aimed at the lowest common denominator.*

The New Drama and the New Theater

The theater has not played a role in the development of European spirit and feeling since the days of German Classicism. This or that exception may be allowed: but we need only mention the single name of Nietzsche, or the brilliant great chain of names that spreads all over Europe, suffering no interruption between Stendhal and Hamsun, to know that the novel and the essay, indeed even the lyric, have had a far more powerful and fundamental influence on the current or developing "formation" [*Bildung*] of the individual than has the theater.

The reason for this may be that no art form, with the exception of the almost defunct form of the verse epic, allows the spirit so little freedom of movement as does the drama, and is so unsuited to our way of thinking and our morality—which can be better understood from any physics manual than from the theatrical harvest of ten recent years. The theater is an apparatus as cumbersome as it is magnificent, with the most contradictory subsidiary interests and an intimidating economic risk; this is why it is conservative to the point of paralysis. We may say with confidence that nine-tenths of the points of view pompously advanced by theater directors, writers, critics, and actors as "laws of stage effect" are nothing but a dramaturgy of cutting real spiritual cloth down to marketable size.

Many of our contemporaries have rebelled against this mindlessness of the stage, with the result that all parts of a stage performance were "discovered" and made, one after the other, the chief part. The actor's theater, the director's theater, the theater of acoustic form and that of optical rhythm, the theater of vitalized stage space, and many others have been offered to us, if often only in theory. These efforts are what is usually meant when people speak of the "new theater." They have taught much that is worthwhile, but about as one-sidedly as the assertion that one should throw a man who has a cold in the fire, which is also fundamentally based on a correct idea.

For the experiences of our senses are almost as conservative as theater directors. What is to be understood through *seeing and hearing* (even if not at first glance) cannot be too far removed from what is already known. As incomparably as something unutterable may be expressed at times in a gesture, a grouping, a picture of feeling, or an event, this always happens only in immediate proximity to the word; as something hovering, so to speak, around its core of meaning, which is the real element of humanity. That is why all-too-radical attempts at reform are condemned to failure, not only because of their "boldness," but because, unfortunately, they are also burdened with more than a little inner banality.

Something similar is also true of the "immediate language" of feelings, passions, and events in the theater. A stubborn prejudice insists that the human spirit and thought be reflected in these things on the stage, but not be allowed direct expression. Happily, film, in the phase when it was imitating the stage, produced such a babble of expressive gestures that it undermined the idea that passions and events speak for themselves and only need to be hung on the line. Even in one's personal life the *outer* attitude of the mind is no more than a provisional and expressively meager translation of the *inner* attitude, and the essence of the person does not reside in his experiences and feelings but in his silent, persistent quarrelling and coming to terms with them.

The spirit has, to be sure, the unpleasant quality of not having come into the world for the theater alone, but for other tasks as well. It has its own events. But there are times when something can be expressed, or even only expressed, through means of the theater: then a "new drama" arises. This certainly does not mean that the theater exists only for the spirit; yet it cannot be overlooked that the business of the theater, the dramatic as licensed craft, would be disturbed by the rigorousness of the spirit's demands. I would answer this by saying that not even the Church consists of nothing but saints; but what kind of peculiar quality of the Church would it be if she were to regard the saints only as unpleasant surprises?

Literati and Literature
Marginal Glosses
1931

Here again Musil investigates, in a more exploratory way, the forms, defi-
ciencies, and ideals of the relationship between the serious writer and soci-
ety in a period when instability has overtaken the way we view the world as
well as the institutions of our culture, of which literature is one. He then
discusses the nature of lyric poetry and how the use of language in poetry
and the essay differs from rational and scientific discourse, and discusses
form and content in poetry.

Preliminary Note

These sketches are intended neither as a theory nor as a discovery; they
represent nothing more than a survey of some phenomena of literature and
the literary scene that in some way are related to each other. We might begin with the question why for us *literati* is a term of opprobrium, and in
addition is often used in a not entirely unobjectionable sense against those
who would like to be men of letters in an irreproachable sense. For among
us, people who live off literature by exploiting it as a kind of business are not
ordinarily called literati, but possess along with their income a neat professional tag, even if it only amounts to being called a writer of subtitles. Those
people are chiefly called literati who do not allow themselves to be guided by
any other consideration than their dependence on literature. They are *only*
literati, and the fact that from this a derogatory appellation not too far removed from the notions of the café or the bohemian could develop certainly
points to relationships within literature, or between literature and the whole
of human life, which must be quite remarkable.

A literature that permits such an imputation to be associated with the
term *literati* is reminiscent of an apple tree that would love to bear cherries
or melons, but please, no apples. What is wrong with the tree? We are all
first and foremost literati. For in the proper sense, literati are the as yet non-
specific functionaries of literature, the basic form that gives rise to all others.
The young person begins as a literatus and not as a writer, not to speak of
his immediately becoming a dramatist, historian, critic, essayist, and so on,
even if one should wish to admit a certain "being born for" one or the other
genre; and the nature of literature is in disarray as soon as this state of affairs is lost sight of. Then one might ask what the disturbances are that

cause the shared basic meaning to get lost in favor of the specialized form. This is the question that will be heard resonating in the following observations, even if only imperfectly and developed only according to certain notions.

Literati as a More General Phenomenon

Usually, where the appellation *literati* is used pejoratively, it is associated with a not unimportant idea that might roughly be expressed thus: literati are people who somehow concern themselves with literature too exclusively and at the cost of their "full humanity"; consequently, they are secondhand people who are not dependent (as writers supposedly are) on life's facts, but on secondhand reports. In other words, the chief features of this idea are the same as those of the notion one has of a scholiast, glosser, or compiler; in this sense the famulus Wagner [in *Faust*—ed.] was a literatus whom Goethe made both immortal and ridiculous. In truth, in the history of culture from antiquity to the present this sort of person has indeed played a role that has not always been edifying. But such a man, who swears by the words of the masters, is characterized by the paltriness of his own accomplishment while possessing comprehensive knowledge of the accomplishments of others. This would almost provide a definition of the literatus of the less desirable sort—if such a description did not also fit the average professor. It also fits strategists who are flops at making decisions, but quite useful instructors in military institutes; one might call them literati in the art of war. It further fits moral rigorists whose minds are entirely filled with precepts, as well as moral libertines whose minds are a sketchpad of liberties: both rigor and libertinage are essential features of literati.

This disproportion between one's own accomplishment and knowing about other people's is stamped differently by different circumstances. Where abilities might be called for, it will replace them with knowledge; where decisions are indicated, it will furnish scruple; where the task lies in developing a theory, it will make do with compilation, or take refuge in a never-ending experimental busyness . . . : in every case it seems to lead to a displacement, by means of which the strain of real achievement, for which talent, will, or circumstance do not suffice, is shifted to a more easily attainable secondary accomplishment that is sufficient to satisfy ambition. It is inherent in the nature of this process that in the course of it the unfruitful and unoriginal, if coupled with a certain achievement-oriented ambition, will always hit upon an active connection to tradition, while not reverting, or to only a small degree, to the most fundamental elements, whether of idea-formation, experience-formation, feeling, or practical decision making.

Literati in the bad sense are nothing but individual cases of this phenomenon, which embraces far greater areas.

Literati and Literature

Such an attempt to incorporate the phenomenon of literati in a context of related phenomena of course leaves open the question of what it is, finally, that makes this context unique, and what particular qualities differentiate belletristic literati from some other kind. If one observes them in order to determine this, looking at them as portraits of a particular social type, one finds the aesthetic literatus, according to the aspect one is looking at, to be differentiated from neighboring types either as a so-called intellectual or as a so-called man of feeling.

This means that he usually evokes in a genuine intellectual, such as for instance your average scholar, the impression of an insufficiency of intellect (usually, to be sure, with the appearance of an excess of feeling); while on the other hand he makes on a proper man of feeling—who finds talking difficult, who can not easily make decisions about anything, and who therefore remains firmly faithful to his words, resolves, and feelings—the impression of an "intellectual," whose feelings are weak, inconstant, and unreal. If one considers these things together, and supplements them from experience, the result is a person whose intellect plays with his feelings, or whose feelings play with his intellect (one cannot distinguish which); whose convictions are wavering, whose logical conclusions are not very dependable, and whose knowledge has vague boundaries, but who makes up for these deficiencies impressively by means of an easy, quick, wide-ranging, and sometimes even sharply penetrating intelligence, and by an ability and readiness like an actor's to immerse himself in mimicking alien areas of life and thought.

Without disparaging the writing profession, one might well object that hardly a single person devoted to it is entirely free of symptoms of this double aspect. But we could also proceed—since act and actor mutually determine each other—by looking at literature. In that case we would find something incomparably more important, the existence of an area with peculiarities corresponding in a significant way to those of the literati. Belles lettres as a whole, and in all its parts, has something infinite and unbounded; it extends outward without beginning or end, and every one of its creations is unique and cannot be replaced by any other, even though they permit comparison with each other to some small degree. Serious literature has no order beyond the historical, and only scattered fragments of an aesthetic-critical order. It knows no logic, but consists only of examples for a secret law or chaos. One could say that its intellectual component consists of memories without a conceptually tangible order. In such an area quotation (appealing to the polished word of the masters, instead of to the factored-out sense) is constitutive, and not merely expressive of a need for rhetorical ornamentation. Historically, the type of the humanist also began with classical and biblical quotation, and even though this kind of quotation, superficially at least, has now gone somewhat out of fashion, actually it has merely withdrawn within, so that all serious literature resembles a pond of quotations in which the currents not only visibly replicate themselves, but also sink into the depths and rise up from them again.

This process must necessarily give rise to some quite remarkable situations. Thus one could probably "dissect" any writer whatever (formally, or according to subject matter, or even according to the intended meaning), and would find in him nothing but bits and pieces of his predecessors; by no means completely "taken apart" and "newly assimilated," but preserved in broken shards. Perhaps pardon should be sought for such expressions, but there is no appropriate explanation or description of this process of literary tradition, a process of which one can state with certainty that even the most independent writer produces nothing that could not be shown to be almost exclusively dependent on traditions of content and form that he had assimilated. On the other hand, it appears that this in no way impairs his originality and personal significance. This phenomenon is most clearly apparent in the lyric poem, which in every instance, if it is beautiful, represents one of the incomparably happy occasions in literature—disregarding the fact that it can be more "unoriginal" than almost any other literary type if one compares its "form" and "content" with those traditional forms and contents in which it is embedded, which are apparently boundless but actually sharply bounded, like a transparent crystal in its transparent melt.

Thus in serious literature the peculiar situation emerges that the general, ongoing tradition and the personal contribution of the individual cannot be separated from each other. In this process the continuum does not grow in any dimension other than extent, nor does the personal element gain a solid position. The whole consists of variations that randomly come to rest on each other.

The Need for Compensation: Originality, Experience, Reportage, and Sublimity

Here we again touch on the question of originality (as we did earlier with the assertion that the literati do not get down to the basic elements). The term *originality* and its equivalents have caused many misunderstanding in literature. It was once maintained of German literature that it consisted of nothing but original geniuses; even in contemporary literature, however, one does not have to seek far to find personalities and conditions making profitable use of the aura of genius, which, in the eyes of an initially resistant public, always manages, in the end, to suffuse what has supposedly never before been present. What argues against this idea can be summarized quite briefly: obviously, it is only meaningful to speak of originality where there is a tradition. For determining the originality and significance of a scientific or mathematical accomplishment there is an objective standard that permits the distance from the accomplishments on which they are based to be judged, and the more rational or susceptible to reason some other area is, the more this relationship will be true in similar ways there as well. But the more such relationships are lacking, the more capricious and indefinable the concept of originality becomes. It is a concept of reciprocity. A literature that consisted only of originals would not be a literature, but then, neither would the originals be original, since one could gather them together into something resembling literature, and do so, moreover, in a routine and imprecise way.

Thus what this particularly luxuriant thriving of "originality" expresses is the systematic weakness of a literature, the weakness of the literary system in question. Part of this too, of course, is the collective suprapersonal notion of originality which has recently been more prominent than any other, and which, as "generation" or "generationism," has confused our ideas.

It is understandable that such a condition of weakness must of necessity also bring about all sorts of confusion in ideas and undertakings, which either exploit this condition or seek to obviate it. Thus, for instance, instead of asking about originality as a characteristic of achievement, one need only ask about individuality as the characteristic of the originator that corresponds to originality, and one is immediately reminded of that most extreme limitation, if not of the denial of the individual, which is today part of the cultural program of all political parties and is associated with the subordination of literature to preexisting views of the world. In this process the mutually antagonistic political camps are one, and the effortless spread of this "politicization," even if originally it only expressed politics' natural claim to dominance (just as many things can apparently be understood as a justified countermovement to the decayed cultural concepts of liberalism), still reveals nothing so much as the weakness and vulnerability of the idea of literature itself: literature has become, almost without resistance, an object of political will because it has no internal objectivity.

Aesthetically, this leads to the question of what the relationship is between the individual and collective components of an artistic achievement, and it can hardly be claimed that this question has been adequately confronted. But belles lettres has taken up a series of positions in relation to it, and over the last few decades this has been a not inconsiderable obstacle to proper understanding. Particularly worthy of emphasis among these efforts are those that might be summarized as anti-intellectual, because, in their desire to justify the writer's activity, they all lead in one way or another to ascribing to him as an uncommon, indeed occult, capability. Because sober human reason is an ordinary capacity of present-day people, these efforts decree that the "intellectual" can only rise as far as the level of "literati," while the genuine writer, or whatever the counterimage might be, must be a person who goes about his business with something that neither is nor needs intelligence.

This is the rough profile of all these cases. One need not always go as far as the past president of the Writers' Academy,[15] who, with self-apologetic intent, presented himself as a kind of seer assisted in his creativity by demons; ordinarily, one is satisfied with the sleight-of-hand term *intuition*, and the most important insinuations, historically, have been precisely those that appear to remain planted on the solid ground of existence. These declare the writer to be merely an especially portly kind of person who is susceptible to an unusual degree to the "true facts of life"; he is said to be, in short, a strong and original nature that somehow, by reason of his own strength, recognizes the great nature of mankind and drinks life, so to speak, from the udder.

What really lies behind this notion, which even today gives rise to all sorts of errors, is simply that in literature there are two kinds of reporting, the intuitive and the intellectual, which must always intermingle, but which in talented individuals are often separate. It is not difficult to find in world literature one's own examples of strong but relatively naive portrayers, and on the other hand those who are "processors," which also includes those ascetic artists of form who seem to get rid of everything personal and ideational in favor of the representation itself. There are also, according to this division, two kinds of immediacy, one relating to the experience itself and one to its intellectual reworking, even if this distinction is mingled with others that cannot be discussed here. This picture is entirely analogous to that offered by the natural sciences, in which there are people with experimental and theoretical talents, both equally necessary, but in the nature of the case almost never combined in equal parts in one and the same person.

This is the present state of affairs, and it was a fateful exaggeration when, about a generation ago—in that period, still important today, that called itself "Naturalism" and "Impressionism" in protest against an art of ideas that had faded to the faintest echo—the value of "facts" and of so-called human documents (the "petits faits" Nietzsche railed against) was one-sidedly considered central; for this marked the entry into our literature of the idea that the writer must be above all a whole person from whom art bubbles out warm, without anyone bothering their heads about how God could really instigate the creation of such a writer producing his cow-warm work without offending against the laws with which He has otherwise bound the human spirit. This small error had no less a consequence than that since that time the concept of literature has been completely lost among us, since, far more than the concept of the writer himself, it assumes the synthesizing (meaning above all the highly rational) elements of the mind.

The false understanding of originality and the protest of the literati against literature, both of which were included in the heart of Impressionism, have survived Impressionism. For a fine recent example, the reactive phenomenon may suffice—no less illustrative for being a single episode—that has been baptized by its inventors "reportorial art." This amounts to renouncing everything that claims to be more than mere reportage. Such objective reporting of life is by no means hostile to the intellect, as Impressionism was (at least in its effect). On the contrary, this objective reportage, intellectual on the journalistic level, is by no means subjective and does not coddle the "personality," but, with every sign of objectivity, it still manages to neglect what Impressionism's subjective reporting of experience also left out of account: that there is no objective reporting of life that does not presuppose an intellectual system by whose aid the report is "created" out of the facts. At that time a vague notion of "personality" was substituted for this intellectual framework; today it might be the framework of the newspaper, or consist of a political intent; it can content itself with a few simple ethical principles, as the group of "Naturalists" once did; at any rate, it is today as little the intellectual framework of literature as ever. Thus with the passage of years the only thing that changes in this skepticism about literature is the way it is expressed.

The truth is that we constantly find ourselves in a state of doubt about the skein of art that has come down to us, and in this lies a tendency to allow life to flow on as it is and however it wishes. With the utmost complacency this tendency gives itself the appearance of principle through the gesture of furnishing a report. But there are also less comfortable phenomena that accompany this condition, phenomena more deeply imbedded in the problematics of literature, such as the way logically hermetic narrative form has loosened into the logically, indeed psychically almost asyntactic form which has gained prominence through Joyce and Proust. This would be the place to treat this development, if there were not another, more comprehensive one that has higher priority. For it is well known that in unstable situations the tendency to devalue something and to overvalue it excessively are in close proximity; so it can come as no surprise that the lack of results by which literature is oppressed—not as a personal activity, but as a whole—has constantly led to the opposite of the aspirations I have been discussing, that is, to an exaggeration of the literary tradition that turns away from the activities of the day, and the elevation of literature as a poetic Elysian Fields in which a person wanders according to laws other than the common ones. In fact this consecratory heightening of the world and turning away from it has, in the period under discussion, formed the exile of pure minds of firm resolve, and if one conjures up their names, which are associated with great stringency and beauty, one realizes that on this boundary the operations undertaken up to this point can be extended only with the greatest caution. Here we touch on the peculiar innermost zone of the majesty of humanism that lies in a somewhat arrogant half light, filled half with truth, half with futility; and the final problem to which the loosely ordered circle of our series of problems has led is really: literature as a reaction to the fact that there is no literature. This question too is a variation of the interpenetration of dependence and independence, but at this point it would be a good idea to change our method of observation.

The Spirit of the Poem

One should never forget that the innermost source of a literature is its lyric poetry, even if one thinks it false to make this a question of artistic ranking. For the custom of regarding the lyric poet as the poet in the true sense of the term is a profound one, even if somewhat archaic. Nowhere is it shown more clearly than in poetry that the writer is a being whose life is lived under conditions that differ from the ordinary.

But we have no idea what a poem actually is. Not even of the outer reaches of poetic effects that are governed by the concepts rhyme, rhythm, and stanza do we have knowledge that would unburden our relation to the poetic experience, let alone understanding much about its inner nature. A certain kind of association of ideas that deviates from the ordinary: it sounds matter-of-fact to say that this is what a poem is, but it is perhaps the safest assertion of whatever could, for the moment, take us further. From an idea no more beautiful than dozens of others, that children walk singing across a bridge under which the lights of boats and reflections from the bank are swimming (itself immeasurably superior to the banal: children are singing on the bridge, lanterns swim on the stream), Goethe forms two most magical lines by a transforming twist: "Lichtlein schwimmen auf dem Strome / Kinder singen auf der Brücke" [Lanterns swimming on the stream / Children singing on the bridge].

If one observes the rhythm here, which the fingers can tap out on a tabletop, it does not have much more meaning than as a supportive accompaniment. The sound picture that is palpably part of the changed impression cannot be separated from it, and has no more of the quality of self-sufficiency than one side of a geometric figure would. Thus one could analyze such a line for other changes, but would find nothing but details that, by themselves, are as good as meaningless. One can only explain that it is from all these details taken together, and through their mutual interpenetration, that the whole arises in a way that remains mysterious. Now there are many people who love to see mystery in poetry; but one can also love clarity, and perhaps in this case one is not quite so hopelessly barred from it. For if one reads the above lines in their first version, and then in their final form, one experiences (along with everything else) that the absolutely tangible contraction the sentences undergo at the moment the right words are found, that the unity and form that vault up like a bolt of lightning out of the diffuse first version, are not so much a sense experience as a transformation of sense that eludes logic. And why would the words be standing there, if not to express a meaning? In the last analysis even the language of a poem is a language too, which means that it is above all a communication; and if one could glimpse the essence of the process in the poem simply in this transforming of meaning, which can be transformed in this way only by means of the poem, then all the details one recognizes, without being able to combine them, as participating in the poem would gain an axis that would make their connection comprehensible.

Much seems to speak for this. The word is not the bearer of a concept to the extent one usually assumes, corrupted by the fact that in certain circumstances the conceptual content can be defined; it is, rather, so long as it is not restricted by definition to technical usage, merely the seal on a loose package of ideas. Even in such a simple and straightforward combination of words as "the heat was intense," the ideational contents of *heat* and *intense*, and even of *was*, are quite variable, depending on whether the sentence applies to a Bessemer furnace or a stove in a room, while on the other hand a heart and the intense warmth of a stove in a room still have something in common. The sentence not only derives its meaning from the words: the words also derive their meaning from the sentence, and the relationship between page and sentence, whole work and page, is no different. To a degree even in scientific language, but most extensively in nonscientific language, the embracing and the embraced develop their meaning mutually out of each other, and the structure of a page of good prose is, analyzed logically, not something frozen but the vibrating of a bridge, which changes with every step one takes on it. In this process it is, as we know, the peculiarity and the task of scientific or logical or discursive thinking or, as one could say here in contradistinction to literature, thinking that is faithful to reality, to give form to the sequence of ideas, to make it unambiguous and inescapable. Logical rules only oversee this process, and even psychologically it is a fairly straightforward habit.

One can also renounce this habit, and give words back their freedom; but even then these words will not simply link up with each other according to whim, for in that case the words are to be sure ambiguous, but their *meanings* are related to each other, and when one grasps one meaning the others peep through beneath it; they never decay into the completely random. In place of conceptual identity in ordinary usage, what dominates in poetic usage is in a certain sense the similarity of the word with itself; and instead of the laws that regulate the logical sequence of thought, a law of enticement is operative. The literary word resembles a person who roams at will: he will pass his time in an adventure, but not without being involved, and he will have to master powerful exertions, for mastery of the halfway definite is in no way easier than mastery of the completely definite.

It has been maintained that in the sequence of thoughts in a poem an affect takes the place of the determinant controlling ideas, and it also seems to be true that a unified affective basic mood is always involved in a poem's composition. But speaking against this, according to the testimony of the poet, is that what makes itself decisively felt in the choice of words is above all the intense work of the intellect. Likewise, the distinction between the word in logical and in artistic usage has been explained (if I remember rightly, by Ernst Kretschmer in his *Medical Psychology* of 1922) according to whether the word appears in the full light of consciousness or is, so to speak, at home on its margin, in a half-rational, half-emotional area which Kretschmer calls the "sphere." But even this assumption—which, by the way, like the much too spatially named term *subconscious* in psychoanalysis, is only a figure of speech, since consciousness is a condition and not an area, almost even an exceptional condition of the inner life—would have to be supplemented by the insight that in our representations not only the interrelationship of conditions, but also the interrelationship of objects, is located between *all* degrees of the "spheric" and whatever is capable of being unequivocally conceptualized. There are words whose sense lies entirely in the experience to which we are indebted for their acquaintance, and this includes many of the moral and aesthetic ideas whose content varies to such an extent from person to person, as well as from one time of life to another, that it can hardly be grasped conceptually without sacrificing the better part of its substance.

In an essay that appeared a long time ago ["Sketch of What the Writer Knows"—ed.] I once called this "nonratioid" thinking, with the intention of distinguishing it from scientific as well as from "ratioid" thinking, whose content corresponds to the capacity of reason, as if wishing by this means to give the province of the essay, and beyond that the province of art, intellectual autonomy. For scientific judgment understandably tends to overestimate the affective-playful element in artistic creation at the expense of the intellectual component, so that the spirit of opinion, belief, intuition, and feeling, which is the spirit of literature, can easily appear as an inferior stage of scientific certainty. But in truth two autonomous realms of experience and knowledge, whose logic is not entirely the same, underlie the two ways of thinking. This division into what can be characterized as ambiguous and unambiguous objects does not contradict, but is only supplemented by the fact that the area of what can be communicated and of human communicability presumably extends on a graduated scale from mathematical language at one end to the almost entirely incomprehensible affective expression of a mentally ill person at the other.

Excluding the pathological, and limiting oneself to what in some way has communicable value for a group of people, one could for instance place on this graduated scale, at the end opposite the purely conceptual, the so-called nonsense poem. This meaningless or objectless poems, advocated from time to time by groups of poets, always with conflicting motives, is especially noticeable in this connection because it can be really beautiful. Thus Hofmannsthal's lines "Den Erben lass verschwenden / an Adler Lamm und Pfau / das Salböl aus den Händen / der toten alten Frau" ["Let the anointing oil from the hands of the dead old woman be squandered by the heirs on eagle, lamb, and peacock"] will surely have for many readers the qualities of a nonsense poem, because without aid it is simply impossible to guess what the poet actually had in mind, even though one cannot avoid a feeling of spiritual empathy. One might reasonably claim that this happens to many people with many poems, at least in part. These lines are not beautiful in this situation because Hofmannsthal had a specific thought in mind; they are beautiful even though one can not derive any idea from them. If one knew what one was supposed to think while reading them, they would perhaps be more beautiful, or possibly less; because the thought and knowledge one brings to these lines already belong to rational thinking and receive their meaning from it. One might, of course, be tempted to regard this not as an example of art, but only of the reader's lack of art; but then one should make the complementary experiment of laying a cipher code over a poem by an expressive poet (Goethe for example), or in some other mechanical way merely tag every tenth word or third line. In eight out of ten cases it is astonishing what vivid half-images this gives rise to. This speaks strongly in favor of the view advanced here that the central event in a poem is the formation of meaning, and that this proceeds according to laws that deviate from those of logical thinking without losing contact with them.

In this manner, the question that the poet's feeling raises against secular rationalism would also be resolved. This rationalism is indeed his enemy, a form of intellectual movement that accords as badly with his own as two different rhythms in body movement would accord with one another. One can perhaps see this most clearly in the extreme that, in lyric poetry, is most opposed to the nonsense poem: the peculiar nature of the didactic poem, which has all the aesthetic indicators of a poem but contains not a drop of feeling, and thus consequently also not a single idea that does *not* come under the laws of the rational mode of understanding. One feels (at least today one feels) that such a thing cannot *be* a poem; but people did not always feel this way, and, between these two contrary poles of the all-too-meaningful and the all-too-meaningless, poetry is spread out in every degree of intermixture, and lets itself be comprehended as the amicable-hostile interpenetration of both. Poetry so mixes "profane" with "irrational" thinking that what can be said to be peculiar to poetry is neither one nor the other, but precisely their combination. This might also furnish the most fruitful explanation of everything previously characterized as anti-intellectualism, including its exaltation and its Romantic-Classic turning away from life.

A special word might be said about this turning away from life. One not infrequently hears the opinion expressed, and always by someone who really has something to say, that great poetry must assume a doctrine, an ideological accord, or firmly established convictions of the general public, if it is to reach its full force (often even with the implication that this is why today there is no great poetry). There is a lot to be said for this. It is illuminating that when the tension of what one wishes to say is relieved by "leaning against" something, energies are released and can incorporate themselves into the expression, and the psychological law that holds that the interests of ambivalent feelings tend to disturb one another probably also plays a role. So it is reasonable to assume that every person who writes must have had the experience that only when the content is completely under control does the form rise to complete freedom of invention. The assertion that this is also true for the development of literature in general can at any rate be admitted in the sense that an especially seductive and pure kind of beauty in the poem arises in those periods that feel themselves ideologically on stable heights. Franz Blei, to whom we are indebted for a great many useful critical observations, in representing this view in his fine *Story of a Life*, even speaks of "poetry injuring itself through simultaneously generating philosophy."

If this were entirely the case, any view that regarded something capable of intellectual enhancement as the soul of the poem would be in trouble; but obviously such "radical classicism" arises only from the need to characterize sharply, by means of the extreme toward which one leans, at least one's own standpoint in a discussion that is already thematically vague. For even if, in poetry, perfection of the form were what was most important, under conditions of totally unrestricted creation and in suspended time, this formation of a given content would still include changes in this content. So there is no genuinely Catholic work of art that would not earn for its creator at least several centuries of hellfire on account of heresy, and later ideologies than Catholicism do not permit the deviations to emerge so clearly only because they themselves are vague.

Thus in the connection that exists between classical beauty and intellectual ferment it is a matter of a relationship, and this is none other than that previously characterized as the breach of meaningfulness by nonsense. Blei says, speaking of Swinburne "and not only of him," so clearly that I would like to quote him,

One can measure by his sometimes sullen, sometimes insincere perceptions how by any conceivable standard the poet's diction is so meaningful that the form of expression makes one completely forget, hardly assimilate, what it is that has been expressed; perhaps Swinburne forgot it himself. But Swinburne's style is not simply musical or sensual; for all his spontaneity, what is most characteristic for this improviser of artfully constructed stanzas is the great precision of expression and assurance of the image. The impression that it has to be the way it is, this way and no other, is so compelling that one can not conceive of him working over the stanza: it arose spontaneously.

This describes in compressed but complete form how even in the classical poem meaning can arise out of meaninglessness, so that not only sensual experience but also meaning that has the "greatest precision" arises out of "insincere perceptions." Nothing justifies the assumption that the gift of thinking or the sense of contemplation so intimately intertwined with art stands in contradiction to imagistic language: these are gifts with different origins and reach their peak in different people or periods, and precisely that poets who have an exceptional command of language often content themselves with an eclectic and ornamental picture of the world may in this way be connected with their *need* for language. But the poem that arises in this way is in most cases really nothing more than something meaningless in front of, so to speak, a collectively reflected background of sense—which does not imply a lack of respect, for practically speaking the rarity of great talents makes any other distinction of value pointless. But one should be clear about this from a theoretical-critical point of view, because the will of the individual is formed in relation to society; and if the sense of a poem grows out of an interpenetration of rational and irrational elements in the way I have described, it is important to hold the demands of both in high regard.

The Significance of Form

It would be simply misleading if these partial observations were to pretend to consistency and completeness; the connections, general as they are, will have to be left to speak for themselves. But for this purpose they also need to be supplemented by a few words about the concepts of form and composition employed. Old conceptual aids from the observation of art, these concepts were in earlier times mostly applied, especially in popular-critical usage, to supposing that a beautiful form is something added to or missing from a beautiful content (or vice versa, unless both are found not to be beautiful). There was a not unknown anthology of German lyric poetry from the 1860s or 1880s in whose preface this was very cleverly discussed, but these good principles were followed by a selection of extraordinarily bad poetry. Later, people again had the idea that form and content constitute a unity that cannot be completely dissolved, and the prevailing view today seems to be that only formed content constitutes the object of observation in art: there is no form that does not emerge from a content, no content that does not emerge from a form, and such amalgams of form and content are the elements out of which the work of art is composed.

The concept of "gestalt" is the scientific basis for this interpenetration of form and content. It signifies that out of the juxtaposition or sequence of elements given by the senses, something can arise that can be neither expressed nor measured by them. As one of the simplest examples, a rectangle can be said to consist of its four sides and a melody of its sounds, but also of their unique internal relations, in the position of the sides in relation to each other, and of the notes to each other. This constitutes the gestalt, and expresses something that cannot be explained on the basis of the expressive possibilities of the individual component parts. As one can also see from this example, gestalt figures are not completely irrational, since they allow comparisons and classification, but they still contain something individual and unique. One could also say, to use an older term that will continue to be used as well, that they are a whole; but it must be added that they are not an additive whole, but in their moment of origin they bring into the world a special quality that differs from that of their elements. One might even add (and this would be important for what follows) that the whole imparts a fuller mental [*geistig*] expression than the elements of which it is composed. For a figure has more character than a line, and a configuration of five tones speaks to the soul more than would an amorphous sequence of the same five tones. The scientific question of where in the ordering of psychological concepts the gestalt phenomenon belongs is controversial, and there are quite varied and opposed opinions; but it is certain that the phenomenon exists, and that important characteristics of artistic expression, for instance rhythm and intonation, are similar to its characteristics. If we therefore draw conclusions, as we shall, about higher and more complicated phenomena in life and art, we should nevertheless not forget that we are temporarily abandoning the precision of the area of this problem that is scientifically circumscribed.

Backed by this reservation, we might now boldly assert that a striving to summarize as mental wholes everything received and emitted, as happens with elementary gestalt perception, everywhere plays an important role in the proper mastering of life's tasks. This belongs in the large orbit of those mentally economizing arrangements that aim, by many routes, at the simplification and economy of actions, and that have their origin in the physiological realm. The "one-two-three" by which a recruit learns any kind of physical routine as separate parts of a process melts, once he has mastered it, into a kind of bodily formula that he can repeat smoothly and as a whole, and the process of mental acquisition is not much different. This way of constructing formulas is also clearly evident in the life of language, where the condition constantly prevails that someone who uses words and sentences sensibly and according to their meaning remains incomprehensible to the majority of his linguistic compatriots because they do not speak in such articulated fashion, but rather talk in tidily packaged bundles. This formula formation is as valid for intellectual as for emotional attitudes, and is no less valid for one's whole personal bearing than it is for details. Imagine, if you are not put off by a graphic example, an ordinary dental procedure in its parts and details, and you will come up with the most insurmountable horrors: the breaking open of bony parts of the body, intrusions of sharp hooks and poisonous substances, stabs in the flesh, the opening of inner canals, and finally the tearing out of a nerve, almost a piece of the soul itself! The whole trick of removing oneself from this mental torture lies in not breaking it down in the imagination but instead, with the casualness of the practiced patient, replacing it with the smooth, round, familiar unity "root-canal treatment," to which, at most, some slight discomfort is attached.

The same thing happens if one hangs a new picture on the wall: for a few days it catches the eye, but then the wall swallows it up and one does not notice it any longer, although presumably one's total impression of the wall will have changed slightly. To express this in terms popular in the literature today, one could say that the wall works synthetically; the picture has for a while a divisive or analytic effect, and the process consists in the greater entity, room wall, swallowing and incorporating the smaller whole, picture, almost without a trace. One is satisfied to call this *habituation,* but since this term does not express the active sense of the process, it does not sufficiently characterize the phenomenon. This active sense clearly consists in one's always "living within one's four walls," in order to do with undivided energy within a stable whole what is called for by the particular task of the moment. One can apparently even imagine this process extended to an ultimate degree, for the peculiar illusion that one calls the tenacity of the life feeling also gives the impression of being such a protective hermetic surface for the mind.

As these examples show, the formation of such entities is naturally not a task for the intelligence only, but is carried out by all the means at our disposal. Here too lies the significance of those so-called completely personal expressions, which extend from the way one puts an end to an unpleasant situation with a shrug of the shoulders to the way one writes a letter or treats another person, and this "forming" of the material of life has its own great importance in enabling a person to finish his tasks, along with acting, thinking, and that retarding inclination that is usually called feeling.

If this does not succeed, if, for instance, the person is what we today call a neurotic, then his failures—which express themselves as hesitation, doubt, scrupulous obsessiveness, anxiety, not being able to forget, and the like—are almost always to be understood also as a failure to develop the forms and formulas that make life easier. And if one turns from this argument back to literature, one can understand to some degree the profound uneasiness that the "analytic mind" encounters in it. The individual, and humanity too, preserve a right similar to the right to a night's sleep by defending themselves against the dissection of the formulas of thought and feeling; changing them does not seem to them an urgent matter. But on the other hand, excess in accepting "whole" states of affairs is just as characteristic of stupidity, especially moral stupidity, as is excessiveness in dissecting things that have unstable natures. This is obviously a question of a mixture, whose proper proportions in life will be no more frequently met with than one meets in literature the proper proportion between credulous narration and analytic investigation: the charm of narration consists in its unbroken flow.

From this viewpoint, the concepts "whole," "gestalt," "form," and "ordering" have so far been used as if they were identical, which in actuality they are not. They come from different fields of research, and are distinct from one another in that each partly characterizes the same phenomenon from different sides, and partly characterizes phenomena that are closely related. Since their use here aims only to indicate and make visible a basis for the concept of the irrational in art, and why its relation to the rational is not one of opposition, the present unity of the object suffices, without depending on details; indeed, these could be rounded off even further. For in the psychology of the self in the course of the last generation, under various kinds of influences, the traditional, very rationalistic model of the soul which had been unintentionally based on the model of logical thinking (it could have been called a centralistic psychology of authority, since it is partially preserved today in juridical and theological modes of thinking) has gradually given way to an image of decentralization.

According to this image, everyone carries out most of his decisions not rationally, with a goal in mind, indeed hardly consciously at all, but by reactions, so to speak, of closed parts, "achievement complexes," as they have also been called,* that "speak" to specific circumstances, unless the whole person does something that the awareness only catches up with afterwards. This is not to be understood in the sense of a "decapitation"; on the contrary, it reinforces the importance of consciousness, reason, the personality, etc. Nevertheless, in this view in a great many actions, and specifically the most personal ones, the person is not led by his self but carries his self along with him: in the voyage of life it clearly occupies a position halfway between captain and passenger. Gestalt and form too display precisely this peculiar position halfway between corporeality and spirit. Whether one is looking at a few expressive geometric lines or the ambiguous repose of an old Egyptian visage, what presses outward, so to speak, from the materially given is no longer merely a sensory impression, nor is it yet a content of clearly defined concepts. One might say: it is corporeality that has not entirely become spirit, and it appears that this is precisely what excites the soul: for by their adherence to the external world the basic experiences of feeling and perception, as well as the abstract experiences of pure thought, nearly exclude the soul.

---

* Not to be confused with the concept of complexes in psychoanalysis. This essay does not use psychoanalytic ideas for various reasons, among them that these ideas have been taken up too uncritically by belles lettres, which at the same time "punish" the "psychology for schools" with disrespect, mostly out of ignorance of the possible ways it could be applied.

In the same fashion, rhythm and melody can doubtless claim to have some spiritual value, but along with it they still have something that has a direct effect on the body. This physical quality dominates in dance, but the spiritual flickers in it like a play of shadows. Even performing a play has no other sense than giving the word a new body through which it may gain a meaning it does not have by itself. The summation of this experience is perhaps expressed in the fact that so many clever people regard art with as little understanding as imbeciles, while on the other hand there are people who can without fail characterize the beauties and weaknesses of a poem, and act accordingly, without being able to express themselves in logical terms. It is misleading to consider this a particularly aesthetic ability, for what such a thing would ultimately consist of would be only a fraternal function of thinking, one intimately interwoven with thinking, even though the extremes tend in opposite directions.

Conclusion

Of course it would be a misunderstanding simply to equate poetry with form. For a scientific thought also has form, and not only the ornamental form of its more or less beautiful presentation, which is what is praised (usually wrongly), but an inherent and architectonic form that shows itself most clearly in that, even when expressed most objectively, it is never perceived by the receiver exactly as the originator intended, but always undergoes a reshaping that adapts it to the receiver's subjective understanding. Still, form in this case does recede strongly behind the invariant, purely rational content. Even in an essay, an "observation," or a "contemplation," the thought is entirely dependent on its form, and it has already been pointed out that this is related to the content that is given expression in a genuine essay, which is not merely science in slippers.

In the lyric poem it is most completely the case that what is to be expressed is only what it is in the way it is expressed. The thought is as incidental as a physical gesture would be; it is not so much that the thought arouses feelings as that its significance consists almost entirely of them. In the novel and drama, on the other hand (and in the mixed forms between essay and treatise; for the "pure essay" is an abstraction for which there are almost no examples), the thought, the discursive network of ideas, stands out baldly. Yet an unpleasant impression of extemporization always still clings to such places in a story, of acting out of character and confusing the space of representation with the private space of the author, if these places are not also components of a form. The difficulties and the attempts to resolve them can be observed especially in the novel, often in complex interpenetrations and layerings; the novel is called upon like no other art form to incorporate the intellectual content of an age.

It is therefore doubtless a platitude that the poet's word has an "elevated" significance, but what is not a platitude is that this is no longer the ordinary word *plus* such an elevation, but originates as a new one, which is neither congruent with the original nor independent of it. The same is true of other, in the more technical sense formal, means of expression in poetry: they too impart something, but in their application the relation between what they impart and what remains, so to speak, intransitively bound to the phenomenon, is reversed. One can just as well regard this process as the adaptation of the mind to realms inaccessible to reason, as the adaptation of these realms to reason; the word in this ceremonious or elevated usage resembles the spear that must be cast from the hand to reach its goal and does not return.

This naturally raises the question what the goal of such a cast might be, or, to speak nonmetaphorically, what the mission of poetry is. It is no longer part of the purpose of this discussion to take a position on this, but what emerges from the argument is the assumption of a specific area of relationships between people and things which poetry proclaims, and to which the means of poetry are adapted. Such "proclaiming" was deliberately not represented as subjective utterance, but in its relation to the assumed object-quality and objectivity. In other words, as poetry imparts experience, it also imparts knowledge. This is not at all the rational knowledge of truth (although it is mingled with it), but both are the result of parallel processes, since there is no such thing as a rational world and a separate irrational world, but only one world containing both.

But rather than conclude with generalities I would like to close with an example* that is quite revealing, that of the primal forms of poetry. Through comparison of archaic with primitive hymns and rhythms, it seems quite probable that the basic characteristics of our lyric poetry have subsisted pretty much unchanged since primitive times. These include the manner of dividing the poem into stanzas and lines, symmetrical construction, parallelism (as it is still manifest today in refrain and rhyme), the use of repetition, even of pleonasm, as a stimulus, the scattering in the poem of meaningless (that is, secret, magic) words, syllables, and series of letters, and finally, too, the peculiarity that the individual component, the sentence or phrase, has no meaning in itself but only acquires meaning through its position in the whole. (Even the sensitive importance of originality has its counterpart, for such songs or dances often belong to an individual or a community, are protected as secrets, and are sold dear!)

---

* For which I am indebted to Professor E. M. von Hornbostel.

These ancient dance songs are usages designed to keep natural occurrences within bounds and to move the gods. Their content says *what* has to be done to accomplish this purpose, while their form determines precisely and in what sequence *how* it must be done. The form is therefore dictated by the course of the event that is its content, and it is well known even today that primitive people anxiously avoid mistakes in form because of the presumed consequences. Thus scholarly research into the primal condition of art, as shown in this example and its brief elucidation, leads to conclusions quite similar to those drawn from observation of current conditions. The comparison also has the advantage of making more concrete the basic relationship between form and content, that every *how* signifies a *what*, than literary analysis can. Today literature is still a process directed at "production," a "being enchanted by models," and not a repeating of life or of views about it that can be better expressed without literature. But while the *what* side has developed in the course of centuries from the originally communal "rainmaking" into research and technology, and has long since produced its own "how one has to go about it," the *how* side has also transformed its thinking and distanced itself from the original magic, but out of it no clear *what* developed. What poetry has to do is still more or less the old "how one has to go about it," and if, in individual particulars, this may be connected with all kinds of changing goals, yet the art of poetry has still to seek a contemporary metamorphosis for its conviction, lost since the days of Orpheus, that it influences the world in a magical way.

ON POLITICS AND SOCIETY

Anschluss with Germany

1919

Like the Austrian Socialists Musil advocated Anschluss (annexation to Germany) in 1919, in political circumstances very different from those of March 1938, when Hitler marched into Austria. At the Paris Peace Conference, the Allies opposed an enlarged Germany, and within Austria conservative elites opposed a merger with Germany.

As I write it is not yet clear whether the peace conference intends to be the culmination of five years of European history or of two and a half millennia, or whether it will bring an end only to the period of the war or to the age of wars; nor are we in a position to influence the outcome. We have thrown away our weapons, and with them our rights, for a right one cannot enforce is no right at all. We stand defenseless before our "judges," protected by nothing but the dignity of spirit that a great nation embodies, by the spirit of humanity which is rising up on all sides, and by the force of example offered by someone whose power is broken and who does not haggle about right and wrong, but breaks camp to move toward the new order. The more deeply we understand this, and the more boldly we allow it to determine our actions, the less we will be the judged and the more we shall rise above the shabby prattle about judges and judged to become the ones who point to new directions. Whether this time humanity will miss the opportunity or not, the task is in any case so clearly posed that it cannot be misunderstood:

it is the necessity of finally achieving a form of organization that does not, like a bad machine, consume the greater part of its energy in internal friction and release only a small remainder for the development of happiness, mind, personality, and the work of humanity. Great deeds almost always contain a negative, reactively determining element, the stamp of a situation that has become intolerable and has at last incurred its own dissolution. Thus the movement that has now begun in reaction to war and social injustice has assumed the forms of the League of Nations and class conflict. But neither parliamentary democracy, nor dictatorship of the proletariat, nor disarmament and courts for the arbitration of conflicts between states, will bring an end to war and social injustice; of this end nothing more can be glimpsed than the direction in which it lies.

What stands in the way is the state—not as an administrative organism, but as a spiritual-moral entity—and it is the task of the impulses that have grouped themselves around the idea of a League of Nations to break out of the evil destiny that attaches itself to the organization of mankind into states. I know that such a contention may be least suited to German ears, for not only does the average German, even in his dreams, still have the functionally efficient machinery of the state clattering and rattling in his ear in exemplary fashion, like a chauffeur, but German thinkers have also credulously deepened the ideology of the state, driving it to the point of idolatry and seeing in it both an institution for the perfection of human nature and a kind of spiritual superperson. One must, therefore, point out very forcefully that this is false. Of course there is a spirit of the Prussian, Austrian, or French state that is more than the spirit of the inhabitants, just as there is an esprit de corps or spirit of the regiment, and speaking of Austria I would have something to say in favor of its importance. But one ought not to forget how far the spirit of the state nearly always lags behind the spirit residing in the best of its inhabitants; how it sent Dostoevsky to Siberia, Flaubert before the penal court, Wilde to the penitentiary, Marx into exile, Robert Mayer to the madhouse, and that in one respect it remains far behind the average person: that is, in its behavior toward other states. The naive moral demands that one not break contracts, not lie, not covet one's neighbor's goods, and not kill, do not yet prevail in relations among states; their place is taken by the single principle of pursuing one's own advantage, which is realized through force, cunning, and businessmen's tactics in applying pressure. As a result, every state is naturally recognized as criminal by the inhabitants of other states, but thanks to relationships that would merit sociological analysis, its appears to its own inhabitants as the embodiment of their honor and moral maturity. It is no wonder that such national organisms behave toward one another with gloomy *grandezza* and feel obliged to preserve their sovereignty and majesty with an inflexibility that, at the very least, ought to be regarded as a morally corrupting tastelessness. What one calls the modern constitutional state is such only internally; toward the outside it is a state of injustice and violence. One would be ashamed to repeat such self-evident propositions, since prattle about "criminal states" has still not been banished to war-hysteria's chamber of horrors along with the whole treatment of the "question of guilt," which searches *intra et extra muros* for individual guilty parties; or even the belief that partial disarmament and courts of arbitration would be sufficient: one would be ashamed, that is, if all this were not enough to demonstrate how little current thinking is ruled by a proper notion of the historical state, and that the progress that is proclaimed so loudly apparently starts out with its face turned toward the past. For the distinctively nonsocial character of the state follows, of course, not from the evil will of its inhabitants but from its nature, structure, and way of functioning: this makes it an almost completely self-enclosed system of social energy, with an infinitely greater variety of vital relationships internally than externally. The state is a form that, in order to be able to provide stability for life to develop, must first encapsulate itself and make itself impermeable. We can see in the opposition between classes how the absence of relations becomes hostility, and we ought not to be reluctant to cite as a comparison the psychology of the complications arising from warlike religious rituals between neighboring villages; for the psychology of martial entanglements between great civilized states is no different.

History teaches us that the achievement of an enduring agreement always requires the formation of a higher community, the giving up of full autonomy by its members, and implementation by positive common interests. The state, too, shaped itself in relation to individuals and partial associations, not merely as something privative whose purpose is to impede excesses, but as something yielding palpable advantages. In this way the German Empire outgrew its federated states, the old Austrian Empire its crown lands, and Switzerland its cantons; and in the same way an organization of humanity will not result from preventive measures, but only from an extensive fusion into new common interests in which the individual state steadily recedes to the level of a body for self-administration. What will finally remain is the organized nation, or let us say rather: the organized language community. For the nation is neither a mystical unity nor an ethnic one, nor is it really a spiritual-intellectual unity either—it has been argued with at least some justice that genius is international, and only narrow-mindedness is national—but as a language community it is a natural association for accomplishing things, the collecting basin within which intellectual exchange develops quickly and most completely. This significance of the nation for intellectual organization holds true even for humanism and communism at their most developed; at most one could object to this, by misunderstanding the word, that mind is something that should not be organized but left to grow indeterminately, like a stretch of landscape, in mutual interaction with people, their lives, their history, and their institutions: but the medium that circulates among these people and brings them nourishment is, precisely, language. Since the spirit of a nation does not hover over the nation as if it were a debating club, but wants to make itself concrete, it requires a homogeneous material apparatus. If parts of a language community live under entirely different conditions and in long-separated cultures, like South America and Spain, it obviously makes no sense to unite them; but where an ancient and never-interrupted cultural association exists between immediate neighbors, as between the German part of Austria and Germany, the consolidation of states is simply one of the decisive stages on the way from the condition that we may call the state animal to the human state.

. .

There are of course people who dispute this.

A small proportion of them are impatient people who call the idea of nationalism a "bourgeois" ideal, and for whom it is a matter of indifference whether German Bohemia belongs to the German Empire or the Czechoslovakian state, since after all Bolshevism is inevitable, or the world will be given some kind of spiritual order; in short, because the consolidation of nations is not really the ultimate or most important thing. These people always skip over a few stages, and are obviously people for whom there is not enough room at any one time for two truths or two plans, because they can transport themselves into a creative trance only by fixation on an extreme.

But mostly the people who deny or disavow the importance of a national idea are nauseated and worn down by its exaggerations. Austrian supranationalism in particular was ordinarily only a reaction against the especially crude form nationalism had assumed in Austria. But precisely this crudeness constitutes evidence in favor of the national idea, for it is the typical form it assumes when it doesn't get what it thinks it is entitled to. The unsatisfied urge of the Czechs to play at games of statehood, which we now see working itself out in their dollhouse imperialism, would really be touching if it were not so reactionary and did not contain so much megalomania and obstinacy.

It recalls the affair of the Königinhof manuscript, when millions of people were swindled by a forger who dazzled them with documents supposedly from some ancient, autonomous culture: because these people would not let any refutation deprive them of their delusion, they ascribed to false evidence almost a higher truth value than to historical evidence: the truth value of glowing desire. And this had its counterpart in the idea of redeeming the "unredeemed" Italians, which was full of sentimental romanticism and paraded with a puerile pathos that was of course entirely inappropriate for grown businessmen and lawyers. But what in Austria was called "German-national" is part of this as well. Its excuse was that it originated as a defensive reaction, and as far as politics is concerned there is in my view a lot to be said for it: but as an ideology it was nothing but a deadly, rampant tumor. A mishmash composed of Wagner, [Houston Stewart] Chamberlain, the Rembrandt German, Felix Dahn,[16] student poetry, anti-Semitism, and the ignorant belittling of other nationalities made up the content of a self-consciousness rubbed raw by constant political conflict. When people raved about raising the German identity in Austria, they did not mean by this, let us say, Rilke, although he is German, Austrian, and "Aryan," but rather the folksy-primitive German. Unfortunately, this mentality continues to live on in many people, above all among the student fraternities; one might be pleased that this mentality was German and not Austrian, yet be obliged to feel sorry for the way in which it was German. Wherever the national ideal becomes the goal of a struggle or a passionate yearning it degenerates into an inhibition, the way a hysterical knot forms in people: an inhibition that is always demanding to be, finally, entirely itself instead of constantly having to be able to dissolve and redefine itself in the normal course of everyday tasks.

What was called the problem of Austria's nationalities was—much like the course of a vendetta—exclusively an increasing entanglement and immobility produced by a single chain of causes, and this is usually given as the reason the state had trouble making progress; but the opposite connection was at least as important: because there was nothing in the life of the state to sweep along the resistance, this single conflict could harden to the point of imperious monomania. Since it had been pushed out of Germany by the victory of the kleindeutsch over the grossdeutsch idea[17] (and after the "Compromise" with Hungary this led to in 1867), the former Austrian Empire was a biologically impossible structure. In "Cisleithanian Austria" (even in the name the old State Chancellery still lives on!) the nations that constituted Austria maintained a sterile equilibrium; none was in a position to assume leadership and stimulate the others to a common and far-reaching shaping of will in economic and cultural questions. In addition, there was the constitutionally required renewal every ten years of the economic relations between Austria and Hungary, which with their endless renegotiations of both vanguard and rearguard conflicts had, according to an informed estimate, held back the rate of economic development by at least a third. Thus the Austro-Hungarian Monarchy could not keep up with the unpolitical, indirect effect of 1848, the unshackling of the middle-class entrepreneurial spirit, which called into being in Germany an energy and vitality that one must acknowledge as having been enormous, even if one quite justifiably condemns its forms and consequences. If Austria had been a state of such tremendous tempo, the interests of its peoples might perhaps have been able to fuse into a dynamic balance; but since Austria was awkward and poorly coordinated and never got up any speed, it fell off the bicycle.

The non-German peoples within Austria-Hungary referred to it as their prison. This is quite remarkable when one knows that even the Magyars asserted this to the very end, although they had long since become the ruling nation within the Monarchy. It is even more astonishing when one knows with what freedom South Slavs and Czechs in Austria were able to vent their anti-Austrian feelings; I could quote wartime newspaper articles that it would have been impossible to write in any other state. Despite all this, a prison? This cannot be explained by two centuries' worth of old memories, but only by deep mistrust of the state: from a fear of smothering, from contempt. If it had been nothing more than nationalistic yearning, the Czechs would not have to include on their agenda the destruction of the Monarchy, and the Serbo-Croatians and Slovenes would have invited their kinfolk in the tiny states beyond the border to join the Monarchy, instead of wanting to leave it themselves. This sleepy state that watched over its peoples with both eyes closed did indeed have real fits of brutality and rule by force; this always occurred when it allowed things to get out of hand and there was no longer a respectable way out. When this happened, it proceeded with police measures, state prosecutors, and absolutist decrees, only to draw back fearfully a few minutes later—shocked by the embittered resistance it encountered—and repudiate its own administrative officials. The intimate history of the Austrian bureaucracy is full of sad, burlesque examples that have succeeded each other for half a century, always in the same way. One may call the spirit of this state absolutist in spite of itself; it would gladly have acted democratically, if only it had understood how. But what was this state? It was not based on a single unified nation or free union of nations, which would have given it a skeleton whose cells it could have constantly renewed from the vitality of its blood. It was not nourished by a spirit emerging from civil society, which could force its way to political influence once it had achieved a certain strength. Despite the talents of its officialdom and many good works in individual instances, Austria really had no brain because it lacked a center for formulating a will and ideas. It was an anonymous administrative organism, really a ghost; a form without substance, permeated by illegitimate influences in the absence of legitimate ones.

. .

In such circumstances there developed what many people quite naively call Austrian culture. They attribute to it a particular refinement that supposedly can flourish only on the soil of a nationally mixed state; most recently, some of them believe they must protect Austrian culture from being absorbed into German "civilization," and even make this an argument for reviving Austria-Hungary in the shape of a Danube Federation, born from the anxiety dreams of big industry.

We may spare ourselves many words in this matter if we make three assertions at the outset. First, neither the Slavs nor the Rumanians nor the Magyars of the Monarchy recognized an Austrian culture. Each nationality acknowledged only its own culture and a German culture it did not like: "Austrian" culture was a specialty of the German Austrian, who likewise did not want to have a German culture. Secondly, even within German Austria one could identify three quite distinct regions in terms of the people and their style of living: Vienna, the Alps, and the Sudetenland; of what was the common culture supposed to have consisted? There were many provinces in Austria in which a common culture blossomed nonetheless; there, as everywhere on earth, people sought a connection to the world of the mind, and the means by which this happened was neither Reichsdeutsch nor Austrian, but simply German culture. Certainly Tirol, the most Catholic of the provinces, although nevertheless somehow touched by the south, had a quality of its own, but what difference did this make to Bukovina or Dalmatia, or the other way around? Austrian culture was an error of perspective from the Viennese point of view; it was a copious collection of distinctive qualities through which one could let the mind roam with advantage, but this should not deceive us into thinking of it as a synthesis. Thirdly, every "old Austrian" who is not utterly deprived of the grace of self-reflection will concede that when he speaks of Austrian values he means nothing other than old Austria as it was *before* 1867. This is the Austria that built the beautiful, broad white roads on which one could travel as through a fairy tale from north to south, from Asia to Europe; this was the Austria in which Grillparzer, Radetzky, and Hebbel lived; this Austria produced the type of a well-educated, well-intentioned administrative official, who went out to the periphery of the Empire not only as magistrate but also as cultural missionary. This Austria was a remnant of the old, capable, in many ways not unattractive authoritarian state. Since then, however, the wheel of world history has turned a bit further and, if everyone in his heart is thinking about this Austria whenever he starts getting excited about Austrian culture, and if, since 1867, among Austria's fifty million inhabitants there has not been one who has spoken with the same conviction about modern, Austro-Hungarian culture, then the whole cultural legend reveals itself to be: romanticism.

As conquerers and colonizers, Germans came into this country more than a thousand years ago, and the connection with Germany constantly rejuvenated their energies. It was therefore only natural that up to the last they occupied the preferred positions in the bureaucracy, as well as in economic life; and it must also be regarded as virtually natural that in this way they eventually came to be stamped with many qualities of a mandarin class. Austria was the land of "privileged" enterprises, a business world that worked with guarantees and letters of protection, and thus lost efficiency. In conjunction with this, it was also the land of "personal connections" and "*Protektion*,"[18] so much so that the front section of the newspapers had nothing to report on middle-class charities that had not secured the backing of some "highly placed patron," and in the advertising section in the back of the paper stood shameless requests in which money was publicly sought for backing. In these circumstances the illegitimate influence of the aristocracy and the ennobled bourgeoisie on the conduct of public affairs was so great that, despite its unruly parliamentarism, one had to regard Austria as a feudally governed state. How far this went can best be seen in the small rituals of everyday life: people loved to use the term "noble" even in characterizing intellectual and spiritual excellence, and taxi drivers addressed their customers as "Your Grace," which made everyone not only smile but regard it as a delicate subtlety, not thinking that they were witnessing something that deserved a thrashing. The Austrian countenance smiled because it no longer had any muscles in its face. There is no need to deny that in this way something elegant, gentle, measured, skeptical, and so forth came into the Viennese sphere; but it was bought at too great a price. If there were nothing but this "Viennese culture" with its *esprit de finesse*, which degenerated more and more into feuilletonism, nothing but this elegance that could no longer separate energy from brutality: then it would be enough to wish it would drown in Germany's tumult.

But of what *does* culture consist? People are always mixing up two quite different concepts: intellectual-spiritual culture, and what they mean by personal culture, the conventions of life, elegant style; in theory, certainly, life culture ought to grow out of and rest on intellectual-spiritual culture, but in reality the two are ordinarily separated. Granted, Austria had more than its fair share of personal culture; but of intellectual-spiritual, or real, culture it had too little. If one compares the resources of Austrian institutions of higher learning with those of German institutions, the number and size of library holdings and public collections of paintings, the opportunities to become acquainted with the art of other countries, the number and quality of periodicals, the intensity and scope of public discussion of intellectual issues, the substance of achievements in the theater; if one thinks of the fact that nearly all Austrian books are produced in Germany, or that nearly all Austrian writers owe their existence to German publishers: then let one ask of what the culture of a state consists if not these accomplishments? The talk about Austrian culture, which is supposed to bloom on the soil of this mongrel state more vigorously than elsewhere, this so often solemnly proclaimed mission of "holy Austria," was a theory that was never validated; that it could be stubbornly clung to in the face of reality was the solace of people who could not pay the baker and stuffed themselves with fairy tales.

So that these attacks will not end up hitting targets they are not aimed at, let me say expressly once again: they are aimed at the cultural values of the state and not at those of the Austrian individual. Even the average Austrian type is valuable; life here is not built in such a helter-skelter fashion; one sees the sky and has space and time. One feels oneself living more deeply in this land than in Germany. And, even in Vienna, people still have something of Stifter's characters in them, and more of the Russian, than Germans have. They are in any case not the worst Germans, those Austrians who adduce such reasons in warning against being absorbed into the solidarity of the German Empire. But they don't see that what they refer to contemptuously as the "Berlin mentality" was only a passing phenomenon in the development of the world and finally even Austria was by no means the state that, by reason of its more profound insight, would have stayed with the mail coach and Weimarean ideals of education. It too introduced railroads and journalism just like everyone else; it was only that one had less success with them in Austria than people did elsewhere. This does not depend on the competence and discipline of the individual; these have always been present in Austria and are still considerable, which already demonstrates the contribution that the Austrian, working on German soil, can make to German culture. Precisely for the sake of the valuable Austrian, the legend of Austrian culture must be destroyed!

The culture of a state does not arise as the average of the culture and cultural capacity of its inhabitants, but depends on its social structure and a multitude of circumstances. It does not consist in the production of intellectual and spiritual values for the sake of the state, but in the creation of institutions that facilitate the production of such values by individual people, and that assure the potential effectiveness of new intellectual and spiritual values. This is about all that a state can do for culture; it needs to be an energetic, vital body that shelters the mind. If one may, metaphorically, reproach Germany with having pandered too much to its physicality since the economic and political euphoria of the 1860s, this could be rectified by a change in its way of thinking; but Austria must change all the tissues in its body, which is much more difficult. For this reason it needs to be absorbed into Germany, even if tomorrow the movement coming from the East were to give the world a new shape that breaks the old boundaries, or if in the West the constraints of yesterday should triumph once again. In both cases, we will be confronted with tremendous tasks, which will require for their solution the most purposefully united energies.

Buridan's Austrian
1919

After the First World War, Austria-Hungary dissolved into nation-states. The small German Austria that remained might have been united with Germany, had the Allies permitted this; the other option for German Austria was to find a way to cooperate with the other successor states of the Habsburg monarchy. In this essay, as in "Anschluss with Germany," the issue is the role of Austrian ideology in keeping imperial elites from adjusting to this new situation.

Buridan was a fourteenth-century French philosopher who proposed that a donkey who found himself equidistant from two equally appealing bundles of hay must inevitably starve.

The good Austrian stands between Buridan's two bundles of hay: a Danubian Federation and a Greater Germany. Since he is an old logician and mentioned honorably in every history of this science, he is not content to compare the caloric value of the two kinds of hay: it is not enough for him simply to determine that the German bundle is more nutritious, even if it would, at first, lie heavily on a weak stomach. Instead, he ponders his dilemma with his nose sniffing the spiritual aroma as well.

Here our good Austrian discovers Austrian culture. Austria has Grillparzer and Karl Kraus. It has Bahr and Hugo von Hofmannsthal. For all eventualities it has *Die neue freie Presse* and the *esprit de finesse* as well. Kralik and Kernstock.[19] It does not, to be sure, have some of its more important sons, those who, spiritually, fled abroad just in time. All the same; there still remains—no, *not* an Austrian culture, but a gifted land that generates an excess of thinkers, writers, actors, waiters, and hairdressers. A land of intellectual and personal taste: who would argue with that?

The mistake begins with the patriotic explanation of this reality. It always runs like this: we are so talented, Orient and Occident are wedded in us, South and North; an enchanting variety, a wonderful mixture of races and nationalities, a community of fairy-tale beauty and a blending of all cultures: this is what we are. And we are old! ("We" of course reaches in our case all the way back to the baroque; what a parvenu by comparison is the *Reich* in Berlin! That Cranach and Grünewald are a bit older, that they and Leibniz and Goethe and a good hundred other greats established the foundations is forgotten.) That things have, nevertheless, always gone a little badly for us stems, aside from our excessive modesty, merely from bad luck. In theory, given our mingling of peoples, we ought to have been the most exemplary state in the world: this is so clear that it is not at all evident why, in practice, we have emerged as a European scandal, right behind Turkey. It was for this reason also that we didn't bother to investigate this seriously, but awaited the day that must inevitably bring us our due. For we knew we were talented. Hjalmar Ekdal[20] as state. The directors of the Austrian Institute for Culture wrote, anno 1916: Austria has the greatest future because in the past it has been able to accomplish so little.

The mistake may be expressed either thus: A state does not have bad luck; or thus: A state is not talent. A state either has energy and health, or it doesn't; these are the only things it can have or not have. Since Austria did not have them, it had talented and cultivated Austrians (in numbers large enough to assure us a good place in Germany), but there was no Austrian culture. The culture of a state consists of the energy with which it collects books and paintings and makes them accessible, the energy with which it establishes schools and research institutes and provides material support for gifted people and assures them of stimulation by means of the intensity with which its blood circulates. Culture does not reside in talent, which is divided up fairly evenly internationally, but in the layer of the social fabric that underlies it. But this stratum in Austria cannot bear any comparison with its counterpart in Germany with respect to functional efficiency. A culture can be created out of a thousand clever people and fifty million dependable business people; but out of fifty million talented and charming people and only a thousand practical, dependable people there arises only a country in which one is clever and dresses well but which is not even in a position to produce a new fashion in clothes. Whoever appeals to the Austrian as a way of justifying Austria believes that the public mind is the sum of private minds, rather than a function intrinsically more difficult to calculate.

Thus class-conscious Austrians prefer to rise up in warning against Germany's public spirit, which is supposedly much too robust. They tell dreadful stories about the deafening clatter of work in Germany, and excessive social bonds that strangle the individual. Living off Austria's subtle decay has of course been delightful, so it is understandable if one or the other artistic carrier of the bacillus of illumination feels spiritually obliged, should Austria be annexed to Germany, to emigrate to Rumania. This idea, at any rate, is better than the notion that Austria could stagger on as a natural preserve in Europe for elegant decline under the name "Danube Federation." But is it even true in the first place that Germany is only the land of working-class terror? At the very least, it is also the land of a much stronger reaction against such terror than Austria would ever be capable of. The nationalist movements in both countries resemble each other down to the strand of hair floating in the soup, but the resistance of the new Germany to this mentality is far more passionate than anything perceptible in Austria. And however that may be, the stalwart German social patriots aren't a source of much comfort either, nor am I pleased with the way German writers have now taken up their pens when—in a questionnaire on the moral recovery of Germany—the issue was to save the capitol: intellect can guide minds and change them, but it cannot create energy, or can do so only over a long period of time.

We ought not confuse this simple set of objective circumstances, this natural sequence of development. Even Buridan's Austrian, despite the fact that he is nobly refined and prepared to be split down the middle from head to hoof, should just this once arrange a truce between his spirituality and the plain truth and do the simple thing simply, despite the fact that he would be capable of ignoring it in a complicated way.

"Nation" as Ideal and as Reality

1921

Musil believed that the importance of nationalism in his generation stemmed from a general failure to come to terms with questions of ideology and soul. Here he tries to define what a nation is, and, in the context of the political traumas of the war and the postwar period, he considers its familiar formulations as state and race. Musil was not a sentimental advocate of Austrian culture and had no interest in a nostalgic return to the past. On the

other hand, he believed that the talk about race and nation that dominated
German politics in his generation was intellectually misguided and morally
pernicious.

1

In setting out to treat the problem of national feeling as a question, even
though since 1914 it has seemed to exist only as an answer—as passionate,
uninhibited affirmation or denial—and in attempting to do so in the midst
of an extremely critical period of our destiny, when it would seem that skepticism about the concept of "nation" ought to be avoided, I must nonetheless
reject the excuse that I am raising the question because I have a new answer
and the prophet in me urges me to proclaim it. In fact, I have only partial
answers, or answers that are only partially satisfactory. But precisely in this
deficiency, which persists despite all efforts to eliminate it, I recognize the
necessity to speak of this matter not, for once, out of settled conviction, but
rather from the unconcealed helplessness in which we find ourselves in spite
of all our fine phrases.

2

Those from whom the nation simply does not exist make it too easy for
themselves. This mentality, which declares itself extraterritorial and supranational in the name of the spirit, pursues ostrich politics in response to the
contempt and slavery that weigh on all of us. This way of thinking sticks its
head in the sand, but cannot prevent the blows meant for us all from striking it where its ostrich feathers are. This individualistic, separatist spirit
overlooks something else: that well-known summer experience of 1914, the
so-called upbeat to a Great Age, and I do not at all mean this entirely ironi-
cally. On the contrary, what was stammered at the outset and later allowed
to degenerate into a cliché—that the war was a strange, somehow religious
experience—undoubtedly corresponds to a fact; that it degenerated says
nothing against the character of the original insight. It became a cliché in
the customary way precisely because we called it a religious experience, and
in doing so gave it an archaizing mask, instead of asking what it actually *was*
that was pounding so strangely and violently on a realm of ideas and feelings that had been asleep for the longest time. Still, it cannot be denied that
mankind (and of course people in all countries in the same way) was touched
at that time by something irrational and foolish, but awesome, that was
alien, not from the familiar earth, and which therefore, even before the actual disillusionments of war arrived, had already been declared a halluci-

nation or a ghost simply because its atmospherically undefined nature prevented it from being held or grasped.

Contained in this perception too was the intoxicating feeling of having, for the first time, something in common with every German. One suddenly became a tiny particle humbly dissolved in a suprapersonal event and, enclosed by the nation, sensed the nation in an absolutely physical way. It was as if mystical primal qualities that had slept through the centuries imprisoned in a word had suddenly awakened to become as real as factories and offices in the morning. One would have to have a short memory, or an elastic conscience, to bury this insight under later reflection. Even those few who wanted to rid themselves of this tremendous pressure could not do so by calm persistence, but only by counterattacking. Anyone who already opposed the war at the outset had to be fanatic; he was spitting in the face of the nation, killing it in cold blood, and thereby demonstrating only an equal, but opposite, fascination.

Are we now to believe that it was nothing when millions of people, who had formerly lived only for their own self-interest and repressed their fear of dying, suddenly, for the sake of the nation, ran with jubilation into the arms of death? One would have to have a very uncultivated ear for life not to have heard this voice of what was actually happening over the pacifist voice of conscience. And even if millions of people should simply have sacrificed themselves, their existence, their goals in life, their neighbors, and everything they possessed in the way of heroism to a mere phantom: can we then simply come to our senses again, stand up and walk away as if after a binge, calling the whole thing just an intoxication, a psychosis, a mass hypnosis, a delusion of capitalism, nationalism, or whatever? We certainly cannot, without repressing an experience that has still not been assimilated. By repressing it we would be sinking the foundations of a monstrous hysteria into the soul of the nation.

3

But also those for whom the idea of supranationality does not exist make things too comfortable for themselves. Does this really need saying?

But if not, why does one so rarely hear a complaint about the fraud that was committed against us at the end of the war by Wilson and his Trojan horse of the Fourteen Points? Of course we were on our knees by then; but at the moment when we put down the weapons which had become so repugnant to us, did they strike something from our hands or cajole us? Was there not an Easter mood around the world, as premature as a warm day in February, the conviction that a new age for humanity was beginning? And this new age too, compared with the shattering disappointment it suffered, was only an intoxication, a psychosis, a mass hypnosis, a delusion.

We had, then, two great, opposing illusions and we experienced the collapse of both more painfully than other nations. Is it so astonishing that this broke us down spiritually? The wild hatred that split the German nation between those who were eager to pull themselves together again and those who were zealously against it; the shrilly contradictory appeals to the national uprising of 1813 and the international revolution in Moscow; the contrast between pacifists waving palms at the Entente and the assassination of our own politicians; the intensely passionate grief over the nation's lost self-sufficiency taking place at the same time as illicit foreign trade and the flourishing of profiteers, dance halls, and a thousand things that, even if not impermissible, nonetheless seemed inappropriate; and finally the tremendous spiritual exhaustion, and the decay of the nation into tired, sullen, and alienated parts. This is no longer merely a matter of the severity of the material injury we have suffered, but indicates spiritual shock.

4

For the task of reconstruction will require a clear, firm soul. If it is true that those illusions and their collapse have weakened us, and that we really do suffer from a spiritual vacuum, then we have no task more urgent than to come to terms with these illusions.

How false the childish excuse, which is, unfortunately, often heard in Germany: We didn't do it! The Emperor, the generals, the diplomats did it! Of course we did it: we let it happen; it happened without our interfering. Here as in other countries. How false too the other excuse one often hears: We simply weren't firm enough, we let ourselves be fooled. This overlooks what was genuinely new, to which the general will wanted to adapt itself at the time. But if one studies the negotiations at Versailles in the French papers, one sees something that was shaping itself cunningly, no, almost mechanically, helplessly and inevitably, something that put this will in question (just as it was doubted among us too), that made it look dubious by bringing up all sorts of old experiences and ensnaring it with a mentality whose mechanisms could only serve to crush the young seedling. Versailles was a focal mirror of European political thought. The individual, however, was the same before 1914, in the summer of 1914, at Brest-Litovsk, with the Fourteen Points, at Versailles; the same in France and Germany. He simply lived through the most terrible contradictions, almost without noticing the transitions. He simply showed himself capable of anything, and allowed it all to happen. In the complete illusion of his own free will, he followed without exercising his will. We did it, they did it; that is, no one did it, just "it" did it.

Let us consider this "it."

That the will of the whole population does not represent the sum of its individual wills is nothing new. We find significance attributed to this idea as early as Lagarde,[21] if not before, and since then it has been an often-discussed and carefully investigated subject. Even a questionnaire expresses not only the voice of the person questioned, but also that of the mechanism doing the asking. So the sum of a people's opinion is not only that of the people themselves, but is codetermined by the apparatus of their bureaucracies, laws, newspapers, and economic and countless other arrangements, down to the apparently most individual and yet still partially dependent accomplishments in literature. A people is the sum of individuals plus their organization, and since this organization leads an independent life in many respects the result is—if one adds to this the largely fortuitous composition of the public atmosphere of ideas at any particular moment—that "it" of which we are speaking. In what follows its constitution should be assumed to be sufficiently known and insufficiently grasped. It is remarkable how rarely these already established truths are made use of, and it would not contribute much, although it would take up a lot of time, if I tried to reiterate them here.

On the other hand, one has the duty to regard with suspicion the ideological garb in which this "it" appears in the period before a cultural renewal.

5

There cannot be many people who, if directly asked, would equate nation with race—everyone knows that nations are racial mixtures—but, strangely enough, the concept of race is nonetheless constantly substituted, quite unabashedly, for the concept of nation, and people make use of "race" as if it were as straightforward as the concept of the cube: therein lies the phenomenon that is to be considered here. I have no desire to hold forth on the question of race, but in order to get at its ethical meaning I will have to refer to the theoretical peculiarities of this idea.

If ordinary tables were, at a given moment, to begin multiplying by propagation rather than by being ordered from a manufacturer, we would immediately see arising from the now-living tables (and on the same evidence by which we recognize a Frisian as a Frisian) races of four-legged square tables, one-legged oval tables, and more. Nothing would have happened except that every two tables produced a third, which resembled them according to a specific law of mixing characteristics, and which possessed the ability to propagate itself in the same way. The fact that in this way some qualities can be passed on in the genetic material through several generations without becoming manifest does not change the fact that this all takes place only in and between individuals. Race has nothing to do with the whole matter, except that it ultimately is present because it can not be anywhere else, just as rain is present when drops fall from the sky. There is no other way for race to enter material existence except through individuals, and race has no other effects than the effects individuals have. Such an existence, however, is only an abstraction, a collective concept. Of course there are races, but the race is constituted by individuals.

If this is the state of affairs, then reversing it is not at all justified. Such an almost theological distortion would run: The individual is constituted by the race. Yet this is precisely the standard formula in everyday use.

According to this formula, there is as little left of a human being as there would be of a stocking if you took away its crisscrossing mesh. Most of the time it may just be a convenient way of communicating, by which a person is first characterized by membership in a group—if it can be family X, why not the Germanic race?—and today it already sounds almost natural for Bismarck to say that "the felling of trees is not a Germanic, but a Slavic trait," or for a Jewish critic of Wassermann's book *My Way as Jew and German*[22] to assert that "it is impossible for a Jew to become a pure German artist." Nevertheless, it is precisely in harmless cases a dangerous concession to a vicious mental habit. We are familiar, of course, with the literature that brought it about and was brought about it. This literature is concerned not with measuring skulls, eye color, or skeletal proportions, which interest only a few, but with qualities like religious sense, integrity, state-building power, scientific ability, intuition, a talent for art, or tolerance of ideas: things of which we hardly know how to say anything at all about what constitutes them. This literature ascribes or denies these things to supposed "races" with the help of an anthropological pig-Latin because it believes it can instill dignity in the nation through its ear by ventriloquizing with the voice of the ages.

One cannot deny that a good part of our national idealism consists in this diseased way of thinking.

It is not hard to see where this must lead. If, in good and evil, the "race" rather than the individual is made responsible for everything, the effect is exactly the same as if one were always making excuses for oneself: the result is not only that truthfulness and intellectual refinement become dulled, but also that all the germ cells of morality degenerate. When virtue is declared to be national property by predestination, the Lord's vineyard is expropriated and no one needs to work in it any more. The individual is flattered into believing that he possesses everything desirable by merely contemplating the virtues of his "race": evidently a fool's paradise, our happy Germany, where roasted virtues fly into our mouths!

It is harder to see where this idea of race comes from. People say anti-Semitism, but that is almost just another word for the phenomenon itself. The essential thing is that behind the phenomenon there lurks a genuine idealism. This is a typical case of the regressive need to refer every idea back to older, eternal ideas that are considered sublime, instead of trying to think it through: in short, precisely what is this country counts as idealism. This produces the person who has fixed recipes and sublimely simple rules for everything, who puts himself above spiritual experience: the Pharisee. A strange and extremely dangerous relationship has arisen among us: lack of respect for the mind in the name of the German Spirit. Broad circles of our people—and one is almost inclined to say the ones with the best intentions—have lost the ability to judge an achievement by its substance; they test it only according to its origins, and thereafter as it fits into their system of prejudices. The broadest is measured by the narrowest, the versatile mind by one of its stillbirths. Attention has turned away from values to their accompanying circumstances, from reality to hypothesis, and those who are called upon to follow have been seized by a sectarian arrogance and preaching. Since only primitive virtues can be associated with something as basic as race, even those minds who pride themselves on having the same blood as their judges will finally no longer be allowed to have the ear of the nation if they do not write like Herr Walter Bloem or think like Herr Hilthy [*sic*],[23] in other words are not true, brave, and chaste and cannot make do with five further Germanic redskin virtues. On the path of this idealism the idea of race has become a self-inflicted German wound, and sucks the marrow out of the nation in an abuse that continues for decades.

6

Beneath all the ideological clothes of the nation, however, the most physical reality is the state. One is almost tempted to say: It *is* the body of the nation; but of course it is more; it is, unfortunately, virtually the soul of the nation as well. Look at the old German *Reich*, but look also at the new Russia. The state is a protective vaccine that rampantly penetrates the remotest organs of the body.

It is striking how in the history of thought, from the Greeks down to the present day, immoderately high regard for the state alternates with excessive contempt for it with almost the regularity of a pendulum. At one time the state is regarded as the highest human institution for education, or the essence of all human goodness; at another, as a Leviathan that swallows up everything higher in life, and is considered, even if unavoidable, an unavoidable evil. It is clear that such stubborn contradictions cannot be of a merely theoretical nature, since otherwise, in the course of time, as with all rational questions, some sort of balance would have been achieved. These contradictions also prove to be independent of the great worldviews: Greece, the Catholic Middle Ages, and the Enlightenment all had to give space within themselves to both views to the same degree. Since it cannot be resolved, the quarrel is probably connected with some emotional consideration, and since, moreover, it shows itself resistant to influence in relation to the deepest distinctions of feeling about the world, it may reach down to a still deeper difference. It seems likely that this difference is to be sought in the opposition between the individual self and the social self, a difference that reaches back before the beginnings of human society to animal society, and that each of us bears within himself. In relation to society every individual is torn between love and hate, even if the individual circumstances often do not allow one of the two to be noticed, or weaken both into indifference.

This contradictory relationship of the person to the state is also expressed in the following terrible problem: if one sets aside the exaggerations of the idea of race, individual people in various countries are almost identical to one another. States also, if one compares them to each other as mechanisms, are nearly always the same. And yet individual *plus* state results in those annihilating contradictions that vent themselves in war, and that in times of peace express themselves in the strange ceremonies of delegations, notes, receptions, and diplomatic demarches which correspond so precisely to the way dogs greet each other on the street. If one wants to resolve this contradiction, that the same people organized in the same way constitute an enduring antagonism, then its cause can only be sought in the form of organization.

Even the most casual examination of this problem reveals that the state is something like a calloused skin, a sealed surface that turns the greater part of the forces at work in its sphere back toward the inside, allowing only a much lesser portion through; an insulator. Exchanges of opinion, communications, intellectual organization, religious community, even socialism, all these "fields of force" are much more diluted outside than inside. This comes from the fact that it is virtually only the state that has developed effective "organs." The nation has almost none; those that it has are the state. Therefore, in most cases, the state thinks, feels, decides, and acts for the individual with a general proxy that evades any form of supervision. For the supervising authority is, if one takes the concept of the state in a sufficiently broad sense, again the state itself. Of course it is not only the government and the executive that constitute this apparatus of the so-called common will, but also the parties and special-interest lobbies of every sort. There is in this a pervasive, so to speak histological law of structure, according to which the elements of organization are only further organizations, and this apparently becomes the more palpable the further it develops in a democratic direction. Democracy is rule not by the *demos*, but by its subsidiary organizations.

But always, when a group acts for individuals, there will be something left over, a sacrifice, a forbearance. This will not be the case only when a strong urge, the commitment to a particular achievement, an excited heartbeat, sweeps it away and will not allow it to break through to consciousness. In such great, nonhomogeneous, ancient groups as states this will occur only in especially intense moments. Ordinarily, the state "oppresses" the human being wherever it comes in contact with him. One does not need to be against the state, and can fully acknowledge its great importance; but nonetheless, in the face of these relationships it remains an ideology contrary to fact to see in the state the representative of the highest values (because they are common to all), and therefore to ascribe to it a kind of superwill, or to regard the state as some sort of institution for human perfectibility. That is the remnant of an idea left over from the age of the authoritarian state, which took refuge in the proverbs of the educators of the young German *Reich* and is unfortunately well on its way to finding new life in socialism, whose ethics seem to be stuck in the altruism of fraternity. It is also a case of that "transforming idealism" that projects the dignity the human being is unable to achieve in his personal life onto its background: onto the race, the Emperor, a social club, the sublimity of the moral law, or some other such tapestry.

7

The ordinary relationship of the individual to so large an organization as the state is that of letting it do as it likes. Indeed, this phrase is one of the formulas of the age. The social life of human beings has become so broad and so dense, and relations so inextricably entangled, that no eye or will is any longer able to penetrate great stretches of it, and outside the tightly restricted circle in which he functions every person remains a child. The citizen's underling mentality was never so circumscribed as it is now, when it is running everything. Whether he likes it or not, the individual has to let things happen, and does nothing. The Englishman and the American did not allow the children of central Europe to starve, but simply let it happen. And we ourselves did not play our role in the atrocities, even if we were the actors, but simply allowed it to happen. If we want to change this, however, we must be clear about the need for change. Anyone who believes—and it seems to be more than a few people, and precisely the most zealous souls—that something could be changed by a warm heart rather than through cold-blooded organization ought to open his newspaper some morning and read in it all the accounts of a single day's suffering and misfortune that it would have been possible to prevent: and if he does not want to concede all this, indeed, if all he possesses is the capacity to make it physically palpable, no, to make it only as clear as the word "empathy" demands of each of us—he would go mad!

The active counterpart to this letting things happen is the summary, general, routine treatment of people. The legal document is the symbol of the indirect relationship between the state and the human being; it is life become odorless, tasteless, and weightless, the button you press; and if this causes a person to die you have not done it, because your whole consciousness was absorbed by the demanding task of operating the button. The act itself is the sentence of the court, the gas attack, the good conscience of our torturers; the act divides the individual in a most unhappy way between private person and functionary. But under present conditions we apparently cannot do without this kind of hygiene.

The ordinary person corrects the monstrosity that arises from this by stealing and by cheating on the rules made for him in any way he can. In fact, aside from this system about all that is left are disreputable influences that are illegitimate, and almost illicit: the free traffic of goods, opinions, and life. Yet in spite of all resistance, again and again ideas develop that finally do bring about a slight change. The heretics had an effect on a church that had become part of the state; free writing had an effect on the bureaucratized spirit. But it is above all the addictions—dominated and ruled by those involving money—that constitute the human counterweight to bureaucratic organization. We should not simply complain about them, but rather understand them as the satanic corrective to that very imperfect god, the state. Augustine drew a distinction between the state and the *civitas dei*, the sphere of the divine kingdom, where the individual withdraws from the clutches of public life. Today the *civitas dei* rushes to the cinema, gives up its life for some celebrity, and cheerfully pushes the state to the edge of its grave with slogans. This is, of course, degeneration. But it is more important to admit to oneself that on the other hand it is only the obverse of the state, something grounded in its essence, a ghostly human sacrifice entombed in the walls of the cathedral.

The existence of the nation was not to be found either as race or in the form of the state, but these are in fact the two places where it has been sought. The idea of what is German rests either on racial fantasies or on a philosophy of self-sacrifice for the sum of all sums, which the state is supposed to be; almost on a form of individual original sin, which can be redeemed only by subsuming the self in the totality. Besides these two ideas there remained a third, the *civitas dei*, and to it corresponded the third view that we have already touched upon, the nation as spirit. Our Ciceros say: The suprapersonal, ideal values, the spirit of the community, the institutions that arise from the common will, the common cultural tradition (of which the complex of the state makes up only a part), are what integrated the nation. Without finding it necessary to deny this—it contains much that is correct—I may perhaps be allowed to contrast it with a picture that is probably closer to the truth. What spirit, for example, does a university share with a penitentiary—and yet these are two institutions in which exponents of the two most strongly developed capabilities may be found today? What spirit does Herr Anton Wildgans[24] have in common with Nietzsche? Surely some spirit, but it would be so difficult to define that it is better left alone. It would be a better idea to note that in the course of an extraordinarily confusing historical period, millions of individuals have stuck their heads into a world that they understand to very different degrees and in very different ways, from which they want completely different things, of which they see little more than the thread of their own livelihood and hear some great general noise, in which here and there something echoes that makes them prick up their ears. This enormous, heterogeneous mass, on which nothing can quite make an impression, which cannot quite express itself, whose composition changes every day as much as the stimuli that act upon it, this mass, nonmass, that oscillates between solid and fluid, this nothing without firm feelings, ideas, or resolution, is, if not itself the nation, at least the really sustaining substance of the nation's life.

Every investiture of the ideal feels itself as a false "we." It is a "we" that does not correspond to reality. "We Germans" is the fiction of a commonality among manual laborers and professors, gangsters and idealists, poets and film directors, a commonality that does not exist. The true "we" is: We are nothing to each other. We are capitalists, proletarians, intellectuals, Catholics . . . and in truth far more—and beyond all measure—caught up in our own special interests than we are concerned with each other. The German peasant stands closer to the French peasant than to the German city dweller, when it comes down to what really moves their souls. We—each nation for itself alone—understand one another very little, and fight or betray one another when we can. We can, to be sure, all be brought together under one hat when we plan to squash it on the head of another nation; then we are enraptured and have a shared mystical experience, but one may assume that the mystical in this experience resides in its being so rarely a reality for us. Once again: this is just as true for the others as it is for us Germans. But in our crises we Germans have the inestimable advantage that we can recognize the real connections more clearly than they, and we should construct our feeling for the fatherland on this truth, and not on the conceit that we are the people of Goethe and Schiller, or of Voltaire and Napoleon.

There is always and in all ages a feeling of insufficient congruence between public life and real life. But can anything at all in public events be the true expression of real life? Am I then, as an individual, that which I do, or am I a compromise between unarticulated energies in me and transforming external forms ready to be realized? In relationship to the whole, this little difference gains a thousandfold in significance. Aside from passive persistence, an unnatural alliance of interests can be held together only through a common interest in using force against others; it does not necessarily need to be the force of war. But if one says that mass hypnosis is at work in times when wars break out, this is only to be understood as an ordered system exploding because of its inadvertently neglected tensions. This explosive stimulus, with which the human being liberated himself and, flying through the air, found himself together with his own kind, was the renunciation of middle-class life, the will for disorder rather than the old order, the leap into adventure, no matter what moral names it might be given. War is the flight from peace.

8

Frankly speaking, however it has been formulated, "nation" is a fantasy.

It is not easy to admit this to ourselves at a time when other nations are puffing themselves up with *their* illusions, and have laid upon us German-speaking people the solidarity of being deprived of our rights, exploited, and dragged off into slavery. It will therefore be objected that even if patriotism, nation, and the like are illusions, this is now better kept quiet. Quite aside from whether there is a nation or not, the assumption that there is one does have value; indeed, precisely because it cannot be denied that in practice the unity of the nation is still a very recent phenomenon, its presence can not be spoken of suggestively enough. This will be said especially by those who see in the nation an ideal that can be realized in the distant future, but that must be shown to the people from time to time in order to purify them. An ideal like this, however, which has in reality developed into a purifying hypnosis only for holidays, as it were, or for occasions on the order of a mobilization, has the same relationship to a person as a house in which a man sleeps only every leap year at Pentecost, while the rest of the time he prefers to sleep in the swampy meadow next to it. Something that has this effect cannot be entirely good and proper.

Indeed, we may say that everything we have seen up to this point has really only been a particular instance of the false application of ideals. Just as the assumption of a race was not conceived progressively, as something to be aimed for, but regressively, as a mystical fetish, so the state was elevated by being relieved of the requirement of being irreverently renewable, like the furnishings of an apartment; the concept of the nation was not admitted institutively, as something to be formed, but rather asserted constitutively as something already present that merely did not express itself tidily. This is a use we make of all our ideals, apparently a leftover from times when it was still hard to win respect for the simplest rules except by declaring them taboos. Even today our ethics bears this prehistoric stamp of the taboo. We stabilize our ideals like Platonic-Pythagorean ideas, immovable and unalterable, and when reality does not conform to them we are in a position to regard this very fact, that reality is only their "impure" realization, as characteristic of their ideality. We strive to conform the incalculable curve of being to the rigid polygon that passes through our moral fixed points by breaking the rectitude of our principles into ever new angles, but still without ever achieving the curve. It may be that the inner life has the same need for fixed connecting points that thought does; but as ideals these have led us to a point where things can hardly go any further, since—as everyone knows—in order to approximate it to reality we must burden each ideal with so many limitations and disclaimers that hardly anything is left.

If a white surface is entirely covered with dark spots, there comes a point when one's mind is working with a dark surface and white spots; in the field of ethics we are still far from this. This "negotiating" with reality is unfortunately exactly the opposite of what our idealists regard as ideality. I call idealism the forming of reality according to ideas (and I would call following successful ideas until the next stage of realization is achieved only idealism in the second degree). Therefore, when life does not live up to a system of ideals, I am not able to see much idealism in them. One should finally realize that it is not that life fails to conform to ideals out of disobedience, as in school, but rather that the mistake must lie with the ideals.

A morality that wants to be more than a patchwork today—something like a merely "civilizational" morality that renounces the beautiful atavism "culture," the refutation of which, incidentally, can be inferred from the foregoing—must be erected on the deformity that European civilization and the enormous growth of its interconnections have imparted to people. I believe that what we have experienced since 1914 will have taught most people that, ethically speaking, the human being is almost formless, unexpectedly malleable, capable of anything: good and evil range equally widely in him, like the pointer on a sensitive scale. It is foreseeable that things will get still worse in this regard, that people will slip further and further away from those already half-impotent ethical constraints that restrain them today. For one may think of the human being as originally a creature just as ready to be good as evil, just as much social as egoistic (leaving aside the matter of how large the dose of egoism is that goes along with the social). But the interests in which he is entangled today are too many, and the impenetrability around him, the insufficient intellectual conductive capacity of the social body, carries with it the fact that, at the moment of any action, only a small part of the possible ethical determinants are at work in him. Today, therefore, every ethical event, if it is a real experience, has "sides." On one side it is good, on the other evil, on a third something that cannot quite be established as being either good or evil. Good appears not as a constant, but as a variable function. Only intellectual dullness has kept us from finding a logical expression for this function, which satisfies our need for the unequivocal without suppressing the many-sidedness of the data. Morality is as unlikely to collapse because of this as mathematics is to die from the same number being the square of two different numbers.

9

We do not, of course, have this morality that would be adequate to our realities. All the same, the consciousness of transition already requires us to treat neither state nor nation as ideals, but rather simply as objects, which have to correspond to their purposes. No one person can say anything binding regarding these purposes, which change over time, except: One leaves it to the culture to develop such purposes out of itself. But this means—if one has the right sort of optimistic pessimism in human affairs, and believes neither that a race of engineers and businessmen can be helped by myth, intuition, or classicism, nor overlooks the energies that rage even in the abuses of this civilization—leaving it to people themselves, insofar as it is in some way compatible with social life, to seek the way for themselves and follow their own interests. This is a principle we begin to apply as early as elementary school, because it has been shown that one educates better pupils this way; and we would need only to extend this, at last, to adults.

Today proletarians, industrialists, ichthyologists, painters, and so on are already organized into international associations, whose linguistically national organizations actually amount to subassociations. The view is slowly beginning to gain ground that economic life constitutes an international unity, and that working for an egoistically nationalist economic policy instead of organizing work on a larger scale is a short-sighted subterfuge. Does one need to add proofs of the internationalism of intellectual interests that already actually exists? And yet diplomatic conferences between countries on dismantling their antagonisms display such a ridiculous discrepancy between effort and result that one really must conclude that these organizations are not suited to lead developments beyond the stage we have reached. The League of Nations in its present form of an association of states reveals itself as ever more grotesque. Getting rid of the state, however, could succeed only through world revolution: but is the program for life after this death of the old order already prepared, or is it not that one almost expects that through a very long course of revolutionary thinking evolution will relieve us of responsibility for the decision? But nothing more nefarious stands in the way of a natural ordering of human society than the arrogance that the two ideals of nation and state show toward human beings. All one can do is work to strengthen whatever is developing that circumvents these ideals, and awaken and keep awake the idea that they superannuated.

One may object that wherever international associations fight their way to prominence there are always powerful material interests behind them, and that any organization, since it requires major financial backing, can come into being only where great material success can be realized. Furthermore, one need only glance at internal politics to see how nothing idealistic works, how only the strongest material interests are able to keep people together, and how, scandalously paired in our political parties, aging beauties of ideas let themselves be supported by the pimps of material needs. One finally tells oneself that even the internal moral order in which every culture originates could only have been created through an act of force that set it up in the first place, and that even in Bolshevism force believes it has to make itself the bearer of the idea. It is possible that even the aspect of a form of life appropriate to our time of which I am speaking here will not be achievable without force. Ideas, however, do not show the path to the future, but only the direction: they are nets thrown over the future to catch what they can; the future always partly rips them, but never wholly.

Then what is our future? Consoling ourselves over time for the injustice we have suffered by getting fat again? Getting revenge without the world-political goals that have eluded us? Or: creating a world-political goal! When the War broke out the church failed, socialism failed, both under the pressure of an either-or ideology that was a superstition. The first people able to find their way out of the blind alley of national imperialism to a new possibility of world order, and able to lend all its efforts to this breath of the future, will soon have the leadership of the world and be able to realize its legitimate wishes. Today no one can foresee in detail the road that leads to this; it is a matter of creating convictions leading in that direction.

Helpless Europe

A Digressive Journey

1922

Translated by Philip H. Beard

*Showing signs of Musil's reading of Spengler (see "Mind and Experience")
as well as echoes of Nietzsche, this essay grapples with the problems and
ethical implications of understanding history as a way of ordering the European world as it had developed since the Enlightenment. The insufficiency
of this perspective had been exposed by the First World War, which made a
homogeneous view of history impossible. For Musil, the main intellectual
task of the 1920s was not to advocate a particular position or ideology, but
to move cooperatively toward an overview beyond the ideologies of state
and nation. Despite his antisystematic style, Musil's intellectual goal repeatedly reveals itself as system and order.*

The author is more modest and less obliging than the title of this piece might lead one to infer. Indeed, I am convinced not only that what I say is wrong, but that what will be said against it will be wrong as well. Nonetheless, a beginning must be made; for the truth is to be found not in the middle of such a subject but around the outside, like a sack which changes shape every time a new opinion is stuffed in, but grows firmer all the while.

1

I begin with a symptom.

For the past ten years we have doubtless been making world history in the most strident fashion, but without actually being able to see it. We haven't really changed much—a little presumptuous before, a little hung over afterwards. First we were bustling good citizens, then we became murderers, killers, thieves, arsonists, and the like, but without really experiencing anything. Is there any doubt about this? Life goes on just as before, only a little more feebly, with a touch of the invalid's caution; the effect of the war was more festive than Dionysian, and the revolution has taken its seat in parliament. So we have been many things, but we haven't changed; we have seen a lot and perceived nothing.

I think there is only one explanation for this: we were lacking the concepts with which to absorb what we experienced; or perhaps lacking the feelings whose magnetism sets the concepts in motion. All that remains of the experience is an astonished restlessness, as if the neural branches that the experiences were beginning to send out had been lopped off before they matured.

A restlessness. Germany swarms with sects. People are looking toward Russia, the Far East, India. They indict the economy, modern civilization, rationalism, nationalism; they see a decline, a waning of the race. War has flattened the curves of our archways. Even Expressionism is dying, and cinema is on the march (Rome before the fall).

In France, England, Italy—to the extent our abominable wire services allow a layman to judge—the bewilderment appears to be just as great, even allowing for individual variations.

2

That is how world history looks from close up: you don't see anything. Of course someone will object that we are standing too close. But it is a metaphor, taken from the visual realm; one can be too close to an object to apprehend it fully. But can one be too close to understanding something to be able to grasp it? The analogy does not hold. Surely our knowledge suffices for us to form a judgment about present and recent events, and in any case we know more about them than later generations will. Following another of its roots, this metaphor would portray us as still too involved. But were we really involved at all?

The proverbial notion of historical distance consists in our having lost ninety-five of every hundred original facts, so the remaining ones can be arranged however one likes. But one manifests "objectivity" by presenting these five surviving facts as if they constituted a fashion of twenty years ago, or as a lively conversation between people out of earshot. We shudder at the grotesqueness of human deeds as soon as they have dried out a little, and we attempt to explain them in terms of all the circumstances that are not "us"—that is, the historical ones.

"Historical" is what one wouldn't do oneself. Its antithesis is "vital," or "dynamic." If our age were an "epoch," one might well ask whether we stand at the beginning, in the middle, or at the end of it. If there was a Gothic Man, with his prehistoric, early, high, and late periods, in what relation does modern man stand to *his* zenith? If there is a German or a Caucasian race, what biological stage is it in? If such rises and declines are ever to become something more than the facile discoveries of hindsight, we will need a symptomatic picture of what, in general, they look like. This would be objectivity of a different sort—but there is a long way to go. Perhaps dynamic historical facts are not at all unambiguous, and only dead facts can be clear? Perhaps dynamic history is ultimately no history at all, that is, not something that can be apprehended by our simplistic historical categories? For here there is a peculiar sense of contingency involved.

3

From our present perspective, there is a sense of contingency in everything that happened. To insist on interpreting every crisis we have lived through as the expression of some comprehensive significance would amount to a considerable overextension of belief in historical necessity. In retrospect it is easy to recognize necessity at work in the breakdown of German diplomacy or military strategy. But everybody realizes that things might just as easily have turned out differently; the judgment often hung by a thread. It is almost as if the events themselves were not necessary at all, but only accommodated necessity after the fact.

I don't mean to philosophize—God forbid, in such serious times!—but I can't help thinking of the famous man who was passing by under the notorious roof from which the tile fell. Was that necessity? It was, and was not. The famous tile's working itself loose, and the notorious man's strolling by, are surely events conforming to natural law and necessity—leaving aside for the moment the doctrine of free and unfree will and predetermination, which simply repeats the whole story all over again. That both happened at precisely the same moment is not that kind of event, unless we are to believe in the hand of God, or in the historical workings of some still higher rational power—which proves that accidents may be deducible from acts of God or from some natural order, but not God and natural laws from accidents.

Plainly stated, what people call historical necessity is clearly something different from the kind of scientific necessity in which a particular v corresponds to a particular p; it is necessary like those things of which it is said that "one leads to another." Laws may be involved somehow—like the interplay of intellectual and economic developments, or the perspectival factor in the visual arts, for instance—but there is always something else present too that is just this way just this one time. Incidentally, we human beings also belong in part to this class of unique events.

4

Such considerations strip from our conception of the world much of its vaunted loftiness. Perhaps we can console ourselves with a prospect.

In the verdant forest a green-clad hunter brings down a brown stag.

Let us attempt to reverse this process. The bullet leaves the rifle, the flash follows, then the report; the stag stumbles, falls on his side, his antlers crash to the ground, and there he lies. Return trip: the stag rights himself—but he can't just get up; he would have to "fall" up; his antlers would first have to execute a mirror-image dance of the motions of their impact, and he would have to begin this ballet with his final velocity but end with the initial one. The bullet would have to fly back fat end first, the exploding gases precipitate into solid form with a backwards bang, and so on. To take back even a single step of the process, it would not be enough to reverse what happened; rather, we would need ultimate authority for reworking the entire world. Gravity would have to pull upwards, the air to be bisected by a vertical plane of earth; the laws of ballistics would require stupendous alterations; in short, a melody played backwards is a melody no longer, and it would take a thorough convulsion of time and space to alter this fact.

The truth is that even putting a dead stag back on its feet requires no mere reversal or indemnification, but something completely unheard of. The world is filled with an indomitable will for the new, obsessed with visions of doing things differently, of progress!

5

According to some people, we have lost our morality. Others say we have lost our innocence, and that along with the apple in paradise we swallowed the bothersome quality of intellectuality. Still others maintain that in order to reachieve a culture such as the Greeks possessed, we must run the entire gamut of civilization. Et cetera.

6

A historical approach that divides events into successive epochs, and then acts as if each epoch corresponded to a historical human type, such as Greek or Gothic or Modern Man, and further implies that each of these types contains its own rise and decline (e.g., early Greek Man, Greek Man, Classical Greek Man, late/degenerative Greek Man, non-Greek Man), and that in them something had blossomed and withered—not merely an unfolding, but an essence that unfolded, a human type, a race or society, an empirically real spirit, a mysterium—such an approach, common today not only among essayists but frequently met with in historical research as well, proceeds from a certain hypothesis:

What is given are only phenomena: certain kinds of buildings, literature, paintings, actions, events, and life-forms, and their evident coexistence and mutual affinity. This phenomenal substrate of a particular time span, epoch, or culture appears at first glance to possess a unique homogeneity, occurring only at that specific time and place. This appearance, however, cannot prevent our noting that the hypothesis is not quite correct: Oriental life elements are known to have influenced the Hellenic sphere, and Hellenic elements continue to suffuse our lives even today. In fact, similar life manifestations (and history concerns itself only with similarities and analogies) form a continuum extending across time and space, a continuum that condenses noticeably only in certain places—precipitating, one is tempted to say, in response to certain circumstances.

For anyone who has had a little experience with the statistical side of the outer or inner world, a view of phenomena of this sort, put in general terms, is reminiscent of the interplay of a constant determinant with variables ones. If this constant determinant is the human constitution, it cannot simultaneously be the causes of the various differing epochs, societies, and the like, in the sense of genuinely active entities and not merely as innocuous collective concepts: the causes must lie in the circumstances.

Botanists, for example, differentiate in an area as small as Lower Austria some three thousand forms of the wild rose, and are unsure whether to classify them into thirty species or three hundred; so uncertain is the concept of "species" even in cases where so many distinct features can be identified. Yet history is supposed to be so presumptuous about such thoroughly ambiguous, obviously "nonessential" features as the complex manifestations of edifices, works, and life-forms? Raising these doubts is not a matter of denying the actual existence of various epochs; in a certain sense each is indeed based on a different kind of person; but it is a question of precisely this "certain sense"!

7

Since 1914, humanity has revealed itself as a mass that is astonishingly more malleable than we had been accustomed to assume.

Previously, full acknowledgment of this discovery was precluded by religious, moral, and political considerations. I still remember quite well a congenial essay by a respectable German writer in which he allows with considerable astonishment that mankind, whom he had conceived differently, is in fact as evil as Dostoevsky's portrayal of it. Others may perhaps recall the importance ascribed to "character" in our moral systems, namely to the demand that human beings submit to being treated as constants; whereas a more complex moral mathematics is not only possible, but probably necessary: from a mode of thought accustomed to the fiction of an "unchanging inner disposition" it is not far to exceptions from the type, from epochs, etc.

This rigid categorization contradicts the experience of psychology and our lives. Psychology demonstrates that the spectrum of human types spreads smoothly and seamlessly from super- to subnormal, and the war demonstrated to all of us in one monstrous mass experiment how easily human beings can move to the most radical extremes and back again without experiencing any basic change. They change—but what changes is not the *self*.

8

The formula for these experiences would have to run roughly like this: the greater the amplitude of expression, the lesser the amplitude internally. It really doesn't take much to make modern civilized man out of his Gothic or ancient Greek forebears. Just a slight overbalance of material circumstances, nonspiritual factors, coincidences, and contingencies, working constantly in the same direction, is sufficient. This being is every bit as capable of cannibalism as of *The Critique of Pure Reason*. We should stop thinking that this creature *does* what it *is*; rather, it becomes, for God knows what reasons, what it does. Man makes his own clothes, but clothes make the man too, and the physiognomy is a membrane responsive to both inner and outer pressure.

This is not, of course, to say that there is no difference between primitive cultures and developed societies; it consists in a greater versatility of the brain that develops only over the course of generations—just as the chin recedes and the stance becomes upright, that is, as a real, functionally determined physiological difference—whereas whether one's brain does Aristotelian or Kantian gymnastics is functionally quite irrelevant. To assume without such reservations the rise, culmination, and decline of a given society or human type is to place the decisive motivators of change too much in the center: we must, more than is ordinarily done, search for them at the periphery, in the "circum-stances," in the "taking of the helm" by particular groups of people or tendencies from within what is, on the whole, a quite homogeneous mix; we must search for contingencies, or more correctly, for "unlawful necessity," where one thing leads to another not by accident, but in a sequential concatenation not governed by any particular law.

(To give an example. Given our technical and commercial structures, we would certainly be capable of building a Gothic cathedral in a few years, or even, if we were aiming for a record and using the latest Gilbreth scaffolding and "scientific techniques," in a matter of weeks. It would sprout uniformly according to a plan, but even if we used the original plans, our cathedral would remain a barren piece of work, because the passage of time would be missing, the change of generations, the inconsistency, the organic result of an inorganic process, and the like. The oddly protracted duration of impulses of will, manifested in the expression of the Gothic soul, originates from the slow, necessarily deliberate technique of actualization, and if we pursue this further we will find technical, commercial, intellectual, and political elements in this single example intertwining in a thousandfold tangle of determinants.)

9

The inclination towards such a view of things is often assumed to be crudely mechanistic, uncultivated, and cynical. I would point out that it harbors a tremendous optimism. For if it turns out that our innermost being does not dangle from the puppet strings of some hobgoblin of fate, but on the contrary that we are draped with a multitude of small, haphazardly linked weights, then we ourselves can tip the scales.

But we have lost this feeling.

10

How?

It was probably evident for the last time during the Enlightenment. In the waning years of the eighteenth century people believed that something existed within us that needed only to be liberated in order to take flight. They called it "reason" [*Vernunft*], and hoped for a "natural religion," a "natural ethics," a "natural education," even a "natural economy." They despised tradition, and imagined themselves capable of rebuilding the world anew from their intellect. Undertaken on far too narrow an intellectual foundation, this attempt collapsed, leaving behind merely a heap of hackneyed rubble. The present epoch has witnessed the abhorrence of this rationalistic attempt—or more precisely the abhorrence of a weaker nine-teenth-century repetition undertaken by the natural sciences—imprinted on the works of Flaubert, Dostoevsky, even of Hamsun. By the time it played itself out, "rationalism" had become the butt of ridicule and contempt.

It is understandable that the failure of the narrow rational program was followed by a thirst for the irrational, for a plenitude of facts, for tangible reality. It took two courses: one was history. In a certain sense the sudden awakening of historical interest represented a reversion from the presump-tuousness of the adult to the open-eared attentiveness of the child: ex-panses; solitude; being led; letting reason grow out of things and into man; a more universal, more conciliatory, but less precise mode of thought in place of ethical-activist brusqueness. But alas, the plenitude of facts became overwhelming; faced with an excess of facts, historical research necessarily grew ever more pragmatic and exact: the result was a nightmare, a moun-tain of facts growing larger by the hour, knowledge won, life lost—a failure of the soul, the avoidance of which, incidentally, had not been entrusted to the historians alone.

For roughly since our grandfathers' generation—that is, in a time of growing pragmatization of all thought, during which philosophy shied away from philosophizing—history had to assume as a side office philosophy's task of interpreting life, and as a result appears afflicted with two guilty con-sciences: a pragmatic one that scoffs at the outmodedness of a philosophy of history, and a philosophical one that sighs about soulless pragmatism, since one can't do without sweeping perspectives that bring order to things.

11

Perhaps a digression may be tolerated here, as it is still part of a writer's prestige to rail at the barrenness of pragmatism.

As we all know, even the "intellectual giants of our Classical past," if the expression be permitted, laid back their ears whenever this school of thought announced its presence. Goethe, who admired Kant, loved Spinoza, and was a natural scientist in his own right, was on better terms with the inductive intellect than are the Goethean dwarves of our day. (His intuition is much abused: in his scientific works one finds no trace of that "other form of knowledge" for which he is so often claimed as a confederate.) Nonetheless, German Classicists felt little affection for English looms, for mathematics or mechanics or, if I recall correctly, for Locke or Hume either, whose so-called skepticism they rejected; but "skepticism" was most likely merely an ex-pression of that positivistic spirit that arose with the natural sciences, mathe-matics, and industry, and was instinctively felt by the Classical authors as subversive. (Even Hebbel,[25] who in other regards stands as an intermediary between our past and present, is thoroughly Classical in this respect.) If I understand our great humanists correctly, they were concerned primarily with some kind of cosmos, a stable order, an intact code of laws—albeit including all possible confusions of the human heart. In any event, they would have found intolerably demeaning the degree of spiritual disorder and ugliness we are confronted with today.

But this rejected spirit of self-sufficient facticity in the sciences, in statistics, machines, mathematics, pragmatism, numbers, this sandhill of facts and anthill model of humanity—has today won out.

For good or ill, the epigonal Goetheans, along with the Goethean parrots and pretenders, will have to make the best of it.

This spirit of facticity dug the second channel for the intellectual countercurrent that was freeing itself from the too-narrow bed of rationalism. But it had begun well before the Enlightenment; the Enlightenment only gave it added impetus.

12

Still, when the terms *pragmatism* and *positivism* are used here, they should not be taken too precisely, and not with their technical philosophical meanings. They are intended to refer not to any theory, but to a phenomenon that occurs in life.

Rationalism did not arise in the Renaissance when physics turned away from Scholastic speculation and toward the discovery of facts and their functional connections; for Scholasticism too had been rationalistic. Rather, what took place was simply a *restitutio in integrum*: rationality was restored from the speculative degeneracy it had suffered to the firm Antean ground of facts, although it was given a direction in which the issues to be treated by philosophy and even by mathematics were primarily initiated by the quantifying natural sciences. Right from the start, the quantitative approach—to use today's terms, the "unholy" and "unspiritual" approach—spread like wildfire. "True knowledge comes only with knowledge of quanta," writes Kepler. The Portuguese Sanchez, who died the year Locke was born, argues that philosophy should join in the aggressive spirit of observation and experiment. The great Galileo, a more versatile thinker than Kepler and by dint of the example he set a watershed between two epochs, and even an artist like da Vinci, share this furious renunciation in favor of factuality, objectivity, sobriety, and the testimony of the intellect and the senses.

We must distinguish this new spirit from the exaggeration it was soon to undergo (Descartes), and, in light of the current intellectual vogue of lamenting mankind's enslavement by barren mechanistic thinking, we must remind ourselves with the greatest urgency that at one time, and for great minds, it held the force and fire of a new, redeeming experience.

13

The formula for this runs: Don't fool yourself; rely on your own senses; get to the core! Through a powerful movement of abstinence the soul received a powerful thrust in a new direction, and we should make no mistake about the ardor and strength that that impulse still manifests today.

True, here too the development tended more towards breadth than depth. As they multiplied, the exact sciences splintered into specializations, and attempts at synthesis, however impressive their individual achievements may have been, could not keep pace; one might almost say that all the disadvantages of a democracy of facts had been established; here too the mountain, the pressure of rising alps, displaced them, as it had already buried the human achievements of history. But it is nearly always presented, quite erroneously, as if it were a merely negative characteristic of our time, that it—briefly put—has no philosophy, and this lack is portrayed as a sign of its inability to produce one. It is much more a sign that can also be evaluated as positive, for pragmatists accustomed to climbing on the firm rungs of facts can only laugh at the philosophies offered by our custodians of culture. This age has no philosophy less because it is unable to produce one than because of its unwillingness to accept offerings that don't fit the facts. (Anyone wishing an example should read the book by the young Berlin philosopher Wolfgang Köhler,[26] modestly characterized as an essay in natural philosophy, entitled *Physical Forms at Rest and in the Stationary Condition.* Those equipped to understand it will see how solutions to perennial metaphysical problems are now being hinted at from the firm ground of the exact sciences.)

Related in this respect to the leading intellectual type of our age, despite all their differences, are the leading practical types, the businessman and the politician. Even capitalism has as its spiritual base dealing only with facts, complete self-reliance, the firm hand, sculpting in solid stone, the independence of the individual as he stands—and it suffers the same after-hours ennui. Politics in particular, as it is understood today, is the absolute opposite of idealism, almost its perversion. Those self-anointed paragons of realpolitik who speculate on the falling of humanity's stock take as real only the base side of human nature, believing it to be all that can be counted on: they place their faith not in conviction, but exclusively in coercion and cunning. What we saw of this during the war, though, and in the most disgusting caricatures, is at bottom precisely the same spirit as the one that ministries of one and the same state employ towards each other whenever their interests on a given issue diverge, and the same as the one adopted by the clever businessman when dealing with his own ilk. At the bottom of this abyss, no longer consciously recognized by the individual, sits like the tip of a cone the diabolical contempt for that impotence of idealism that characterizes not only the degenerate members of today's society, but so often its strongest representatives as well. This contempt bespeaks as much the profound self-confidence of our age as its desperate situation. It is a swimming underwater in a sea of reality, a grim holding-one's-breath-just-a-little-longer—of course with the risk that the swimmer will never come to the surface again.

14

For the task of taming this strain of humanity and leading it towards balance and constancy, the task of creating order in this chaos, of giving sense and meaning to life, what was available? Nothing but history, and only in a subordinate capacity! It did not have the concepts for the task. The philosophy of history was rejected, and purely historical categories were not yet sufficiently developed; the conceptual tools for ordering life were lacking. So we reintroduced subjective, conjectural stock notions from the philosophy of history—but through the back door, uncritically. Concepts like reason, progress, humanity, and necessity held ghostly sway over our view of life, together with ethical values that are arbitrary or at best standardized by public opinion: a veneer of order covering chaos. That is how the familiar shift to methodological immanence in the historical sciences could at the beginning have had the effect of a salvation. Initially, history's new doctrine of approaching "periods" without preconceived notions, "gleaning judgment and measure from the intrinsic nature of the times," seemed to embody progress. Immersing oneself, getting into things, understanding phenomena from the inside, without imposing external syntheses: never had a generation been so prepared and eager for this task as our own. The consequence, to borrow Eucken's words, was the weakening of our own essence and resolve through our striving to adapt to foreign ways. Just the thing during a period of our development bursting with problems of its own!

15

And so we arrive at the present day. The life that surrounds us is devoid of ordering concepts. We are inundated by a jumble of facts from the past, facts from the specialized sciences, facts from life. Popular philosophy and topical discussion are either content with the liberal scraps of an unfounded faith in reason and progress, or invent the familiar fetishes of epoch, nation, race, Catholicism, the intuitive man—all of which share, negatively, a predilection for sentimental carping at the intellect and, positively, a need to seek a foothold, to find gigantic skeletons, however ethereal, on which to hang the impressions that constituted our one remaining bit of substance. (This is, incidentally, the core of the literary dispute over culture versus civilization; it is also one of the major reasons why Expressionism was not much more than a charade: a soil that remained fundamentally impressionist could nurture it no further.) So timid have we become in matters of straightforward judgment and the shaping of reality that we habitually came to view even the present as history. Every new "ism" that crops up is hailed as the harbinger of a new humanity, and the end of every school year rings in a new epoch!

Thus everything belonging to the realm of the mind finds itself nowadays in profound disorder. Acting from tradition, and hardly aware of the reasons anymore, people attack the spirit of facts and numbers without offering anything but its negation to replace it. For if we proclaim—and who doesn't, to some degree?—that our age lacks synthesis, or culture, or a sense of religiosity, or community, this is hardly more than singing the praises of the "good old days," since no one can say what cultures, religions, or communities would look like today if our laboratories and airplanes and the whole mammoth body of our society were to include them within their synthesis, and not simply dismiss them as outdated. This is merely to demand that the present surrender itself. Uncertainty, enervation, and a pessimistic cast are today the hallmarks of soul.

Naturally this is all reflected in an unprecedented intellectual fragmentation. Our age accommodates side by side and in totally uncoordinated fashion such oppositions as individualism and social solidarity, aristocracy and socialism, pacifism and militarism, the lionizing of "culture" and the bustle of civilization, nationalism and internationalism, religion and natural science, intuition and rationalism, and so on ad infinitum. Excuse the analogy, but our age has an upset stomach, and it keeps regurgitating bits and pieces of the same food without digesting it. Even a casual glance reveals that this kind of antitypicality—this posing of problems as pairs of opposites, this agglomeration, or these "either-or" formulations—means that too little intellectual work is being done. There is in every either-or a certain naiveté, which may well befit the evaluator but ill-becomes the thinker, for whom opposites dissolve in series of transitions. And indeed, corresponding to this mode of inquiry on the practical level, an intellectual profile of our society shows a splinter-group collectivism carried to the extreme. Every reading circle has its poet; the political parties of the farmers and the manual laborers have their different philosophies; there are perhaps a hundred publishing houses in Germany, each with its more or less loosely organized circle of readers; the clergy has its network, but the followers of [Rudolf] Steiner[27] too have their millions, and the universities their prestige. I even once read something in a waiters' union newsletter about how the weltanschauung of the restaurant worker must forever be upheld.

It is a Babylonian madhouse; a thousand disparate voices, ideas, and tunes assault the wanderer's ear from a thousand windows at once, and it is clear that the individual is turned into the playground of anarchic forces, and morality and the intellect disintegrate.

But in the cellar of this madhouse we hear the hammering of a Hephaestian urge to create; humanity's archetypal dreams are being realized, like flight, our seven-league boots; seeing through solid bodies, and an incredible wealth of fantasies such as in centuries past were the blissful magic of dreams. Our age creates these wonders, but it no longer feels them.

It is a time of fulfillment, and fulfillments are always disappointments; our time lacks a sense of longing, a sense of some challenge it hasn't yet mastered, but which gnaws at its heart.

16

The War, it seems to me, erupted like a disease in this social organism; an enormous pent-up energy, without access to our collective soul, finally dug itself this gangrenous fistula channel to it. I have read a warning about viewing the War as a crisis of European culture, claiming it to be a specifically German view (Robert Curtius, citing others for support in his highly readable treatise, *Syndicalism among French Intellectuals*).[28] But how seriously we should take this warning depends on the meaning we give its content. The War may have had a thousand different causes, but it is undeniable that each of them—nationalism, patriotism, economic imperialism, the mentality of the generals and the diplomats, and all the rest—is tied to certain spiritual preconditions that characterize a shared, and therefore codetermining, situation.

Above all, one of the most telling symptoms of the catastrophe was simultaneously the expression of a particular ideological situation: the totally laissez-faire attitude toward the teams of specialists running the machinery of the state. It was like sleeping in the Pullman car of a train and being awakened only by the crash. It is not only the "thinking citizen" who has become accustomed to this laissez-faire attitude toward these "action-oriented minions" of the state: the ideologies that coexist side by side, always barking at each other but never biting, have as well. This is the other side of the incorporation of the individual into society: the stress of trying to resolve every moral dilemma by ourselves would drive us insane. On the other hand, some of these dilemmas should no more be left to the "experts" than questions of marriage or eternity, and such cases must be clearly labeled. The way the world careened into the War evinced above all a debilitating lack of intellectual and spiritual organization: our unwillingness to take the signs seriously, to recognize the uncontrolled forces and counterforces, stemmed from a situation in which ideological discourse, thanks to its confusion and vapidity, was considered effete, while the forces championing realpolitik at least had the advantage of a certain middle-class legitimacy.

Another indication was the dimensions the catastrophe immediately assumed. Only where everything was ready and longing for an earthquake, a firestorm, and whirlwinds of emotion, could the conflagration spread with such sudden and appalling speed. Anyone who witnessed the outbreak of the War in its full intensity will agree that it was essentially a flight from peace.

17

Of course it would be senseless to reduce a catastrophe of such enormous proportions to a single formula. We still know very little about the sociology of war; all cultures have experienced it, and for that reason alone it is difficult to regard any particular war as the debacle of a particular cultural situation. Clearly, war is tolerated as something traditional, perhaps even as a periodically recurring institution. An altogether different question is how war can break out in a time whose spirit, if we disregard aberrations like the "Knockabouts," was so decidedly pacifist. Moreover, there have been wars that were, in a manner of speaking, only tolerated, while others whose social nature is quite different spread like wildfire. Nowadays commonsensical moderating forces are at work to discredit war as useless and irrational—no doubt weighty arguments in an age so attuned to utility and reason. But this sort of pacificist, I believe, underestimates the explosive inner force that lies behind wars of the second kind, the apparently human need to rip existence to shreds from time to time and toss them to the winds, seeing where they fall. In peacetime this craving for a "metaphysical bang," if I may call it that, piles up as a residue of discontent. In cases where, far and wide, not a trace of oppression or economic despair is to be found, but only flourishing prosperity all around, I can discern in this craving nothing but a revolution of the soul against order. In some periods it leads to religious rebellions; in others, to war.

If we examine the phenomenon from this angle, we are obliged to add that what is at issue is not (that is, it is only apparently) the collapse of a particular ideology and mentality—for instance, that of the bourgeoisie today, or of Catholicism in 1618—or the content of this or that of ideology, but rather the periodic breakdown of all of them. They are forever incongruent with life, and life shakes them off in recurring crises the way swelling mollusks shed their outgrown shells.

Today, despite the weariness left behind by the war we have just barely got over, we can see this threat approaching anew. It is not only the French mind that reveals toward its authorities an apathetic attitude worse than any that existed before the War; we too have seen only the subject matter of our concerns altered by our recent history. Our confused and uncertain mode of acting and reacting survives unchanged.

No values stood firm; accountability was lodged nowhere; life was tossed ecstatically into the flames. Yet it seems mistaken to assume that we could improve the situation by an expiative *restitutio in integrum,* by the demand for more accountability, goodness, Christianity, humanity, in short by any increase in what we showed too little of before; for what was lacking was not our vision of the ideal, but its preconditions. This insight, it seems to me, is the one our age ought to burn into its soul. The solution lies neither in waiting for a new ideology nor in the clash of the ones that are quarrelling today, but in the creation of social conditions that safeguard the stability and depth of ideological endeavors in general. What we lack is not substance but function!

Never again will a homogeneous ideology, a "culture," arise in our Western society on its own. Even if it did once exist in the distant past (although we probably imagine it as too perfect), water flows downhill, not up. Prospering societies undergo a progressive intellectual and spiritual self-necrosis. Ever more people and opinions participate in the cultivation of ideas, and thanks to man's exploration of early times and the linking of distant sources, more and more propositional wellsprings open up. What is called "civilization" in the derogatory sense is mostly nothing but the burdening of individuals with questions whose very words they hardly understand (witness political democracy, or the newspapers). That the individual reacts in a completely pathological fashion is only natural: nowadays we expect the average businessman to make intellectual decisions whose conscientious deliberation would boggle the mind of a Leibniz! But it would be hard to deny meanwhile that each of these ideas that crisscross from various directions has a certain practical value, and suppression is a loss while receptivity is a gain. Therefore, if we want to promote the interaction and linking of ideological elements rather than leaving them to chance, we are faced with an enormous organizational problem.

This essential organizing function of society, however, rests in our time exclusively with the sciences, in the realm of pure intellect; in the humanistic area not even creative people recognize the need for it. On the contrary, precisely in humanistic circles (here used abbreviatively in contrast to unequivocally intellectual work) there exists no more stubborn prejudice than the belief that civilization's entire misdirection, and above all its spiritual dissolution, can be blamed on the scientific spirit our society panders to. Science may be accused of creating all manner of imbalances and deleterious side effects, but whenever one maintains that it has a "corrupting" influence, what one invariably means is that science gradually dissolves values that were previously accepted as integral and emotionally safe. But science can only have this effect where these values already have cracks in their emotional premises. The cause lies not in *its* nature, but in *theirs!* In its essence, the scientific spirit is just as syncretic as analytic; indeed, it represents probably the strongest binding force in human relations, a fact its dilettantish detractors overlook with surprising frequency. The difficulty, then, cannot be anything other than a skewed relationship, an abiding miscommunication between the intellect and the soul. We do not have too much intellect and too little soul, but too little intellect in matters of the soul. The grievance that is held against science is really that the pathway of our thinking habitually circumvents our self as it connects thought with thought, fact with fact; *we exclude our ego, our self, from our thoughts and actions.* Therein lies, of course, the essence of our objectivity; it connects things one with the other, and even where it sets us in relation to them, or, as in psychology, takes us as its very object, it does so in a way that excludes the personality. Objectivity sacrifices, in a sense, the inner aspect of objects. General laws are impersonal; or, according to an appealing indirect formulation by Walther Strich,[29] one can't vouch for a truth with one's whole person. Thus objectivity cannot create a human order, but only a factual, impersonal one.

In fact this protest had already appeared in full force during that wide-ranging transition to the modern age referred to previously, in which objectivity was in the ascendant. Religion—to paraphrase Schwenkfeld [*sic*], Sebastian Franck, and Valentin Weigel[30] in their common opposition to Luther, the errant mystic—is not theology, but "renewal of the entire human being." This is the protest of our feelings, our will, our vital and changeable faculties, all our innate humanity, setting itself off against calcified, rigid theological "knowledge." Moreover, stripped of all theological connections and their related specializations, this protest has always been the mainspring of all mysticism. All those words such as love, contemplation, awakening, and the liked describe in their profound vagueness and tender plenitude nothing but a deeper embedding of thought in the emotional sphere, a more personal relation to the experiencing subject.

But the entire literature of nonmystical wisdom as well, from K'ung Fu-tzu to Emerson and beyond, displays a related experiential content and a similar attitude toward the scientific spirit. One might even maintain that here too runs one of the lines separating morality from ethics. In accord with its prescriptive nature, morality is tied to experiences that can be replicated, and these are precisely what characterize rationality as well, for a concept can only take hold in areas where explicitness and, figuratively speaking, replicability obtain. Thus there exists a profound connection between the civilizing character of morality and of the scientific spirit, whereas the truly ethical experience, such as love, introspection, or humility, is, even where it is of a social nature, something difficult to transmit, something quite personal and almost antisocial. "In Christ was an outward and an inward man, and everything he did in relation to the outward world was from the outlook of the outward man, and the inward man stood by motionless and detached," says Meister Eckehart. What passes for ethics in our current literature is for the most part a narrow foundation of real ethics, with a skyscraper of morality above it.

What genuine ethics there are today lead a very meager life in art, in essayism, and in the chaos of private relationships. Music trundles emotions back and forth in which are rooted the ideas of cosmos and soul; painting seeks to detach itself from the "object," the carrier of the rationality bacillus; literature presents the image of a stagnating spiritual condition, devoid of progress despite repeated attempts. All in all, a dull dissatisfaction that periodically whips itself up into evanescent peaks, a fermenting mass in which the same fragments keep forcing their way to the top, but with no chemist on hand to clarify the mixture.

Our way of thinking is, for the moment, in no way equipped to change this situation. History, as indicated earlier, itself in need of assistance from ordering concepts, is only abused as an expedient in the search for them, while the humanism we practice is also at most only secondarily concerned with comparative perspectives, ethics, and the analysis of vital phenomena, seeking instead to grasp personalities, epochs, and cultures as totalities and set them up as models. If people are taught to appreciate Goethe or Lessing as self-contained, unique totalities, the exemplary quality of these great personages certainly has some "educational value," but transmitted by itself is no different than if in the study of physics one would present only the biographies of Newton or Kepler. The essential objective value is neglected; the biographical view is never complemented by the ideographical one, which is pretty much consigned to subjective arbitrariness and predilection, in our academies as it is in life. But the lines of Goethe, "Ist auf deinem Psalter, / Vater der Liebe, ein Ton / Seinem Ohr vernehmlich, / So erquicke sein Herz!" [If on your psaltery, / Father of love, is a tone / To which his ear might hearken, / Then pray arouse his heart!], certainly don't exist by themselves, nor merely in connection with the young and mildly irksome Herr Plessing and all Goethe's other biographers, nor are they simply part of German Classicism and the literary tradition; they form, rather, a stitch in the fabric of human love or human kindness, whose series run through our world of images from the earliest beginnings to today, and the real essence of Goethe's verse is defined by its position in this sequence.

Such an ordering of art, ethics, and mysticism, that is, of the world of feelings and ideas, certainly demands comparisons and analyses and summaries, and to that extent is rational and related to the strongest instincts of our age, but it does not run counter to the soul. It has its own goal, and this is not the kind of explicitness that would compress ethos into morality, or feeling into causal psychology; it aims at an overview of the reasons, the connections, the limitations, the flowing meanings of human motives and actions—an explication of life.

Perhaps it will seem odd for this survey of our situation to conclude with the plea for discipline. But a time that has not accomplished such work or acquired such discipline will never be able to contend with the immense organizational tasks confronting our age.

ON CULTURE AND THEORY

Mind and Experience
Notes for Readers Who Have Eluded the Decline of the West
1921

Oswald Spengler's Decline of the West *appeared between 1918 and 1922. Musil sees Spengler as exemplifying the typical vices of German intellectual life in the 1920s. Although critical of the exaggerated importance Spengler accords intuition, Musil attempts to delineate what would be a legitimate balance between thinking and feeling, and to clarify the distinction between civilization and culture that was so familiar in the irrationalist polemics of German intellectuals of the time.*

1

In his treatise on the necessary limits to the application of aesthetic forms, Schiller writes that "the capriciousness of belletristic thinking is a very bad thing."

Mathematical subjects, however, have the advantage over others in that they allow us to distinguish between real knowledge and the imitative fluency that belletristic minds can so quickly establish in any field. Spengler writes that something or other "may be less evident in the popular branches of a mathematical system, but the numerical constructs of a higher order to which each of them . . . directly ascends, such as the Indian decimal system, the ancient groups of conic sections, prime numbers, and regular polyhedrons, in the West number domains, multidimensional spaces, the highly transcendent forms of transformational and set theory, the group of non-Euclidean geometries . . ." and so forth, and this sounds so expert that a nonmathematician understands immediately that only a mathematician can talk this way. But in fact, the way Spengler enumerates these higher-order numerical constructs is no more expert than a zoologist's including dogs, tables, chairs, and analogies of the fourth degree under the rubric "four-footed." Or Spengler writes, "From this splendid intuition . . . there follows the final and conclusive version of . . . Western mathematics: the extension and spiritualization of function theory to group theory." But group theory is really not a continuation of function theory at all! Or, Spengler says, "Groups are . . . ," but what he defines are not "groups," but (under certain conditions) sets, and without the slightest precision! But where he does define a set as "the conception of a set of homogeneous elements," he mistakenly believes this to be the definition of a number domain! Or he writes, "Within function theory, on the other hand, the concept of the transformation of groups is of decisive importance, and the musician will confirm that analogous constructs constitute an essential part of the modern theory of composition." But of course there is no such thing in function theory as the concept of the transformation of groups; there is only the intellectual object "transformation groups," and even that not in function theory, but in group theory. Which is simultaneously an example of the universality and the style of Spengler's way of arguing.

2

After such examples one would certainly find it hard to believe that I am claiming the privilege of taking Spengler literally. But there are people who will. For there is a favorable prejudice—I want to use the word *spiritual*, let us say then in spiritual circles, but I mean in literary circles—toward offenses against mathematics, logic, and precision. Among crimes against the spirit, these are happily counted among the honorable political ones; the prosecutor actually finds himself in the role of the accused. Let us be generous, then: Spengler is speaking approximately; he works with analogies, and these are always right in some sense or other. If an author is bent on referring to concepts by the wrong names or even confusing them with each other, one can eventually get used to it. But some key symbol, some kind of ultimately unequivocal connection between thought and word, must be sustained. Even this is lacking. The examples I have adduced, without having to look very hard, are only a selection among many; they are not errors of detail, but *a way of thinking*.

There are lemon-yellow butterflies, and there are lemon-yellow Chinese. In a certain sense, then, one can say that the butterfly is the winged, middle-European, dwarf Chinese. Butterflies and Chinese are both familiar as images of sexual desire. Here the thought is formulated for the first time of the previously unrecognized commonality between the great ages of lepidopteral fauna and Chinese culture. That butterflies have wings and the Chinese do not is only a superficial phenomenon. If ever a zoologist had understood anything about the ultimate and deepest ideas of technology, it would not have been left to me to be the first to disclose the significance of the fact that butterflies did not invent gunpowder precisely because the Chinese had done so already. The suicidal predilection of certain kinds of nocturnal moths for bright light is a relic of this morphological connection to Sinology, a connection hard to explain in terms of everyday reason.

It really makes no difference what it is that is to be proved by such means. I wanted to show, using the example of mathematics, how much trust should be placed in Spengler's way of arguing, since Spengler himself says that only the example of mathematics can corroborate it.

3

I move on now to the epistemological conclusions that Spengler draws from his observations on physics.

He argues "that even words such as quantity, position, process, and change of state are specifically Western conceptions that dominate the character of scientific facts and the way in which they are known, to say nothing of complex concepts like work, tension, quantum of effect, quantity of heat, and probability, each of which contains its own total vision of the physical world *in nuce*." He says, "The experiment, the systematic management of experience, is highly dogmatic; it already assumes a particular aspect of nature." Or:

The self-contained, highly persuasive complex "unassailable truths" is, in a very significant sense, dependent on the course of development, on general, national, and private destinies. . . . Every great physicist, who as a personality always gives his discoveries his own particular stamp, every hypothesis, which without an individual flavor is entirely impossible, every problem that finds its way into the hands of this researcher and no other—all these signify just so many providential interventions for the shape of the theory. Anyone who disputes this has no conception of how many conditional elements are contained in the absolute forces of mechanics.

Aside from a few ambiguities, Spengler is entirely justified in such observations. He is mistaken only in thinking they are new; their substance is familiar to anyone who knows anything about the epistemological work of the past fifty years.

But when this leads him to conclude that decisions in physics are *"questions of style. . . .* There are physical systems, just as there are tragedies and symphonies. Here too there are schools, traditions, manners, and conventions, as in painting,"* he turns a dead horse into an Irish stew.

Spengler says: There is no reality. Nature is a function of culture. Cultures are the ultimate realities accessible to us. The skepticism of our final phase must be historical. But why did the fulcrums in the age of Archimedes or wedges in the Paleolithic age work exactly the way they do today? Why is it that even a monkey can use a lever or a stone as if he knew the theories of statics and the strength of materials, and how can a panther deduce his prey from a spoor as if he knew about causality? If we are not willing to assume that a common culture unites monkeys, Stone Age man, Archimedes, and the panther, there is presumably nothing left but to assume that there is a common regulative principle that lies outside the subject; in other words, an experience that is capable of being amplified and refined, the possibility of knowledge, some sort of conception of truth, progress, ascent; in short, precisely that *mixture* of subjective and objective factors in knowledge whose separation constitutes the painstaking work of sorting out the theory of knowledge, work that Spengler has dispensed with because it most decisively interferes with the free flight of ideas.

At one point Spengler emphasizes that knowledge is not only content but also dynamic activity: but what he neglects to an incredible degree is that it also *is* content. What characterizes and defines our intellectual situation is precisely the wealth of contents that can no longer be mastered, the swollen facticity of knowledge (including moral facts), the spilling out of experience over the surfaces of nature, the impossibility of achieving an overview, the chaos of things that cannot be denied. We will perish from this, or overcome it by becoming a spiritually stronger type of human being. But then it makes no sense from a human point of view to try to wish away this enormous danger and hope by stealing from the facts, through a false skepticism, the weight of their facticity.

4

Since a large part of natural laws is the result of spatial measurements, it would of course be an amazing accomplishment if it were possible to show not only that the essence of space is experienced differently in every culture, but also that it actually *is* different. If this were so, the claim that nature is a function of culture would, as it were, be demonstrated together with its roots.

Spengler does in fact claim to have "destroyed the illusion of a single, enduring space surrounding all human beings, by means of which we could completely understand each other conceptually," and to have demonstrated that "an extensiveness in itself. . . , independent of the knower's specific feeling for form," is "an illusion."

He points to the existence of non-Euclidean geometries. From this it follows that there are a number of concepts of space, which are defined precisely by the fact that these geometries are valid for them. Let us call these mathematical spaces. They arise from variations in certain qualities of the traditional Euclidean concept of space, but they may, nonetheless, be employed for the reliable calculation of physical, that is real, facts. However, we ordinarily make a distinction here: the space chosen for representation, just like other mathematical symbols, is first of all only a conceptual bridge for processes in another space, that of profane reality. Let us call this space empirical-metrical, for it is nothing but experiential space under the dominant aspect of measurement. One can easily convince oneself of this by bearing in mind that beside empirical-metrical space (and in a sense preceding it), there are other kinds of spaces that are still seen, touched, and heard, in all gradations from primary impression to fully conscious perception. These spaces are not Euclidean at all: in visual space, for instance, parallel lines intersect, length is dependent on the relative position of the line, the three dimensions are not of equal value, and specific illusions crop up that often reveal themselves as illusions only when confronted with experience from another realm of the senses.

It is not my intention to develop this idea further and show how the whole of experiential space arises from it, or why this is considered Euclidean, or with what competence more profound mathematical-physical experience again calls it into question. It is enough for me to establish that this would provide material for numerous epistemological and psychological studies, whose results would certainly not yield the solution, but would point to it. Thus Spengler is right not only that there are a number of different mathematical-physical spaces, but also that the "variety of different ways of seeing" that he claims does indeed exist; he is mistaken only in taking this to be a new basis for spatial theory. Here again he has taken the point of departure of an intellectual task for its conclusion. If he did not regard "the foolish methods of experimental psychology" as one of his unworthy "hunting grounds for mediocre minds," and epistemological studies as "academic trivia," it would not have been so easy for him to make this mistake. I will pass over his analogous observations about our time, as well as "the mystery of the origin of space" for the sake of a broader context, since on the level of detail the same pattern merely repeats itself.

5

First a digression.

Up to now I have appealed repeatedly to experience. There are people who respond to this with a shrug of the shoulders: empirical philosophy! A philosophical trend that is only one among many, and not particularly privileged to possess the truth. Spengler would indulgently dismiss this insistence on facts as a symptom of Western culture. But the choir of soulful anti-intellectuals—from Goethe (or so they claim) to the smallest intellectual pipsqueak and religious zealot of today—has long since unanimously intuited: there is nothing so contemptible as empiricism.

Before I reply to this, however, I wish to say that I would consider it inappropriate to ridicule a significant work that has a life of its own—and I take Spengler's to be such a book—because of its weaknesses, and then slide my own pot onto the fire and quickly cook up my own better ideas; much more superficially than the author did, of course, since space, time, and sense of importance are limited. So I would like to make clear that I am not evaluating Spengler, but attacking him. I attack him where he is representative. Where he is superficial. When one attacks Spengler, one is attacking the age from which he springs and which he flatters, for his faults are its faults. An age, however, is not to be refuted; I say this not out of agnosticism, but rather because no one person has the time to come to terms with it. All one can do is keep an eye on it and perhaps rap it on the knuckles here and there.

The kind of experience this produces in Spengler's case has nothing to do with historical distinctions in philosophy. No system of thought may stand in contradiction to experience or proper inferences drawn from it: in this sense, every serious philosophy is empirical. How, in this context, the concept of experience is to be grasped with precision, how one is to separate a priori elements from experiential elements in the narrower sense of the term, and in what sense we ought to speak of an a priori at all—these questions require wide-ranging and open-ended discussion. But they may also be set aside for the reason that the widespread aversion of which we were speaking is not directed against theoretical works with which almost no one is familiar but against a particular attitude that, favored by the successes of the natural sciences, has increasingly dominated civilized humanity since the eighteenth century. Experience that is relevant for science (there were also thinkers who claimed to have experienced God) is, under specifiable conditions, vouchsafed to everyone. I would therefore like to add, not without some pleasure in being nasty, that this experience is trivial.

In this sense, empirical thought naturally narrows the mind. Having to rely on building from the bottom up, on the safe, the accessible, the smoothed-down—great theoretical ideas are relatively rare—empirical thought easily acquires, along with precision, a certain Philistinism. This constant reaching for the lower before the higher becomes (since reaching for the higher rarely succeeds) its only move. A certain philosophical sluggishness is part of empirical thinking—where it does not become a high intellectual virtue: one stitches fragments of experience together, hoping that someday a system will develop out of them that has by no means been demonstrated. One goes around in circles, and settles again and again for merely ordering phenomena in groups of other phenomena. And even if, in this process, satisfying the metaphysical need does not, as one generally assumes, have to be so hopeless that one must be content with the appearance alone, there is no denying that for the sake of finding causes one often finds trivial causes, and comes up with explanations that are valid only, as it were, in terms of the jargon. These then become the showpieces of the struggle against the narrow scientific spirit, intellectualism, rationalism, and so forth. But of course every intellectual style carries its camp-following caricatures along with it, and the other side's are infinitely greater. If in the empiricist one only sees Lucifer banished to the depths by God, one should not forget the main argument in Lucifer's favor: the inadequacy of all philosophical angels. In honor of a higher angel, I took Spengler as an example, in order to portray one of these angels as well as I could, in partially plucked condition.

6

Epistemological objections are of course valid only on the assumption that knowledge is at issue. But are we then always knowing? When we read Emerson, Maeterlinck, or Novalis—I count even Nietzsche in this company, and to give a contemporary example I will mention Rudolf Kassner[31]—we experience the most powerful movement of the mind; but this cannot be called knowing. The convergence to clarity is missing; the impression does not let itself be compressed and precipitated out. These are intellectual paraphrases of something that one can assimilate on the human level, but can restate only in intellectual paraphrases.

The reason lies in the fact that representations in this area have no fixed meaning but are, rather, more or less individual experiences, which we understand only insofar as we recall similar experiences. They must be experienced anew every time, but they are always reexperienced only partially, and by no means definitively understood. Ideas are always like that when they do not have a firm basis in what can be perceived through the senses, or in the purely rational, but rest instead on feelings and impressions that are difficult to reproduce. Obviously, all expressions of practical life belong in this category; every discussion, every argument, every decision, every relation between two people rests, as we like to say, on imponderables. If we summarize such conceptions and circumstances in such a context—as the essay does, or "opinion," or "personal" conviction—complicated constructs arise, which of course disintegrate as easily as complicated groups of atoms.

The moment we enter this territory, logical method reveals itself as dethroned. The higher a thought stands in this realm, the more the rational component retreats in relation to the experiential component. For this reason I once referred to this as the "nonratioid realm" (in the fourth volume of the journal *Summa*,[32] where one can find a few more incidental observations on the subject), but of course that is valid only in the sense I have just described. The pulsating idea replaces the rigid concept, analogies appear in place of equations, probability in place of truth: the essential construction is no longer systematic, but creative. This realm includes all gradations from the almost scientific, such as is found the essays of Taine or Macaulay but ultimately also in almost any piece of historical writing, to presentiment and willfulness, or those treatises that dispense only stimulation, such as poets sometimes write today. The content converges accordingly at times almost to clarity and at times diverges to complete disparity, creating only intellectual structures and diffuse agitation.

Anyone who has educated himself by means of such works will know how much can be extracted from them through order, analysis, or comparison—in short, through thinking—despite the fact that their finest substance is lost in the process. He will also know how much rationality they contain, aside from the obvious rationality required just to state them. (I leave aside the case in which areas previously dominated only by an idea, or even by literature, are suddenly conquered almost completely by reason, as in the case of psychoanalysis.) If it were not presumptuous, in view of the current disparity between the accomplishments of the nonratioid realm and the purely rational accomplishments of science, I would say that wherever human understanding is deprived, as it were, of all its creature comforts, it must be that much more flexible, and where everything is fluid it must grasp and discriminate that much more sharply. To set the spirit in opposition to reason [*Verstand*] is a pernicious misunderstanding; the humanly essential questions are only confused by all the scribbling about rationalism and antirationalism. The only possible longing in which one does not lose as much as one gains is the longing for suprarationalism.

Very little is being done to clarify these fundamental questions. Philosophers are uncomfortable exploring the methodology of a realm whose facts consist of experiences with which most of them are not familiar in the necessary variety. Thus there has not been to my knowledge any attempt whatsoever to investigate the logic of the analogical and the irrational. "There is scientific experience and life experience," says Spengler, "and there is a seldom acknowledged distinction between experience [*Erlebnis*] and knowing [*Erkennen*]." "Comparisons could be the blessing of historical thinking. . . . Their techniques would have to be worked out in the context of a comprehensive idea and thus to the point of strict necessity, of logical mastery." I admire the passionate resoluteness that wants to press the whole of world history into new forms of thought. That it does not succeed is not Spengler's fault alone, but lies also in the lack of any preparatory work.

7

Once it is clear that, depending on the object, either the conceptuality or the fluctuating character of the experience in an idea is the main thing, we can then understand without any mysticism the distinction Spengler and others make between dead and living knowledge. What we can learn as if we were in school—knowledge, rational order, conceptually defined objects and relations—we may assimilate or not; we can remember it or forget it. This knowledge can be placed in us like a true, smoothly polished die, or taken out again: such thoughts are, in a certain sense, dead. This is the reverse of the feeling that they are valid quite apart from us. Precision and correctness kill; what can be defined—concept, fossil, skeleton—is dead. An exclusively rational thinker has probably never had occasion to experience this in his sphere of interest. But in intellectual fields, where the proposition is valid that to know is to remember (or—I referred to this earlier—the Hegelian triad of thesis, antithesis, and synthesis, which is not valid precisely where he applied it, namely in the ratioid realm), one has this experience at every step. Here the word does not signify anything fixed; it is the living word, full of meaning and intellectual relation in the moment, bathed in will and feeling. An hour later it says nothing, although it says everything that a concept can say. We may well call such a way of thinking dynamic, alive.

8

Spengler says,

One can at will analyze, define, order, limit according to cause and effect. This is a work, the rest is a creation. Form and law, metaphor and concept, symbol and formula have very different qualities. What appears here is the relationship between life and death, creating and destroying. Reason and concept kill because they "know." They make what is known into a rigid object that can be measured and parceled out. Contemplation is inspired. It internalizes in the individual a living, inwardly felt unity. Writing poetry and doing historical research are related, as are calculation and knowledge. . . . The artist, the genuine historian, looks to see how something comes into being. In the qualities of what is observed, he experiences becoming once again.

This leads in addition to something closely connected to the distinction between living and dead ways of knowing, or as Spengler says, between contemplating and knowing: I once called it the distinction between causality and motivation. Causality seeks the rule in what is regular, confirms what is permanently stable and fixed. Motivation makes the motive comprehensible in that it releases the impulse to similar action, feeling, or thinking. This forms the basis of the distinction I have already mentioned between scientific experience and life experience. I would, however, like to mention that the common confusion between scientific and literary psychology also lies in this direction. Around 1900 every writer wanted to be a "profound psychologist"; around 1920 psychology is considered a term of abuse. This is a battle of illusions. Causal psychology was always only rarely employed as an artistic method. But the rest of what is referred to as "psychology" is simply knowledge of people and the capacity for motivation. Not a horse trader's understanding of people, which rests on what is humanly typical, but rather that of the human being who is spared nothing or from whom nothing is withheld.

9

The opposites of life and death, contemplating and knowing, form and law, symbol and formula have already been mentioned. I would add to these the pairs becoming-being, movement-rest, self-other, soul-world, direction-space, time–clock time, will-knowledge, destiny-causality, organic logic–logic (also opposed to each other as logic of time and logic of space), appearance-system. This is an almost complete list of the structural ideas with whose aid Spengler cuts cross-sections through the basic given, whose essence remains the same from whichever side he seizes it.

I will resist the temptation to demonstrate this, because it would get me entangled in the difficulties that Spengler passed over. Moreover, anyone can imitate Spengler's philosophy according to a ruthlessly simple scheme. One need only take the predicate "is in a certain sense," "becomes in a certain sense," or "has in a certain sense," set aside minor differences of expression, combine every idea that has been brought up with all the others, and then affirm the combination of all concepts that stand in the first position in their pairs and likewise all those in the second position in relation to each other, and finally negate every combination of a concept in the first position with one in a second position. The conscientious application of these rules will effortlessly yield Spengler's philosophy, and even somewhat more. For example: life is contemplated, has form, is symbol, is becoming, etc. Causal relation is dead, is known, has laws, has become, etc. Life has no system, destiny cannot be known, and so on and so on. Spengler will say this demonstrates the inadequacy of rationality; but that is what I am saying too.

It is only against the reproach, which has been brought against Spengler, of unavowed dependence on Bergson that I would like to come to the defense of Bergson—*his* case is another matter. But what does bear on the fundamental problem belongs neither to Spengler nor Bergson alone, but reaches further back beyond German Romantic philosophy and Goethe (whom Spengler invokes).

10

Intuition is a question in itself. I propose that all German writers refrain from using this word for two years. Things have reached a point today where anyone who wants to claim something he cannot prove and has not worked out invokes intuition. During this period of abstinence perhaps someone could sort out the innumerable meanings of the word.

Perhaps then we will be able to better appreciate something that is now so gladly overlooked: that there is also such a thing as a purely rational intuition. Here too, however methodical its preparations may have been, the decisive case of inspiration breaks in on consciousness suddenly, as if from the outside. Heightened states of feeling enhance even strictly rational thought, which apparently has nothing to do with feelings at all. How much more is this the case with what is referred to here as nonratioid thinking, whose pungency and speed of inner propagation absolutely depend on the vitality of the words, on a cloud of thoughts and feelings that surround a trivial conceptual kernel. Or think of those moments of knowledge that "illuminate life in a flash"—showpieces of intuition; but even here one will see that it is not a matter of another kind of intellectual activity suddenly erupting, but of the condition of the whole person, which had long since become critical, suddenly reversing itself. The relevant, presumably igniting idea is usually only the flash of the explosion that accompanies great inner transformations.

"Something that cannot be known, described, defined, . . . but only felt and inwardly experienced, which one either never comprehends or of which one is fully certain"; "at a stroke, out of a feeling that cannot be learned, that is removed from any intended effect. . . , that appears rarely enough in its highest moments," says Spengler. This is only one gradation on the great scale that leads from this point to holy simplicity, beatific vision, and the other great forms of conceiving the world by way of the condition of the believer, the lover, and the ethical person; with a very significant ancillary branch to the pathological, reaching from common forms of cyclothymia to serious states of insanity.

This is an analytic attitude toward the process of intuition. People will object that this is of interest to scholars who might wish to determine it among themselves, but that what matters humanly is not analyzing psychological form but synthesizing the substance that has been achieved within it. The world in which we live and participate every day, this world of authorized conditions of intellect and soul, is only a makeshift substitute for another world to which our true relationship has been lost. One sometimes feels that none of this is important; for hours or days it melts in the glow of a different attitude toward the world and people. One becomes straw and breath, the world a trembling soap bubble. In every such moment all things arise anew; one recognizes that to regard them as fixed entities is inner death. The horse drawing the wagon and the passerby communicate. Or at least human beings do not measure one another, or sniff each other like spies reconnoitering, but rather know about each other like the hand or leg of a body. This is the mood of philosophically creative *or* philosophically eclectic conditions. One may interpret them intellectually as a belated Christian, or demonstrate in them the Heraclitean flux, or for that matter read anything and everything into or out of them; among other things, an entirely new ethos. Do we believe in it? No. We play "literature" with it, galvanizing Buddha, Christ, and other imprecisions. Around it, reason rages with thousands of horsepower. People defy reason and claim to have another authority in a locked chest: this is the cistern of intuition. One should finally open it and see what's in it. It may be a new world.

One rarely finds attempts as beautiful and powerful as Spengler's to give this form. But that finally the entire substance of intuition amounts to the fact that one cannot say or treat what is most important; that one is skeptical to the extreme in matters of reason (thus precisely against something that has nothing to be said for it except that it is true!), but on the other hand unspeakably credulous toward everything that happens to pop into one's mind; that one doubts mathematics but believes in art-historical fabrications of truth like culture and style; that, despite intuition, one does the same thing the empiricist does in comparing and combining facts, only worse, shooting with smoke instead of bullets: this is the clinical picture of the mind, the aesthetic mind, of our age, softened by immoderate, advanced addiction to intuition.

11

The idea that cultures finally collapse from inner exhaustion is plausible even without metaphysics. Likewise, that corresponding phases can be distinguished in rising and declining cultures.

Spiritual tension holds people together; once it is gone and no longer necessary, the organism collapses. That something similar happens in the life of society is not to be doubted. It becomes a disorganized heap if directing energies no longer shape it.

All cultures arose in relatively small geographical regions and societies, and spread out from there. In this there is a tendency toward dilution and exhaustion; the same tendency can be found in the effects of time over generations. Ideas (nonratioid) cannot be transmitted in the same way as knowledge: they require identical mental conditions, but in reality at most only analogous dispositions of the soul are present, so they are constantly undergoing change. So long as ideas are new this may perhaps enrich them; later it corrupts them. Along the way, ideas do realize themselves in arrangements and forms of life; but to realize an idea already means to partly destroy it. All realizations of ideas are distortions, and as they become older they become more vacuous and incomprehensible, for form and idea have quite different rhythms; thus the forms of an older layer always intrude in the ideas of a more recent layer and compete with them for influence.

This is one of the reasons why late periods are so fragmented, and why in such civilized eras cultures decay like mountains.

12

Progress itself is not something that unfolds in a single line. Along with the natural weakening an idea suffers as it becomes diffuse, there is also the crisscrossing of influences from new sources of ideas. The innermost core of the life of every age, an inchoate, swelling mass, is poured into molds forged by much earlier times. Every present period is simultaneously now and yet millennia old. This millipede moves on political, economic, cultural, biological, and countless other legs, each of which has a different tempo and rhythm. One can see this as a unified picture and elaborate it in terms of a single cause by always keeping to a central perspective, as Spengler does, but one can also find satisfaction in the exact opposite. There is no plan in this, no reason: fine. Does that really make it any uglier than if there were a plan? Is agnosticism comfortable? It can be true or false, for it is a rational matter, penetrating or superficial; but whether it is humanly profound or not is no longer a quality of knowledge but rather one of those—in my shorthand, nonratioid—complexes that arise on the base of such rational convictions. Such a confusion, for example, has virtually immortalized itself in the common view of (philosophical) materialism, which is regarded to this day as shallow and emotionally constricted, although naturally it can be just as full of feeling as believing in angels.

It is now perhaps possible to understand what I mean when I ask that such theories (insofar as they are not explicitly true or false) be treated as nothing more than experimental intellectual principles for forming the inner life, instead of—as always happens today—ascribing an emotional quality to theory in such a simple and clumsy way. What people refer to as intellectualism in the negative sense, the fashionable intellectual haste of our time, the withering of thoughts before they ripen, is caused in part by the fact that we seek depth with our thoughts and truth with our feelings without noticing that we have it backwards, and are often disappointed at not getting anywhere. Sweeping ideological attempts like Spengler's are quite beautiful, but they suffer today from the fact that far too few of the inner possibilities have had the ground prepared for them. One simply explains the World War or our collapse first by this, then by that cluster of causes; but this is deceptive. Just as fraudulent as explaining a simple physical event by a chain of causes. In reality, even in the first links of the chain of causality the causes have already flowed and dissolved beyond the scope of our vision. In the physical realm we have found an accommodation (the concept of function). In the spiritual realm we are completely helpless. Intellectuality leaves us in the lurch. But not because intellect is shallow (as if everything else had not left us in the lurch as well!) but because we have not worked at it.

13

How to distinguish between culture and civilization is to my way of thinking an old and really fruitless quarrel. If one wants to make such a distinction, I believe it is best to say culture where a *single* ideology reigns and a form of life is still coherent, and to define civilization, on the other hand, as a cultural situation that has become diffuse. Every civilization is preceded by a culture, which decays in it. Every civilization is characterized by a certain technical mastery over nature and a very complicated system of social relations—one that requires a great deal of intelligence, but also devours.

An immediate relation to the essence of things is almost always ascribed to culture, a kind of fateful security of human demeanor and an assurance that is still instinctive, in comparison to which reason, the fundamental symptom of civilization, is supposed to possess a somewhat lamentable uncertainty and indirectness. One knows the symptoms this view relies on: the great rituals of myth and religion that, from a distance, seem self-contained, and on the other hand the ceremoniousness of expressing through reason what a glance, a silence, or a resolve can express much better. A person is not only intellect, but also will, feeling, lack of awareness, and often mere actuality, like the drifting of clouds in the sky. But those who see in people only what is not achieved by reason would finally have to seek the ideal in an anthill or beehive state, against whose mythos, harmony, and intuitive certainty of rhythm everything human presumably amounts to nothing.

As I have said, I take the growth in the number of people involved to be the main cause of the transition from culture to civilization. It is clear that to permeate a hundred million people presents quite different problems from permeating a hundred thousand. The negative aspects of civilization are connected for the most part to the fact that its capacity to lead and influence no longer corresponds to this volume of the social body. Consider the high points before the War: the railroad, the telegraph, the telephone, flying machines, newspapers, the book trade, the system of schools and higher education, military service: all completely inadequate. The distinction between the big city and the benighted mentality of the countryside is greater than that between races. The complete impossibility, even in one's own stratum, of penetrating the assumptions of another circle of thought without devoting an incredible amount of time to it. Result: narrow conscientiousness or impetuous superficiality. Intellectual organization cannot keep up with the growth in the number of people: this explains ninety-eight out of a hundred of all the phenomena of civilization. No initiative is able to penetrate the social body for long stretches and get responses from the whole. It doesn't matter what one does: Christ could come down to earth again; it is out of the question that his coming would have any effect. The life-and-death question is: the politics of intellectual and spiritual organization. This is the primary task for activist and socialist alike. If this problem is not solved, all other efforts will be in vain, for it is the precondition for their having any impact at all.

14

I summarize myself; never before in my life have I found it necessary to do so *post facto*.

I have attacked a very popular book.

I had promised myself—I am not, after all, writing a review—to demonstrate errors of the age in a famous individual instance. Superficiality: casting the cloak of spirituality, under which the marionette is hiding; overflowing of a lyrical imprecision into the quadrant of reason. For great as the distinction is, for example, between the passionate observer of the contemporary scene, who digests into solid clumps what is in the intellectual air, and the bookworm who in the manner of worms daily eats a multiple of his own intellectual weight and consumes sciences, and who of course can only excrete this in a loose form—these are merely opposite, but in their meaning identical, phenomena of an age that does not know how to use its reason. It is not an age with too much understanding, as has been said again and again, but one that does not have its understanding in the right place. With Expressionism, to give another example, our age made flat and superficial a really fundamental insight into art, because those who wanted to introduce intellect into literature could not think. They couldn't because they thought in airy words whose content lacked any empirical restraint. Naturalism offered reality without spirit, Expressionism spirit without reality: both are nonspirit. On the other hand, however, a certain dried-fish rationality has come among us, and the two opponents are worthy of each other.

I refer once again to the distinction between ratioid and nonratioid, which I did not invent, but have simply named so poorly. Here lies the root from which the fateful question of intuition grows, and that of understanding things through the feelings, which are nothing other than peculiarities of the nonratioid realm falsely understood. Here lies the key to "education" [*Bildung*]. This is where the rickety idealism of our age and its god have come out. This would be the way to understand why the pointless battle in contemporary civilization between scientific thinking and the claims of the soul can be solved only by adding something, a plan, a direction to work in, a different valuing of science as well as literature!

And to Oswald Spengler I declare publicly, and as a sign of my affection, that the only reason other writers do not make so many mistakes is because they lack the necessary reach to touch both shores in order to cover so much.

The German as Symptom
1923

This series of unpublished drafts contain Musil's most complete account of the ideological crisis of modern culture. Despite their unfinished and fragmentary quality, this is also Musil's most sustained attempt at a comprehensive statement of his views on such topics as epistemology, human nature, capitalism, and mysticism. His critique of ideology (and his understanding of it as the shaper of human experience) is central here, and he concludes with his fullest account of the "other condition."

Recall one fact above all: around 1900 (the last spiritual and intellectual movement of great vital force in Germany), people believed in the future. In a social future. In a new art. The fin de siècle gave the period a veneer of morbidity and decadence: but both these negative definitions were only contingent expressions for the will to be different, to do things differently from the way people had done them in the past.

If we consider what has become of this and what remains of it, or if we leaf through back issues of magazines that were "modern" then, it is hard to understand how so much genuine ability and accomplishment could be concealed for so long beneath the illusion of decadence.

If we attempt to analyze this situation we immediately encounter a great variety of quite different elements, among them some that are thoroughly contradictory. Nietzsche and Carlyle intersected with socialism, decadence with the spirit of a nature-cult club, Maeterlinck, Emerson, and Romanticism with veneration of the machine. Foreign influences were interwoven here in Germany in equally colorful ways. All this is extremely difficult to analyze, but what I have to say requires only the highlighting of individual traits.

Secret underground forces or trivial causes? A thousand little causes, but the given of a problematic situation.

These are only the events in the most effervescent part. The others quite confused and tangled up in one another.

Complaints and regressive suggestions symptom of pos[itivism.]

Above all: people believed in the future. People really wanted to make it happen. Even where they yielded voluptuously to an incipient decline, they at least wanted to make use of this interval for demonic activities that strike us today like the tawdry furniture of a disreputable bar in the sober light of morning. Compare this to the feelings of decline today, which are gray, ashen, passive, and joyless by comparison. Desire, will, hope—in a word a state of power that was sthenic, imagined or real, distinguished that period from today.

Secondly, we were international. State, nation, race, and family were cast aside, even if we ourselves did not often take the trouble to carry out the gesture. We were also summarily irreligious, since religion too was something that belonged back in the past.

The connections are easy to understand: We believed in progress. Progress is international. It was a matter not simply of a historical juxtaposition of these two things, but of facts. Scientific progress is international, as is artistic progress.

Scientifically: Frenchmen, Englishmen, Germans. Italians and Americans catching up. Germany perhaps even in the lead.

Artistically: Germany behind France, Russia, Scandinavia. Vacuum after Classicism and Romanticism were demolished. Everything vital came from abroad.

We may say: Intellectual life is international. Only a period of discouragement, an age that has given up on itself, that wants to "preserve," that has been driven onto the defensive, can be intellectually nationalist. Such a period is essentially "conservative." A person who has progress in his heart is international.

Later we were confronted with the question of whether there is any such thing as "intellectual progress." And we also get nowhere if we regard what is essential in the phenomena just enumerated as simply a certain "directedness." Feelings, illusions, intentions, and thoughts bore this mark of being directed; they ran (apparently or really) parallel, and somehow pointed to the future. (A concept that seems to me important for the sociological analysis of intellectual movements.)

Here an interpolation is necessary.

Even today the proletariat and its intellectuals remain international in their sentiments, and only the bourgeoisie is once again (stated physically) aimless and chaotic.

Moreover, the phenomenon with which these ideas are connected took place only in a small stratum of the bourgeoisie, and could thus be discounted as inconsequential from the outset.

But naturally the intellectual leadership of the proletariat was intimately associated with this thin layer; even Russia, apparently, did not produce anything intellectually whose substance was not derived from it. The proletarian is either bourgeois or antibourgeois. He did not produce a new ideology: aside from Marxism, which is, all in all, half true, the dross of bourgeois ideologies was mixed in with his ideology. Much as it was in the movements for educating the masses and in school reform. (I say this as a political supporter of the proletarian movement.)

The effect of the thin layer of which and to which I am speaking is socially very complicated and circuitous, but it is real. It may be that intellectual repercussions eventually emerge even from political movements that are carried out stupidly; but that does not excuse us in the least from the task of trying to improve things through preliminary intellectual work.

The sulking intellectuals, just like those who have fled into the church of communism, are today betraying their responsibilities.

Let's take a look at the path from hope to hopelessness that lies between 1890 and 1923.

What seemed then to be the trend has dissipated; a skein has come unravelled. It is apparent that even then everything was already present: one thing after another, it all came into being, and today it is once again all present at the same time.

I take my examples once again from the literary sphere: there was irrationalism along with rationalism. The idea of the experimental novel, and S. Fischer's authors,[33] expecting redemption through feelings, through a human short circuit. Nietzsche and socialism. The materialist view of history and the early stages of idealism. Humanism and anti-Semitism (or racial theory). Thus, internationalism and nationalism as well. European art and regional art. The poetry of the metropolis and the Catholic church. Monism, Free Christianity—church.

We can also trace it back to personalities, who are themselves blends of elements. I would mention as the most influential: Nietzsche, Marx, Bergson, Bismarck.

Following Naturalism there was a weak form of Neo-Romanticism, and an equally weak Neo-idealism; then came Expressionism.

An art of ideas, but the ideas were not there, and it chose the wrong means.

A major formula: rationalism and irrationalism.

Whereas people around 1900 believed in the advent of a new man, people today are desperate and without hope. We have all the historical possibilities and no contemporary reality.

I attempted to show (in this journal, number. . . , and in *Annals of the M. Society*, vol. #)[34] that the intensity with which the enthusiasm for war in

1914 set fire to both the new world and the old had a principal source in this spiritual despair. What has been said so far about the spiritual situation of Germany was, with variations, most certainly a phenomenon of the whole of Western civilization. Obviously there are other ways of looking at such a complex phenomenon as the War, but this perspective surely is an important one.

I have repeatedly tried to fathom this despair, which expressed itself in the most varied forms. As a general formula, I would adduce that European life and European ideology are not commensurate with one another.

One must first of all account for the importance of an ideology. Every day there comes a moment when a person lays his hands in his lap and all his busyness collapses like ashes. The work accomplished is, from the soul's point of view, entirely imaginary. But as an ideology this is impossible. One looks for—symptoms. Instead of seeing in it a symptom of the future.

People have tried to discover the poetry of work, of money, of noise, of haste, and the like. In vain. These things are poetic only for the observer who is not working, poor, silent, nonparticipating.

On the other hand, it is conceivable that people would, as it were, wean themselves away from the soul and develop constitutions suited to this life. Love would then become procreation with the help of an irritation of the skin that was just impersonal, like freezing or burning. I have no interest in getting too excited about this future possibility, but it is a fact that we suffer from its being something that is not real, but nonetheless possible!

I believe that the average person is a far more avid metaphysician than he admits. "Avid" is probably not the right epithet, but a dull accompanying awareness of his curious situation rarely leaves him. His own mortality, the minuteness of our little ball of earth in the cosmos, the mystery of personality, the question of an afterlife, the sense and senselessness of existence: these are questions that the individual ordinarily brushes aside his whole life long as in any case unanswerable, but that he nonetheless feels surrounding him all his life like the walls of a room.

I also believe that few people remain completely untouched by the thought that instead of the life they lead there might also be another, where all actions proceed from a very personal state of excitement. Where actions have meaning, not just causes. And where a person, to use a trivial word, is happy, and not just nervously tormenting himself.

To allow people to find this attitude—to approach it, after which each person could adjust it for his individual case—is the task of ideology. Guiding the soul. Informing the soul.

In the *Annals* essay mentioned above I suggested that the lack of congruence between ideology and practical life must lead from time to time to explosions (to "metaphysical blowouts").

Now I am, of course, aware of the enormous literature whose content consists of expressions for this incongruity. It embraces the familiar sea of complaints about our soullessness, mechanization, calculatedness, lack of religion, and so on. But I know of hardly a single sensible book that tries to see this problem as a problem, a new problem, and not as an old, failed solution.

Generally speaking, the cure is sought regressively. (Nation, virtue, religion, antagonism to science.) Only very rarely is it made explicit that a new problem has been posed here, that its solution has not *yet* been found.

And I am equally unaware of any productive examination of what is really lacking, from the absence of which all suffering comes: the soul. (But "soul" only a special case of "ideology.")

Take care that this doesn't simply turn into the afflictions of the bourgeoisie and its literature!

The ideological situation today is individualistic. No single ideology dominates. Countless individual names, which are brought together only in the individual formulations of individual thinkers, are picked out singly at random.

Therefore the chaotic situation. Comparable to a madhouse.

A few aids:

Drawing power of the church. A truth can last 2,000 years—but an ideology can't!

Nation: ⎫

State: ⎬ Bland philosophical idealism.

Communist church: ⎭

No one can grasp the spiritual needs, which are incomprehensible even in a positive sense. Two attempts to create a philosophy out of the age—pragmatism and positivism—have remained unfruitful.

Money is orderly self-seeking. Cap[italism]: greatest organization of bearish speculation.

Selfishness is as old as human associations. Money is the most recent attempt to limit it.

Abolishing capitalism means abolishing order. Demand a new order of selfishness. It is nonsense to think that selfishness would be abolished along with capitalism. This is the way utopian socialists weasel out of their real task.

Every existing order says: Man is good, man is altruistic. It calls its own requirements good, and accordingly the person who is subordinated to them is *illis ipsis* good. (Moreover, the new order is continually depositing itself on the remains of older ones.) We may say: Because the forms of order are evil (namely, expressions of dominant groups), they produce good people (= the person who is subordinate, submissive to external evil) (polarity, dualism of good and evil).

In a natural order there must, according to human nature (as political animal [ζοον πολιτικον] and individualist), be a ma[ximum] of individuality along with a ma[ximum] of communality. Such a requirement is vague to the point of rubbish; but we can't do any more either than vary the given situation in a direction we anticipate. Beyond that, opinions and feelings about what is good and evil vary so widely that one must let people do as they like as much as possible. There is no worldview. The strongest feeling is that a perspective is being formed, the feeling of a process underway: one must try to come out of it with a mi[nimum] of hindrances.

In some such way capitalism must unite with a mentality that absorbs egoism, lack of discipline, and the *omnes contra omnes* into its good conscience.

Capitalism today is unspeakably cruel, but has altruistic phrases in its mouth.

The French point to the profiteers among us, and we answer with nationalist phrases, etc.

If I want to have a worldview, then I must view the world. That is, I must establish the facts. The smallest fact from the connection between the soul and hormonal balance gives me more perspectives than an idealistic system. But the facts are not finished; they are hardly even begun—A worldview that waits for facts believes in progress. It is simply curious. It is also relative. Positively skeptical (not *ignoramibus*). Sense of: free research.

But there can be no doubt that through the empirical sciences we gain new perspectives on the age-old metaphysical problems.

Here Kant's thing-in-itself has done enormous harm. It demonstrated that a way of formulating the question was impossible, and people believe that one can pose questions only in this way. Ways of formulating questions are elastic.

People say that the soul does not progress. The individual is not essentially different in A.D. 1923 from the individual of 1923 B.C.

What phil[osophy] has accomplished up to now has really been only a mopping-up operation. Developments since the seventeenth century have as yet penetrated it only slightly, and still do not correspond to the latest phase, the rampant proliferation of facts. Of course this development had an influence on philosophy. Philosophy has fallen behind the facts, which tempts people to believe that facts are antiphilosophical. They are simply very heterogeneous (but just that *is* their phil[osophy]).

The proper philosophy of our time is that we have no philosophy.

Here contact with the practical person. He has anticipated this and, not being influenced by any philosophy, is in some cases adroit to the point of corruption.

I shall mention a few frequently encountered types (and I am speaking throughout of only the most contemporary things).

The engineer—this is always overlooked—is not only a rationalist, but also a man of facts. In his profession there is a great deal that is irrational. In themselves, facts are altogether irrational; they are only regulators of rationality.

The businessman calculates rationally, to be sure, but he is also a man of will, and as such he calculates only in terms of man's most dependable qualities, that is, his lower ones. Business depends in large part on coercion. Egalitarianism and individualism.

Therein lies the common ground with the politician. Cunning and coercion. I hear what the men in French headquarters say: civilian protests! A couple of machine guns at every railroad station, a company of soldiers in every town, and ideals faced with the power of force break down; in a few months ideals emerge that have subordinated themselves to the means of coercion.

In the last analysis, this is the melody of humanity. To abolish force would mean to become soft. The challenge is to inspire man to greatness despite the fact that he is a swine.

This matter has still another important side.

The capacity to calculate soberly and evaluate is only one of man's important attitudes.

In contrast to facts, actions, business, the politics of force (and it is politics even when force serves the cunning of goodness) stand love and poetry. These are conditions that rise above the transactions of the world.

Since people are inclined to take these as literary inventions, I want to recall their venerable aunts, the religions. I offer a few examples: . . . /from the Loyola introduction/

There is nothing in this that could not also seem profane, and thus it is also true that there is an element in secular life that is religious in the most important sense. It has simply always been fused with the business of the church. Without this element religions could hardly exist, but this element can do without religions.

The moment this element comes into play, our soul is in play. Things belonging in this context concern us in a way quite different from other things.

Irreligious times, like the Enlightenment, which lack this element, are unbearably Philistine.

It reaches from mysticism to the willful obscurities of Dostoevsky.

Historically it can be traced in the most varied forms. Let me indicate a few: It extends into the present: Emerson, Maeter[linck], German Romanticism/traced back to the School of Chartres;[35] significant here the parallelism of the situation; natural science without soul. The even more ancient Greek-Levantine past. Also appears as opposition of the individual to the state/Renaissance, Protestantism.

But I cannot claim that salvation lies in the tidy organization of this area. That is only one of the possibilities. The challenge is to create an organization that protects the possibilities. Belief in humanity. Doing away with half-witted ideologies of state and nation. Recognizing the situation, not inhibiting it!

The German as Symptom

1

Introduction: I believe mankind does the second (nation-soul) only because it has forgotten the first (self-soul). Unfortunately I have only the one answer: . . .

2

Opposed to this is the fact that we look for the German and do not find him; a European symptom (sympt[om] of Western civilization).

Let no one object that the English do not find it necessary to search for the essence of the Englishman, or the French for that of the Frenchman: that we find it necessary is an advantage.

We are fragmented, the others more homogeneous? I want to show that precisely this fragmentation is a quality of the future, and that the others will have to acquire it if they are not entirely godforsaken. (We cannot do without Locke simply because we have Kant. They can, perhaps. But even Bergson, to take one example, cannot be understood without his older German relatives.)

The essential German? A question of conscience. Squeezed between East and West and, moreover, having fallen under the wheels of world history, people today catechize themselves with a zeal that recalls the most beautiful ages of the German religious renaissance.

[. . . ed.]

1

No scient[ific] theory can be constructed purely by induction.

But through hypothesis and verification. An act of faith, an act of the imagination, is required in order to form a hypothesis even in the purely rational sphere. (But we should not distort this familiar fact the way Sp[engler] did.)

A much greater proportion of faith, imputation, and assumption before the fact is necessary in private and public life. We live according to rules, principles, and guidelines that we allow life to modify; we even exchange them, but few people develop new ones, and even these are limited. Life shapes itself in ready-made forms: it is socially preformed. The feeling of love, for instance, finds modes, modifications, degrees, etc., already prepared, into which it pours itself and in which it becomes reality. Without guidelines the individual disintegrates.

For this the expression "bonding" has become widespread: life is socially bound, and flexible for the individual only to a limited extent. An officer, a member of a student society, a believing Catholic or Jew, a proper man or a moral one, each has prescribed for him in every situation in life a much narrower range of possible reactions. This concentrates energy.

The principal bond today is the profession. By characterizing a person's profession and adding a bit more, we can say today what is most important about a person. When we learn that a man is a judge or a businessman, and hear in addition that he is good at his work or not, perhaps also that he is a "nice" fellow or a "clever" one, we know most of what can be known about a person living today. The consciousness of being a . . . consoles us in the empty hours; d[it]to to entertainment.

There are also some leisure-hour professions. All of them really are professions, which then appear with the modifier amateur: for instance, stamp collecting, tennis, setting records on the mount of Venus.

Outside these bonds the individual cannot raise an arm or lift a finger. He collapses like a deflated balloon or, if inflated by an impulse, he deforms himself immediately in some single, random direction. He has (aside from this) no shaping or guiding ideas.

Now it is clear that historical development has led to the destruction of bonds that were present or should have been present. The struggle between church and state ended with both of them being inwardly powerless; the boundaries between social strata have become confused, etc.

Thus, lack of faith is not just a religious matter at all, but includes the secular as well.

Regarding the new bonds: Nation, state.
Ideologies: Catholicism, Marxism.
One cannot believe Various attempts: morality, human-
by an act of will. ity. Above all: (Ideological
surrogates:) one cannot advise a
person who is not bound: bind yourself, and one cannot crawl back into discarded bonds. (They are not rational but credulous, and the like).

In principle, however, this is a universally human matter and not a German one.

I have repeatedly attempted to argue for evaluating this chaotic situation positively. Primal dreams, and the like. Such a time cannot be bad or weak. It is customary, however, to see in it only a symptom of decline. Bonds, regulators of life that ought to have been present, no longer are; capitalism has dissolved them; now the individual only calculates, and his so-called great scientific accomplishments are nothing but excesses of this drive to calculate. Art changes hysterically, and the like.

Here pos[sibly] already "facts."

If we look back at these events, we come up against a sharp boundary around 1880–90. From there the countermood has carried over into the contemporary situation.

If we look back still further, we arrive at the age of faith in reason. We can say: The attempt to master the problems of life through speculation. Premature and failed. At the same time, however, the problem of classicism-empiricism.

We can trace the present back to this undigested situation.

If we trace the line back still further, we encounter the original élan of empiricism.

And *still* further back (I am indebted for this reference to . . .): the School of Chartres.

In this the exemplary separation of natural science and mysticism.

The word *mysticism* is likely to cause offense. Secular mysticism.

Experiment of the ratioid and n[on]-r[atioid]. Role of art. True attitude toward art.

Corrective role of facts. Today's person the person of facts.

Seen from this perspective: the calculating, capitalistic, evil person. Mass organization in a bearish market, creative! Natural corrective to the believer, his alter ego, his provisional quality.

Merely exaggerated, pathologically hypertroph[ied]. To be dismantled by redressing defects of organization.

A r[atioid] + n[on]r[atioid] epoch will come!

The German as Symptom

Structure

1 The Problem

1. If the following thoughts bore only the heading "T[he] G[erman]," one would have some idea what might be expected of them: a certain selection of desirable or undesirable qualities would be claimed as German, and from these a series of more or less brilliant pseudoproofs would be derived— prominent and familiar individual traits of our life.

"As Symptom" was added for two simple reasons.

a. (negative) I don't believe in the distinction between the German and the Negro.

α. Race.   Only results. They
β. Nation.   point to older articles, essays.

b. (positive). The concepts of race, nation, people [*Volk*], and culture contain questions and not answers: they are not sociological elements, but rather complex results. Nonetheless, people refer to them as if they were unities. Vacuum. "Nation" as phenomenon of ironic internationalism. This the second reason.

2. Here then one question is posed; the urgency of the question should not be overlooked. Once somewhat ridiculous, today it has become a wan-

dering question of conscience. The best symptom is that the readiness for spiritual communion it bespeaks recalls the Reformation.

Where the conscience feels uneasy, impulses are in conflict with one another; larger stabilizing perspectives and principles are lacking.

In its vivification of general concepts related to early Catholic Scholasticism, nationalism is only a special case of forced yearning for belief. If we summarize all the attempts that involve a forced yearning for belief, going back to Romanticism, Scholasticism, and Platonic ideas (attempts to find some kind of footing retroactively), our time is characterized by spiritual romanticism. Although the positivism of everyday life would not take these things seriously: they are literature. (Even socialism is taken seriously by this positivism only insofar as it is not romantic, but represents tangible interests.)

3. Now in the midst of conflicts of conscience, the individual can indeed find an anchor in the principles of a community. The self-enclosed and self-supporting community of the nation, however, no longer offers anything of the sort to lean on. What has become clear in the German case—this moral situation that no longer finds a point of reference in itself, but looks for one in the past (race, nation, religion, old-fashioned simplicity and strength, uncorrupted goodness)—is the latent spiritual situation of Europe as a whole. To regard the Germans as a symptom means, in other words, to raise the whole problem of civilization.

I will attempt to place this problem in a different light from the one in which it is ordinarily seen.

T[he] G[erman] a[s] S[ymptom]

1. *The Problem.* The original title of this essay, when it was still a challenge presented to me, was simply: "The German." I soon gave it the additional "as Symptom" for two simple reasons.

The first is that I do not believe, am not able to believe, that the German is *essentially* different from, for example, the American or the Negro. I deliberately choose the latter example as the most remote instance, for it is not at all a question of explaining away palpably existing differences, but of evaluating them correctly. But when people speak of essential differences today, they mean either differences of race or differences of culture. And differences in anatomical physiognomy are, of course, crass in their most extreme features; but no one has been able to demonstrate skeletal distinctions that are racially constant, and comparative psychology yields more similarities than differences in the essential qualities that constitute mental achievement. The racial "theories" that play such a large and fateful role in the practical and popular-science constructs of our time are rejected as unsupported and unsupportable by the sciences in whose field they lie.

But if heredity offers only very inadequate help in explaining the obvious differences between two peoples, then the difference can only be social in the widest sense. If it cannot be grasped as "race" and "people," then perhaps as "culture" and "nation," together with their influence. It is recognized, however, that even this thought is repeatedly crossed out or cancelled. Thus profession, estate, and class brought about all sorts of spiritual as well as physical similarities and differences, which, cutting across national unities, established international connections that are today probably stronger and more natural than national ones. One hardly need say more in the age of capitalism and the international proletariat, as well as of the separation between big cities and the rest of the country.

Thus these concepts of race and culture, people and nation (even the useless explanatory concept of "epoch," borrowed from cultural history) conspicuously point to something real, but, equally manifestly, characterize nothing firmly tangible or even simple. Because of this we cannot make any reasonable use of them other than seeing in them questions, and not answers; not substrata of phenomena, but complicated phenomena in themselves; not sociological elements, but results; in other words: products and not producers. It is immediately apparent that probably no one would think anything else. But why is it then that today the invocation of the national, whether as race or culture, in any case as a mysterious unity, is a phenomenon of thoroughly ironic internationalism? It is as if at a certain point anxiety arose over a vacuum, into which this reaction rushed; what is it and where did it come from? This is the second reason why the question of the German is to be spoken of here as a symptom.

We should not overlook the urgency of this question. But where conscience strikes, there, we may conclude, impulses are in conflict with one another, and the wider intellectual perspective and principles that could provide order are lacking. That this is actually so today (and particularly that the War—even if economic and political causes played the dominant role in it, as they do in all such matters—and the decline since could never have spread so powerfully without the lack of a spiritual order) is so generally accepted that particular indications are superfluous. I would nonetheless point to our time's yearning for belief, of which nationalism is only a particular case. And since we happen to have been speaking of the racial theory that has most often been imputed to lie at its base, we may also mention at the same time the peculiar spiritual affinity between them.

For if one knows a little about the extraordinary difficulties confronting the descr[iptive] natural sciences when they try to classify the almost limitless propinquity of individual phenomena in schemes according to race, species, genus, and the like, and if one knows how much in need of clarification these concepts are in themselves, then the thoughtless levity with which the far more complicated problem of the individual social phenomenon is explained today recalls in caricature the time when people ascribed real validity to universal concepts, and, in a reversal not without its greatness, used them to explain the world of the individual.

This warped similarity of modes of thinking is not without analogy to the fervor of belief; whereas thinking, like faith, stands in crass opposition to the superficial positivism that largely fills up our industrious days and smiles with inner certainty over such regressions. If one compares this positivism with our attempts at spirituality (which have been roused from torpor to the point of reaching back to the Scholastics or to Platonic ideas), our time is characterized in this case too by a tremendous spiritual romanticism that flees from the present into any and every past, looking for the holy grail of a lost security. But what is generally deduced from this is the disintegration of an earlier condition that is supposed to have been more solid, the loss of dogmas and guidelines, the dissolution of bonds; in a word, a decline, and I would like to demonstrate that this despondent assumption is not necessary. The condition of the European mind today is in my view not one of decline, but rather of a not-yet-completed transition: not overripeness, but immaturity.

2   The Theorem of Shapelessness

1. Supporting idea: for the proper evaluation of cultural phenomena. (Perhaps this has meaning only as a corrective to a way of looking at things.)

2. It is comprehensible—because it is only a transfer of habits of mind that have proved themselves elsewhere—that even specific periods and cultures that are distinguished from one another in characteristic ways should be traced back to various substrata as the simplest kinds of causes. In this sense one speaks of Egyptian, Hellenistic, or Gothic Man, of nations and races, of mysterious epochs or cultures. This kind of historical phrenology has become very popular; it roughly amounts to saying that the thieving person has in his cerebrum a physiological substratum for theft, and the honorable person an organ segment for honor.

Just a slight exaggeration of this way of thinking and we stop where we are now, with a new generation arriving every five years.

As opposed to this, it is time to develop a fundamentally different way of looking at things, which, formulated in an extreme way, contains the following assertions: The substratum, the individual person, is everywhere just one and the same, throughout all cultures and in all historical forms. The ways in which cultures, and thus also people, distinguish themselves from each other come from the outside, not the inside.

To put it crassly: if a generation of contemporary Europeans were transplanted at the age of their earliest childhood impressions to the Egyptian year 5000 B.C., and then given over absolutely to the influences of religion, art, form of the state, economic methods, social traditions, etc., in other words to the whole organizational and extra-organizational apparatus then existing, world history would begin once again at the year 5000 and would at first repeat itself for a while.

3. Difficult to demonstrate, except in extreme cases. But a series of indirect considerations supports it.

a. Humbolt[36] tells . . . this recalls—tenderness of peasants—the widespread existence of such paradoxical mixtures of feelings. We can change our standpoint and say: The mixture of feelings is not paradoxical at all, but normal; it is only from the perspective of the extreme development of one element that the extreme development of another element seems monstrous.

In fact, even among us, cruel and tender, etc., can barely be distinguished. Great poets confirm for us that the moral personality is quite malleable, with more possibilities than the rest cure of everyday life would lead us to suspect.

b. Scient[ific] comp[arative] psychology also shows that the transitions between types are fluid.

It does not find really constitutive differences between peoples, for instance not even a difference in the sharpness of senses between a civilized people and a people of hunters. (More agreement than difference in really constitutive qualities.)

c. The science of temperaments and other psychological documents. Extensive accord in thinking, works of art, private expressions, typicality of historical event, stream of tradition.

d. Experience since 1914 has taught us of what contradictory excesses of expression the same human material is capable. In fact, no one will seriously believe that the German republican of 1923 is a different person from the submissive German subject of 1914, or that the Frenchman who in 1923 committed the worse excesses against civilization is different from the person who in 1914 believed he was fighting for civilization. One cannot even say that he has been dissembling.

4. What then is the cause of such varied human phenomena?

It has already been mentioned that it comes from outside, but one should not understand this in the sense of some environmental theory, in which a geographical basin "forms" the people living in it: that comes from the same need for inadmissible simplification as racial theory.

But we will get close to the truth (some temperament and heredity may be left over) if we regard as variative those peculiarities that constitute the totality of the retroactive effects, from which the person learns what he himself has created. To eliminate the activity in this way in favor of the reaction sounds impossible or stupid, but in fact houses build houses, people don't. The hundredth house arises because and in the same way that ninety-nine houses arose before it; and if the hundredth house is an innovation, it derives from a literary discussion and not from a house.

In other words, this is the commonplace that development takes place according to the primer of tradition, and in cautious departure from its direction.

The totality of these derivations of which we are speaking embraces, of course, everything: economic forms, political organization, all institutions, habits, remedies, books, actions, events, that is to say the whole ineffable interplay of giving and receiving between . . . , which each of us knows from experience.

Whatever we do is done in the forms of our time and is determined by it. Wilson's humanitarian intentions in the Peace of Versailles took on the forms of the European state mentality, although they were transformed into their opposite thereby; but in any case these humane intentions were already colored by the age.

If we consider this relationship in terms of the thought process of cause/effect/countereffect, and put first what is temporally and logically the final member of the sequence, we of course come up against resistance; but we can reassure ourselves that the categories of causality in this conception have also proved unsuitable in other ways. This relationship between person and environment is less difficult if one thinks of it functionally, in which case we are accustomed [to seeing] the dependence as mutual. But it is best to keep to what one has experienced oneself, without philosophical justification, and this is roughly as follows:

If we attempt to subtract from ourselves those conventions conditioned by our time, what remains is something completely unshaped; for even what is most personal in us is related to the environmental system as a deviation. A person exists only in forms given to him from the outside. "He polishes himself on the world" is much too mild an image; it ought to read: He pours himself into its mold. It is social organization which through its forms gives the individual the possibility of expressing himself at all, and it is only through expression that he becomes a human being. The terrible cruelty . . . inescapable. . . . We can judge by this how fatal is the error made by many pious souls, that today more depends on changing the person than his forms of organization.

Secondly, let us attempt to construct from an ex[ample] what the beginning of a new epoch might be like. There are a great many secret polygamists among us, but officially, even before their own consciences, many of them are in favor of monogamy (according to the motto of the rule with tolerated exceptions, which dominates our whole morality). This is already an unstable condition, and it is conceivable that (in a situation that would weaken the conservative parties and the churches) the propaganda of a few determined reformers against marriage could suddenly lead to changes in the law from which, presumably, the most profound spiritual innovations might be expected. "It is conceivable," however, means: among other things would have to   , the emancipation of woman would have to be far advanced, Social Democracy would have to start getting serious about its old demand, which again assumes changes in the economic situation whose scope cannot be imagined. And whether the newspapers would smother the movement at the outset or support it cannot be foreseen: in other words, the beginning of an epoch depends on a thousand accidents. But if everything were present, perhaps the spiritual innovations would not take place anyway in the last analysis, because "reforms" do not make people change unless they lie in the path of a broad current of spiritual energy, and this in turn again depends on a million accidents.

Lawless coincidence of many facts. If it is absent, propaganda is a quite negligible factor.

5. This view of historical events is apparently antiheroic. It is a philosophy of the petit bourgeois: small causes, great effects.

In truth, the philosophy of history of great causes, with its lovely intellectual pathos, is only apparently heroic. For it does not take the facts as they are.

Path of history not that of a billiard ball. Rather, it is like the path of clouds, which is influenced by so many circumstances that at any moment a new one can change it.

It is like the person . . . every step with necessity, but without necessity of the whole.(!)

What emerges: *Where* am I.

So then the whole heroic business is to be sought in this: we can't change laws, but situations, yes!

What has been created depends on contingencies, but its impact thereafter is determined.

2   The Theorem of Human Shapelessness

Contrast sharply with one another: Various substrata as causes. A substratum and every day, every determination, as a cause

In this connection I call upon a few thoughts that—if they should be correct and developed—could be characterized as a th[eorem] of h[uman] s[hapelessness].

I would argue that a cannibal transplanted to a European environment as an infant would probably become a good European, and the sensitive Rainer Maria Rilke would have become a good cannibal had a fate unfortunate for us thrown him as a child among people of the South Seas. I believe the same about a Hellenistic infant of the fourth century B.C. whom a miracle might bestow on a mother on the Kurfürstendamm in 1923, or a young Englishman presented to an Egyptian mother of the year 5000. As is apparent, such a belief is difficult to demonstrate, but there are nonetheless reasons that support it.

I recall a charming anecdote Wilhelm [sic] von Humboldt[37] tells in the incomparably great description of his Orinoco journey. Somewhere on the return trip he took a young Indian into his service, who not only proved to be extraordinarily intelligent and skillful in maintaining delicate instruments, but also attracted notice by his gentle and pleasant demeanor. But when the other natives shied away from him because at a meal of monkeys he had spoken all too enthusiastically about the comparative charms of various roasted hand surfaces, it turned out that the new arrival belonged to a notorious tribe of cannibals. I am convinced that even his gastronomical observations, aside from their gruesome content, were also sensitive and delicate (restrained); at any rate, the memories of notes that I made, as I recall, from Frobenius's[38] book on Africa, point in the same direction. Frobenius speaks of kidnapped children who were brought up with the children of the kidnappers and gently fattened, in order eventually, as youths, to serve as a meal at a religious sacrifice. One need only think of the delicacy, indeed tenderness (for them quite unaccustomed), with which our coarse young peasants bring up a young pig that they will one day slaughter, in order to really understand completely how widespread such apparently paradoxical mixtures of feeling are. In fact, cruel and tender, friendliness and caution, devotion and rejection, or a hundred elements of such pairs of feelings are, among us too, hardly to be clearly distinguished from each other. As comparative psychology knows, the transitions between human types are fluid, and, as some poets know, even the individual moral personality is quite unstable, and contains far more possibilities for good and evil than its everyday state of rest would lead us to assume. The last nine years have taught all of us, I believe, what excesses of cruelty and trespass not only secret neuropaths but also good, ordinary people are capable of.

This is not, of course, to be taken in the sense of a theory of environment that excludes everything else: but the dependence of the individual on the influences of his environment is extraordinarily great. I personally believe that only a few determinants are to be found in the person himself, and today it is not yet possible to sort them out in a satisfactory way. What we call temperaments—although, to be sure, we are not yet able to classify them adequately, or explain them—furnish a limited number of such fundamental predispositions, and these remain similar throughout the course of history, as the relationship between ancient speculation on the subject and what we say about it today shows. In a similar way, inventions from ancient times such as bows, ships, and carts, even if we assume they were developed over a long period of time, display thinking of extraordinary genius. Artworks of the Stone Age, or the private lives of ancient Egyptians, speak to our feelings in as lively and precise a fashion as those of today, and the attitudes that reproduce themselves in the facts of history have remained astoundingly constant. Finally, there is also a familiar broad and steady stream of tradition that flows through the whole of Western and parts of Oriental culture, down to our ways of speaking, or the way we decorate the façades of our houses.

What has changed, and comes to mind as the difference among historical periods seems, then, to be less the people than the most impersonal (or suprapersonal) products of their collective social life; and we must be clear about what this means, for example in distinction to that insidious way of talking that speaks of a Gothic person or an ancient Greek as the cause of the Gothic or the ancient world, just as people have naively turned race into the "cause" of the individual. Not long ago I tried to reduce the true relationship between the individual and his social expression to the formula: A small amplitude of the inner being corresponds to a great amplitude of expression. Without denying that mankind has assumed very different forms, which one would have to be blind to overlook, and indeed setting out from precisely that assumption, one can argue that even this is almost all too easy, and that people do this with trivial changes in themselves, just as a breeze can move water in any direction. Clothes make people, and then such people make such clothes once again, and the order is just as often reversed: what the characteristic physiognomies of the various periods have brought forth is a thoroughly inextricable interplay of giving and receiving between the individual and his world, essence and accident, drive and force, self and expression. Precisely the shapelessness of his disposition requires the individual to accommodate himself to forms, to take on the character, customs, morality, life-style, and the whole apparatus of an organization. It is a well-known saying that in our machine age machines rule people, and this explanation has been offered for the horrors of war and politics as well. This is very true: power and impotence are one. The terrible cruelty of our forms of political and economic organization, which do violence to the feelings of the individual, is so inescapable because this organization is all there is that offers the individual a surface and the possibility of expressing himself. For we may say that the human being first becomes human through the way he expresses himself, and society shapes forms of this expression. (It is really a symbiosis.)

This is a different view from one that explains the individual as a simple, deterministic product of the crossing of races, or as an individual case of epochs and cultures. It seems to lack the dignity of necessity which makes the other view so pompous, and its law of world history is really nothing more than the old Austrian state's principle of "muddling through." The *path of history* is in fact not that of a billiard ball, which, once struck, follows a predictable course, but resembles rather the path of a cloud, which also follows the laws of physics but is equally influenced by something that can only be called a coinciding of facts. For everywhere the wind blows from e[ast] to w[est], because in the e[ast] there is a ma[ximum] and in the w[est] a mi[nimum] in air pressure; but that a place lies between both, where no nearby mountain mass diverts the air's course, or where otherwise competing influences make themselves felt, all these circumstances constituting the weather: all these elements, when they come together, even if they are calculable, are really facts and not laws. It is the same when a person wanders through the streets, attracted here by shadows, there by a group, further on by a strange profiling of faces; when another person "accidentally" crosses his path and tells him something that leads him to decide on a specific route—and he finds himself at last at a point he neither knows nor wanted to get to: every step of *this* route also occurred out of necessity, but the sequence of these individual necessities has no coherence. That I suddenly stand where I am is a fact, a result, and if one calls it necessary, because in the last analysis everything has its causes, then this bears the character of preserving something in the name of causality; but it is quite useless, since we will never be able to make good on it.

The individual possesses this quality of the actual, the individual, of what has happened, what has run its course (in both senses) as a typological mixture, as do historical events, nations, and cultures. It appears that the question of the European: What am I? really means: Where am I? It is not a matter of a phase in a process governed by laws, and not a matter of a destiny, but simply of a situation.

People are not capable of changing laws; but they certainly can change situations in this sense, no matter how many imminent laws may have contributed to them.

Emphasize that the theor[em] of shapelessness is a vulgar philosophy. Against false phil[osophical] pathos, greatness, sublimity! Spengler appears sublime! (as sublime as a canary). These people's primary demand is that every conception must be sublime.

Poss[ibly] at the end of 3.

Not the state, but the individual should change!

Active and passive factors from 3?

3   The Situation of Our Generation
(OUR GENERATION AND SHAPELESSNESS)

I don't want to act as if I am prestidigitating a rabbit out of a hat when I have hidden it there myself. So I confess that all these thoughts are nothing but impressions that our life has made on me and that I have made various efforts to expand upon. It is about this original material of impressions that I would now like to speak.

The observing glance seeking to account for this first comes to rest on the period just before 1900. The older people among us lived through it, the younger awakened spiritually and intellectually in its immediate aftermath.

It was a time of great ethical and aesthetic activity. People believed in the future, in a social future, and in a new art. Of course people often gave this belief the appearance of morbidity and decadence, but both these negative determinations were only accidental expressions for the will to be different and do things differently from the way people had done them in the past. People believed in the future, and wanted to make it happen. Even where people voluptuously yielded to the vision of an age in decline that began with the turn of the century, they at least wanted to make use of this period as long as it lasted for demonic and immoral purposes that today, of course, seem like satanically red plush furniture. But whatever we still possess today that rises above the Philistinism of the age of Heyse[39] we owe almost entirely to those years. Compared to that time, today's feelings of decline seem gray, ashen, dispirited, and joyless. Desire, will, hope, and a part-imaginary, part-real state of energy are what distinguish that period from ours.

At that time too people were internationally minded, and summarily rejected state, nation, race, family, and religion because they resisted all bonds handed down from the past. Moreover, people believed in progress, in the life of the mind, in the value of what they accomplished: the mood of such an age is always international. For mankind's forward intellectual march has constantly distributed its steps among the various nations, and only a dejected age can be intellectually nationalist and conservative: it wants to conserve because it has given up hope. This is the second result of a comparison. This is as true for Germany as for France.

But if we examine what was actually accomplished, we find perhaps a slight excess of talent, but this was not the decisive factor: for on the one hand the effect of the greatest talents—Nietzsche, for example—was already an aftereffect even then, and on the other hand the same people are to some extent still working today. But there existed at that time the same illusions about the unity of will that later appeared in Expressionism. The most contradictory tendencies crisscrossed each other: The hero cult of Nietzsche and Carlyle confronted socialism, which was then more respectable in literature than it is today. Decadence contrasted with the movement of raw youth back to nature. The late Romanticism of an Emerson coexisted with the machine worship of a modern generation. Literature contained realists alongside aesthetes, immoralists alongside the transfixed morality of Stefan George, pantheists alongside the Catholic Rilke, and the idea of a pseudo-scientific experimental novel alongside a pronounced hostility to thought, which took comfort in the belief that the poet must directly affect the feelings, and receive his inspiration directly from the feelings.

What has happened since then is simply that, one by one, these tangled threads have unravelled from their skein. Partly there is a number of, on average, quite measurable and limited intellectual personalities left over from before, and partly we have experienced, one after the other, the movements of Neo-Romanticism, Neo-idealism, and Expressionism. They were all (without wanting to underestimate the last, which has produced many worthwhile things) weaker in intensity and extent than the original movement, and contained nothing that had not already been present—even if with a weaker emphasis—in the latter.

If we consider this, we must say that very little of intellectual substance has changed, but rather that, figuratively speaking, there was originally present in this intellectual-spiritual mixture a kind of polarized condition, an illusory sense of unified purposiveness, which later dissipated and was replaced in the days of Expressionism by something newer and weaker. Today this has in turn dissipated once again, and been succeeded by an "undirected condition," a leftover abject confusion, like iron filings scattered in an un-magnetized field. I myself believe that we are not far from again sinking into the apathetic condition of German culture before 1890: a brief con-tinuation of the political and economic depression might perhaps suffice. The crudest phenomena of capitalism are already making themselves felt in the realm of the spirit, and critical concepts as well as ideological attitudes have become dulled.

There is the possibility of believing in secret pulsations of progress, which stretch and release the creative energies of the ages and are intended to explain the remarkable fact that the births of great minds—for example the great German musicians, or the masters of Ital[ian] painting—are bunched together in relatively narrow time frames (Stendhal). But such an explanation probably offers no advantage over the obscurity of occultism, for what is the substratum of this pulsation supposed to be? It is much more natural to regard it as one of those highly composite social phenomena that crystallize and dissolve from a thousand causes that we can never fully enu-merate. Or as a natural tendency constantly suppressed by circumstances, but which can develop quickly under favorable conditions? But let us ask ourselves about some of the causes that are still present today! There is the ambitious economy of a new *Reich,* whose enterprising mercantile spirit had room for intellectual commodities as well. The beginnings of a new po-litical development still do not reach back very far, and the thought that a new German culture might also be part of it may be music to the young. Germany had entered the rank of world powers and sought, receptively but self-consciously, to borrow the best from their cultures. It seems to me idle to enumerate more such reasons, which are more or less extrapolations from private experience to the life of a great social body, and cannot be made properly objective, but above all can never entirely account for the facts. How can we, for example, explain the existence at just the right moment of a theater director like Brahm? Of a publisher like S. Fischer? Of art dealers like P. Cassirer? In short, the existence of the right man at the right place /But: the universal drive to do things raises more people to the heights; few remain: but in other times there were none at all. / This results in a remark-able dilemma. That movement (Impressionism, Naturalism, Modernism)—we may leave open whether it was self-contained or a wave in a greater movement—will doubtless be awarded the honor of being regarded as a valid historical event, or mini-event. In every such movement a thousand functions of the most varied degrees of importance must be staffed by ap-propriate men in order for it to come into being. All these functions are ultimately just as indispensable as those of the visible top functionaries, and experience shows that even these positions are by no means easy to fill.

Where is the border between the historical personalities and their circumstances? (One can also formulate this question in this way: What would have become of the great man in another age?) It is a matter of a coincidence, which either has a common origin we cannot imagine but which we label with a beautiful name like "spirit of an age," or is a situation complicated by so many causes that we cannot analyze them completely. This is confirmed by its fragility and their rapid disappearance. We realize that "so much is involved in it" that we cannot enumerate it all. There are, however, ultimately, onetime events and events in all degrees, from the unique to those that recur according to some law.

But there are also active and passive factors in history; what does not appear by itself may be introduced. Everything that has been said here about this period concerns a thin layer of people and interests; around them is the whole insistent apparatus of organization and everyday life, which, like a fossil, bears the traces of a thousand past lives. Hidden in the existence of a clearinghouse are great quarrels from the past about its permissibility, struggles over economic and political ideas. The walls of our streets radiate a mixture of countless ideologies: only scattered parts of the movement of which I speak, not its best part, have penetrated the masses; and the masses have closed ranks over it again. The active factors of history change the passive ones a little bit, expend their energies on them, and sink into them. Thus a polarized spiritual situation passes over into a diffuse one.

What we have seen here on a small scale may be demonstrated in quite similar fashion with large examples, for instance the rise and decline of Scholasticism.

What role, then, does ideology play in this? Is it only a cork swimming on the surface, in whose inexplicable movements we can discern the far less comprehensible movements of the masses beneath, or can a more important role be attributed to it?

(4. Role of ideology in everyday life. It reveals and forms the character of everyday life. If it is set in its real significance: What existed around 1900 was not ideology, but doubtless the beginning of one; contemporary situation

Ideological symptoms)

4

(A. ROLE OF IDEOLOGY IN LIFE)

Ideology is the soul of life, even of everyday life. It not only reveals the character of this life, but forms it as well. Even today, despite the fact that the whole world makes fun of it.

Ideology is: intellectual ordering of the feelings; an objective connection among them that makes the subjective connection easier. It can be philosophical or religious or a traditional mixture of both. This definition is not entirely precise, but it is serviceable. An order of the feelings is conceivable, a harmonious organization of the spiritual life—which Nietzsche sometimes advocated—on the basis of tradition and instinct, but without a supporting intellectual system. Here I would also call this an ideology, although it would no longer be one. But experience teaches that such ways of organizing life never exist "without teaching," whether we look for them in the historical dimension or in the ethnological. These ways need not necessarily be systematic; sometimes they are fragmented into aphorisms, as in the teachings of Christ and the Chinese sages. (What we experience in the immediacy of everyday social life as "blood certainty" is only relatively instinctive, on the basis of a secure bonding through social ideas.)

I want to point out the important role that ideology plays in life.

Even in the purely rational natural sciences a theory cannot be constructed on the basis of pure induction, simply from the facts. A universal regulative law is never derived from individual facts without the aid of an idea going in the opposite direction, an idea that always includes from the outset an act of faith, of imagination, of acceptance. *Hypotheses non fingo* [I do not make hypotheses—ed.] was an error even with Newton, as modern spatial analysis demonstrates. A much greater degree of faith, imputation, and assumption before the fact is necessary for both private and public life; without it a person could hardly move an arm or lift a finger, for the simplest kind of life—walking past a beggar, friendliness or hostility to a subordinate, one's choice of pleasure—is full of decisions, each of which would require a lifetime for reason to establish free of doubt. Moreover, each day there comes the moment when a person must lay his hands in his lap, and then all his activity would fall like ashes into a bottomless void were it not held together by the certainty of having done the right thing and of just being empty between two fillings, like a pitcher used for pouring. For this reason the individual is today a far more involved metaphysician than he is usually willing to concede. A dull, persistent feeling of his strange cosmic situation seldom leaves him. Death, the tininess of the earth, the dubious illusion of the self, the senselessness of existence, which becomes more pressing with the years: these are questions at which the average person scoffs, but which he nonetheless feels surrounding him all his life like the walls of a dark room.

We can speak more generally of bonds that support the life of the individual than we can of ideologies. Life is made easier when it socially bound, and when it is individually mobile only to a limited extent. A believing

Catholic or Jew, an officer, a fraternity brother [*Burschenschafter*], an honorable businessman, or an important person, is in every situation capable of a far smaller number of reactions than is a free spirit: this saves and stores energy. Principles, guidelines, models, and limitations are storehouses of energy. To see how shapeless a person would be without them, think for a moment of a process like love; it is only the actual seizing of the little woman that is determined by this notion, whereas the whole complex we call love, with all its gradations, types, perversions, and subcategories, is determined by social conventions (even if only in opposition to them). Even our feelings form like fluids in containers that generations have formed, and these containers receive our shapelessness.

B. THE CONTEMPORARY SITUATION

Today the principal bond is the profession. Once a profession has been indicated together with a brief tag, such as talented or untalented, entertaining or not entertaining, respectable or not respectable, almost everything about a person today for which his life offers occasion has been said. Perhaps in his free hours he also collects stamps, plays tennis, or chases women: but he pursues even these activities as an amateur profession, and just as methodically and exclusively as his real one. Outside these bonds the individual collapses like a deflated balloon, or, if he is seized by some external impulse, he immediately deforms himself in its direction. Haste, encapsulation in one's profession, and the shouting of leisure hours cover over a profound anxiety that would otherwise make itself felt.

If we consider the intellectual and spiritual content of the present, in which the individual more or less takes part (but always a very mixed part), a mingling of the most contradictory thoughts, feelings, and directional forces becomes apparent. The ideological situation is enormously particularistic, indeed individualistic. Components of the great old ideologies such as Christianity or Buddhism, as well as countless other kinds of ideologies, which have been brought together in individual philosophic and artistic personalities, fly around in the air, as it were. No single ideology reigns. Individual parts are singled out. One can call it an inexpressible multiplicity.

C. THE CUSTOMARY INTERPRETATION

This is explained by saying that bonds that had once been present, or ought to have been present, have been destroyed by progress. Thus the struggle between church and state ended with a situation in which both were inwardly exhausted, and only bar the way with their corpses; the bonds of class have loosened, allowing members of different classes to intermingle; science has destroyed faith, capitalism has broken up older forms without creating a new one, and so forth. And, finally, the War was the collapse of this undermined humanity. These are all negative determinations, and the remedies suggested are also essentially negative.

The literature of our time is clearly full of remedies. It has poured out an ocean of complaints about our soullessness, about our mechanization, our calculatedness, our irreligion; and the accomplishments of science as well as art are regarded as excesses of these conditions. All the individual does now is calculate, and even his supposedly great scientific achievements are said to be nothing but excesses of this drive to calculate. Except for socialism, the remedy is nearly always sought regressively in turning away from the present. For the liberated man the old bonds are recommended: faith, prescientific thinking, simplicity, humanity, altruism, national solidarity, subordination of the citizen to the state: the abandonment of capitalist individualism and its frame of mind. Even socialism is full of this.

People believe there is a degeneration they must cure.

D. ANOTHER INTERPRETATION

It is rarely recognized that these phenomena represent a new problem that does not yet have a solution. I know hardly a single presentation that sees this problem of the present as a problem, a new problem, and not as a failed solution.

Diversity as a quality of the future.

5   The Age of Facts

Put positively, our time's lack of faith means: The age believes only in facts. Its conception of reality recognizes only what is, as it were, really real. An unofficial ideology that has taken shape.

The following sequence for the decline has been established: First, there was a time that believed in God simply and unequivocally. Then came a time that had to demonstrate God's existence through reason. Then a time that was content as long as reason was unable to disprove God's existence. And finally our own, which would believe in God only if it could encounter him regularly in a laboratory.

But then consider occultism. Either it asserts unbelievable things and proves them with considerations that are, for informed people, equally unbelievable, or it asserts unbelievable things because a small circle of occultists has seen them. I assume that few people pay attention to these things, and they don't because they are fantasies and not facts. The spiritual development of Western humanity represents nothing more than the very large model of this small life experiment. We have learned that the considerations of reason deceive, as soon as its snares are set too far out in the empty space of thought, and on the other hand that there is a considerable distinction between verifiable facts and improbable ones. People had bad experiences before they stumbled upon faith in facts.

"I believe only in facts" means nothing more than: I want to proceed with certainty. The proposition that was written down on December 21, 1613, that theology must take care to explain the Bible in a way consistent with the established facts of the natural sciences, brought the Inquisition down on Galileo. (When facts can be safely relied on, under what conditions they should really be regarded as facts, and within what wrapping of subjectivities they still remain facts, are questions of philosophy that will not be touched on here, but I don't want to pass over the senselessness of the popular reproach that contemporary academic phil[osophy] occupies itself most often with precisely this problem.) This apparently brought great happiness at first. What evokes weariness today inspired great élan in the seventeenth century, as many historical examples show; it was a new spirit, and not mindlessness. People had doubtless grown tired of speculation; the new direction of thought by no means resolved the difficulties with which they had tortured themselves, but it pushed them aside. The way of formulating questions changed, indicating a change in the direction of interest; and a tremendous success, which began to accompany this new way of formulating problems from the outset, steadily attracted more attention. This is how natural science began at the turn of the seventeenth century. We should not forget that it is only three centuries old, while the Scholastics required seven centuries to reach their synthesis in Albertus Magnus and Thomas Aquinas.

Of course we should not imagine that a new way of thinking simply solves the old questions one after another, but rather that underneath the mountain and debris of the old way of thinking a new way develops that rises up until the last fragments of the old mantle fall away from it. With the so-called end of Scholasticism the new way of thinking was still a long way off. But from Descartes to Fichte, indeed even down to our own day, an aftereffect of the old way continued to be preserved as a goal, even if only informally, in the existence and construction of great systems of thought, while the natural sciences had to feel that their real picture of life was not covered by philosophy.

The reproach that our age is unphilosophical is based on the old dignity of philosophy, which was accustomed to great deductive systems. We may characterize all systems of modern phil[osophy] as powerful logical thought structures resting on a very narrow foundation of experience; none of them is able to ignore the development of the empirical sciences. But if one wants to attain such a system, a genuine worldview, the first requirement is really to have viewed the world, to know the facts. The smallest fact about the connection between character and hormonal balance offers more insight into the soul than a five-story idealistic system does. Kant's critique of the thing-in-itself: correct, but in this sense one of the ways of formulating questions that are circumvented. All these facts, however, are not finished and decided, but have hardly begun to be looked into. In their totality they are, to the philosophical glance, far from united. Philosophy has remained a little (!) behind the facts, and that misled people into believing that meaning concerned with facts was somehow antiphilosophical. But the appropriate philosophy of the contemporary period is that we have no philosophy!

It would be wrong to be saying this if there were no hope that in time we will get beyond the cardinal speculative questions by means of experience, get around them, perhaps, see them from new angles, and thus learn to pose questions differently. Psychology, mathematics, and physics have achieved new perspectives on the problems of time and space; the structure of matter has been dissolved into a network of new relations; the problems of life and individuality have to some extent been brought out of the darkness: indeed, even with so specific a metaphysical problem as the transformation of the physical world into the psychic, a solution of extraordinary range has been adumbrated by extending the application of psychology's gestalt theory to physics, physical chemistry, and physiology. It lies in the nature of things, of facts, that such research in the direction of further development will always remain open; empirical knowledge is never definitive. But a domination by the metaphysical that approximates the domination by the physical that we see today might represent some kind of progress in comparison to the perfection philosophy has up to now achieved! Naturally, in the course of time, systems would continue to displace each other, just as they do in the natural sciences; but they would be solidly grounded, and would change only in order to create room for new certainties. This may seem like a fantastic utopia, but . . . . Many indications suggest that this age is already underway in the sciences, and even in philosophy. This expectation is the deepest sense of the demand that research remain free. And of the imminent belief in progress of the sci[ences].

Today, of course, we are only stepping out of our baby shoes. We are an early phase.

It is easy to understand that an age that has not understood its newness should be distressed by a belief that it has lost something it once possessed. In addition, we usually do not attempt to view such a long period of development as I have attempted to characterize here, but only the connection with what is historically most recent. This would, however, be a premature attempt to philosophize in the old speculative way with mechanistic methods. The popular philosophy of our fathers' generation was oriented toward Darwinism and atomism; aside from the fact that these were themselves quite inadequate attempts at solutions, and filled only a tiny chamber in the armory of the empirical sciences, the way they were exploited philosophically was simply a caricature. But the reaction, which does not recognize the attempt as premature but regards it as corrupt in its very direction, truly throws the baby out with the bathwater. It is an episode, and of no significance.

Not what is here referred to as the phil[osophy] of facts, but rather specul[ative] phil[osophy], stimulated by the development of the factual sciences.

More important for us Germans is the dismissive attitude our classical authors took toward the new spirit. It was received by the writers of German Classicism in the double form of the philosophy of the Enlightenment and the age of the machine that began with phil[osophical] empiricism. About the first I have little more to say in this context, except that it too was an attempt condemned to fail because of its still inadequate means, even if there were accomplishments that were individually significant. Goethe's love for the individual and concrete was the proper reaction to it. What seems less justified is that the writers of Classicism paid no attention at all to developments in thought and life that were already quite visibly underway in their time. Mathematics, English philosophy, national economy, weaving looms, and business affairs did not seem worthy of their attention. Because of this, something of a provincial mentality, something narrow and petit bourgeois, inheres in this sublime flight of the German spirit that arose in a feudal and bourgeois ministate. Pos[sibly] in spite of Kant, who was the tremendous systematizer of this period. His thing-in-itself a rock fortress, around which the stream flowed. There is in the unity of the great achievements of these great men something that is by no means a mistake, but that probably becomes one in the disciples of German Classicism, which we all are: for what in Goethe's field of vision was a small dead space displaces an important arc of the horizon a hundred years later.

On the other hand, what lay behind this rejection was simply the feeling, which was justified at the time, that such a direction of the spirit and intellectual orientation provided no philosophy of life, while the German Classical writers furnished the basis on which the ideal of humanity has been established. How justified this mistrust was is dramatically demonstrated today by the fact that our educational systems in the *Realschulen* and the humanistic *Gymnasia* are at gross cross-purposes, and compete for importance without achieving any kind of synthesis.

Partly out of itself, partly because of the aftereffect of Classical resistance, and partly for reasons to be discussed later, the new way of thinking signified by the catchword "philosophy of facts" has, up to now, proved unfruitful in the sphere of the philosophy of life. Our poets, artists, and philosophical pathetics feel alienated from it, and look past it as they look backwards. Indeed, we may say that those among them who have all too eagerly seized on the new spirit are the less good ones. The exemplary synthesis is missing. But how, in the midst of such confusions, should the perspective of scientific thought and practical life be raised to the sphere of observation of life? The age take on form?

This split (intensified by the ever greater complexity to which political and intellectual democracy have evolved and by the lack of preparation to cope with it), this provisional inability to take a final step, is the main cause of the disunited, fragmented, and discontented spiritual situation of our time.

6   Capitalism and Facts

I have been discussing the development of the natural sciences, of machines, newspapers, and democracy, the lack of unity in opinion, and the atomization of all ideologies. I could easily have summarized all this under the heading "Age of Capitalism." In fact, not only all these phenomena, but also all their lamented effects can be summarized under this concept.

The formula of this age of capitalism relevant to "facts" runs: Money is the measure of all things. Its negative formulation is: Human action no longer contains its own measure. Words about the far-reaching validity of this formula are superfluous; it has been discussed often enough. I would merely like to emphasize the extent to which, among the best people, "success" is decisive today even for "understanding." Backbone of value.

It seems more important to bring out the positive, one should not hesitate to say the good, that is inherent in this situation. It is the most powerful and elastic form of organization that human beings have so far devised.

In this connection, however, it is nothing but an ordered selfishness; the most monstrous organization of selfishness according to the ordering of energies to amass money. In the absence of any other valid system of order it is absolutely indispensable. Where money doesn't do the ordering—for example, in a bureaucratic monarchy or the academic world—nepotism and favoritism immediately jump in. If money were abolished today, "the hegemony of that which has prerogatives to distribute" would be left untouched. During the recent period of revolution and confusion, a kind of natural economy involving every imaginable form of favoritism established itself everywhere. This point needs to be made, since many people seem to believe that abolishing money would abolish selfishness. But selfishness is as old and eternal as its opposite, social feelings. Money is not the cause of selfishness, but its consequence; although nothing has made this feeling monstrous the way money and its products have.

The connection with "facts" is that selfishness is the most dependable quality of human life. Leaving aside some ineffectual exceptions, through the stimuli of desire and intimidation the individual can be made to do anything. To say that these qualities can be dependably counted on is more than a play on words. Calculation assumes fixed quantities, or the calculability of such quantities. Calculating, measuring, and weighing are possible only where the objects on which these operations are performed remain constant, where they do not vary between two measurements or during the calculation (when that happens, every effort of discernment is directed toward finding a connection to some invariable quantity). Approximately valid. The connection with $\pi\alpha\nu\tau\alpha\ \rho\varepsilon$ [all things flow—ed.] will be left aside here.

The development of our modern knowledge of nature rests on attention having been directed at fixed functional variations among measurable quantities (for instance between the length of a pendulum and period of oscillation, duration, and height of fall). Better stated: The ancients did the same thing, for exactly the same may be said of their system of statics. Modern physics is a continuation of ancient physics. In between, however, lies not only a hole in the continuity of the tradition, but also a philosophical interlude, which I would like to demonstrate with the distinction between two conceptual sequences in an example that has become historic, that of the falling body. After antiquity, for example, it was possible to subordinate stone as an individual entity to the concept of "stone," and this in turn to the higher concept "body," and body to the higher concept of "matter," and it was assumed that this led to an explanation of its behavior. In modern science, what is examined is not the behavior of the stone, but rather a detail of this behavior, the relationship of time and path. But since this detail was abstracted from the totality of the individual object, its connection with such abstractions was revealed from quite different things. Dissimilar processes, such as the perpendicular falling of a stone and the circling of the planets, proved to be the same, and this was a tremendous shock to the old way of thinking. The elliptical orbit of the stars entered into a relation of kinship with all other possible forms of oscillation, and the method of abstraction and this new kind of comparison tore the fabric of the world asunder, displaying entirely new interweavings of warp and woof that appeared to lie behind them. The same capacity to abstract, to treat actions for themselves, as a means, is also apparent in the ethical attitude of the present, where it knows itself to be free from the traditional Christian ethic, just as in war or business.

This divergence between thinking oriented toward facts and speculative thinking should not, however, keep us from noticing that underlying both is the same drive for certainty: only the method has changed. The essence of language, and the innermost principle of so-called logical axioms and laws, are the most unequivocal possible signification; but this also constitutes the nature of what is referred to here in a wider sense as facts. Lack of ambiguity, the repeatability of experience, and fixity of the object are the preconditions of calculating and measuring, as they are of the discipline of thinking in general.

This need for the unequivocal, repeatable, and fixed is satisfied in the realm of the soul by violence. And a special form of this violence, shockingly flexible, highly developed, and creative in many respects, is capitalism. To describe this I have already advanced the broader concept of an order that takes account of selfishness. This principle of order is as old as human association itself. Whoever wants to build in stone where people are concerned must use violence or desire. This reckoning with people's bad capacities is a bearish speculation. A bearish order is trained vulgarity. It is the order of the modern world. I let you win so I can win more; or I let you win more so I can win something: this cunning of the reflective parasite is the soul of the most respectable business negotiations. Granting or obtaining advantages. Those that absolutely depend on harming others are numerous. Even the most modest, most justified profit of a seller, who procures goods in danger and at the risk of his existence, and has acquired some stake in things— whether he is an entrepreneur or a wage slave—is claimed without regard for the personal situation of the person who needs the goods, thus exploiting it; indeed, the opposite would not only appear to be, but under today's conditions actually would be, a mental disorder that would justifiably call for appointment of a guardian.

One reason: abstraction. The other: weariness in the face of ideologies.

("Put the screws on," "tighten the screws," "cold-bloodedly pursuing a policy of tightening the screws," "not recoiling at the use of strong methods, even broken glass")

The same is also true of politicians, whether it is a matter of domestic politics or foreign policy. The commanding officer who with threats keeps malleable the population of the territory behind the front calculates with these people no less bearishly than the industrial combine that starves striking workers, or the political party that misappropriates a campaign fund. War is the continuation of politics by the *same* means, and peace would remain, even after a general disarmament, an armed peace. This is the type of politician who first supplies arms and then negotiates, and can imagine a flourishing relationship in no other terms than the hegemony of a single part. He says that he is only taking account of the facts, and not being utopian.

Let's be fair to this man of facts who only calculates bearishly with his fellow human beings. He's a clean-cut, precise type, averse to chatter, and for all his reprehensibility often appealing. If one wants to oppose him all the same, the important thing is to define this opposition correctly.

BETTER ORGANIZATION

1. Understood as Age of Capitalism.

2. Money has become the measure of all things, and things no longer contain a measure of human value in themselves. The fundamental connection of capitalism with the scientific character of the age, on the one hand, and with its political excesses on the other is, however, this:

3. Money is the concentration of potential advantages and disadvantages, therefore ordered selfishness. Selfishness, however, is the most dependable fact in human life. Desire and intimidation.

4. {Both these methods correspond in the spiritual realm, and to the need for unambiguousness, repeatability, and fixity

5. that has become so characteristic of our thought.} Whatever makes use of selfishness is violence, and capitalism is a particular form of violence. It is the most tremendous organization of selfishness.

6. This principle of order is as old as human association itself. To grant advantages or gain them by trickery is the soul of business; to threaten with reprisals the soul of foreign policy (domestic politics falls in between). Both cases signify bearish speculation. When the representatives of these views say that they reckon only with facts and are not utopians, they express

7. thereby only the spirit that has made our science great. For the notion that in life only advantages and disadvantages can be calculated is more than playing with words. A great spiritual attitude expresses itself in them or influences

9. [*sic*] them. The old struggle for unambiguous order, which already underlies soc[ial] axioms. The ethical connection with science is, however, an even more intimate one. It cannot be made comprehensible without a small

8. [*sic*] epistemological excursus. Dissolving into abstractions.

10. The same capacity for abstraction in ethical behavior.

11. Without this ability to abstract, the barbarousness of propositions like [11] [*sic*] is impossible to understand. But the cruelty of life as a whole cannot be understood without them.

12. One should not be unfair to the man of facts. He is a clean-cut type. He is hard (even in relation to his own people). Exponent of a way of thinking that has brought about successes never dreamed of. That he acts the way he thinks is his natural ethic. And so he feels the way he thinks. For we feel the way we think. And in opposition to this natural inclination there are only pulverized ideologies, which so contradict one another that he assumes they can do nothing more than babble.

If one wants to oppose him, the most important thing is to define the opposing position correctly.

7   The Opponents of Facts

There are people who deny facts and call that thinking. We should not begin with them, although many writers and even properly philosophical philosophers belong in this group.

Then there are people who blame our rationality and desire to be less rational. They have various arguments.

One is that because we are constantly calculating everything, we also calculate with people. This is certainly not entirely false, but violence is older than calculation, and is itself already a naive calculation about calculation. The Fall of Man is, therefore, dated too late. Then they also overlook that the men of facts whom they find especially unpleasant, the engineers and businessmen, are not nearly as rational as they think, in the sense of a preponderance of the intellectual: one need only compare them with a Scholastic (a high Scholastic). There is in their activity a great deal that is irrational, indeed even antirational. In itself, a fact is not rational at all; it is only a regulator of rationality and is ordinarily important for rationality only in a series. And the engineer is often distinguished from the theoretician precisely because he allows thinking to break off at some point and makes his construction by means of an assumption, an approximate value, or a process of abbreviation that is a leap across the undemonstrable, and this is then validated by its success. The age of positivism is distinguished from the age of Scholasticism precisely by being more practical, more factual, and not thinking so much. By comparison, our age is as much an age of thinking a lot as it is one of thinking less. Much the same may be said of the businessman: will, decisiveness, is just as important in his activity as calculation; he is a man of facts also in the sense that he creates facts. One of the elements of his life is the freedom he creates for himself, the autonomous businessman, free from intellectual quarrels and the opinions of all among his fellow men on whom he is not immediately dependent (in his strong type). If he does not quite properly count, then, as a representative of rationalism, this seems to have a further significance, a more comprehensive human attitude than thinking.

In the last analysis, the formulation as "antirational" is also misguided, because without rationality there would be no order, no language, no clarity or stability. All that remained would be a limitless vague feeling.

From another point of view the opposite of the contemporary spiritual condition, in the form of love and goodness, has been called for. This demand for love, human goodness, and the like, even if it was only superficially understood, surfaced with great vehemence in the midst of the War. Insofar as it is reawakened Rousseauism—man is good—it does not need to be discussed here, where the presupposition is human (and therefore also moral) shapelessness. The people to be warned against are all those who wish to reform society on the basis of this false assumption, for they will miss their goal.

Nonetheless, the true opposition to the factual attitude is not far from this last determination. There is a human state that is fundamentally opposed to rationalizing, calculating, goal-oriented activity, estimating, pressure, craving, and base anxiety.

It is difficult to describe.

One aspect of the truth resides in all the characterizations (as love, goodness, irrationality, religiosity) that have been disputed here, and for the complete truth we have today no thought at our command.

I would like to call it simply the "other condition."

In contrast to it, all thinking and desire appear as one.

If we try to characterize this contrast soberly and thoughtfully, we could describe the ordinary condition as narrowly focussed and goal-oriented: a strut, a thin line connects the individual with his object and attaches itself to both the object and the person at only a single point, while all the rest of the person's being remains untouched. This is true of knowledge as well as desire, and in fact both are often condemned together as two aspects of the same evil.

It is a well-known fact that a person is completely transformed depending on whether one observes him sympathetically or unsympathetically, and our science may be characterized as observation without sympathy, for that is an important essence of the demand that it not be fantastical. People will of course ask whether even lifeless things actually change, depending on whether we observe them with or without love, and I would answer yes. It reaches into the rational. Knowing/reknowing *credo ut intelligas* (Ans[elm] of Canterbury).[40] A tone and ductus, a tension and coloration, changes in the external world, depending on the disposition of the observer's feeling. This seems to be confirmed by experiences in daily life as well as by the observation of nervous and mental disturbances and the description of religious states of mind. In itself it is not particularly surprising that the appearance of the world depends on emotional factors, since we know this from sensory data. This dependence obviously remains within narrow limits, and precisely because it is irrelevant to the practical attitude it has not received much attention from investigative thought.

We have a great many accounts of this other condition. What seems to be common to all of them is that the border between self and nonself is less sharp than usual, and that there is a certain inversion of relationships. (Egoism and measuring.) Whereas ordinarily the self masters the world, in the other condition the world flows into the self, or mingles with it or bears it, and the like (passively instead of actively).

One participates in things (understands their language). In this condition understanding [Verstehen] is not impersonal (objective), but extremely personal, like an agreement between subject and object.

In this condition one really knows everything in advance, and the things merely confirm it. (Knowing is reknowing.)

(Actively instead of passively   Nietzsche's Dionysian ecstasy)

It is possible that this masculine-feminine principle lay at the basis of the ancient mystery cults.

I will not continue with this description, because the means of making it reasonably comprehensive are not available to me at the moment. But one can see that it involves a greater degree of subjectivity, and this is distinguished from the proportion of ordinary egoism in the same way that the measuring attitude and so forth contrasts with the other attitude. Embraces both the egoistic and the altruistic attitude. In itself, the self is something quite vague, and experienced in various ways. We can perhaps say that in all objective relationships the self is, in a certain sense, bracketed (that is also the point), and that this is explained by characterizing this ordinary condition as an "alienation"; although this could certainly not always be claimed for strong actions of the will. But one can claim it for the feelings [Affekte]. We can perhaps distinguish evil will from good will to some extent as a hot from a cold will, as a will that retroactively associates with one's self, that permits empathy, that is refashioned by someone who has been lacking in empathy, as a will that not only recognizes, but experiences its sacrifice. The good person in another sense, the lover, is, of course, not good out of opposition to egoism, for in that other world egoism does not exist at all; the other person, properly received, serves to heighten one's own egoism. And the same is true of evil. There is evil that is good, just as there is evil that is evil.

If we attempt to summarize, we may already say:

That the condition is characterized as active as well as passive; but never indifferent. (Contemplative-Dionysian.)

That it shows heightening of subjectivity as well as diminution; in both cases, however, no objectivity. Double subjectivity. From the perspective of the external world, then, a broad contact that oscillates back and forth, in which the outer world dominates or retreats; but never indifference. The opposite of objectivity is excess of self or excess of object, but not subjectivity. It is a matter of dividing things differently: the division between subject and object is a result of the rational attitude (obviously a matter of the emotional-rational [distinction].

We may say that it is just as much a dereification of the self as of the world.

It is a matter of evaluating differently. The opposition egoism-altruism loses its meaning; likewise, the opposition good-evil. In its place we can put the pair: enhancement-diminution.

Also, in place of what is useful we can put: what enhances.

Part of this too is a falling away of everything petty.

In the contemplative branch, a frequent feeling of sinking or being engulfed [*Versinken*], of perishing [*Eingehen*], of being borne up.

From what I have discussed so far, a series of questions naturally follows:

I touch first of all on the question, What role do the feelings that we have in our normal relation to the world play in the contemplative relation?

For example, love. I believe that one must properly distinguish psychologically between the affect and the result of its appearance in the whole person, the attitude in which emotion is emphasized. Only those bodily feelings we name after the affected parts are really purely affective, such as toothache or backache. Put better, they are an amalgam of sensations with feelings of pleasure or aversion. Those conditions that originate in inner sensations of our body, such as digestion or circulation, establish a state of feeling or mood: they are no longer localized, have no connection to the outside world (which is probably what makes the difference), but on the other hand an internal relation to the self that is that much more intense (for example, bad moods, depression). They pass over as something special into conditions that never become conscious to us at all, as for example in personal moods conditioned by hormonal balance. All these various states of feeling in a person are closely related to sensory experience as well as to willing and thinking: those in the first group primarily with the sensory apparatus and defense or desire; those in the second have only a shadow of sensation, while, on the other hand, they determine a kind of muscle tone of the will and also of the sphere of thinking.

What in life we call affect—for example, love, anger, hatred, anxiety, aversion, shame, etc.—are obviously alloys. They are related to these feelings-sensations in being tied to their object in a fairly unambiguous way; a something hurts, a something is loved or regretted. At the same time they are, for various reasons, characterized as physical conditions and general feelings; not a part of the body, but the whole self is affected; every time in a different, characteristic way. Not, to be sure, distinguished as sharply as pleasure and aversion, which is why a misguided older psychology was inclined to assume that it was only a matter of desire or aversion in connection with various objects. It is difficult to say in psychological descriptive terms which feelings, and how many, may be distinguished in this way as different. In their organic part they may well be related in many ways, and partially identical. It is easier to answer biologically or sociologically, by assuming that the various socially important attitudes have also clearly defined themselves emotionally: I believe that here an older part of the reaction is always combined with a more recent one. Love, hatred, anger, courage, and shame were already a phenomenon in primitive social relationships (even among animals); we may assume that later developments have added very little. If we consider "love," for instance, we may distinguish simple sexual "craving" as its core; in anger, the will to annihilate, in hatred the same "will to annihilate" and the will to retaliate, just as in aversion there is a kernel of "anxiety." We may assume that the more basic components of these amalgams are most unequivocally bound up with specific bodily conditions, and that these bodily conditions infuse the various major feelings we have today. What is it, then, that is added to them? What is it, for instance, that distinguishes the most primitive love affect from purely sexual desire? Obviously, the presence of contradictory affects. But superstitious ways of thinking are components of even the most primitive hatred! The desire to rape is mixed with hesitation, with tenderness; one might almost say, the masculine with a feminine. Can we not say metaphorically: Masculine is the movement of the arms, feminine is the falling into the arms. The man is masculine with a feminine admixture, the woman feminine with a masculine admixture. The anger of today's person is an inhibited will to annihilate, etc. This mixture of contradictions arises from the fact that the affected personality has various moods at the same time; it reacts in differently constituted proportions, which apparently or really blend together in typical cases into typical conditions and patterns of behavior. On a still higher level of complication, then, there is often no way of distinguishing whether a condition of feeling indicates love or something else. (Therefore, among other things, what is formless can so easily take on shape.) The basic behavior patterns were associated with specific social situations; what occurred as they became complicated was not competition among the basic feelings, as if they had to be mixed in in specific dosages, but the whole process was intimately intertwined with the simultaneous development of the intellectual faculty. As in the "kernels" of feeling mentioned previously, ways of thinking about the world are already involved, for the gaze of the loved one or the enemy heightens feeling, and it does so most on the higher levels. Thoughts and intellectual dispositions form inseparable components of the higher feelings. "Feeling strongly" means even today, of course, still having the capacity for certain emotional dispositions, but it also means being seized and influenced in a far-reaching way in the totality of one's mental personality.

What role then do these feelings play in the contemplative attitude?

Let us recall that they are in a certain sense cancelled out. Desire will be weakened by love; on the other hand, the core that surges around it will be expanded. Diffusion of affect and a specific dilution. The loved ones unite in God, as one used to say, or as we might say today: in the world.

But are there, in the condition of contemplation, any feelings of disgust? Religious tradition speaks of them, but this is perhaps disgust at the failure of the contemplative condition to appear. Is there anger, hatred, shame in the condition of contemplation? That people have so often applied the name "condition of love" to it shows that, at least ordinarily, such feelings don't enter in. Therefore, too, the close historical connection between contemplation and bliss.

In my view dejection (see disgust) does exist, for example in the form of humility (sweet humility) as a condition within contemplation. It is hard to deny that with a corresponding epithet there can also be anger (a gentle, loving anger). Also unhappiness at the diminution of the condition by oneself or the other. Thus it may be assumed that the condition is not only one of desire; it will more nearly contain everything we could associate with the epithet "ecstatic." Ecstatic love, ecstatic anger, ecstatic regret, shame, anxiety.

But there is certainly no ecstatic or contemplative envy, and just as little hatred, avarice, social uncertainty, probably not remorse in the ordinary sense of moral conscience, either. Jealousy   Missing feelings.

Another way of arranging this comes up here—great feelings and petty ones—which is related to it, probably a product of the contemplative plus the normal condition.

Why are these feelings missing? Envy is, biologically speaking, inhibited *struggle of life* [in English in original—trans.]; as are hatred, greed, in part jealousy also. We might therefore assume: combative feelings are missing. This would also explain the feminine component in the contemplative love of the man. And justify the characterization: condition of love.

But also missing are feelings such as vanity, everything that could be considered base, a large part of the feeling of possessiveness, feeling oneself ridiculous, and the like. Under what heading should we summarize all these? We could say: Everything corrosive, everything that diminishes the personality, but also inflated vanity: thus everything disproportionate, everything that disturbs a certain harmony. (In a group of descriptions there is a great deal of talk about "harmony.") (We might also recall the notion of "exalted feeling.") Or: feelings of inferiority and overcompensating for them. Humility and dejection are, to be sure, feelings of inferiority, but as blissful, ecstatic, and compensated feelings, not overcompensated ones.

But also missing, as we have seen, are the feelings that appear as social reactions, and that are rooted in the objective attitude toward knowledge. Vanity, ridicule, and possessive feelings enter in here as well. The contemplative person has no conscience because this reaction is simply not possible for one who finds himself in a state of continuous ethical action. One thinks of the frequent predicate: "withdrawn" [*weltabgewandt*]. Let us say simply: Moral feelings.

If we review these considerations, we can already see that what comes into play are neither new feelings nor particular cases of the loss of basic feelings, for desire as well as aversion are present, sthenic as well as asthenic affects. But of the feelings that may be considered biological in origin aggressive feelings are missing, and missing too (and hard to distinguish from them) are the moral feelings, the derivates of social life. The feelings that are present have suffered a certain dilution, but are much more diffused throughout the whole person.

We may compare to this the disparity in thinking that expresses itself in the fact that in the contemplative condition one can philosophize, but not add. This coincides, as we pointed out earlier, with "dispersion," and we may suppose that the characteristic emotional attitude is strongly influenced by the intellectual attitude, and that this is therefore a matter of the complications belonging to a higher level mentioned earlier, and less a matter of a fundamental change in feeling.

We could also of course assume that knowledge is lacking because the combative attitude is missing, and that its absence is based on some abnormality of feeling. But we must not forget that it is a question not of a constitutive condition, but of transitory conditions. Falling into the contemplative state may be constitutionally facilitated, in some cases periodically, in others due to illness, but one should not overlook the fact that the capacity for contemplation is widespread, and that through an act of will one can assume one or another condition. What we are dealing with, then, appears to be not an abnormality but another use of our capacities.

The conflict between these two attitudes is probably as old as our history. It is in the broadest sense the conflict between religion and state.

8   Profane Religiosity

What is the meaning of the conflict between these two attitudes?

The contemplative attitude has always been associated with the hypothesis of the presence of a god. But, as is evident, it is independent of this presupposition. Even the worldly, the erotic condition of love leads many people far into this realm who don't believe in another world at all. One therefore has the duty first of all to investigate this condition as such, independently of the hypothesis. Ordinarily we might even say that in the consolidation of the divine realm and of theology something is brought in from the order of ordinary realms, and something of the logical consistency of the normal attitude: this has been repeatedly articulated in the struggle of the mystics against the theologians.

What, then, is the meaning of the conflict between these two attitudes in the individual, if it has nothing to do with God?

It goes without saying that the normal attitude serves social life and the mastering of the world.

What does it mean to turn away from the world, to rise above the world, to renounce conflict, if it does not serve union with God?

It has no goal, for it has always contained a hidden unreal and unattainable goal.

It has no sense, for the theologians only gave it a pseudosense.

It is then a drive, a need, a suppressed half of the individual, that repeatedly strives to assert itself.

This other half is, however, biologically incomprehensible, for (even if not from lack of goal or purpose) a world in the condition of contemplation would perish from defenselessness. The theories about this are extremely simple: the lost state of being God's children, the lost paradise: they contain the admission that this condition is not to be achieved by earthly means.

We can perhaps make the assumption that here the two fundamental drives of every living creature stand out as the striving for food and individual survival, which includes conflict, but also flight as well? and the drive to reproduce, which in any case transcends the individual! The first created the rational world, the second, love. But since "love" appears only periodically, or among mankind only from case to case, it created not a total worldview but only the exception to the existing one. This would also satisfactorily explain to the positivist the connection with thinking and so on.

Three Basic Drives?
Aggression
Protection
Procreation

But one could equally well construct an opposition between *struggle of life* and rest, digestion, and the like in the animal/human being, and derive from that the antagonism of the two basic attitudes.

It is rather pointless, since the problem has not yet been addressed, and we cannot predict which connections will be compelling for a more comprehensive and penetrating, even if initial, treatment.

But it is not superfluous to emphasize that the problem must be looked at from this side as well. For the methods of scientific investigation have almost always been rejected in favor of the visions of contemplation, with the claim that it involves a different (intuitive) way of knowing, an envisioning and the like. Be that as it may, it *has* been demonstrated that no firm internal coherence of this contemplative realm has ever been established from this point of view. No one has ever progressed beyond exhortations and programs. This alone is sufficient justification for applying, for a change, the other way of looking at things, and allows us to surmise that the contemplative attitude may be explained by means of the normal one, but not the other way around.

But there is probably still another fruitful way of looking at this, which for the most part remains within the particular way of thinking of the other realm itself. I have often tried to give some definite idea of this, namely a way that begins with the essence of ideals or ideality.

Ideals possess the strange quality that if they were completely realized they would turn into nonsense. One could easily follow a commandment such as "Thou shalt not kill" to the point of dying of starvation; and I might establish the formula that for the proper functioning of the mesh of our ideals, as in the case of a strainer, the holes are just as important as the mesh. With moral propositions it can be demonstrated in every case that the exceptions are part of the rule; but also what we call ideals in the real sense, the great driving ideas of individual and social life, contain no end of demands that would lead to ruin, if we did not consider them unreal from the outset.

Toward a New Aesthetic
Observations on a Dramaturgy of Film
1925

*Set in the context of a review of a book by his friend Béla Balázs (Der
sichtbare Mensch [Visible man]), this essay is Musil's most important statement on aesthetics and the "other condition." It offers his clearest description of the distinction between the normal relation to experience and the
"other condition."*

1

I know that theory is not dull, but signifies broad perspectives of freedom for every
art. It is the explorer's map in art, showing all the ways and possibilities, and un-
masking what looked like compelling necessity as one accidental path among a hundred others. It is theory that gives courage for voyages of Columbus and makes
every step into an act of free will.

Why the mistrust of theory? Theory need not even be true to inspire great
works. Almost all the great discoveries of humanity have begun with false hypotheses. It is, moreover, quite easy to discard a theory when it no longer works.
But the accumulation of random experimentation bars the way like a heavy, impenetrable barrier. No art has ever become great without theory.

By that I do not mean to say that the artist must necessarily be "learned," and I
also know the common (all too common!) view of the value of "unconscious creation." But it is a matter of the intellectual and spiritual level of consciousness on
which one writes "unconsciously."

I have nothing to add to these excellent words of introduction, except that
among us Germans their spirit is not very widespread. We have accomplished great things in the scientific study of art; and the casual insights of
artists who create in ateliers and coffeehouses are often very colorful. But
the thinkers who could mediate between these two domains in a stimulating and systematic way are missing among us almost entirely. This gives
Balázs's book a meaning that reaches far beyond film. In Hungary a famous
writer, Balázs is to us a stranger, thanks to the shabby relations between
Hungarian and German literature. Balázs came to Vienna when the Habsburg Monarchy began to collapse in Hungary; he had to earn his living as
a journalist, and became in this way, among other things, a film critic. To
this circumstance he owes the great experience and the simple, persuasive
style that make his book an extraordinarily knowledgeable guide through
the major and minor dramaturgical problems of film. The capacity to ob-

serve an experience not only rigorously, but also tenderly; the ingenious style, which creates an atmosphere that immediately relates each impression to many others, and above all the clear, profound, ordered layering of this atmosphere—these are personal qualities of Balázs the writer. Like a stealthy hunter stalking his prey he tells us about the life of the films that pass through our theaters in endless herds, but describes them at the same time as their first anatomist and biologist. And because he experiences and reflects on them, experientially and scientifically, his uncommon talent creates in the wasteland of film criticism an unexpected paradigm that is also valid for literary criticism, which he touches upon whenever he distinguishes film from literature.

The observations I shall add in what follows refer primarily to this boundary region in which film and literature overlap. The question whether film is an autonomous art or not—for Balázs the point of departure for efforts to make it into one—raises questions common to all the arts. In fact, film has become the popular art of our time. "Not in the sense, unfortunately, that film rises out of the spirit of the people, but rather that the spirit of the people arises out of film," says Balázs. And the churches and holy places of all the religions have not covered the world with as dense a network in millennia as film has in three decades.

2

Above all—and one could complete in this paradoxical way every proof that film is an art—what speaks for film is its truncated essense as an event reduced to moving shadows which nonetheless generates the illusion of life. Every art involves such a bifurcation. Silent like a fish and pale like something subterranean, film swims in the pond of the only-visible. Painting, on the other hand, is silent and transfixed; twenty Gothic or baroque sculptures brought together in a single room (with their gestures crossed like swords) give more clearly the impression of a collection of catatonics in a madhouse. And when one considers the movements of sound even in a piece of classical music (quite apart from music seen from the point of view of social expression), they display a not-yet-described madness whose peculiarity cannot be compared to anything. How is it that such a fundamentally strange splitting-off from the fullness of life becomes art? Today we can already touch on the answer, but we do not yet possess it completely. It is probably connected to those processes (closely related to each other) that psychology calls condensation and displacement, whereby either heterogeneous images stimulated by the same affect are lumped together in masses, to which the sum of the affect attaches itself in some way (for example, the animal people and multiple animals of primitive cultures, dreams, and hallucinations, in which two or more people simultaneously appear as one), or the other way around, a single image (part) appears as representative of a complex and seems laden with the inexplicably high affective value of the whole (the magical role of hair, fingernails, shadows, reflections in the mirror, and the like).

A stage of development bound up with this, through which every art form passes, can be better understood, at least in its general tendency, from the well-known peculiarities of cognition. We know that in general the weaker the impression made on us by material offered to our perception, the more clearly the relations contained within it become apparent. Rhythm is clearer in a scanned vowel than in a word, and clearest in the sound of a beat, which is, to be sure, acoustically complex but, as it were, psychically simple; similarly, relations of line and surface stand out more clearly in a statue than in a living body. In everyday usage abstraction means, roughly, disregarding something or neglecting all aspects of something save one. In this one aspect there then appear, without our doing anything in particular, relations for which we may also retain the passive name of abstraction (which expresses the one-sidedness and separateness of art), although it is just as much a matter of an increase in impressions as a reduction.

Insofar as art is abstraction, it is by that very fact also a summary leading to a new context. If the context is limited to the surface sense impressions of life, there then arise those relations of color, surfaces, sound, rhythm, and so on whose further transformation generally signifies the formal development of an art. We may leave aside to what extent the patterns arising from this awaken specific feelings ("liking" for instance), or to what extent the basic experiences we have just assumed illuminate these experiences, or the extent to which both effects combine with each other and with others: in any case, the formal aspect never exists independently, even though it has often been seen as the essential element in art—as the real object of aesthetics. What remains of a poem after the logical meaning has been removed is known to be just as much a pile of rubble as what remains of its sense if its vocalization and rhythm are exchanged for everyday speech; and something similar is true for all the arts. If the formal relations of an art suddenly emerge in isolation, there arises that frightened astonishment at an irrational world which I spoke of earlier, half in jest.

3

We do not, of course, actually experience this astonishment at works of art as complicated, impractical, or even grotesque constructs. And therein lies the reminder that we immediately compensate for the disequilibrium in our awareness of reality that every work of art invokes by balancing it in another direction. We omit what has been excised and make the part into a new whole, the abnormal into a new norm, what is disturbed into another equilibrium of the soul. We are accustomed to having the effect of the work of art described as an elevated, perhaps even as an alleviated, condition of life; we used to call this condition imagination [*Phantasie*], and maybe today we call it illusion. But one rarely, if ever, strikes upon the recognition of the possibility that this illusion, for all its distinctive qualities, is analogous to what psychiatry means by illusion, that is, a "disturbance" in which elements of reality are reconstituted as an unreal whole that usurps the value of reality. People would rather regard art as decoration than as a negation of real life. The concepts of purposeless beauty or of beautiful illusion, which continue to play an important role in our view of art, have something of a holiday mood about them. If I am not mistaken, the root of this lies in the beginning of the reign of Christianity, when art suffered from the jealousy of true believers and was allowed by its defenders to escape, as it were, into a second-class existence. Later, the aesthetic of our Classical period, which suffered from a culture of deference toward petty princes (how strange the mixture of boldness and caution often is in Schiller!), directed its energies more toward again assuring this "purposeless illusion" a proper place and dignity than toward emphasizing art's tendency to deny life.

Nevertheless, the means employed by the arts already display this opposition to the normal attitude toward the world, even if this opposition is presented as harmless. Apart from condensation and displacement, both of which arise from a precivilized phase of humanity, rhythm and monotony (which play such an important role) aim for example at a narrowing of consciousness similar to mild hypnosis, with the same goal of overvaluing the suggestion given through depression of the psychic environment. All these means have their origins in quite ancient cultural conditions, and taken together they signify an extraconceptual correspondence of the human being with the world along with abnormal or correlative movements. We can see this at any moment when we find ourselves lost in a work of art and the normal controlling consciousness suddenly switches on. If one reads the brilliant descriptions of the thinking of primitive peoples that Lévy-Bruhl has given in his book, *Les fonctions mentales des sociétés primitives*,* in particular his characterization of that special attitude toward things that he calls participation, the connection with the experience of art becomes at many points so palpable that one could believe that art was a late form of

* In German: *Das Denken der Naturvölker*, Braumüller, Wien.

development of that early world. It would be unusually important for research in the field of aesthetics to devote its attention to the clarification of
these connections, which, on the other side, are profoundly bound up with
psychopathology.* These fundamental experiences have of course long since
been remolded in the course of human development: they have faded and
been mixed with others, so that it is hardly still possible to dissolve them
into their elements. They have embedded themselves in a new social context, that is, that of being art, something that is apparently so fixed and defined in its social roles and significance that one hardly even feels the need to
reflect on the nature of these relations.

At its core, however, is another attitude toward the world. Softly quote a
poem to yourself on the floor of a stock exchange, and the stock exchange
will become for a moment just as meaningless as the poem is in it.

4

A remarkable example is offered by a fundamental experience that belongs
to film, that exotic life described in Balázs's book, a life in which things gain
in visual isolation. "In the world of speaking human beings, silent things are
far more lifeless and insignificant than the human being. They are allowed
only a life of the second or third order, and even that only in rare moments
of especially clear-sighted sensitivity in the people who observe them. . . .
But in the shared silence inanimate things become almost homogeneous
with people, and gain thereby in vitality and significance. This is the riddle
of that special film atmosphere, which lies beyond the capacities of literature." One might be tempted to see in this only the description of an emphasis of attention, but the subsequent clarification draws out the meaning
quite unambiguously: "The precondition for this is that the image of each
object actually signifies an inner condition," that "in film all things have
a symbolic meaning. . . . One could simply say meaning. For symbolic
means as much as having significance, going beyond its own sense to a still
further sense. What is decisive in this for film is that all things, without
exception, are necessarily symbolic. For all things make a physiognomic impression on us, whether we are conscious of it or not. Just as time and space
can never be excluded from our world of experience, so does the physiognomic adhere to every phenomenon. It is a necessary category of our
perception."

* Stimulating in this context is Ernst Kretschmer's *Medizinische Psychologie*, G. Tieme,
Leipzig. This little book, which I make use of frequently here, offers valuable suggestions toward a psychology of feelings, a subject that up to now has been treated with too little success
by experimental psychology and too one-sidedly by psychoanalysis.

What is this "physiognomic impression," this "symbolic face" of things? First of all, it is certainly something that can be explained within the compass of normal psychology: some kind of emotional tone associated with the processes I have characterized as abstraction and splitting. But psychological connections are almost always so intertwined that although a whole is determined by its parts, the parts are also determined by the whole; thus, if impressions become overvalued and alienating as soon as they are separated from their customary setting, this invites the presumption of another, apocryphal context into which they move. In this case it would be a kind of soft spot in the image of the world that normally surrounds us with the appearance of unshakable certainty; for what I have quoted very much recalls that transformation of our consciousness to which Novalis and his friends owed their great and wonderful experiences.

One could in fact call this symbolic face of things the mysticism of film, or at least its romanticism, if it played more than an episodic role in the shadowy realm of living photography. What is extraordinary is that a book on the practice of film reaches this point at all, and touches quite consciously on the border between these two worlds.

5

The uncertain history of this division in human experience has unfortunately never been pursued and portrayed without prejudice—whether by rationalist hairsplitters or addicts of religion. It seems, however, that a bifurcation runs throughout the whole of human history, dividing it into two spiritual conditions, which, even though they have influenced each other in many ways and entered into compromises, have nonetheless never properly mixed with each other. One of the two is familiar as the normal condition of our relationship to the world, to people, and to ourselves. We have evolved— if one were to describe this condition in relation to the other—by means of the *sharpness* of our mind to what we are: lords of an earth on which we were originally a nothing among monsters. Activity, boldness, cunning, deceit, restlessness, evil, a talent for the hunt, lust for war, and the like are the moral qualities to which we owe this ascent. Today we demote these qualities to the status of vices as soon as they appear in excess within our communities of interests; but they dominate the interactions of these unions of interest with each other as they always have (war, exploitation, and the like); and—what is far more difficult to change—they penetrate even the spiritual attitude of people in our civilization to the ultimate degree. Measuring, calculating, and tracking, that positive, causal, mechanical way of thinking that is so often held against the people of our day, is an expression of the same aboriginal mistrust and struggle for existence as the dominant role of money as regulator of a world in which only the lower qualities of the human being count as solid and calculable; money is to be used, so to speak, as the only reliable material for constructing society. The popular task of "improving" man is far more difficult than is generally assumed; it cannot be done just with the proper attitude toward avoiding evil, for without his evil qualities there is nothing left of the human being that we are but a formless heap. Even morality itself is, in its most profound nature, totally alloyed with and compromised by the sharp and evil basic qualities of our spirit; even its form, as rule, norm, command, threat, law, or the quantifying and weighing of good as well as evil, reveals the shaping influence of the metric, calculating, mistrusting, annihilating will of the spirit.

In contrast to this spiritual condition stands another, no less demonstrable historically even if it has left a less powerful imprint on our past. It has been characterized by many names, all of which are vaguely in agreement. It has been called the condition of love, of goodness, of renunciation of the world, of contemplation, of vision, of approach to God, of entrancement, of will-lessness, of meditation, and many other aspects of a fundamental experience that recurs in the religion, mysticism, and ethics of all historical peoples as universally as it has, remarkably, remained undeveloped. This other spiritual condition is always described with as much passion as imprecision, and one might be tempted to see in this shadowy double of our world only a daydream, had it not left its traces in countless details of our ordinary life and did it not constitute the marrow of our morality and idealism lying within the fibrous threads of evil. Today, if one does not have one's own thorough researches as a base, one must renounce the temptation to try to say more about the nature and meaning of this other condition; for until recently our knowledge of it was about as extensive as the rest of our knowledge about the world in the tenth century. But if one simply extracts a few main, common characteristics from the purely descriptive accounts of a literature that is thousands of years old, one finds again and again the presence of another world, like a solid ocean bottom from which the restless waves of the ordinary world have drawn back; and in the image of this world there is neither measure nor precision, neither purpose nor cause: good and evil simply fall away, without any pretense of superiority, and in place of all these relations enters a secret rising and ebbing of our being with that of things and other people.

It is in this condition that the image of each object becomes not a practical goal, but a wordless experience; and the descriptions quoted earlier of the symbolic face of things and their awakening in the stillness of the image belong without a doubt in this context. It is uncommonly interesting to find the fleeting traces of this experience revealed on the territory of film, which, in the most ordinary sense, is still such a realm of speculation. It would be a mistake to want to see in the suddenly glimpsed physiognomy of things simply the surprise induced by the isolated optical experience; this is only a means, for there too it is a matter of exploding the normal totality of experience. And this is a basic capacity of every form of art.

6

This observation, apparently far from our subject, touches on a dangerous field of what are today widely disseminated false doctrines. The experimental field of contemporary efforts—in dance, on the stage, in nonrepresentational painting, sculpture, and poetry, through intuitive contemplation, education of the senses, religious renaissance, and the like—is directed at freeing the human spirit from reason [Verstand] and placing it once again in immediate relationship to creation. Today these efforts seem to express a yearning that first became important in connection with the related efforts of Expressionism. But if one looks a few decades further back, one sees that this critique of "reason" in the name of liberating the "soul" was already present at that time; even then it wanted to help "soul" achieve more immediate expression than the empty term, caught in a conceptual tangle, allowed, and led the human spirit to freedom by all the side roads, just not by the main one. The real seeds of this striving for emancipation were already present in Impressionism, at least in its literary manifestations, and had been planted by the influence of German Romanticism, Emerson, and the mystical eclectic Maeterlinck. Even the religious renaissance, the highpoint of which is probably past today, was underway at that time. Admittedly, it was a reaction against the increasing mechanization of existence, the crisis of a Midas existence in which everything became, if not money, at least reinforced concrete. But the unrecognized underlying sense was nothing more than one of those constantly recurring attempts to seek a closer approximation to the "other condition," which, in its various forms, as church, art, ethics, or eroticism, breaks into our existence with tremendous power, but has become completely confused and corrupt.

The decisive error, however, was committed—and is still committed today—in imagining that what needs to be repressed is "thinking"; this has remained a lively prejudice right up to the present, above all in the world of art. It is an oblique angle of attack that does not aim at the center of the problem. A great deal depends upon defining these oppositions correctly, and since these difficulties are still entwined in the intellectual discussions of our day, I might take the liberty of discussing them.

Above all, we must remember that not only our intellect [*Verstand*] but also our senses are "intellectual." It is common knowledge that we see what we know: ciphers, signs, abbreviations, summaries, the principal attributes of a concept: imbued and sustained merely by isolated dominant sensory impressions and a vague outline of the rest. Something similar happens with hearing; if our comprehension is not just ahead of the sound, as the prompter anticipates the actor, it is difficult for us to get the sense: for instance, in a language in which we are not too comfortable even when we know the individual words. Even in movements we perceive general characteristics, but we grasp what is atypical so poorly that, for example, nothing requires more effort than describing a gesture so that someone else can picture it. Even smells and tastes, if they are not very penetrating, can be distinguished only poorly without the help of something specific with which to compare them. And the same is even truer for actual emotional [*seelische*] experiences, of which one may say without exception that the form they assume in different people is that of the picture these people had already formed beforehand. This goes so far that without preformed stable representations—and these are concepts—really only a chaos remains; and since on the other hand concepts are dependent on experience, there arises a condition of mutual formation, like that between a fluid and an elastic container, an equilibrium without firm support for which we have still not found any adequate description, so that it is fundamentally as mysterious as the surface of a swamp.

We find ourselves, then, in a divided situation. It is not thinking but, rather, simply the need for practical orientation that drives us to general formulations, to formulas for concepts no more than to formulas for our gestures and sense impressions, which fall asleep after a few repetitions just as do the representational processes that are tied to words. But then hostility should not be directed against thinking, as almost always happens in such contexts, but must seek to free itself from the individual's practical, factual, normal condition. But if this does occur, nothing remains but the dark realm of the "other condition," in which everything provisionally ceases. This is the true and apparently unavoidable antithesis.

One should note in this connection that all attempts to find a way out of this antithesis, as they were stated above, are defined negatively: purpose*less* movement is the essence of dance, *non*representational seeing that of revolutionary painting; the positive assertion, the active determinant of essence, is missing, or idle studio chatter. This refers us back still further to the concept of purpose*less* beauty and art in general: apparently a world in itself, the world of beauty is nonetheless incomplete, marked off, and secretly negative. What is most likely to deceive us about this is the soul system of music, with its formal pseudototality, and in fact music was always (this has not always been admitted, but is constantly demonstrable) the model for the "free" experiments in the other arts. There is in music an apparently complete world independent of the intellect, a pure sensing and feeling, and without doubt the other arts also display this heightened perceptiveness and responsiveness, which seem to run their course in a space in the soul that is heremetically sealed and walled off from the ordinary. Nonetheless, art as form is probably a special limiting and grouping of the contents of ordinary life; art enriches life, but remains within its compass. Intermediate shades, oscillations, modulations, gradations of light, spatial relationships, axes of rotation; in literature the irrational simultaneous effect of words that illuminate each other: as in an old painting, when it is varnished, events emerge that had been invisible, so these things escape the dull, confining picture and the formulaic nature of existence. But if one thinks of the brush of a painter who sees in the world nothing but subjects, or of a poet from whose chalice of words all ideas that had been firmly knotted together by concepts spill forth in a disorderly way, or of the musician for whom the slightest clinker is a metaphysical convulsion: then one quickly comes to the limit on the other side. All of these hypersensitive types leave the impression of debilitated drug addicts or old drunks, who have nothing to hang on to when they are sober. In this way art frees itself from the formulaic limitation of sensation and concept, but this condition cannot be "stretched" to totality. As little as mystical experience can without the rational scaffolding of a religious dogmatism, or music without the scaffolding of teaching.

Thus is condemned the essence of all-too-optimistic attempts at "liberation."

7

Now it is true that the possibility of expressing ourselves is already conditioned beforehand by the thoughts and feelings we want to express, and precisely this allows us some hope that film will contribute to a new culture of the senses. Even in everyday life we learn from every experience that touches us that the expression of existence generates that which takes on its form, whether it is the way a movie hero flings back his scarf, thereby revealing to the street urchin the meaning of soul, or the amorous word that arouses love. That clothes make the man is a maxim down to the most elementary level. Were one, nonetheless, to take this proposition literally, in the much-used sense that one becomes a fundamentally different person by dancing, filming, or doing anything artistic and "expressive" than one is through the medium of printer's ink, it would lead to a fantastic unreality, and completely contradict our experience of never being able to express ourselves entirely, whether in feelings or in words. One does not become different. In each of these "cultures" by which we are so richly blessed, certain components of our normal total experience take the lead with all the resultant consequences, which are in part very refreshing and fulfilling; but nothing happens beyond this. Where more is demanded there immediately arises what can only be called the motoric phrase, eurhythmic babble.

Film, of course, is subject to this danger as well. The pretentious quality of formulaic gestures constitutes the greater part of kitsch in film, just as it constitutes a higher form of kitsch in dance. What is unbearable in film and dance (and, moreover, mutatis mutandis, to a degree in music as well) begins where anger becomes rolling of the eyes, virtue is beauty, and the entire soul is a paved avenue of familiar allegories. If one looks more closely, one discovers that this rarely appears in film, where it is a question of the immediacy of experience; on the other hand, it almost always appears where there is an effort to link these individual experiences together and work out the relations among them. When we look at a film, it unfolds the whole infinity and inexpressibility possessed by everything that exists— placed under glass, as it were, by the fact that one only *sees* it (there are exemplary instances of this in Balázs). In making connections and working out relations among impressions, on the other hand, film is apparently chained more strongly than any other art to the cheapest rationality and platitude. It appears to make the soul more immediately visible, and thoughts into experience; but in truth the interpretation of each individual gesture is dependent on the wealth of interpretive resources that the spectator brings with him; the comprehensibility of the action increases, the more undifferentiated it is (just as it does in the theater, where this is taken to be especially dramatic). Thus the expressive power increases with the poverty of expression, and the typicality of film is nothing but a coarse indicator of the stereotypical quality of everyday life. Because of that, it seems to me, film will always in certain regards be on a lower level than (and at a fixed distance below) the literature of the same period, and film realizes its destiny not as a deliverance from literature, but as sharing its destiny.

8

By literature I do not mean simply the specific sum total of images that, as the critics maintain, have formal laws different from music or painting, while the aestheticians struggle to demonstrate that they are fundamentally the same. I refer rather to the spiritual endowment, the level of soul of people of our time, that content of life mentioned previously, the staging and productive limitation of which is the significance of the various forms of art. In the legitimate attempt to study the distinctive qualities of the various arts, what they have in common is often overlooked, or else reduced to a general and practically empty concept, such as that of "aesthetic response." The different arts, however, must in some way have deep roots in common with each other (and even with ordinary speech), since they are nothing more than various forms of expression by the same people; they must therefore also somehow be translatable into one another, and replaceable by each other. Of course a picture cannot be described completely, any more than a poem can be reproduced in prose; indeed one may regard it as precisely the distinguishing characteristic for the autonomy of an art form that is, to use Balázs's words, "an irreplaceable possibility of expression"; or one may use this incommensurability as the criterion for the choice of an expressive medium, as I have attempted to do in studies not yet published.

But even when an art is as turned in on itself as music is, full of objectless form, abnormally heightened feeling, and inexpressible meaning: at some point one asks oneself what it all adds up to, sets it in relation to the whole person, orders it for oneself in some way or other. And the opposition to literature as an art corrupted by intellect, so frequently harped upon, disappears if one analyzes this "some way or other," for the process in literature follows very much the same course. There are beautiful poems that few people understand at first glance; on the contrary, at first one understands nothing at all aside from details; only later does the sense "begin to dawn," as that very nice expression has it: at the moment of comprehension there is a mixing together of meaning, perceived sensuous form, and emotional excitement; afterward, the experience is in part conceptually assimilated and fixed, and in part leaves behind a vague, usually unconscious deposit, which in some later situation in life can suddenly revive. Even on a page of prose really deserving of the name, one can recognize that a general excitement is communicated *before* the meaning.

Sensuousness and meaning have, then, in literature simply a different relative importance; one can say that in literature the sensuous form merely colors and heightens the meaning, which is communicated in the main by conceptual representations, and that this at least is the opposite in the other arts. But the more time one lets pass before comparing the effects, the more this distinction disappears, and it seems to me that it is impossible to select any particular moment as the legitimate one for making the comparison, including the popular moment of the immediate experience itself. One could almost make a better claim for the period of the aftereffect. For the distinction between a trained musician, for example, and a musically uneducated person may also be enormous in the moment when they hear the same music. (Incidentally: it is an intellectual, that is to say heightened, awareness, while the emotional excitement, insofar as we have any standards for it at all, need demonstrate no distinctions.) Similarly, the surface of a canvas has many more relations for the trained than the untrained eye. But one should not overlook that the bad artist, the dilettante, or the sentimental spectator can have, in many cases, an experience that is sensitively articulated and emotionally quite powerful. It is downright funny how *much* such people experience, and it probably amounts to the same thing that, in periods of decline, art—like every other function—is apparently practiced and judged with extraordinary subtlety, ramification, and connoisseurship. Nietzsche summarized this quite nicely in the formula: the detail darkens the whole and increases at its expense. That is historically valid for everything from letter writing to the conduct of war, and from lyric poetry to coitus and gastronomy. It encumbers every attempt to define the value of the work of art aesthetically, in itself, formally, in the experience of the moment. One should also not lend credence to the frequently heard opinion that the conceptual, the intellectual, is art's late fall from grace, while formal and sensuous art is art's original state of paradise. On the contrary, the formal is relatively late, and all naive art, like that of children and savages, has a notable tendency toward the portrayal of what is known and thought rather than what is perceived: it aims for "the totality." But however that may be, in a process of being transported outside oneself such as experiencing art represents, the point of contact with the normal condition, and the transition back into it, deserve at least as much attention as the experience itself.

9

This point of view, of course, constitutes the most extreme contrast to treating the aesthetic process as an immediate experience, and certainly can not claim anything more than advancing another point of view. In contrast, one can go even further, and assert that every work of art offers not merely an immediate experience but an experience that can never be completely repeated, that cannot be fixed but is individual, even anarchic. It takes its uniqueness and momentary quality from everything I have said so far: it has no tendency at all to become ordinary experience [*Erfahrung*], but extends itself rather in another dimension. The person dancing or listening, who yields himself to the moment of the music, the viewer, the person transported, is liberated from everything before and after; he finds himself in a different relationship to his experience. He does not take it into himself, but rather loses himself in it, and precisely this other attitude is often referred to, with special emphasis, as "experiencing" [*erleben*].

I will now attempt to conclude from both directions.

We may take as a point of departure the average, ordinary condition that is regarded as orderly, whose most important characteristics include the fact that we acquire experiences. I have already said that between the experience that one has and the concepts with whose help one has it there exists a peculiarly labile relationship; each new experience escapes the formula of previous experiences, and is at the same time formed in their image. This is as valid for ethics as it is for physics or psychology. What we call our spiritual and intellectual being finds itself continuously in this process of expansion and contraction. In it art has the task of ceaselessly reforming and renewing the image of the world and of our behavior in it, in that through art's unique experiences [*Erlebnisse*] it breaks out of the rigid formulas of ordinary experience [*Erfahrung*]. Music does this more subtly, literature most aggressively and directly because it works without mediation with the material of formulation itself. Even if art in general requires a condition in which we have less abstract experience than concrete experience, the task of this concrete experience is, in this context, still only that of a source of energy, whose content flows away from it.

The complaints about the intellectualizing of art, which are directed primarily against literature, are justified insofar as among all the arts literature stands closest to thinking, and abstract thought is in its very essence a formulaic abbreviation. Every concept signifies this, and the more general the concepts, the emptier they are of any specific content. This is the emptying of life by thought at which these complaints are directed. It appears, however, that this emptying concerns not only thinking, but also feeling as well, and one can, completely analogously, characterize kitsch as well as moral narrow-mindedness as formulaic abbreviations of the feelings. This tendency toward rigid formulas is the enemy of the saint as well as the artist, of the scholar as well as the legislator, and they should not devalue each other but rather unite in their efforts.

But this opposition of the individual experience to the formula of its group does not by any means dispose of that other dimension belonging to the experience in itself, without any desire to become part of the larger structure of experience as a purely objective condition. The distinction between experience with concepts and experience without (traces of feeling, habit, imitation) is no longer in play here, since both are, after all, experience. It is rather a matter, as was explained above, of a different relationship of the experiencer to the experience, which does not need to change its content but contains in a certain sense an indicator, a vector, another direction. Now it is certainly not necessary to describe expressly how this neutral attitude, for so one can call it, is distinguished from that other attitude that has a continuation outside itself; but if in the search for expression another dimension is ascribed to it, it seems more correct to say that it is really without dimension. For, strictly speaking, no purely neutral state has any connection with other states; but if a neutral state should establish such a connection, it assimilates itself to consciousness or allies itself with the remainder of the self; it loses, in a word, precisely the quality that matters.

This is, of course, only an abstract fiction, but practically speaking it corresponds to the fact that we use the experiences of such heightened states as pleasure, recreation, relaxation, and retreat, to sum them up in a word, merely as interruptions. How remarkable it is that we nonetheless have the tendency to value these experiences as fragments of a different totality, as elements of a way of experiencing that reaches into a different dimension from ordinary experience, and that gives these elements a different direction; for this is assumed by all attempts to posit a different inwardness as attainable, a world without words, an unconceptualized culture and soul. This is an analogy that leads one to think that even in ethics there is a hostile distinction between creative sources and their acculturation to moral norms (for example, the criminal as a good person in literature after Dostoevsky). There has always also been a similar opposition between religious experience and orthodox belief. There is, in fact, insofar as I am able to achieve an overview, only one condition that is able to satisfy these sublime demands and the consequences that can be derived from them: this is that "other condition," beyond that "border between two worlds" of which I have spoken.

Whoever has concerned himself with these phenomena knows that the term "ordinary experience" is foreign to them. If, as seems appropriate here, one sets aside any sort of mystical interpretation, one will hardly be able to claim that ordinary experience is not in any way involved, for this would contradict our understanding of physiological processes. On the other hand, one can surely say that in this "other condition" ordinary experience is felt to be essentially alien and hostile; causal, goal-oriented connections do not build up this condition, but destroy it. (Example: the most fleeting profane thought instantly destroys contemplation.) At the same time, this condition is characterized by a unique excitement about life. The ordinary affect or the ordinary actuality of experiencing such unique states seems peripheral to them, not reaching to their depths. The feelings do not point to things outside the self, but rather signify inner conditions: the world is not experienced as a field of objective relations, but rather as a consequence of self-oriented experiences. The vector, the pointer I spoke of earlier, has inverted itself and is directed inward.

To have some notion of this one does not even need to study the literature of mysticism, for almost every person has experienced this at some time as "the rapture of love" (as opposed to the "love flame" of desire), even if he looks back on this later as a passing anomaly. If one takes art as a comparison, one must characterize profound artistic excitement in much the same way. As soon as an object steps out of the sphere of mundane observation and into that of the creative attitude, it changes itself without changing; nor can one apparently say either that the object changes feeling, but rather feeling changes the object. One can see this distinction especially clearly in artistic genres that unite both attitudes, for example, the novel.*

Thus the second extreme of a possible view of art points in the direction of the "other" condition, and it contains the valuation of this condition as pure actuality and excitement, as a component that reaches beyond the improvisations of the senses and feelings. This condition is never of long duration except in pathological form; it is a hypothetical borderline case, which one approaches only to fall back repeatedly into the normal condition, and precisely this distinguishes art from mysticism, that art never entirely loses its connection with the ordinary attitude. It seems, then, like a dependent condition, like a bridge arching away from solid ground as if it possessed a corresponding pier in the realm of the imaginary.

Woman Yesterday and Tomorrow
1929

Dedicated to Franz Blei

This is a playful analysis of the changes that have shaped the lives and roles of women in European society since the late nineteenth century. A brilliant analysis of society, social change, and fashion, this piece is also a satire on the male imagination.

What we call the new woman is a rather intricate being; she consists at the very least of a new woman, a new man, a new child, and a new society. I

---

* For these reasons it does not seem to me out of the question to look for a psychological explanation of what is described here as the "other condition." The way of experiencing what was previously reserved for mysticism as normal naturally only concealed what was to be understood. And if this were done, then the concept of intuition, which has been so misused in writings on art (and which has simply been avoided here, although it was always hiding in the wings), would be brought out of the shadows.

must confess that I ought to have thought of this before I took on the task of writing about her; it is, moreover, not even entirely certain that there really is a new woman, or whether she only considers herself one for the moment.

So I will only be able to touch on a few selected questions that particularly interest me, and among these the one that has interested me longest is the problem of the old-fashioned woman: more specifically, the woman most recently outdated among those of us living today. The old-fashioned woman was, as far as one important question is concerned, more consistent than the modern woman: she was covered from her neck to the soles of her feet, while the new woman is partly naked. If you ask a sixty-year-old man to recall his youth, he will tell you that today's woman can neither dress nor undress; and there is a truth in this about which we should not let ourselves be deceived by the depictions of old fashions, in which the women look so incomprehensibly ridiculous that the present time seems to us, if one may say so, a miracle of modernity. These are creations from which the life has fled; they are time-lapse snapshots of love in which the form as such startles us, as always happens when it is no longer bathed in the flow of feelings. If, however, we free ourselves from contemporary prejudices without transporting ourselves back into the past, and regard these clothes and hats somewhat as we have learned to regard baroque statues, we may still not be able to discover any refined taste in them, but might yet find an uncommon dynamism. Precisely in their historical desiccation these folded, puffed, frilled, and layered masses of clothes have the effect of being what they are: an uncannily artificial enlargement of the erotic surface. The work of art that nature produces in bringing forth animal and human forms and the enticements of love through the folding in or out of a leaf of skin is here exaggerated in a somewhat tasteless but effective way. The dress of the old-fashioned woman, like her morality, had the task of capturing and dispersing the urgent desire of the male. It distributed the simple beam of this desire over a great surface (and morally over a hundred difficulties), as land is irrigated for miles around by a single stream. And, according to the law that gives desire and will a special place among human powers (since obstacles increase rather than diminish them), this dress multiplied desire to an absolutely ridiculous degree, so that acts of undressing that don't strike us at all were for earlier people shattering adventures. But one should recall, and not only just to laugh at them, the charming love stories of Stendhal's Renaissance novellas: their torchlike glow also arises from the extraordinary difficulties that rarely (and then only furtively) permitted the lovers to embrace at night, in mortal danger. These are intensifications that today we are in the process of losing permanently, even if they have lately only been present in the form of an almost senseless rigidity.

I would like to recount an example of this senselessness for which I am

indebted to a man who suffered from groundless emotional troubles connected with the history of his youth. He had spent this youth, the period on
the borderline between boyhood and adolescence, in a boys' boarding school,
and he mistrustfully portrayed the way in which he and his comrades—it
must have been toward the end of the 1890s—imagined "woman." An old
library of stories, some kind of "treasury of world literature," was the
source from which they drank, and all the women appearing there were
beautiful, had thin waists, tiny hands and feet, and very long hair. In character they were part proud, part gentle, part gay, and part melancholy, but
above all feminine and, at the end of the story, as sweet and soft as baked
apples. They formed the expectations of these young men, who had not yet
had an opportunity to look into life for themselves, and something extraordinary came to light. On the man's side, what went with such women was a
mustache, which was to be pressed against her lips, and this mustache was,
according to the prescription of nature, something these young males could,
after all, soon look forward to; in this way they came to wish for it as an
anticipatory desire, as I believe it is called today. And since, according to
these stories, the mustache had to be blond or black, and soft and long, the
man who told me this story wished for a mustache one sweep of which was
blond while the other, out of prudence, was black. From one time to the
next this mustache also grew longer; at first it was only as long as the mustache of a hero whose description he had read in one of the stories, but when
a rival of equal rank from a second story appeared, it became as long as both
mustaches together, and finally as long as the sum of all existing mustaches,
even a little longer. At this point, through a happy insight, the boy was
fortunate enough to recognize that such a mustache was something one
could no longer wish for at all, and later the memory shocked him that he
could have unwittingly stumbled into such an extraordinary degeneration of
the imagination. Illuminated by this experience, he found that women in-
stilled fear in him; the tininess of their feet, hands, and mouths, and the
smallness of their waists were (with the strong emphasis on all those parts
that physiology characterizes as cushions of fat) fantasies in which there lay
a tendency toward an unbounded diminution that emptied the heart. The
waist could now no longer be small enough, the ideal mouth had the size
and roundness of the head of a pin, and the tiny hands and feet sat with the
impotence of little butterflies on the luxuriant chalice of the body.

There was no doubt a kernel of madness in this ideal, and anyone who
knows a little about psychology will perhaps be reminded of the insatiable
striving for security which is, according to the Adlerian school, one of the
signs of the neurotic. But this form of madness can hardly be regarded as an
illness, for this kind of senseless growth appears in all human activity when-

ever it leaves its natural base, where it arose along with a number of other, contrary, interests; it is a development in the direction of excess without abundance. Thus mysticism transforms itself into ascetic torment, intellectual superiority into a chess game, and joy in the body or in combat is twisted into the slavery of sports records. From the moment the grotesque shadow of this one-dimensional attitude fell upon love as well, no other conclusion can be drawn than that the ideal form that had up till then had meaning was already dissolving.

Since then, enough has been written about the new woman for us to be able to describe the transition in a few words. The concept of love that had been valid through the centuries, down to the time of the parents and grandparents of the two generations living today, was that of the knight who seeks and finds his lady, although in the course of time the hard trials he had to pass for her sake shifted steadily into the domain of bad novels, and, besides, the original Christian-chivalric ideal had distributed itself in such a way that the chivalric attainments fell to the man and the Christian ones to the woman. This concept of love, which hardly ever existed in real life, although life continued to follow it, is presumably now over. With it disappears the limitation of the age of love for women to the brief span between their seventeenth and thirty-fourth years, which is today already almost incomprehensible. This limitation goes back to an ambitious and exaggerated concept of love radiant with the suggestion that it could only be satisfied by life in full bloom. Significantly, the social position of woman went through a similar process of becoming hollowed out, and consequently exaggerated. One must bear in mind that originally the household's circle of activity was sufficiently great and varied to require a whole person; but in the course of time only petty chores were left, which, however, were always connected with the concept of the housewife as manager that had long since grown too big for them. In this way, finally, a somewhat ridiculous little housewife who gossiped vacuously about her chores grew out of the powerful ally of the man. Inevitably bound up with this destiny was a similar fate in relation to the children. The problematic question of the child, or the generation problem, as it is called today, probably does not lie where we ordinarily look for it, in the way children today mature early, and the related early need for independence, or in some sort of wave motion of culture that pits parents and children against each other: it probably lies instead quite simply in the fact that today the most that is bequeathed is money and property, whereas earlier it was almost all aspects of life. We could almost say that the problem of generations is closely connected with the transition from a family house, which outlived the generations, represented status and wealth, and left its stamp on those who lived in it, to the nomad's rented apartment in big cities.

But this development also undermined the motherhood which had given woman dignity, as well as compensation for the early sacrifice of her youthfulness. Now she lacked the supporting framework, so that only the purely spiritual claim to authority remained. But even if this claim were realized in the most spiritual way possible, the unhurried and self-evident quality of the nonspiritual, material world is not part of it, and disappointments in the relationships between parents and children have become unavoidable because this relationship is much too overburdened with feelings. Limiting the number of children leads in the same direction, overburdening with moral claims relationships between spouses and between parents and children that have lost in outward spaciousness. On the other hand, the decline in fertility is a direct result of the changed economic and living conditions themselves, so that one sees from this example quite clearly how the impulses for development come together from quite different sources. This interpretation implies many other consequences: the untenable legal position of women, women's work, the influence that the needs of the former lower orders have today on customs and manners, the general striving for more flexible moral concepts, the turning away from individualism, and finally again "love" itself, which after its high points in the eighteenth century and Romanticism has fallen into the hands of mindless scribblers of novels and dramas. This wide-ranging interrelationship of so many details guarantees that the changes that have taken place in the meantime are not merely an oscillation, but represent a permanent departure from what had been before; but in the midst of such confusion to try to predict where they will lead would demand the zeal of a prophet.

We are all more or less familiar with the flood of publications, the speeches, the establishing of parties, and the individual actions out of which, in the course of a lifetime, what we call the new woman, or the new status of woman, has emerged. But what is most striking is that it actually came about quite differently. It was the War that liberated the mass of women from their deference to masculine ideals, and thus from the ideal of woman as well. The decisive battle was in the last analysis fought not by the pioneers of emancipation but by the tailors. Nor did woman liberate herself by taking over the man's fields of activity, as it had earlier appeared; her decisive acts were to seize hold of his pleasures and take off her clothes. Only in this phase did the new woman step out of the special status of literature and the separatism of social reform, and quickly become reality in the eyes of the people; a course of revolution that warns us to be a bit cautious.

If we consider the situation as it stands at the moment, with this caution and that eternal empathy claimed by a person who fears a tiny mouse but must nevertheless bring down the world, we might roughly say the follow-ing: Woman is tired of being the ideal of the man who no longer has suffi-cient energy to idealize, and she has taken over the task of thinking herself through as her own ideal image. The panting adulation of older men even seems funny to her, and therein lies a great purification of the atmosphere. She no longer wants to be an ideal at all but to create ideals, to contribute to their formation just as men do, even if, at the moment, with no particular success. She is still somewhat girlishly uncertain in her new activity; she stays in school, on the average, only halfway through the *Gymnasium* or the university, and populates the unregulated professions. Currently she has taken up the boyish instincts of men, is boyishly thin, comradely, sportively hard, and childlike. In front of the countless dressed-up people who sit in a theater, walk past store windows, or look at newspapers, she strips stark naked; but in front of the few people she meets swimming she still puts on a little something, whose extent has lately even been increasing again. These are violations of consistency, but they won't make any difference.

Of more importance, the relationship to children is currently limited, in the main, to preventing them: the new woman has come into being some-what more quickly than the new mother. But it seems that the extremely charming sobriety that has always been characteristic of woman when she acted naturally and not according to male fantasies (for delicate beings are often a little detached in order to protect themselves, and leave tilting at windmills to those who have been provided with bigger bones) will also ex-press itself in a reasonable form of child rearing with which the children will be quite happy. This sense of reality on the part of a category of human being who for centuries was condemned to play the ideal of another is today perhaps the most important aspect of this question. I am not on the side of those who complain about the matter-of-factness of young women. The hu-man body cannot in the long run experience itself only as the receiver of sense stimuli; it always turns to becoming the portrayer, the actor of itself in all the relationships it enters. Thus, its natural drive always combines with a specific system of ideas and feelings, and through the centuries this ideologizing is like a fountain that rises and falls. Today it is close to its deep-est point, almost swallowed up; but it will doubtless rise again in a new combination. Countless and quite different possibilities are available, and the future really conceals them only like a veil, and not like a city wall fortified with prejudices.

Ruminations of a Slow-witted Mind
1933

As the Nazis seized power in Germany, intellectual conscience and collectivity replaced "serious writer" and "society" in Musil's immediate response to the situation. It is striking that Musil intended this essay for publication in the leading intellectual journal in Germany, Die neue Rundschau, of which he had once been an editor. (Political events quickly made publication unthinkable.) His years of close observation of politics, culture, and society furnish an original and striking picture of this political, cultural, and social cataclysm. These are heavily corrected drafts.

The orientation and leadership of the revolutionary "renewal of the German mind," whose witnesses and participants we are, point in two directions. One, after seizing power, would like to talk the mind into helping out with internal development and promises it a golden age if it joins up; indeed it even offers it the prospect of a certain voice in decision making. The other direction, on the contrary, attests its mistrust of the intellect by declaring that the revolutionary process will continue indefinitely, and (especially in the short run) has room for the mind in its task; or it might also assure the intellect that it is not needed at all because a new mind has already turned up, and that the old one might as well jump into the fire and either burn to ashes or purify itself into its elements. What has happened up to the moment these words are being written leaves no doubt that the second direction is on the march, the first its musical accompaniment. Nor can it be otherwise than that a Movement that has manifested itself so powerfully [National Socialism—ed.] demands above all that the intellect completely assimilate and subordinate itself to the Movement. But then again, it is possible that the intellect cannot do this without renouncing itself. Surely there must be some sort of boundary here, since nothing happens that is not contingent; so it is a good test for the intellect that today it has everywhere been saddled with a kind of kangaroo-court mentality that judges it not according to its own laws, but according to the law of the Movement.

With an unparalleled sense of sacrifice Germany has, within a period of a few weeks, renounced researchers and scholars not a few of whom are, by all the values that have guided intellectual life for centuries, irreplaceable, and no discussion of these conditions of vital importance can pass over what has happened with indifference. There are no two ways about it: either one says that the German Jews have an honorable role in German intellectual life, or one must say that this intellectual life is from the bottom up so corrupt that there is no longer any room for judgment in it. For if those among us who have ourselves long been participants in this intellectual life examine our own experience, it shows us that in the mind's struggle with mindlessness there have been people of every descent in comparable numbers on both sides, and there is no way we can suddenly revoke our experience. What has happened seems to us unjust, but even if we wanted to ascribe justice to it, the way justice is being used would still appear to us uncivilized, in a manner that unfortunately coincides most exactly with an offense against a morality that has today been pushed aside, the morality of the humane.

Humaneness these days is a value that casts suspicion on whoever possesses it, just like internationalism, freedom, and objectivity. Indeed, whoever defends one of these ideas is suspected of harboring the others, because he shows he has not understood the indivisibility of the transformation that has occurred. This transformation sets one totality in place of another, and as it has furnished the final argument against every single objection, it is also the essence of what is called, lumping everything together, the "corrupt system." Such an argument may not be correct, it may lead to all sorts of consequences, it is not even logical in its form, but none of this bothers it because it feels itself to be a "transvaluation of all values."

And this feeling is no conceit. Darkly but visibly it contains something that might roughly be expressed thus: that the whole is lord of the parts, that it not only precedes them but somehow leads the way, that it is not merely their master but also what completes their meaning. That was always a biological view, and for many kinds of reasons this notion, that every whole is more than a sum of its parts, or of some analogously indifferent collectivity, indeed, that the world builds itself as much from whole entities as from details, has found a broad area of application in the philosophy of our time. But in political events this emerging but far from completed awareness had come about because of the inability of democracy at difficult moments to impose, either in reality or suggestively, the ring of wholeness around the struggle, which has become incalculable, of each against the other. This incapacity, to be sure, has not yet been generally demonstrated, since the stronger democracies still stand; nonetheless it is collectivism, the anti-individualistic and anti-atomistic disposition of the totality, that has today, in various forms and strength, spread over half the world. That is also the real agenda of this German movement, which does everything in its power to avoid having its new nationalism understood as a reaction on the model of its older relatives.

One can perform the experiment of trying to imagine National Socialism politically replaced by something else. A feeling independent of desires and fears, that indeed will often run counter to them, that nevertheless as a rule responds that such a change, returning to the *status quo ante* of some still earlier condition, can no longer be achieved. The only explanation for this feeling is doubtless that National Socialism is having its mission and its hour, that it is not just a drumroll but a stage of history. In our time a great many people who earlier thought differently have engaged in such an experiment in thinking. But there is also something else to consider: has not, morally speaking, something quite remarkable happened in the last few weeks? The basic rights of the morally responsible person, freedom of speech and expression, the entire edifice of inalienable convictions: millions who were accustomed to believe passionately in these things saw them abolished at a stroke, without lifting a finger for them! They had sworn to lay down their lives for their principles, and they hardly lifted a finger! They felt their minds being plundered, but realized suddenly that their bodies were more important.

During the days this was going on, Germany offered a picture half of storming conquerors, half of a people bewildered. One could even speak with confidence of cowards, for the problem is precisely that earlier, during the War, a large number of these cowards had disregarded every danger in order to appear as heroes; from which one can conclude that the shrines that they now seemed to be losing were no longer sacred, and also that contemporary man is less independent than he thinks, and acquires solidity only in groups. Both conclusions are germane to National Socialism. But no false mythology is permissible here: it was not "yesterday" that capitulated in such a cowardly fashion and has now been done away with, but people who go on living and who now set the same task for the new spirit that the old one failed to master.

Reservations of a Slow-witted Mind

If today a man of intellect ("man of intellect" is intended to characterize profession and habits, as one says "man of the cloth" along with "clergyman") observes the revolutionary renewal of German culture in which he is both witness and participant, he can, supported by an entirely natural need for self-preservation, distinguish two directions in this Movement and its leadership. One, after seizing power, would like to win over the intellect to help with internal development, promising not only a Golden Age if it joins up, but also the prospect of certain participatory privileges. These pacify the man of intellect and win him over. The other direction intimidates and frightens him, for it declares that the revolutionary process will go on forever, that for the time being even the man of intellect will be included in its task, indeed that along with the new politics a new mind is already present and the old one has nothing left to do but throw itself into the fire in order to burn to ashes or be purified into its elements.

Both aspirations really seem to be present in the process of social transformation, even though neither they nor their effect can be clearly separated from each other. One part of those who until yesterday bore the burdens and carried the dignity of the intellect now finds itself beyond the pale. The majority in the country has obviously had its breath taken away by events, but already here and there the voices of new converts are beginning to be heard, bearing witness in more or less happy tones to how good it is to find the bandwagon, even at the last minute. I am here speaking especially of the arts, but the same effect of surprise that is so remarkably connected with this revolution can also be glimpsed in other realms of the mind, even if it expresses itself differently.

But the men of intellect have had no opportunity—or they have not taken advantage of it—to become acquainted in time with the new spirit, and this has created difficulties on both sides, especially theirs. They are reproached with having slept while others were waking up. This they could not understand, for sleepiness and inattention were precisely not among the many errors clinging to the period after the War, or the ten years before it. On the contrary, they had been open to the point of excess, quick, flexible, always concerned not to miss even the most trivial thing, and precisely because public life had lost character and depth, it did not easily refuse or reject anything. So one can really only assume that with their eyes wide open the men of intellect saw nothing, and had the bad luck to overlook just those things that the future would reveal to be the most important.

At first glance this phenomenon appears so strange that one should not be surprised at the unusual explanations put forward for it. The most basic is the anti-Semitic. It says straight out that we men of intellect were so corrupted by Jewishness that we no longer heard or saw anything that had not been passed through a Jewish filter. I will take this for granted here—I can't add the problem of the real relationship between these groups to the one I am discussing here—but I ask myself how such a suggestion could have arisen. I count up us men of intellect (leaving aside those to whom I must ascribe artistic and intellectual significance regardless of circumstances, whether I am for or against any particular case), and I find approximately three times as many "Aryans" as "non-Aryans." I pick out those who have been unquestionably overestimated as well as underestimated and find among them members of both camps. As a control, I look at what is merely the writing industry: there I find in the theater a preponderance of Jewish authors, but in the novel I find a lucrative, unconsciously sanctimonious, incredibly pernicious cerebral industry that is almost exclusively in the hands of Aryans.

Accordingly, we Aryans are amply represented on the side of achievement as well as on the side of nonachievement, leaving open the question whether at the point of transition, where an ambitious literary presence combines with a commercial, officious nature, one or the other predominates; it is conceivable that the phenomena of such a transition zone have been excessively generalized. A distribution similar to that among authors is also found among publishers, if one counts together the active ones and those capable of being aroused to action. They have, to be sure, beaten the drum for a lot of inferior work, but almost alone they had the courage and instinct to stand up for everything that was good.

Who, therefore, was doing the filtering? Were the sources from which our culture flowed corrupted? Goethe, Nietzsche, Novalis, Hölderlin, Büchner, Keller, Stifter, Hebbel, d'Annunzio, Flaubert, Stendhal, Balzac, Dickens, Thackeray, Sterne, Swinburne, Verlaine, Baudelaire, Hamsun, Ibsen, Garborg, Jacobsen, Brandes, Dostoevsky, Tolstoy, Gogol: [41] these grandfathers of today withstood much stricter terms of comparison than the one being demanded now! And there remains one last group that could possibly have been the cause of spiritual injury: criticism and journalism, and there sparks fly! Book reviewing left largely to scribblers who scratched each other's backs, or to beginners satisfied with the smallest honorarium; theater criticism in such a state that in a metropolis like Berlin one could address eight-tenths of the critics as ignoramuses; a minuscule sense of responsibility in questions of art; attention lazily attaching itself to the person who involved no risks, or else inclining to the conspicuous and superficially rewarding; the entertainment portion of a kind that is really to be characterized as poisoning the people: who would not be inclined to greet with joy the most ruthless changes in this area? And these workshops of public opinion and this industrialization of the spirit (whose distribution centers are radio and film) really could pave the way for a wholesale reform. But if one wants to intervene successfully as well as give truth its due one must speak the truth, and that involves two corollaries. The first: even though such errors might be most apparent in the great liberal press, they were far worse in the concerns of the provincial papers and party sheets; one might say that there they were bad sedately and quietly, while in the big cities they were carried out raucously. And the second corollary: in the areas of these enterprises dealing with the arts there were men here and there who preserved their independence as well as they could, who had more to give than is usual, and who helped make the hell of public life in some degree habitable for us. If I call up the memory of such men, as I came across them, I have to say that there appear to have been a fair number of Jews among them. I am simply saying this not from theoretical considerations, but from the shared experience of a quarter century of German literature, and I might add that the enthusiasm and aptitude of a personality for a cause are by no means everyday occurrences, and do not simply grow back like branches after one strips a tree to its trunk.

I consider it an obligation of decency to say this, if this is what one has experienced; and yet it could be that I might perhaps be avoiding this obligation, especially at a moment when everything one says is suspected of being partisan, if I were not completely convinced that anti-Semitism is not an accidental part of the [National Socialist] Movement's program but is included in it as the result of a consistency that is related to other things as well, and if I did not fear for the power of this movement of renewal that with anti-Semitism it is rushing at a red cloth instead of the real enemy! I must go still further, and identify myself even more with the intellectual, who today, with his humanistic scruples, already seems to belong to the past, by declaring that the real reason he did not see what was coming was the peculiarly cryptic character of the intellectual underpinnings of this revolution. The French Revolution was preceded by famous writers; it was not the Revolution that made them famous, and active discussion in the aristocracy and the bourgeoisie paved the way for the new ideas. The year 1848 was the essence of intellect for those who wanted the revolution as well as for those who didn't. Even Marxism produced a literature long before the Marxist revolution, which despite its one-sidedness contained much that compelled even grudging respect. On the other hand it would be to misunderstand the sources of energy of this third German revolution [after those of 1848 and 1918—ed.] by looking for its sources in German intellectual life. Its sources are to be found there in part, but they do not manifest themselves as a jet springing powerfully from a stone, but in the first instance as the flowing together of many unobtrusive channels. With the best will in the world one cannot place [Houston Stewart] Chamberlain's *Foundations of the Nineteenth Century* or Langbehn's Rembrandt Germans in revolutionary opposition to their time, or connect them to suppression at the time of their appearance; their time, rather, placed a disproportionately high value on them.

For this reason Germany's fate depends on . . . proper proportion [of] intellect [and] pol[itics]

But does a transvaluation originate suddenly? It's not very probable; historical experience speaks for

5. [sic] Nothing is as remotely dangerous as the false mythologizing of current events. Transvaluation of *all* values, a new age has dawned (or even, as one says, broken camp), a new race has arrived, history has spoken, the spirit is purified, the *Volk* will bring forth, and similar things, are nothing but dangerous mythologizing.

A kind of theory of catastrophe is imputed to events, their sort of having sprung up overnight. Ideas about geologic eras are attributed to the developments of twenty years, the argument no better than this: We know almost nothing about how mammalian fauna and flora succeeded those of the insects, so it looks as if it happened by enchantment and perhaps it really did happen abruptly, therefore everything really great on earth happens by sudden magic. In response to this one can only point out that this time it wasn't like that, because we were looking on.

6. Transvaluations of a weltanschauung arise either through gradual development or relatively quickly under some particular pressure, and usually both are going on simultaneously. One need only ask oneself how one changes one's own views. And those of the collectivity also arise only in the heads of individuals, and not in some mythical collective head; this is apparently the most important fact for every kind of collectivist observation, for up to now no one has succeeded in treating /evaluating/ it correctly.

The analogy between the individual life and that of the collectivity is quite far-reaching. The thinking, feeling, willing of a whole arise out of those of the individual, while general processes and procedures work on his soul which are themselves analogous to /correspond to/ are almost imitations of/ the processes and procedures of the individual soul. Especially the role of ideas is the same in the one case as in the other. Their task is on the one hand to keep the individual and the whole in agreement with reality; this expresses itself in logic as well as in the parameters of research, which represent nothing but the collective perception and its technical working out. On the other hand ideas are connected with the feelings whose representative /mirror image/ they are, but which they also must lead and finally bring together in a powerful unity, which should be congruent externally and internally and yet still be creative. This hasty and summary description suffices to set forth a few problems quite differently from the way they are seen today.

/The effect of the affect is: to exclude what does not fit, attract what does. To shape the formation of ideas firmly and harmoniously. Harmony with what today is called bringing into line, eliminating opposition [*Gleichschaltung*]. / The great collective hypnoses.

Will, finally, as deliberate will (otherwise it is = result of affect): from the various attitudes toward affect through experience and revision

7. What is called the revol[utionary] renewal of the Ger[man] mind is not fact, happening, deed, occurrence, event, but will.

Fact is only the affect and its effect through suggestion.

Fact is will that originates directly from the affect and an ideology "that [this will] has created for itself in haste"—as one could say if it were the case of an individual person; but in politics it is no different. The man of action does not come out of the study; he will always enter the lists in an unprepared, indeed often false, suit of intellectual armor. This is especially true today, when no single person can any longer bring together in himself enough of the knowledge and capabilities of all. It depends on the candor of others, on his own capacity for learning, on how the adventure turns out that every politics, once decided and entered upon, represents. Whoever has will, has struggled and succumbed and triumphed, knows that it always turns out different than one had anticipated. The will of an insane person is never able to adapt, the will of a strong man adapts not only his tactics to his opposition (circumstances), but sometimes even his spirit (target of his operations?). This does not make him paler or make him take on the color of the study, for again it would be a misunderstanding of his function to make a state philosopher out of a statesman. Especially the modern statesman, who must work masterfully with the dangerous means of crudest suggestion [but] must also possess the opposite ability, to sensitively pick up the finer impressions that crowd around him after his victory.

8. In this or similar fashion one must separate, within the will that has assumed power in Germany, the energy of feeling from its intellectual envelope. The driving effect is directed toward power, unity, greatness; it wants to bring meaning and will into German life; it is a bundle of affects, of what one could call on the personal level a character trait, a disposition of character. This affect has appeared in reaction to a quite specific condition, the national impotence since the War, and wants to take its place. Therefore the ideas connected with this condition must necessarily be the first point of attack by the intention to dislodge it: these are the ideas of democracy, internationalism, the progress of objectivity, etc., in other words the European cultural tradition as it attempted (inadequately) to become reality in the German [Weimar—ed.] Republic. Possibly it would be more proper to direct this hatred against the inadequate realization, but psychologically the

ideas themselves are a closer target. But what ideas are being advanced in place of the supplanted ones? They have the most admirable unity, which lends a strong affect to this entire way of thinking, but their intellectual value will be disputed by anyone who has some idea of standards of thinking; not because these ideas were still too new and incomprehensible, but on the contrary because they are a compilation of extremely well known ones. Affect is a compiler.

One is obliged to say this as soon as one reckons with the fact that the future of the Movement and the future of Germany are linked with each other for the unforeseeable future. The core, the racial theory, has been derived not from empirical research (biology) but from observations about life, from moral ideas that had earlier received a polit[ical] stamp. For research, the concept of race is an extraordinarily difficult one, even today not capable of clear definition; for the "renewal" /Movement/, it is dogma and axiom. Added to this is reverence for the "soil" as bringer of culture. Added to it also a romantic relationship to the past, as well as ideas with which Catholicism had once armed the reaction against a liberalism that was then still dangerous. But anti-Catholic convictions are also part of it. Of great importance is the only all-too-natural distaste for the spread of knowledge, which, given the need for immediacy of feeling, is all too insipid; knowledge that has today become unencompassable, and that dissolves or weakens people. This distaste strives everywhere for simplicity. There is much that is healthy in this simplicity, and much that is right in this or that. But until yesterday there was still in every one of these ideas a bit of "intellectualism," that is to say a word, an assertion in that talking back and forth that forms an all-too-dripping atmosphere above the all-too-dry ground of knowledge. And the method that was intended to purify and sum up these elements is roughly this, that one could base a weltanschauung equally well on the inferiority of woman or on the beauty of the stars.

9. It is hard to imagine that someone should, at the moment of success, part from a conception of things to which one owes this success, and which had already attracted to him masses of enthusiastic, like-minded comrades. A politician who is hailed by half of Germany and wants to convert the other half to his worldview is supposed to distinguish between his talent for leadership and his view of the world? Is supposed to realize that the ideas he has unleashed through propaganda are damaging once he has achieved power, and be prepared to recognize a misshapen totality of the German intellect as power? He, who has just cut a mighty swath through this power? He would be more likely to think of the intellect as an arrogant fiction of scribblers, and truly there is much that makes it look that way!

What is "intellect," anyway? It has always been only hazily understood.

The best has often been regarded as stupid, the mediocre quite often as significant. Intellect simply does not have an identity card. Indeed, questions that to all appearances should be quite simple are among the most complicated, such as that a malicious book can be good and a good-natured one bad.

Use analogy to the individual psyche again!

Assertion that everything is pol[itical] is just as false as the opposite, that intellect should get involved in pol[itics]. Truth easily leads to inhumanity: for N[ational] S[ocialism] very important.

Exchange of Roles

Can a renewal of the nation occur without poets, without philosophers, without scholars, without artists? Can a new spirit take shape without its most important parts? For it cannot be passed over in silence that nearly all those who until yesterday bore the dignities and burdens of the spirit look at what is happening today in part with hostility, in part with mistrust, and in part watchfully. The exceptions are not important, especially if one takes into account the enticements and threats that are now besieging the intellect. Is it that they do not understand their time, or that their time does not understand them? On the whole, silence lies over intellectual Germany, while the political (not only) assures that it has renewed the intellect (will have renewed it, but also that it has renewed it enormously already, even before the new edifice of the state has risen above its foundations). Indeed, many intellectuals are on the lookout for a political transformation that could again come to their aid. A remarkable exchange of roles has taken place (and this revolution will truly take its place not only in political but also in intellectual history).

The Dependency of Intellect

Correction:
An idea conquers. One can imagine it so to speak experimentally:

Although they are bound together as one, two intellectual tendencies can be distinguished in the leadership of the Movement: one is conservative, the other revolutionary. The first, after seizing power, would like to talk intellect into participating, the second says to it: If you don't want to yourself, you have abdicated! And if you won't be my brother I'll bash your skull in! In world history there are examples of both. Intellect allows itself to be influenced by politics, indeed it even allows itself to be annihilated and created. There is little point in railing against this; as a matter of fact it would mean not knowing what intellect is; one must know that too if one wants to conduct politics without losses, but intellect is tough and uneducable and manages by underhanded means and incredible detours to come back again to its past:

The burning of the library at Alexandria, the smashing of Greek sculptures, provide the most perfect examples of how one can bring the intellect into harmony with public developments. At its peak the intellect was dependent on institutions such as libraries and schools, and the people who embodied it were dependent on the benevolence and sufferance of the public. A change in the will of the times (summarily stated) sufficed to sweep everything away. A child of the spirit arrived [Christianity—ed.]: not like the father. Remarkably pathological, and with a deep expression on its face. Grown to manhood a thousand years later, this child would have given much to know more about its father.

If we wish to avoid this "remorse of the centuries"—and this goes not only for us who live now, for history is full of similar instances—we have to make halfway clear to ourselves how the mind is dependent on its own laws and how it depends on those of its environment. If one understands how to take into consideration what *doesn't* fit, it would be an excellent comparison to imagine in a similar but more personal way processes in the mind of the public at large, as well as the relationship between mind and corporeality in general. The thinking, feeling, and willing of the nation are constituted collectively by those of individuals, but they also determine these activities in the individual. The relation of the mind to its body: the mind is dependent on feelings and moods which in part never become conscious at all. But it can also influence them. /The tendencies of the mind are dependent on those of the body. (? lazy body, active mind)/ The experiences of the mind, its growth out of experiences, are to a great extent independent.

Up to now I have taken the sense of reality to be the most highly developed sense in the contemporary German. But in a surprising way he is also a romantic.

The division: reason and perception—drives and feelings. In between, acting and knowing, connected with both. This also repeats itself on the large scale.

To be considered is that what I would like to treat as affect is actually already mind, namely sectarian spirit.

When a state is in a revolutionary condition, drives and feelings predominate. We know from the life of individuals of what excesses they are capable. If a totality has a basic mood that is unified and favorable, if inhibitions are weakened, then these drives and feelings proliferate with the same ruthlessness. There are manias, deliriums, obsessions. There are insane communities of healthy elements. Cure: sobering up through pain, and intercepting affects by means of a new ideological statics.

How do revolutions become stable if one looks at them psychologically? The resistances change the program. Quite often the program is sharpened by the resistances. It is always changed. That is, many drives are inhibited, feed others and favored ones. The field pulls itself apart. The same picture on the side of the resistances. In the end state, the character of a construction, or that of a compromise predominates accordingly.

On both sides, toward the end the elemental, gross interests predominate. This means: revolutions always begin by wanting to change human nature, and it is precisely this they change the least.

and we cannot suddenly stop trusting what we have always seen
Politics prescribing the law for the intellect: this is new.

Revaluation	Councillor of appeasement!
Do they happen suddenly?	Moderation!
Must they have a central value?	Intellect!
	People of every descent
	= outdated feeling (Enlightenment philosophy)

One must either say that German Jews have the greatest share in intellectual life or characterize it as corrupt.

Its intellectual source.
Then that one has to understand everything from the perspective of post-[19]14 becomes forming of the will

locate the repressive relationship in a time that overestimates it.

1. The rev[olutionary] influence . . . allows its mov[ement] and lead[ership] to . . . But both directions seem to be united in this, that pol[itics] has the right and the duty to play around with intellect for its own purposes. Also corresponding to this is the effect

+ putting down, getting rid of

2. A[dolf Hitler] fills whomever stays on the sidelines with concern, no, with desperation about Germany's future. It is an error to believe that he is only a source of agitation; he is a major totemic object. We fear for the drive for renewal . . . table . . . enemy—but every attempt to demonstrate this is answered by claiming that we were under the influence of the Jews.

Today one can perhaps only perform the simplest duty and bear witness in the narrowest area:

3. Portrayal. There is an infinite amount to be done. But not simply go on growing.

4. One must also state that the [National Socialist] Movement is not intellectual but mixed in its origin. Highly summarized.

Also that it contains everything. That evil rushes toward it.

It won't do to distinguish between writers of the right and left

5. But with all these questions one comes upon a ticklish relation of the intellectual to the political. The pol[itical] is in this case an intention of will and its realization. Intellect possesses no such identity card. It is a loose summation, a by no means transparent integration (interpenetration) from the highest to the most idiotic. In the pure, unfeeling sci[ences] intellect at least has the criterion of truth, but even there it must swallow rebukes (Russia). In the aesthetic realm, questions that are perfectly clear to the feelings, such as striking worthlessness, are extremely difficult to answer theoretically. I will try to set down on paper some notes on the relation of intellect to events. /The future depends on politics comprehending the intellect/ Today everything is called into question: objectivity, impartiality, autonomy. . . .

6. I was always opposed to activism, that is, to the direct intervention of intellect in politics and active life; and I have been opposed to it out of intellectual activism. From estimating the task and [its] possibility. One thing isn't right for everyone. You do not write with your foot; you do not stand on your hand. My political foresight is quite average. This point of view had not only a portion of the intellectuals against it, but today it has politics as well. The primacy of politics is insisted upon.

7. But how was it then? How did ideas get into politics? By and large, from the intellect. It was the intellect that has the idea of freedom, of hu-

manity . . . it also has the idea of cruelty, of struggle . . . Then politics took them up, changed them, alienated them. That's autonomy.

8. The intellect has strict laws.
If it becomes ambiguous (morbid) it ought to be an unambiguous ambiguity (which I have striven for).
Offense kills.

9. This does not mean overlooking the reverse case of dependency. Precisely today's example.

As conclusion would come the relationship between affect and intellect. The affect that has formed a mind of its own and now comes in contact with the larger one.

1. Exchange of roles

2. Challenge and duty to speak. To exercise criticism. I consider myself by no means the most suitable person. But I have the feeling that it is a duty. Silence, any longer, the source of misunderstandings. And/or: I presume no mandate, but it can only help if I express a few impressions as simply as possible. /Mandate: I was never the spokesman for others, but certain impressions are quite obviously shared./

3. Perhaps one might express the first /most comprehensive/ as a boundless astonishment.

Openly portray our deplorable situation.

I will pass over those who have suddenly noticed that they always wanted something like this: I can imagine that as honorable.

But they bring all the chaos of their diverging viewpoints into the [National Socialist] Movement and the others are more important.

Had we lived at the time of the French Rev[olution], we would have known Rousseau, some of us would have loved him, some would have considered him overestimated. We would already have learned earlier, through Galiani[42] and others, to see what was cooking. We would have come just after the phil[osophical] emancipation. We have lived through the Marxist revolution, its partial success, partial failure. Even those among us who, like myself, have denied the materialistic view of history as one-sided, and therefore wrong, have yet been able to learn from it. But we have little contact with the cultural ideas of 1933, positive or negative. That is the heart of the matter.

4. Have we slept through our time?

There were many errors in the postwar period, but precisely this was not one of them. On the contrary: journalistic adaptability and adroitness in searching out new things. Intellect had perhaps no character, but it was still quite curious.

If I might apply this to myself, the probability that something has been slept through can be excluded with a probability verging on certainty. No, it was with our eyes wide open that we saw nothing!

5. There remains a second assumption: that we were so totally under the thumb of the Jews that we could see nothing.

Today one must treat this idea with respect: give the state what belongs to the state. I will therefore take it to be true that we were under the control of the Jews. In fact it has a central significance. But whatever can that mean?

We were surrounded by a layer of middlemen (newspapers, reviewers, publishers, friends) who filtered things in a Jewish way. Since we ourselves for the most part are not Jews.

Let's look at this a bit more closely:

Publishers: Until now we were of the opinion that there was a limited circle of intellectually stimulating and stimulatable publishers, and if I go over them without naming names (Fischer j [Jewish], Insel a [Aryan], DVA [Deutsche Verlagsanstalt] a, Row[ohlt] 1/2 2 [Ernst and Paul] Cassirer, j j, Diederichs a, Kiepenh[auer] a, G. Müller a, Verlag der Mar. Ges.[43] a, the list contains more Aryans than Jews.

Newspapers: We thought we saw: excrescences of capitalism. The spirit of the taste-makers industry (much as in film). Allied with the Jewish through the mercantile. A devaluation of its onetime association with the liberals. We were not opposed to a reform from top to bottom. But we saw the same thing in the large, purely Aryan business concerns in the provinces, but in a much coarser way. They fed off the middleman industry (matrices for printing, feuilleton correspondents).

Enthusiasm
Province and metropolis

Now in these businesses there were in the field of the arts men who, as much as they could, preserved their independence, made hell habitable, and, if I let their names run through my head, I find a surprising number of Jews among them.

Call it, as far as I'm concerned, the Jewish protest against Jewishness. But even should such an indispensable person have four Jewish grandparents!

6. /Still under the formulations of 5./
I insert the question: from whom did we gain our intellectual education? Goethe, Nietzsche, Noval[is], Hölderlin, Büchner, Keller, d'Annunzio, Flaubert, Stendhal, Balzac, Dickens, Thackeray, Sterne, Hamsun, Ibsen, Garborg, Jacobsen? Brandes! Dostoevsky, Tolstoy, Gogol . . . : hardly a single Jew among them!

The relationship of these grandfathers of today

7. /under 5/ contemporary so-called older generation or since 1900 or those who have arrived. Th[omas] Mann, H[einrich] Mann, Hofmannsthal, Schnitzler, Altenberg, Kraus, Hauptmann, Stehr, Wassermann, Hesse, Rilke, George, Roth, Döblin, Mus[il], Flake, Benn, Brecht, Kaiser, Borchardt, Werfel [44]

for good or evil the crème de la crème

11	12	Aryans	This does not quite correspond to the currently ac-
6	5	Jews	cepted percentage, but there can be no question of a
2		half-Jews	preponderance, a preferment!

8. (sub 5) philosophy: our education drawn from: Kant and Leibniz, not Spinoza
Bergson—but cf. German romanticism
Husserl ⎫
Freud ⎬ but we are neither phenomenologists nor
Cassirer ⎭ psychoanalysts

9. So it is hard to see in what way we could have been taken over by the Jews. However one may define the concept "Jewish," with which I shall not concern myself here. Why is it that we nonetheless saw nothing? /Because there was nothing there/. . . for us . . ./ Because this revol[ution] arose in a

quite peculiar way, from sectarian spirit, not from the general one, which was also the case, incidentally, with the Marxist revolution.

Except that I feel it as a duty of decency . . .

Because things were different from the way the revol[ution] and in part we imagined them.

This also accounts in great part for the embarrassment of intellectuals toward this revolution. This is the real problem /task/.

9 corrected . . . just as little . . . taken over by the Jews as slept through . . . I would like moreover to insert here a random example   Schlegel.
One can easily recognize the contemporary connections.
The having-been-present before the influence of the Jews /and moreover also system/
As always . . . departure. Things are different.

10. So why was nothing seen
Embarrassment. Task set.

11. I am no more prepared to write than someone else. It is only an effort owed to duty.
[Houston Stewart] Chamberlain. Clever and untenable.
The Rembrandt German [Julius Langbehn—ed.]. Both favored by the "system." Ernst Jünger, Blüher[45] likewise.
All these things elements of the present undefined mix. Until yesterday elements of intellectualism.

What has shown itself up to now, not worth much.

The best comparison would be to the inferiority of women
astrology
together with the "Away from Rome" movement, therefore anticlerical anti-Semitism as well.

12. Beside that, a growing apocryphal literature.
I regret not knowing it well enough to be able to present it histor[ically], but what I am writing is only meant to be the clarifying /and mediating/ confession of impressions, and moreover one can generalize from individual

cases if one does not ignore method[ological] criteria. A few elements of the mix:

  a. It is typical sectarian literature:—Industrious, knowledgeable, and paranoid. Feeling itself overlooked.

  b. Substituting other reasons for this as the real ones. Religious reaction to liberalism, freemasonry. The version of popular anti-Semitism, which is a reaction to the emancipation [of the Jews—ed.]. The idea of *das Volk*, in connection with politics. Emphasis on the racial community, the great common past, and in an isolated section of the populace [*das Volk*] Romanticism: romantic-historical Wagner.

  c. Ethnologically, racial theory.—Proceeding not from empirical research but from moral ideas. One arrives at race from biology as well as from politics. In this period racial theory as something scien[tific], highly dubious, develops; political-sectarian matters as something postulated /treated/ as certain

  When the decades-long suppression of the [National Socialist] Movement is spoken of, here is a reason. But could it have been otherwise?

  d. Literarily: one must not forget that the period of triumphant liberal[ism] in Germany produced little. Nietzsche was its antipode. Hebbel?

  The literature of family magazines.

  The change came from outside, but awakened powerful indigenous movement.

  At that time socialism had a certain youthful energy. Became a popular [*völkisch*] movement in Germany. [Gerhart] Hauptmann representative of this.

  The literature of family magazines was still preserved. Numerically it remained at least as influential as the other [i.e., the popular, *völkisch* kind—ed.].

  Space was won during the ensuing period of exhaustion. The homeland movement [*Heimatsbewegung*] that arose from pedagogical and also from political sources.

  High lit[erature] did not prevail, did not become a model. Properly so. Conditions were not as they ought to have been.

Infantilism of kitsch.

  In addition to individual writers generally held in high regard, sometimes rightly, sometimes wrongly, a so-called asphalt literature arose and on the other side [literature of] the soil.[46]

One could describe it: asphalt, a good liter[ary] tradition,
                  degenerated;
                  soil, a false   ″   ″
                  with an honorable will

One sees that one cannot simply play one off against the other.

13. Two results should be retained here:
a. The primacy of the moral. Unreservedly welcome. A meaning, a will, is to be brought into the phenomena of life. Instead of the free market, which was always the lack of a better one, something better will be put. The individual is to learn national responsibility, the nation too, one hopes, responsibility toward the individual.

b. The close connection of this beautiful impulse with sectarian details. We have seen enough of anti-Semitism, we are now seeing cultural purification setting in. It is bound up with contempt for real intellectual accomplishments and with the overestimation of lesser accomplishment that is bound up with popular clubs.

14. One hears calming voices that these are excesses, frothing, fermenting of must.

If I correctly understand its prehistory, this is false. The [National Socialist] Movement has only two possibilities:

To betray its belief. Make compromises. Compromises are changes dictated by the other.

To change its belief or destroy the German spirit. That would be a change arising from its own internal will and self-knowledge. A general adapts not only his tactics, but also the goal of his operations to circumstances.

I would like to offer for consideration some questions connected with this:

15. I have spoken up to now of "us intellectuals," of spirit and the like, and this of course has nothing to do with my opinion of myself. But the question cannot be avoided: Is there something like spirit or intellect that is relatively independent of politics and of its own (cultural-pol[itical]) group formations as well?

The objections to this are of course obvious: intellect was also the ideology of the political big shots. And intellect smells of internationalism, whereas in truth it can be attained only through blood and national solidarity.

Now I am no political bigwig, I belonged to the opposition. Still, I would like to try sketchily to trace this concept back to its principles: /underscore some of the principles that . . . underlie it./

16. In a nation (in the case of lit[erature]: language community) specific ways of thinking, feeling, desiring, and acting are present and constitute its condition, along with procedures that have become firmly established.

Characterize as in some sense long known.

The comparison with the individual psyche is not merely a metaphor. The intellectual controversy takes place on the larger scale much as it does in the individual head + influence of institutions, which is always a furthering influence, but under certain conditions also falsifying.

Successful action has the effect of endowing dispositions.

Feeling and desiring, affectivity, determine thinking in the individual directly, but on the larger scale chiefly through suggestion.

The greatest possible exclusion of affectivity is science;

—— —— —— involvement —— —— literature.

17. Truth deserves special mention. It is not supposed to be relative; today no one, or at most the lib[eral], wants that. It should therefore be removed from the moods and strivings of the spirit (not subjective). Truth attains this only through agreement with the external world, with the greatest possible area of facts.

Therefore not by agreement among the people, but through accord with reality.

Here lies an error. A romanticism and the like.

A national geometry exists just as little as does a proletarian.

17'. But literature is supposed to be national? Inasmuch as literature builds on hum[an] truth it is more than national. More of this later. For now:

18. When will and feelings are firmly defined, a work of literature has character. But not even that: because feelings become insincere. Literature has spirit when it adapts this character /takes it under protection . . ./ to perpetual new discoveries, to new forms of life. Mind is a perpetual process, character its mass, inhibition, etc. But mind has yet another brake: tradition. But intellect does not change for the sake of change. And art does not by any means exist only to have intellect; it is also an individual reaction. It is dependent on social conventions.

This ought not to become a definition. One reflects in vain one's whole life long. But one can determine roughly what the essentials are. And it should be shown how fragile this is.

What else should there be?

Paradox: excluding the capable ⎫
In contradiction to science,   ⎬   typical affective
excluding science   ⎭   action

Advantage of the [National Socialist] Movement: one cannot imagine what might come after it. Another advantage: the general cowardice and lack of character. Also of official bodies.

The sportsman as well as the clergyman. The same people who could be brave. Nothing else speaks so much in favor of a person's having to have "composure." The moral incorruptibility of the spirit. It can be destroyed, but it cannot change. Ex[amples] of Bolshevism and fascism.

The weltanschauung of the mind as false weakening among worldviews. The concepts of humanism, freedom, internationalism among others in this light.

The outward appearance of the inductively intellectual. (Needs deductive elements.)

What could be done in lit[erature] (academic reviews, promotion).

Wanting to answer not so much the question of what spirit or intellect is, as the question of the relation it finds itself in regarding what is going on in society. Similarly with the individual. He has momentary tasks, for instance in regard to actions, and long-range tasks of development.

Pos[sibly]: How hard it would be as cultural dictator.

Necessary to train character, but possible only in accord with the intellect.

The *Führer* principle and art arising from the people.

To the extent that they have reason, they become unfeeling; to the extent they feel passionately, they lose reason.

Headed downwards for a long time. Autumn rain. Art cannot be commandeered. Form the outward appearance of intellect—induction. But on the other hand not just partial solutions either.

Can be changed

Mind is moral

——   unpolitical

Remarkably consistent paradox: excluding those Jews who accomplish something.

ADDRESSES 1927–1937

Address at the Memorial Service
for Rilke in Berlin
1927

After Rilke's death, on December 29, 1926, there was a debate in a literature club founded by Rudolf Leonhardt as to whether there should be a memorial service in Rilke's honor. Among others involved, Musil was for, Brecht against, the proposal. The ceremony took place on January 16, 1927, in the Renaissance Theater in Berlin. After Musil spoke, Roma Bahn recited some of Rilke's prose and verse.

When the news of the death of the great poet Rainer Maria Rilke arrived in Germany, and on the following days, when one consulted the newspapers to see how this message was being received by German literary history—for, let us not deceive ourselves, today the process of fame is decided at this low level since, as far as literature is concerned, there is hardly any intellectual level above it—one found what I would characterize as an honorable second-class public funeral.

People seemed to want to say—you know how the degree to which you prick up your ears is determined by where it is in the paper, and the kind of type—here something noteworthy has happened, but beyond that we don't have much more to say. The "more" was left to the literature page, which indeed acquitted itself honorably. But imagine how different other cases

237

would have been! How it would have been made a matter of national mourning, and how the rest of the world would have been called upon to witness our grief! The heads of the state would have fallen over themselves in paying respect, lead articles would have been launched, biographical salvos would have thundered: we would have been, in a word, inconsolable, even if it had not been entirely clear to all the participants why. It would, in short, have been an occasion.

Rilke's death was not an occasion. When he died he did not furnish the nation any solemn entertainment. Let us ponder this for a few moments.

. .

When I perceived how trifling the loss of Rilke was valued in the public reckoning—it hardly counted as much as a movie premiere—I confess that my first thought was to answer the question why we have come together today by saying: Because we wish to honor the greatest lyric poet the Germans have seen since the Middle Ages.

It would be permissible to say something like this, but at the same time it is not permissible.

Allow me to begin with this distinction. It is not meant to circumscribe Rilke's greatness in any way, or to codify or compromise it; it is only meant to set to rights the concept of poetic greatness to the extent that it has today become blurred, so that we do not display a false respect and erect Rilke's image over a groundless foundation.

The modern custom that we Germans must always have a "greatest" poet—a kind of "big wheel" of literature—is a wicked piece of thoughtlessness which is not a little to blame for the nonrecognition of Rilke's importance. God knows where this custom comes from! It could just as well have arisen from the cult of Goethe as from physical exercise, or from the peerless, unsurpassable quality of "Brand X" cigarettes as easily as from the tennis rankings. It is obvious that the concept of artistic or intellectual greatness can never be decided by numbers or a tape measure, nor according to the range of the work or the compass of the subjects treated—according to the author's glove size, as it were. Still, there is no question that writing a lot matters more to us than writing a little. No one has proclaimed in such noble fashion as Rilke, who always selflessly encouraged his young colleagues, that the concept of artistic greatness is not exclusive.

Consider for a moment that the slender work of Novalis and Hölderlin was created at the same time as Goethe's mighty work was being accomplished; that Büchner's terse sketches came into being simultaneously with Hebbel's cosmic casting of the dice in his dramas. I do not believe you will feel that one of these could be replaced by the other, or dispensed with for the sake of the other; they are almost entirely removed from notions of "more," "less," "greater," "more profound," "more beautiful"—in short from every kind of ranking. This is the meaning of what an extravagant age called the Parnassus, what an age that loved freedom and dignity called the Republic of the Mind. The height of poetry is not a peak on which one climbs higher and higher, but a circle, within which there is only what is unequally equal, unique, irreplaceable; a noble anarchy and the fraternity of a guild. The stricter an age is in what it calls poetry, the fewer the differences it will allow beyond this. Our age, however, is quite tolerant in what it calls poetry; in some circumstances it is already enough for Papa to be a poet. Corresponding to this on the other side is that this age has carried to an extreme the idea of the Star, of crack horses in the publishing stable, of the Champion in literature—even if this featherweight idea cannot, of course, make the same claims on our attention as the heavyweights of boxing!

Rainer Maria Rilke was poorly suited for this age. This great lyric poet did nothing but perfect the German poem for the first time. He was not a peak of this age, he was one of the pinnacles on which the destiny of the spirit strides across ages. . . . He belongs in the context of centuries of German poetry, not in the context of the day.

．．

When I say he perfected the German poem I do not have in mind a superlative, but something quite specific. Nor do I mean that perfection of which I spoke that is characteristic for every true work of literature, even when this work, taken in itself, is imperfect. I mean a quality quite specific to a Rilke poem, a perfection in the narrower sense that is first of all determined by its historical position.

The modern German poem has had a peculiar development. Without question it achieved a peak right at the beginning, in Goethe, but it became the unlucky star of an entire century of German poetry that Goethe was exceedingly tolerant of the occasional, of improvisation, of light social verse. Such verses were, of course, charming in expressing whatever seized his fancy, and admirable in the fullness of what his many-sided nature was able to animate; but he never drew back from either loosely plumping down the rest of the poem or simply rounding it off as a rimed memorandum. That was in his nature. It was, far more, in the character of his age. That age, which we are accustomed to regard as our Classical period, which in a certain sense it was, was in another sense an age of experiments, of restlessness, of hopes, of great asseverations, of activity. In that earlier time, in marked contrast to our own, both men and women had a breast. One wept upon it; one threw oneself upon it. A characteristic impulsiveness and exuberance went along with harmless social games, magnanimity with ingenious slovenliness. This period zealously imported classical, Persian, Arabian, Provençal, medieval Latin, English, Italian, and Spanish poetic models in order to find in them a domestic form for its domestic restlessness. Today it is hard for us to imagine what in their day a German hexameter, or a madrigal, ballad, or romance meant in terms of the delight in invention or discovery, or the extent to which, by their mere happy presence, these discoveries were able to reward poets and readers alike. Today, when the forms of lyric poetry have been drastically reduced and have also congealed, all this has completely atrophied. But this might also lead us to conclude that the conviction of perfection that many people still believe they feel today contains a small hallucinatory complement.

In the transition from the Classical period to the present, the consequence is irrefutable. What our literary history has, with the impartiality of a stamp collector, preserved from this transitional period as the German poem—these Rückerts, Anastasius Grüns, Lenaus, Feuchterslebens, Freiligraths, Geibels, Gilms, Linggs, Pichlers, Zedlitzes, Scheffels, Baumbachs, Wilbrandts, and Wildenbruchs—you may make an exception for this or that poem, assume about one or the other that you could transport yourself into the situation of the time and, so to speak, enjoy the poem in this distorted position: still, this poetry remains, on the whole, a collection of lyric instruments of torture for use in the schools. Ghasels and canzone romp around in it, as well as sonnets and rondelles. You find in it a quite intellectual, willful relation to form, and also a relation to ideational content that has very little of the intellectual about it. Insights whose triviality one would notice immediately if they were expressed in prose are warmed up by means of rhyme and meter, roasted all over by stanzas, possibly even shrivelled up by a refrain that keeps recurring like a fit of insanity.

This period was the cradle of the German belief that form could ennoble content, that elevated diction was superior to plain, that to glue the plaster ornament of verse onto a shallow thought was something special. I think I may say that the formlessness of our own time is the natural reaction to this, although of course in abandoning beauty of form our age has also abandoned, in part, beauty of content. Here I cannot permit myself to go into detail, but I think almost all of you know the feeling of aversion that this poetry, with few exceptions, leaves in the young reader who is forced to admire in it the cultural history of his people.

In comparison with other countries, the enormous and well-deserved authority of Goethe has, without question, retarded the development of the

German novel by a good fifty years; without being able to help it, except that those coming after only looked at the backs of the heads of their originals! In the same way, the misunderstood authority of Classicism led to a fateful tolerance for the failure of its followers. This tolerance, which is part of our higher culture, allows every lyric evildoer, whenever the moment is favorable, to call upon ancestors who have been ennobled by history. Here I am speaking of one of the most wretched burdens of German poetry. The present epoch arose immediately out of the post-Classical one, even if at first it reacted against it. It was only from abroad, through Verlaine and Baudelaire, Poe and Whitman, that the Germans again learned what a poem was. This influence was powerful: there was tremendous introspection and self-discovery. But in the long run, what are introspections, no matter how penetrating, compared with a solidly entrenched education in false perception? You see, this is always the case with a literature that does not have a solid internal anchor in a country: introspection leads to a struggle against the reigning favorites of idleness and superficiality. Introspection conquers: the dead favorites litter the field of battle. Then the tension of conscience yields for a moment, and the dead not only spring back to life but they have— precisely because they had been dead for a while—something well-preserved about them, something industriously immortal and venerably moving. In our case, furthermore, no one knows whether these dead might not even have, finally, classical qualities.

I believe that many signs in the present point unmistakably to this being a very good time for such resurrection. The tautness of German literature is in a long-term period of slackening. At this point, I run the danger of talking about current matters. But what is it then that I am talking about? About the intangible, paralyzing difficulties that stand in the way of a renovator of the German poem!

· ·

I have taken it upon myself to say a few words more about such difficulties, because they have special importance and currency.

A short while ago an Academy of Literature was founded—with Ludwig Fulda[47] at its head! About its membership, one can only say that the importance of the poets who were excluded or who excluded themselves at least balances the importance of those who belong. I know the inner and outer natural worth of my Apollonian colleagues pretty well; I also know tolerably well the directions, circles, and currents of taste into which contemporary German literature is divided; but it has been impossible for me to find an objective principle that would explain how this collection of academicians was arrived at. All I have been able to determine, using every means available to contemporary literary research, was that the selection was apparently influenced—by very disparate influences.

And now let us ponder this. This Academy was presumably intended to be, in a noble sense, conservative. It was meant to oppose the commercialization of literature, the clamor of the marketplace, the success of the inferior. In this or that uncertainty it could offer literature protection from the state. All this would of course have been possible with simpler, less pompous, more thoroughgoing, and more up-to-date means. For instance, it is not entirely clear why the state requires the aid of literature to protect literature from persecution by the state. Well, we can all agree on that! But one thing we cannot agree with under any circumstances is that one thinks one is helping poetry by perpetuating the principle of being uncritical.

I would not want to say anything bitter against Ludwig Fulda. In his lifetime he has abused both the German language and the human prerogative of freedom of thought; but he didn't know it. For twenty-five years he was such a dependable thermometer that one could say of a literary piece, instead of having to expend a lot of words: It's like Fulda. Perhaps one can still understand this, even today: then I could apply this critical standard to the Academy of Literature, and instead of using a lot of words simply say: There's a lot of Fulda in this monster!

But now comes the serious part. From among Rilke, Hofmannsthal, Hauptmann, Borchardt, George, Däubler,[48] and all the others among our literary aristocracy who are not members, a part has taken leave in order to follow the seductive call of this Academy. Not, of course, because of the temptation, but out of a sense of duty. For us in Germany this is self-explanatory; not, to be sure, without further explanation, but for fine and worthy reasons. Everything that could be said in favor of an academy was mentioned in these arguments, but one thing I do not see in them: the understanding that inner purity, inner clarity, dignity, and incorruptible seriousness constitute literature's highest good.

Among the members of the Academy there are those who, individually, possess these characteristics in high degree. But that they nevertheless do not find it necessary to apply these qualities to the whole intellectual atmosphere around them is incredibly indicative of the way our literature has developed, of its insecurity and lack of structure that we have never been able to shake off. There you have in cross-section the entire moral of German literary history! And I need not tell you that literary history is part of cultural history.

And if I must also lay myself open to the reproach of having strayed far from my subject, I did so not without an inner connection, and also not entirely without profit, for at the same time we have to some extent become acquainted with the environment for which Rilke wrote his great work that is so threatened by misunderstandings.

I would like to use my remaining time to say a few clarifying words about the most important of these misunderstandings.

When I spoke of the perfection to which Rilke has raised the German poem, what I had in mind was at first only an external characteristic. I can describe it to you if I may remind you of the extremely distinctive impression one has on first reading Rilke's works. Not only hardly a poem, but hardly a line or a word sinks below the level of the others, and one has the same experience through the entire sequence of his books. There arises from this an almost painful tension, like a daring presumption, which in addition is achieved not with any large orchestral display but as if it were quite natural, accompanied only by the simple sound of the verse's flute.

Neither before nor after him has this high and sustained tension of impression, this jewellike stillness within a movement that never pauses, been attained. Neither the older German poem nor George nor Borchardt possess this free burning of the fire, without flickering or darkness. The German lyric genius carves a furrow like a stroke of lightning, but piles up the soil around it carefully or carelessly; it ignites like lightning, but only scratches surfaces like lightning; it leads up the mountain, but in order to lead up the mountain one must first always be down below. Compared with this, Rilke's poem has an expansive openness: its condition endures like an elevated pause.

It was in this sense that I spoke of his perfection and achievement. This characterizes a particular quality, and not, to begin with, rank or value. In the realm of the aesthetic, as you know, even imperfection and lack of completion have their value. Indeed, paradoxical as it may sound (even if in reality it means nothing more than our inability to characterize things more precisely), this inner smoothness and absence of wrinkles, this character the poem has of being poured forth from a mold, is often found as well in the poetry of those scribblers who write a poem as smoothly as a barber shaves a cheek. Even more paradoxically, people have not always noticed the difference!

There was a time when every better sort of young man with moist eyes wrote poems in the manner of Rilke. It was not at all difficult; a certain way of walking. I think the Charleston is harder. There have always been sharp-eyed critics who noticed this, and assigned Rilke a place among the artsy-craftsy practitioners of verse. But the time when people imitated him was short, and the time people undervalued him lasted his entire life. When Rilke was young, Dehmel[49] was considered someone, and Rilke—an Austrian! If one was well disposed towards him, one added something about Slavic melancholy. When he was mature, taste had changed; Rilke was then considered a delicate, ripely aged liqueur for grownup ladies, while youth thought it had other problems.

It is certainly not to be denied that youth too had a good deal of affection for him, but it cannot be overlooked that in this affection youth was really succumbing to a weakness. Today I do not see Rilke's spirit at work anywhere. What we have today by way of tension of feeling and conscience is not Rilke's kind of tension. So it is possible that he will be loved again because he is considered relaxing! He is, however, too demanding for that. He makes more than infantile claims on love. I would at least like to indicate this, if not demonstrate it.

. .

I could do so by inviting you to follow Rilke's path from the first and early poems to the *Duino Elegies*. If we did so, we would see in an uncommonly gripping way how early he matured—just like the young Werfel. But how his development really begins from that point on! From the very beginning both the inner and outer forms (even though there are experiments that are tried and abandoned) are traced out like a delicate rib cage; pale; movingly intertwined with typically youthful features; astonishing in the inversion that there is far more mannerism in his first efforts than in the later recurrences! At times one might say that the young Rilke was imitating Rilke. But then you experience the uncanny spectacle of how, for the artist, this sketch fills out. How porcelain turns to marble. How everything that was there from the beginning and hardly changed is shaped by an ever-deepening thought. In a word, you experience the incredibly rare spectacle of something being shaped through a process of inner completion.

Rather than following the stages of this process in detail—for which the best guide would be the poet himself—I would like to try instead to bring out the profound connections I am speaking of in the phenomenon of Rilke's accomplished poetry by returning once again, but this time from the inside, to the unusual impression it evokes.

I called this impression, in my first tentative words, a clear stillness in a never-pausing movement, a daring presumption, an elevated enduring, a broad openness, an almost painful tension. And one might well add that tensions most easily take on the character of pain when they cannot be entirely understood or resolved, when they form a knot in the discharge of our feelings. The affect of a Rilke poem is of a very particular kind. We can understand it if we realize that this poem really never has a lyrical motif, nor is its goal ever a particular object in the world. It speaks of a violin, a stone, a blond girl, of flamingos, wells, cities, blind people, madmen, beggars, angels, the maimed, knights, rich men, kings . . . ; it becomes a poem of love, of renunciation, of piety, of the tumult of battle, of simple description, even description laden with cultural reminiscence . . . ; it becomes a song, a legend, a ballad . . . It is never identical with the content of the poem; rather, what releases and guides the lyric affect is always something like the incomprehensible existence of these notions and objects, their incomprehensible juxtaposition and invisible interweaving.

In this gentle lyric affect, one thing becomes the likeness of the other. In Rilke stones or trees not only become people—as they have done always and everywhere poetry has been written—but people also become things or nameless beings, and in this way, moved by an equally nameless breath, achieve the ultimate degree of humanity. We might say: In the feeling of this great poet everything is likeness, but nothing is *only* likeness. The spheres of the different orders of being, separated from ordinary thinking, seem to unite in a single sphere. Something is never compared with something else—as two different and separate things, which they remain in the comparison—for, even if this sometimes does happen, and one thing is said to be like another, it seems at that very moment to have already *been* the other since primordial times. The particular qualities become universal qualities. They have detached themselves from objects and circumstances, they hover in fire and in the fire's wind.

This has been called mysticism, pantheism, panpsychism . . . ; but such concepts add something that is superfluous and lead to fuzziness. Let us rather remain with what is familiar to us: What *is* it really that these images have? Upon the most sober investigation? What emerges is remarkable enough: the metaphorical here becomes serious to a high degree.

Let me begin with an example chosen at random: Say a writer compares a particular November evening he is talking about with a soft woollen cloth. Another writer could just as easily compare a particular woollen cloth to a November evening. In all such cases, the charm consists in the reinvigoration of a somewhat worn-out area of feelings and ideas by the addition of elements from a new area. Of course the cloth is not a November evening, this we know, but in its effect it is related to it, and that is a pleasant little sleight of hand.

There is a certain tragicomedy inherent in this human inclination for metaphor. If the nipples of the breast are compared to doves' beaks or corals, one can only say, strictly speaking: God forbid that it were true! The consequences would be inconceivable. One gathers the impression from similes involving people that a person cannot endure being in the place where, just at that particular moment, he happens to be. He will never admit this; he embraces the serious life; but while doing so he sometimes thinks of another!

It is a lovely, even if somewhat old-fashioned, trope to say: Her teeth were like ivory. Substitute for it another expression, objectively descriptive and sober but accurate, and it would be, most undesirably: She had the teeth of an elephant! More cautiously, but still awkward: Her teeth possessed the optical quality of an elephant's teeth, except for the form. Most cautiously: They had I don't know what in common. Obviously, this is the usual activity of a metaphor: we detach the desirable quality and leave the undesirable behind without wanting to be reminded of it, and we dissolve solid qualities into the nature of rumor.

The lack of seriousness with which art is reproached, in comparison with reality, and what in art really is distracting, superficial, "the very latest" in fashion and servility . . . : I am happy to be able to demonstrate by so simple an example, worthy of inclusion in any school grammar or poetics text, how all this is reflected in the use we make of metaphor.

This use is connected with a specific way of looking at the world (and as part of this: art as recreation, distraction, spontaneous exaltation). But now I ask you: Instead of saying the November evening is like a cloth *or* that the cloth is like a November evening, could one not say both at the same time? What my question is asking is what Rilke was perpetually doing.

In his poetry, things are woven as in a tapestry. If one observes them, they are separate, but if one regards the background, it connects the things with each other. Then their appearance changes, and strange relationships arise among them.

This has nothing to do either with philosophy or skepticism, nor with anything other than experience.

In conclusion I would like to describe to you a feeling about life. But I must say at the start that I can only indicate it. As little as it will seem to be like Rilke, you will find more of it in his poems than in my words. Up to now I have really spoken of only a single beauty among the many interrelated ones in his works; but I must be satisfied with pointing to this single beauty, since even it is already part of a broad pattern of development. And just this, this involvement of the smallest in the greatest, is Rilke.

A solid world, within which feelings are what move and change: this is the normal notion. But actually both, feelings and world, are *not* solid, even if within quite different limits. That the world becomes a solid wall for the feelings has its good reasons, but is somewhat arbitrary. And we really know this quite well. It is no longer so extraordinary to think that no one knows today what he might be capable of tomorrow. In the last few decades the knowledge that the gradations from moral rule to crime, from health to sickness, from admiration to contempt for the same thing are a continuum, without fixed demarcations, has, through the professional literature and other influences, become for many people a matter of course.

I don't want to exaggerate. If we consider the individual, this "being capable of anything" is subject to very strong inhibitions. But if we regard the history of mankind, that is, the history of normality par excellence, there can be no doubt: fashions, styles, feelings of the moment, periods, and systems of morality succeed each other in such a manner, or exist simultaneously in such variety, that the impression can hardly be avoided that humanity is a bilious mass that will assume *any* shape, depending on circumstances. Of course we have an eminent interest in denying this, which is the practical and moral interest of the then-prevailing situation. To shape reality firmly and unequivocally constitutes the everlasting activity of life, and at the same time its drive for self-preservation.

It cannot to be overlooked that the difficulties inherent in this grow stronger whenever the feelings are involved. We therefore exclude them wherever possible when we are after truth, order, and progress. But there are times when we cautiously bring them back in again, for instance in a poem, or in love. These processes are, as we know, quite illogical, but one may suppose that clarity of knowledge can only prevail at all where the feelings are generally stable. I cannot develop this further here, but you will have noticed that our intercourse with feelings is no longer quite comfortable. And since this has not remained hidden from the sharpened understanding of our time, there are many signs that might already lead us to expect that we are facing the posing of a great problem not only of the intellect, but also of the soul.

And now there is a poem that signifies in the world of the firm and solid a complementarity, a recuperation, an adornment, a stimulation, a breaking out, in short, an interruption and an exclusion; one might also say that it is a matter of specific and individual feelings. And there is a poem that cannot forget the restlessness, inconstancy, and fragmentation that is concealed in the whole of life; one could say that here it is a matter, even if only partially, of that feeling as a totality on which the world rests like an island.

This is the poem of Rilke. This is what he means when he says God, and when he speaks of a flamingo he means it too; *this* is why all things and processes in his poems are related to one another and exchange places like the stars that move without our perceiving it. In a certain sense Rilke was the most religious poet since Novalis, but I am not sure whether he had any religion at all. He saw differently: in a new, more inward way. And someday he will be seen to have been not only a great poet, but a greater leader on the path that leads from the religious world-feeling of the Middle Ages through the humanistic ideal of culture to a worldview yet to come.

Postscript to the Printed Version

A speech is not the spoken printed word. It is intertwined with the elements of immediate effect, of the here-and-now, with the identities of the audience and of the speaker, who is asserting himself in such a way that without these elements what remains is not a score but merely a fragment. At least there are speeches of this kind, and the one I presented here was meant in this way.

The consequence ought to have been to put it out of existence after it had accomplished its task; not only consideration of one's own advantage, but also the sense of art itself would demand this. If I have nevertheless decided on the opposite course, indeed if I abstain from any attempt at change before I give the extinguished word over to print, I do so from the consideration that even if I were to round it out with everything that, on first glance, it lacks, this talk would still remain a fragment.

The most important extension, and the one I feel most deprived of, lies in the continuation of the thought that was only begun. If one were to investigate the dynamic quality of thought in Rilke's verse, what I was able to indicate about the use of metaphor would have to be recapitulated on a larger, and thus much more significant scale. This meaning does not unfold by learning up against the wall of some ideology, humanity, or world opinion for protection, but arises with no support or hold from any side as something left over, free and hovering, from intellectual movement. The "insideness" [*Inseitigkeit*] of Rilke's poem has just as peculiar and striking a configuration as the outer form, even though it is far less accessible to analysis and description. Were one to set up a series, with the didactic poem, the allegory, and the political poem at one end, that is, forms that are the product of an already complete knowledge and will, Rilke's poem would stand at the opposite end, as pure process and shaping of spiritual powers, which in him, for the first time, find name and voice. Between them would lie both the poem intended to arouse "great feelings" and the poem meant to elevate "great ideas," both of which our age already regards as the quintessence of the soul's power, and which lift their glances—back up over their shoulder, for they contain the powers of intensification, but not those of creation.

It was in such a sense that I called Rilke a poet who leads us into the future. For it appears that the development of the spirit, which seems to many today to be in decline, but still must carry its equilibrium somewhere within itself, will body forth this equilibrium as a dynamic one. We are not to be called again to this or that specific ideological fixity, but to the unfolding of the creation and possibilities of the spirit. In view of such inner images, which arise out of Rilke's poems not like a prophecy but as an anticipatory scent, it seems to me immaterial to track down relationships of form or even derivations of form, or to argue about the evaluation of individual elements. Even the exceptional falling off that Rilke's work suffers in the *Sonnets to Orpheus*, and suffers to such a degree that the poet at times appears as a fastidious epigone, signifies little; for this uncertainty that threatens his form at the very moment when he wants to approach the present is extraordinarily indicative of his entranced nature.

This explanation—in its entirety, as I have attempted it here—is not only mine, which might speak in favor of readers not inclined to share my opinion—but I mostly follow in the path set out by several highly distinguished predecessors. Nor does Rilke either stand alone on his path, nor is it the only possible and therefore the only right path that leads into the future. Nor am I unaware that highly intelligent critics would make evaluations quite different from mine on particular matters. To all of this I can only repeat what apparently did not come through in the lecture, that the greatness of a poet lies beyond all questions of degree and is always absolute, for which reason also it never excludes the value and significance of others. One may say that the nature of true poetry is always beyond measure; great poems are pointers, and it would be a foolish criticism that would first want to take note of the demarcation of this mandate from others rather than follow the mandate itself across all boundaries. Today the real meaning of Rilke's work is often still misunderstood even by his friends; this is what I wanted to point out. But it already lies near the surface of our general consciousness. And if I may close with a personal observation, it was these two impressions that gave me confidence that in such a situation even this small push and my inadequate pointing out of this misunderstanding might have some modest value.

That in doing this I presented the picture of a great and not always understood poet against the background of contemporary literature appeared to me a necessity for understanding him, even if it might look to others like an absence of tact. These others are the well-known kibitzers for whom no gamble is too high, and consequently no grief too deep. People may perhaps be of different minds whether, on the occasion of a great loss, one should seek to weep, or to understand what it is that is disappearing. It seemed to me that it was not those who were spiritually the most closely related to the great departed poet who missed the piety in my exposition.

The Serious Writer in Our Time
1934

This is a corrected fair copy of a lecture given in Vienna to celebrate the twentieth anniversary of the Society for the Protection of German Writers in Austria, December 16, 1934.

Honored colleagues!

1

To my regret I must come before you to inform you of my indisposition like the director excusing a singer, because it not only interferes with my speaking, but it has also interfered with my preparing this lecture as befits the worthiness of its subject and of your presence. Still, I hope to be able to share with you some thoughts that are worth being thought today.

2

And because I am speaking about the serious writer and about today the beginning is easy, because I can confidently claim that we don't know what either one is.

Perhaps I may explain this first as it concerns the serious writer. Some years ago I published a trifle in which I described what great moral, but also what great economic, significance is owed to the assumption that somewhere there is such a thing as the serious writer. Publishing houses and the book trade; printers, binderies, and paper factories; copy editors and the feuilleton pages of newspapers; theater and film; offices that dispatch manuscripts; offices that dispatch matrices for printing; offices that dispatch illustrations; governmental supervisory and administrative offices; the hiring of secondary-school and university teachers; cartels, unions, libraries, and their personnel; and, not least, the existence of remunerative scribbling for entertainment: this enormous and unbounded edifice erected above writing and reading, which assures so many people of an adequate or a lavish livelihood, rests entirely on maintaining the feeling of being in the service of some great cause. For without this feeling not nearly so many people could read with a light heart the bad books they prefer, and in doing so make reading a worthy part of the life of our nation. In this endeavor nobody has any idea who really is a superior writer, if one inflates the notion to correspond to such grand importance, and nobody know what a serious writer is. There are among the living perhaps a dozen such caryatids, supporting on their shoulders a monstrous economic apparatus. The exact number doesn't matter; but it is certain that these writers don't, for the most part, feel at all right about holding it up. They are recognized by only a relatively small circle of initiates; in several well-known instances their income is that of beggars, and the greatest paradox is that everything that lives off them seems to have made it its business to kill them off as quickly as possible. It is on account of these parasites that some undeserving writers receive prizes and that radio networks arrange homages for others. This was most clearly expressed by a lady who disseminates culture by arranging public gatherings, when she was once asked how it happened that she had passed over a particular poet, since helping him ought really to have been close to her heart. "What can I tell you?" she replied. "I have such sensitive feelings. He upsets me!"

Is this description an exaggeration? It expresses a truth so naked that it deserves to be forbidden at least by a law against nudity, if no other!

3

And we know just as little about "today." In part this is, as always, obvious, because we are too close to the present; for the rest, however, one can also say that in this particular case we are mired especially deeply in the today we fell into nearly two decades ago.

I would like, nevertheless, to try to dig out some of the major peculiarities of this condition. Whether the age in which we live is prodigious is a question I would modestly prefer to leave unanswered; but it is most certainly an age of violence. It began, rather abruptly, in the summer of 1914. Suddenly violence appeared, and since that time it has not abandoned mankind again but has been assimilated into it to a degree that, before that summer, would have been considered un-European. And its first appearance, even at that time, was already accompanied by two remarkable emotions: first, a paralyzing feeling of catastrophe. What was called European culture suddenly had a crack, became the plunder of peace. Second, there arose simultaneously the even more astonishing feeling of a firm new solidarity within the smaller framework of individual nations, and this occurred as strongly and indiscriminately as a previously forgotten mystical emotion rises up from primeval depths. I said this at the time, and after the collapse I also warned against underestimating this emotion; other disinterested observers noticed its first appearance in ways similar to mine.

It is not difficult to recognize in both these emotions the affective impetus of much that has assumed great importance since.

And I would call this development since the War, which embraces a new solidarity as well as doubts about the old, "collective solidarity," in order to emphasize in it what most involves the "free spirit." Mussolini is supposed to have been the first person to have used this term, in connection with the Total State. But collectivism appeared not only as a claim on behalf of the state, but also as a claim of nationhood and a claim of class, assuming different forms according to the differing historical circumstances in Italy, Russia, and Germany, forms that indeed stand in sharpest contrast to each other. But common to all is the preponderance of collective interests as a totality, as opposed to individual interests, and the greater or lesser ruthlessness with which these collective interests have asserted themselves in our epoch.

This claim as such is not new, but its variety and strength and a certain one-sidedness in its arguments are. Because man is by nature as much a collective as an individual being, indeed precisely because scientific thought, notwithstanding the significance of individual thought, is perhaps the most collective thing there is, the idea of collectivity had of course its model in ethics long before it received its new form. Lessing, for instance, in *The Education of the Human Race*, demanded the education of mankind as a whole, in the infinitude of its being, to a final state of perfection. Kant saw the possibility of fulfilling the moral law only in the infinite progress of mankind. And according to Schiller, the great man was the representative of the species.

In view of such dicta the observation does occur to one that since that time collectivism has moved from infinity up pretty close to us! Nor can we pass over in silence that in the period of our Classicism collectivism depended on "humanity" and "personality," whereas today its appearance is anti-individualistic and anti-atomistic, and it is not exactly a passionate respecter of humanity.

We shall have to come back to this—

4

—but first, for diversion, let us cast a small side-glance at the sphere closest to us, the literary.

There we see one trait of the development I have described, in that in narrative prose, especially the novel, it has not been possible for quite some time to take the destiny of individuals as seriously as it had been taken earlier. We might think by way of comparison of Dickens or Meredith.

To be sure, the conscience of the cosy narrator has also deteriorated because the totality of intellectual development has turned away from the world of things to law, statistics, and the like; but the major reason doubtless remains that for a very long time social development has not taken the individual human being as seriously as the Biedermeier period of Classicism did. The individual understands himself to be woven into the fabric of the whole both economically and professionally. The idea that—somehow—he is no longer so very important is already within him, and the War added a most forceful lesson on the subject.

5

A second side-glance: this expresses itself as weakness of character. For this I would like to point to a few vivid examples.

Let us call to mind the war hero, such as our time has produced. On the whole he demonstrated the most incredible powers of resistance and readiness for self-sacrifice, but his bravery was—if one overlooks the exceptions, as is only fair—not individualistic. The mass model in the War was great courage, which could definitely also be cowardly; today one runs as far away as possible, and tomorrow plunges in again courageously. This might perhaps be called Homeric (for the Homeric hero could scream with fear while still obeying his moral heroic code). However that may be, and however far it may or may not be comparable: what we experienced in the War was our lack of self-sufficiency and our dependency on a mass that threw us forwards and backwards, and within which we obeyed commands of whose logic we had no idea, but whose justification we recognized in a summary way.

This was made clear in the spectacle offered by the most recent upheaval in Germany, when half a brave and great nation presented the picture of headstrong victors, the other half of intimated, helpless human beings. One has to say: Even of cowards; for that is precisely where the problem lies, that such cowards had been heroes and could become heroes again. The man of today shows himself to be even less self-sufficient than he himself imagines, and becomes firmly self-confident only in association with others.

And part of this as well, finally, is the "giving in" of the spirit, an astonishing lack of "civil courage" that came to light. What had people not renounced or abandoned in those years, readily or hesitantly, that had previously been part of their ineradicable convictions and deepest principles! There is not a single principle of humanity, morality, justice, truth, national commonality, or respect for others and their accomplishments that was not among them. One waited for the "Göttingen Seven" of 1837,[50] but they did not appear. The individual, the "personality," the mind, behaved the way the body had behaved under artillery fire: it ducked. It seemed pointless to jump up and raise one's arms to heaven. And it probably really would have been pointless. But what a difference has come about since the Classical days when the mind reigned supreme in Germany!

It is also indicative that the only important way the self persisted did not emanate from the "free spirit" but from religious alliances, which is to say, aside from the particular spirit of religiosity, from organized associations, and this again points to the lack of self-sufficiency, the need to be led, the external and the consequent internal dependency of people today.

6

These have been rather more than side-glances that we have cast, and from which we bring away something that permits discussion, without going beyond the scope of the permissible, of a glimmering insight into why the absence of character in people today is inevitable.

But beyond that, perhaps something more general may be asserted as well. I once wrote down a sequence of ideas—even before there were middle-class political movements, or when they were just beginning—that went something like this: the increase in the number of people united in a common sphere of activity, and the increase in the forces and institutions that unite them, must keep step with each other if a gradual decline is not to set in. In certain circumstances this cannot be left to happen by itself. The misery of the War and the postwar period made this palpable and brought this development to a head; but even without this misery a reaction to the "liberal" management of human affairs would have had to occur at some time. In this sense, collectivism could also be understood as embodying attempts at discipline, in the same way that its tendency to violent interventions through shaking those concepts of the culture that forbid it is understandable.

This is of course only in the smallest degree a causal explanation. Such an explanation would have to adduce the concrete circumstances out of whose variety the various collectivisms arose, and would have to take into account the development of their ideologies. But what I have permitted myself to give some indication of is merely, as it were, the borderline where general intellectual developments come together with these specific ones. Nor is there any sort of mythology of history lurking behind this. As long as Western humanity still has a future, it will always give birth to the critical method at the critical moment: this is not metaphysics but an analytic conclusion from the assumption that things have not yet declined, and will not do so in the near future. This is, to be sure, optimistic; and today, when there is so much optimism, many people might find it difficult to make a confession of optimism. However, wanting to be understood is one of the few undisputed functions still left to the mind, and the mind will for the most part assume that humanity possesses some kind of goal, some kind of task, some kind of meaningful intent that we neither see nor don't quite not see; in a word, the mind's optimism, as it observes the world, is roughly expressable as: We err forwards!

But this should not allow us to forget that different conclusions can be drawn from the moral situation we posited for collectivism. If the moral powers of the individual in relation to the environment are too weak, it is not only possible to strengthen the external framework, but the possibility also exists for an elevating influence on the individual, and a third possibility is for both to happen. Part of our present history is its attitude toward this last alternative, and this also determines the situation that the serious writer has found in this alternative. It is always, of course, this third possibility, the influence from inside *and* outside, which in reality always has been and always will be employed; but the difference between then and now is that since the days of Classicism upright personal conduct has been the aim of the mind [*Geist*], that even legislation has left the individual a broad area of freedom, and that the upright relation to the whole was supposed, for the most part, to be included in this upright personal behavior, while today it works the other way around. This is, therefore, a major change in direction: the same thing is seized from the opposite end.

If one were simply to trace anti-individualism, and the distaste for democracy that is closely associated with it, back to this, one might conclude that the principles need not lie so very far apart. In none of its forms can collectivism be called completely undemocratic; it is rather a new form of democracy, or at least that is one of its ambitions, among others; or perhaps there is no form of government that is not in some fashion necessarily democratic. There is, too, a remarkable contradiction, which can have escaped no one, that all collective forms are associated with a high degree of devotion to a great individual, the personality of genius, and they express this in the principle of the leader and the concomitant pyramidal structure of the state. Therefore great scientific and artistic individuality ought to be compatible with collectivism too, but clearly this has yielded astonishing difficulties.

In themselves, strongly stamped forms of power are entirely compatible with the cult of the spirit and the cult of individuality, as the example of the Renaissance teaches; it was in the Renaissance that the theories of genius and the great individual arose in the first place, so possibly the beginning and end of these ideas might coincide with a rule of power.

But however one may philosophize, events did not arise theoretically but actually and ambiguously, like all reality. So we must supplement the harmless sentence, that in collectivism the influence that forms people externally predominates, by saying that in many places today the individual, as citizen, is so completely organized that there is almost nothing left of him but the vanishingly small point where all the various public demands come together. The majority of rights has been withdrawn from the individual sphere and handed over to the public sphere, and it is out of this that a highly problematic relation of politics to creative powers outside politics has arisen that is probably endemic to all forms of collectivism, even though the power applied not only is as varied as wind velocity ten and a pleasant breeze, but also seems to be associated with a view that includes all gradations between the honorably regretful insight into the indispensability of compulsion and the naked worship of power.

Man is evidently not an ant, and therefore the bearer of collectivity will also ultimately be the individual; but when the mind tries to prepare itself for this it sometimes falls into deplorable uncertainty, for it does not yet know where it itself begins and where it ends.

7

In discussing these matters we have been intensively involved with the relation of the serious writer to the present. For political reasons, the ideas of humanity, internationalism, freedom, and objectivity, among others, have become unpopular in many places. They are considered bourgeois, liberal, outmoded. They are suppressed, excluded from the educational process, starved. Not all at once; some here, some there. But for the serious writer these are the concepts of his tradition, with whose aid he has with great effort consolidated his personal self. He does not need to agree with them all, he can endeavor to change them; but he still remains dependent on all of them, far more than a person depends on the ground he walks on. The serious writer is not only the expression of a momentary attitude of mind, even should it herald a new age. His tradition is not decades old, but millennia. The love letter of a Phoenician girl could have been written today. More profound things about the German soul are expressed in an Egyptian statue than in all the exhibitions of German art. And the mind's history preserves its own course through all the vagaries of politics.

Ultimately this is all expressed in a paradox that there is no way of resolving: for were one to concede all the various demands that amount to the serious writer assimilating himself into the reigning ideology of a community as completely as possible, the final result would be not only that every country would have its own national writers, but that quite different sorts of procedures would be characterized by the word *literature*.

But we have almost come this far if, overnight, the literary constellation is overturned, and serious writers whose place one knew in some starry cloud or other suddenly become stars of the first magnitude, by which the astonished wanderer, gazing upwards, is to direct his path.

8

But here of course it must be conceded that art has always been affected by the political and economic order of its time. We can easily distinguish in Goethe between what is Goethe and what is Biedermeier, and an ancient classical poem can be distinguished in kind from a Goethean imitation: something impersonal or suprapersonal is mixed in with the personal.

On the other hand, for us (to be sure, for a particular "us") even this suprapersonal is still attainable, to a degree. A Chinese saying that originated a thousand years before our calendar is by no means only the affair of an alien time for us, and there are quite remote poems by monks of the Middle Ages in which there glows a religiosity barely still comprehensible to a European, but whose flaming up again one could imagine at any moment.

The problem of art's internationalism and the problem of its transcending time are only two expressions of the same quality, and one might well classify Hofmannsthal in such a series, but never a superior writer who owed the value of his ranking only to a constellation of circumstances external to art. Thus our experience has taught us—politically, an experience without prejudice!—to believe in something specific, an aroma of "art" or "genius," which the individual writer may have more or less of, but which is entirely independent of place, time, nation, and race. We think we feel this immediately, and nothing is so reliable as the concordant sagacity of informed people, the "select circle" of which Schiller spoke, the "smallest troop" of Goethe. It may be that the future of our culture resides today in such experience.

But even in the smallest circle this concurrence is not always dependable. And it might perhaps be objected that it is precisely our own time period that happens to be very receptive to history, and that might easily fall victim to such an illusion. Our age has been reproached for lowering its receptivity as far as primitive art, and it should start doing something else. Our parents were still laughing themselves healthy over El Greco or Van Gogh, and they even laughed over Ibsen, while they thought Hamerling[51] was great, even if they hadn't gotten around to puting up a monument to him!

One can sometimes get dizzy; it's like being on a narrow board over bottomless depths.

9

In this task our concepts still do not provide us with any dependable support. There are aesthetic and critical concepts for whose future application, after they themselves have been more precisely elaborated, there are great prospects. But that will still require all kinds of work. I would indeed say that not even the essence of truth has yet been sufficiently described; and the essence of beauty will follow only at a respectful distance. Sometimes one is helped by indirect hints, such as, for example, the one that points toward literary history, which is a remarkable institution for rewarding the dead, since from them a certain trait of greatness (insofar as they possess it) arises spontaneously, whereby, in spite of all the errors that also inhere in literary history, what emerges with remarkable agreement is that the right way of thinking does not influence this characteristic of greatness at all.

In the sphere of aesthetic values, a child may easily ask more than nine wise men can answer. It is, nevertheless, perhaps worthwhile for the child to ask—but not to decree the answers himself.

10

One can really only counsel patience to literature, and, since our little Austria indeed can claim at present to have become a kind of Noah's ark of German culture, one might also expect a feeling of attentive tenderness. A diminution of the wrongs, a considerate separation of the good from the merely complaisant—well, some things might well be added, but there is much that cannot be done at all. Perhaps the most important thing is to provide oneself with ideas that are to some extent unruffled about what it is that is fluctuating back and forth.

Our literature would not be at all prepared if it were now suddenly to be esteemed. It is not emerging from a terribly good period. Around 1900 it was morbid, aristocratic, and psychological, but also social and analytic; and around 1920 it was centered on the spirit, the chaotic, the miserable, the dynamic, and the like. In terms of criticism, it was looked after either by a collection of the most splendid eulogies, or else particular terms seemed to attract critics the way the whirlpool attracts the skipper, although these terms were exchanged for a new set every ten years or so. In externals, this literature ambled along according to the secret law of canine breeds, cocktails, and the varieties of dance. Intellectual production was heavily mercantilized. Classicism's ideal of education [*Bildung*] was largely replaced by the ideal of entertainment, even if it was entertainment with a patina of art. But if one left that path and entered the silent grove of the "serious" people, one was astonished at how many of them really did not belong there. Taking everything together, this literature directed itself more and more according to the laws of minimal human capacity.

But amidst all this bustle much was going on that was serious and good, and much that contained serious and good things; still, it is understandable that this was less noticed, even by those who carried a "cultural protest" in their hearts against everything that was going on.

To be brief about it, even in the protest that might be considered justified there were all kinds of adulterating ingredients that destroyed its proper effect. I would like to single out a few of them.

11

At some time or other the idea fixed itself in the minds of us Germans that—let's say by way of illustration—if a writer should hit upon the idea of putting a policeman on stage as a murderer, the police would instantly protest. Where does this come from? It calls to mind the popular anecdote about the naive spectator who wants to have the villain of the play arrested; and if the high and highest circles had not forever protected themselves against allowing their ilk to appear on stage, one might say that it was because of inadequate comprehension. The separation between reality and illusion, or perhaps more properly between life and the observation of life, between movement in inner and outer space, this separation, which is of such fundamental importance for literature, is something we have never recognized. Not only has it not been recognized by the great, for whom it was perhaps a kind of caution applied in a precautionary way, but also not by the small, for how often have friends of the people demanded of the superior writer, on the other hand, that he radiate action and not shape experiences for a few: princes did not even wish to see their uniforms faithfully depicted, while the others, in contrast, demanded that even their thoughts be rendered!

The second confusion became immeasurably more influential; one does not have far to seek for striking examples. This confusion finds its prop in that politics as well as literature has an ideological component. In the rarest cases politics produces this itself (by borrowing it from someplace else), and this later gives rise to the error that the mind is itself—I mean, specific positions taken by the mind—political. Think, for instance, of the concept of Liberalism. Its origin is liberality, a great intellectual virtue: Goethe called someone a liberal man, without of course meaning what one calls a Liberal. In this way most ideas have been transposed from their free element to politics, and have for many people so taken on the appearance of politics that these people no longer have any patience with an unpolitical way of thinking or feeling. But it is quite important for politics to maintain this thinking and feeling as its reservoir.

But a *thematic* separation of the spheres of literature and politics can hardly still be effected, and potentially does not even exist; therefore the difference in the way they function must become all the more vivid in everyone's feeling.

12

I recall the old example of the beautifully painted picture of some horrible object: it is a platitude that the picture is beautiful. But what if a beautiful face were to contain a reprehensible sentiment? It would be the same, of course. The face contains this sentiment not as a sentiment but as raw material, as a principle that is in no way self-sufficient and that has become unreal. It can happen that a serious writer does suddenly represent with the greatest devotion what he detests as a private person. One could state flatly that his mind is capable of anything, but it is also capable of detaching everything from its ordinary meaning, while the dilettante is characterized by a constancy of feeling, and for that reason too is easily borne to the skies in periods when everyone is marching to the same step.

Here I would like to recall that just as there are beautiful paintings of ugly objects, there can also be worthless paintings of beautiful objects. Let this be whispered to those portrayers of health and nature who rhapsodize about the chaffinch bursting into song.

The work of art is an abstraction from life and its ties; the enjoyment and understanding of art assumes an ability and a will to abstract that is not often met with, even in artistically minded people, although it always sets in as soon as they scent "something." What is represented truthfully can only be built on the basis of this abstraction. All our higher feelings apparently originated from simple and instinctive feelings sometimes coming into conflict with each other and preventing immediate gratification. Art carries this on in similar fashion, preserving people's sense of not yet having come to closure: it keeps their impulse for progress alive.

I would say that whoever cannot look with pleasure at even the nastiest but wittiest caricature of himself has not yet quite understood this!

13

This spirit—and it is only one member of the mind's family—can of course be subordinated and assimilated only to a certain extent without relinquishing itself. The readiest example of how it can be destroyed is the burning of the library at Alexandria, and the pulling down of pagan statues is the most perfect expression for how the spirit can be brought into harmony with general progress. The spirit of antiquity, at the high level of its cultivation at the time, was dependent on institutions like libraries and schools; and the individuals who incorporated it were dependent on the toleration and good will of their contemporaries. A change in the will of the times (summarily speaking) was enough to sweep everything away. But a few centuries later: A child of spirit came into being. Unlike its ancestors. Remarkably pathological and with a deep expression on his face. Grown to manhood a few centuries later, this child would have given much to know more about its father.

14

But I would not want to close with this threatening picture.

Wilhelm von Humboldt characterized significant individuality as a power of the spirit that springs up without reference to the course of events and begins a new series. He saw nodal points and points of origin in creative people who absorb past things and release them in a new form that can no longer be traced back past their point of origin.

This picture is individualistic in nature, but it also places this individualism entirely within the totality. I would hope and assume that the truth it contains, applied in appropriate form and to purely intellectual endeavors, will become effective a second time in the course of European development!

Basel, Supplement to the Lecture

Honored ladies and gentlemen!

When a short time ago the request was transmitted to me asking me to repeat in your thriving city, so firmly rooted in tradition, a lecture that I had given almost a year earlier in Vienna, I found it very difficult to decide whether to accept the invitation. I question whether fruit that was once

fresh can be trotted out without losing the better part of its taste; but because, nevertheless, I could not deny myself the pleasure of speaking before
you, and since the time for decision was very short, I am now doing penance
with an oppressed conscience.

The lecture of which I am speaking—since I must in any case omit its
original introduction, which was all too specifically designed for local conditions, let me beg your indulgence by saying a few words in advance about
the circumstances in which it came about, and which gave rise as well to its
sketchy and at the same time circumscribed nature. This lecture was given
approximately eleven months ago at the celebration of the twentieth anniversary of the Society for the Protection of German Writers in Austria. The
SPGW is a remaining branch of the once influential but no longer extant
SPGW and Association of Writers, which in Austria embodies the greatest
tradition for individual writers, but which, although it was by nature unpolitical, was rendered innocuous at the beginning of the new political era.

At that time we were all uncertain as to how the notion of the authoritarian—our language really wants to say: of authority, but since in the intellectual sphere this would have to be an intellectual authority, the language
has apparently made an involuntary fine distinction in characterizing the
higher authority of power, according to which one would really have to
speak of "authoritarity"!—at all events, many people found themselves uncertain how this notion of the authoritarian, which was still new in Austria,
was to be interpreted. The example of Germany, despite all the contrasts, did
not appear so entirely remote, and many people feared a restoration of the
monarchy, too; moreover, as is always the case on such occasions, groups of
intellectuals closely connected with the political powers-that-be had stepped
from the background into the foreground and demonstrated, indeed to some
extent appeased, their hearty appetites.

So there was at the time a good deal of apprehension that was not voiced,
and I believe that the success of my lecture was due chiefly to my having
spoken at all, as well as to my having pointed out impartially, without taking
a part either for or against political events, that there are other things to be
gained—or lost, but in any case to be considered—than the things that politically agitated times place in the forefront. The success of the lecture was
surprising, not only at the time but also later; I received offers to repeat it,
to publish it, to give it in other places, to have it translated. But with the sole
exception of today I always resisted, and I did so from the intense feeling
that I owed this success more to the circumstances of my words than to their
content. If, for instance, someone says yes or no to a proposal of marriage,
those are words that are decisive for one's life, but if one were to publish
them in print, their import would not be felt!

I must also mention here that the apprehensions that I said were quite widespread at that time were not realized. The political regime that has been operating in Austria since then may properly be called tolerant, although of course even a tolerant political regime always proceeds in more or less the same way: in all questions of culture it first carves out a preliminary advantage for itself, and then with great impartiality it parcels out the rest to itself and everyone else. By this I mean that the free spirit—which in German spheres has long since no longer been that "we free spirits" with which Nietzsche once did his enchanting, but is, with the greatest diffidence, merely spirit that doesn't belong to some corporation or other—I mean only that not a hair of its head has actually been touched, but that it also does not exactly have a share in the government's hair restorer.

I might also raise the objection that the spirit or intellect, in supraperson, is not free of responsibility for not enjoying greater respect today; for in periods when it was in favor it was to a large extent in charge of managing its own reputation. But this also brings up this problem called "intellect and the present time," or in somewhat more restricted form "the serious writer in our time," which, even in this more limited form, furnishes much too large a title for my brief lecture. In many places today we see the intellect exposed to interdiction by politics, or at least by political leadership, and we have no idea whether this will be not the case in most places tomorrow. The manner in which this happens, and the mind's future prospects, are quite varied. If I also emphasize the necessary independence of intellectual development from political development, I of course do not mean in the least to say that they have no connection. All Europe's political systems are by no means a matter of indifference to me personally, and I do not judge that the future of culture in them will be the same. But I might put it this way: The preponderance of politics, whether it inclines to the good or the barbaric, places the unpolitical mind, or—these exist, at least!—the unpolitical regions of the mind, in the same difficulty of consciousness about itself and of making one's own self prevail. We will no longer get very far with gilded rhetoric. It will be necessary to call to mind the truth in its broadest compass, indeed to discover this truth anew. The moment people began to doubt whether a straight line really is the shortest connection between two points—a thing one obviously should never be permitted to doubt!—was for mathematics the starting point of a whole new development; and we find ourselves, we writers, painters, and philosophers, under a similar compulsion to question ourselves about our basic principles everywhere where the state itself has gone out among the artists and philosophers!

This compulsion embraces a great deal. This I may well say beforehand. And this lecture, which arose from the particular events of a time, and from things that were then important, embraces only a tiny piece of the territory. It represents a chain of connections, and the only thing I believe is that this chain can be usefully interlinked with the many others still to be woven.

After last year's introductory words, this is how I began:

[Lecture. Paris]
1935

These are the notes for a short talk Musil gave before the International Writers Congress for the Defense of Culture in Paris in July 1935. Aldous Huxley, Heinrich Mann, André Gide, and André Malraux were among the other participants. Musil's compressed talk was poorly received, especially his association of Bolshevism and fascism; he had not understood that the congress was primarily political, and had prepared an abstract and nonpolitical presentation. He never expanded these notes (taken from a corrected typescript).

The question of how culture is to be protected, and against what, is inexhaustible. For it involves the nature and development of culture and, equally, the damage to which it is exposed by friend and foe alike.

What I want to say about this here today is unpolitical. All my life I have stayed away from politics because I feel I have no talent for it. I cannot understand the objection that politics has a claim on everyone because it is something that concerns everyone. Hygiene too concerns everyone, and yet it is not something I have ever expressed myself about in public, because I have no more talent as a hygienist than I do as an economic leader or geologist.

I am therefore positing, as I proceed to the borderline between politics and culture, a subordinate kind of person, an unproblematic underling, and yet even such a person still finds himself—here I am thinking of the serious writer in the German tongue as the example with which I am most familiar— in a far from unproblematic situation vis-à-vis the political powers of his nation. Its chief political power still clearly demands of him at the moment that complete subordination that, in a word from which his German grand-

parents were apparently exempt, has been called "total." But this subordination not only is understandably forbidden him if he belongs to a state other
than the German *Reich*, it also demands of him, in addition, a certain kind
of cultural subordination. Thus, for example, my Austrian homeland expects from its serious writers, more or less, that they be Austrian-homeland
writers, and there are constructors of cultural history who show us that an
Austrian writer has always been different from a German one.

Something similar is going on in other countries. The claims of the most
disparate fatherlands, each with its own political and social priorities, have
set themselves above the concept of culture.

This produces a question that has various forms, but is basically always
the same: Does one derive the concept of culture by subtracting what is national, civic, etc., from national, civic, fascist, or proletarian culture (as so to
speak that "which is left over"), or is the concept of culture something independent, which can be realized in many different ways?

I believe that disinterested reflection would, for all sorts of reasons, have
to decide in favor of the second alternative.

The history of our time is developing in the direction of an intensified
collectivism. I need not say how highly differentiated the forms of this collectivism are, and how differently its value for the future is apparently to be
judged. Politicians are accustomed to regard a glorious culture as the natural
spoils of their politics, as in earlier times women fell to the victors. I, on the
other hand, think the glory very much depends, from the cultural side, on
the noble art of female self-defense.

The idea of a many-stranded development of history in a collectivistic
direction can be carried further: but sometimes the simpler and more limited view imposes itself, that the whole is nothing but an encroaching and an
encroachment of politics. Today everything feels threatened, and mobilizes
all the means at its command.

Culture too is among the draftees.

And it is not only that state, class, nation, race, and Christianity lay claim
to us today, but these have themselves gone among the artists and scholars.

Today politics does not derive its goals from culture, but brings them
along itself and parcels them out. It teaches us the one and only way to
write, paint, and philosophize.

Of course, we are also sensitive to the claims of the totality, and the duty
of the individual to accommodate himself. This makes recognition of boundaries that much more important. Imagining what belongs to culture and what

does not is easier the more one has a specific culture in view, and harder the more it is a question of what culture ought to be, or what should be capable of producing it.

Culture is not bound to any political form. It is receptive to specific demands or inhibitions from any of them. There are no cultural axioms (especially not axioms of feeling) that could not be replaced by others, so that on this new basis a different culture would be possible. The decisive factor lies with the whole, as one cannot say of a person according to isolated principles or actions whether he is an idiot, or a genius, or a born criminal. I would especially remind you of Nietzsche's observation, in his posthumous fragments, that "the victory of a moral ideal is achieved by the same immoral means as every victory: force, lies, slander, and injustice."

We transgress against this observation not only whenever we get upset over some crudity or perversity of what is new, but also when we confuse this personal anger with the laws of the history of creation. It is easy to regard what one is accustomed to as necessity.

Part of the aversion towards strongly authoritarian forms of government, Bolshevism and fascism, is merely a consequence of our being accustomed to parliamentary-democratic forms. These evoke the same kind of affection as a suit that is perhaps a little worn but has become comfortable. These forms provide culture with a high degree of freedom. But they provide the same measure of freedom to its pests and parasites. There is no need to equate the essence of culture with parliamentary-democratic forms of government, come hell or high water. Even enlightened absolutism is good, it is just that the absolute must be enlightened.

So if one does not proceed from a traditional ideal of culture, and even assumes that today this ideal is exposed to strong metamorphosing tendencies, and if in addition one does not exactly know what culture is—since for those of us who create, culture is something handed down, something experienced, by no means agreeable in every respect, thus rather a will that lives in us and above us than a definable idea—in which direction should one turn?

I do not believe that this means that everything is left to one's discretion.

Culture presupposes a continuity, and respect even for what one is fighting. Even that is hard to leave out of account.

In that case, it may perhaps also be asserted that culture has always been supranational. The history of the arts and sciences is one long example of this. Even the culture of primitive societies shows this phenomenon. Especially at its highest levels, culture is dependent on supranational connections, and genius too is distributed in the same way as the occurrence of other rarities.

And if culture itself were not international, it would certainly be, within a single people, something supratemporal that often jumps over long flat stretches, and connects with things that lie far back in the past. From this we may conclude that those who serve culture are forbidden to identify themselves totally with a momentary condition of their national culture.

And culture is not a tradition that can simply be passed from hand to hand, as the traditionalists claim, but involves a peculiar process: it is not so much that creative people take over what comes from other times and places as that these are rather newly born within them.

We know further that the bearers of this process are individual people. The community is involved in a most important way, but the individual is at least its independent instrument. This, however, opens up a larger and much more familiar circle of conditions for the rise of a culture, all those to which the individual power of creation is subjected. I don't want to go into this further, but here many politically misused, outworn, and then rejected concepts recur, purified of historical elements, as indispensable psychological assumptions. Thus, for example, freedom, openness, courage, incorruptibility, responsibility, and criticism, criticism even more against what seduces us than against what repels us. These concepts must even include the love of truth, and I mention this especially because what we call culture is not directly subservient to the criterion of truth; but no great culture can rest on a distorted relationship to truth.

If a political regime does not support such qualities in everyone, they will not appear even in extraordinary talents.

To have an effect on recognizing such social conditions, the only thing that might work in culture's self-defense is whatever can be attained by nonpolitical means. It is, at any rate, the most important thing for judging political forms as far as their cultural value and cultural prospects are concerned.

On Stupidity

1937

This lecture was given at the invitation of the Austrian Werkbund in Vienna on March 11, and repeated March 17, 1937.

Ladies and gentlemen,

Anyone who presumes to speak about stupidity today runs the risk of coming to grief in a number of ways. It may be interpreted as insolence on his part; it may even be interpreted as disturbing the progress of our time. I myself wrote some years ago that "if it were not so hard to distinguish stupidity from talent, progress, hope, or improvement, no one would want to be stupid." That was in 1931; and who will dare question that since then the world has seen still more progress and improvements! And so a question gradually arises that refuses to be put off: Just what *is* stupidity?

Nor do I wish to disregard the fact that as a serious writer I have been acquainted with stupidity far longer, indeed I might even say that many is the time stupidity and I have enjoyed a collegial relationship! Moreover, as soon as a man opens his eyes in literature he is confronted by a barely describable resistance that seems to have the ability to assume any form: whether personal, as in the worthy figure of a professor of literature who, accustomed to fix his sights on unverifiable centuries, creates havoc when he misses his target in the present; or it might perchance be the vacuously general, like the transformation of critical judgment by business, since God, in that goodness of his that is so hard for us to understand, has also bestowed the language of mankind on the creators of sound movies. I have described such phenomena before at one time or another, and there is no need to repeat or add to it (and anyway this would probably be impossible, in view of the penchant for greatness everything has today): it is enough to stress as a definite conclusion that the fact that a people is not artistically inclined does not first express itself in bad times, or in coarse ways; so that it is only in degree that oppression and censorship differ from honorary doctorates, membership in learned academies, and the awarding of prizes.

I have always suspected that this polymorphous resistance to art and the finer things on the part of a people that prides itself on being art loving is nothing but stupidity about art; perhaps of a special kind, a particular art-stupidity, and perhaps also a particular stupidity of feeling, but one that in any case expresses itself in such a way that what we call aesthetic sensibility would at the same time be aesthetic stupidity; and even today I don't see many reasons to depart from this view. Of course not everything by which such a thoroughly human affair as art is deformed can be dumped in the lap of stupidity; as the experiences of recent years in particular have taught us, space must be reserved for the various kinds of weakness of character as well. But the objection that the idea of stupidity has no business here because it relates to reason and not to feelings, while art depends on feelings, can not be entertained. It would be a mistake. Even aesthetic enjoyment is a combination of feeling and judgment. And I ask your indulgence if I may add to this great formulation, which I have borrowed from Kant, not only the reminder that Kant speaks of an aesthetic power of *judgment*, and a *judgment* of taste, but also if I may repeat the contradictions to which this leads:

Thesis: the judgment of taste is not grounded in concepts, for otherwise it could be the subject of dispute (subject to being decided by demonstration or proof).

Antithesis: it *is* grounded in concepts, for otherwise it could not even be argued about (a striving for unanimity).

And now I would ask whether a similar judgment with a similar antinomy does not also lie at the root of politics, and of the disorder of life in general? And may one not, where judgment and reason reside, also expect to find their big and little sisters, the various kinds of stupidity? So much concerning their importance. Erasmus of Rotterdam wrote in his charming *Praise of Folly*, a work undiminished even today, that except for certain stupidities no one would even be born!

. .

Many people reveal a sense of the domination stupidity has over us, a domination as offensive to modesty as it is powerful, when they show themselves amicably and conspiratorially surprised as soon as they hear that a person in whom they have placed their trust intends to conjure up this monster by its true name. I was not only able to initially conduct this experiment on myself, but soon discovered its historical validity when, in searching for predecessors who had worked on stupidity—of whom I could find strikingly few; wise men apparently prefer to write about wisdom—a scholarly friend sent me the printed version of a lecture delivered in 1866. Its author was J. E. Erdmann, the pupil of Hegel and professor at the University of Halle. This lecture, which is called "On Stupidity," starts right off with the report that even when it was announced it was greeted with laughter. Having discovered that this can happen even to a Hegelian, I am convinced that there are peculiar circumstances connected with people who demonstrate such an attitude toward those who wish to speak about stupidity, and I find myself quite insecure in the face of my conviction that I have provoked powerful and deeply ambivalent psychological forces.

So when confronted with stupidity I would rather confess my Achilles' heel right away: I don't know what it is. I have not discovered any theory of stupidity with whose aid I could presume to save the world; in fact, even within the limits of scientific discretion, I have not come across an investigation that has taken stupidity as its subject, nor have I found even some kind of unanimity that would, for better or worse, have resulted from treating related things with regard to the notion of stupidity. This might be due to my ignorance, but more likely the question, "What is stupidity?" corresponds as little to our current ways of thinking as do the questions of what goodness, beauty, or electricity are. There is, nevertheless, more than a little attraction in putting together such a notion, and answering as soberly as possible a question as basic as this one, which is preliminary to all life; and for that reason, one day the question devolved upon me as to what stupidity might *really* be—not how it makes a show of itself. (Describing that would have suited my professional duty and skill much better.) But since I did not want to help my endeavor along in a literary fashion, and could not in a scientific one, I have done so in the most naive way possible, which of course always suggests itself in such cases: I pursued the word *stupid* and its relatives, seeking out the most common examples; and then I endeavored to correlate what I had written down. Unfortunately, such a procedure always has about it something of chasing after cabbage-whites: you pursue for a while what you think you are observing without losing it from sight; but since other, quite similar butterflies appear from other directions on quite similar zigzag courses, you soon no longer know whether you are still chasing the same one. So too, examples from the "stupidity" family cannot always be distinguished according to whether they really are related to each other in some fundamental way or whether they lead the observer from one to another only inadvertently and superficially, and it will not be such an easy matter to find a single hat covering all of them of which one could say: This hat *really* belongs to a blockhead.

. .

Under these circumstances it is almost immaterial how one begins, so let us begin somehow; the best place might be with the initial difficulty, which is that anyone who wants to talk about stupidity, or profitably participate in a conversation about it, must assume about himself that he is not stupid; and he also makes a show of considering himself clever, although doing so is generally considered a sign of stupidity! If one investigates this question of why making a show of being clever should be considered stupid, the first answer that comes to mind is one that seems to have the dust of ancestral furniture about it, for it maintains that appearing not to be clever is the better part of caution. This profoundly mistrustful caution, which today is, at first glance, no longer even remotely comprehensible, probably derives from situations in which it really *was* smarter for the weak person not to be considered clever; his cleverness might be seen as endangering the life of the strong person! Stupidity, on the other hand, lulls mistrust to sleep; it "disarms," as we still say today. Traces of such venerable craftiness and artful stupidity are also still to be found in dependent relationships in which the relative strengths are so disproportionately divided that the weaker person seeks his salvation by acting more stupid than he is: these traces show themselves, for instance, in the peasant's so-called slyness, the servant's dealings with his culture-tongued master and mistress, the soldier's relations to his superior officer, the pupil's to his teacher, and the child's to its parents. It irritates the person who has power less if the weak person is not able than if he is not willing. Stupidity even drives the strong person "to despair," in other words, to what is unmistakably a condition of weakness!

This is most admirably consonant with the way cleverness easily "harnesses" the strong person. Cleverness in the submissive person is esteemed, but only so long as it is connected with unconditional devotion. The instant devotion lacks this certificate of good character, and is no longer clearly serving the advantage of the dominant person, it is less often called clever than immodest, insolent, or malicious; and a relationship often arises that looks as if this devotion were at least opposing the dominating party's honor and authority, even if it poses no real threat to the latter's security. In education this takes the form of a rebellious but talented pupil being treated more vehemently than one who is obstinate out of dullness. In morality it has led to the idea that a person's will must be the more evil, the better the knowledge against which it is acting. Even justice has not been entirely untouched by this individual prejudice, and judges the clever execution of a crime, for the most part with particular disfavor, as "crafty" and "crude in feeling." And in politics examples are not far to seek.

But stupidity also—this objection will probably have to be raised here—can irritate, and is by no means soothing in all circumstances. Put briefly, stupidity usually arouses impatience, but in exceptional cases it also arouses cruelty; and the excesses of this pathological, aversion-instilling cruelty, which are ordinarily characterized as sadism, often enough show stupid people in the role of victim. This evidently comes about because they fall prey to cruel people more easily than others do, but it also seems to have some connection with an absence of resistance that is palpable in every direction, and that drives the imagination wild the way the smell of blood excites lust for the hunt: this entices the stupid person into a desert in which cruelty goes "too far" almost for the sole reason that it loses all sense of limits. This is a quality of suffering in the very bringer of suffering, a weakness embedded in his brutality; and although the priority we give to the indignation of offended sympathy rarely allows us to notice it, cruelty too, like love, calls for two people in harmony with each other.

This would certainly be an important enough matter for discussion in a mankind as plagued as ours is by its "cowardly cruelty toward the weak" (and this is also the most usual conceptual paraphrase for sadism); but with a view to pursuing the main course of the argument, and with the hasty gathering of first examples, what has been said so far must already be seen as a digression, from which, by and large, nothing more is to be gained than that it can be stupid to praise oneself as clever, but that it is also not always clever to acquire a reputation for being stupid. Nothing here can be generalized; or the only admissible generalization would be that the cleverest thing of all is to make oneself as inconspicuous as possible in this world! And this final summing up of all wisdom has in fact not infrequently been made. But more often only partial or metaphorically representative use is made of this reclusive result, and then observation is led into the sphere of the commandments of modesty, and of even more encompassing commandments, without having to leave the realm of stupidity and cleverness entirely.

Many people take themselves to be clever but don't say so, as much from fear of appearing stupid as from fear of offending decency. And if they should feel impelled to speak about it they talk around it, as when they say of themselves, "I'm *no stupider* than other people." Still more popular is to apply the observation, as objectively and matter-of-factly as possible, "I may indeed say of myself that I possess a normal intelligence." And sometimes the conviction of one's own cleverness also appears in a roundabout way, as for instance in the expression, "I won't let myself be made a fool of!" It is even more remarkable that it is not only the secretive individual who in his own mind sees himself as extremely clever and well equipped, but also the person who plays an active public role, who, as soon as he gets the power to, says or has said about himself that he is inordinately clever, inspired, dignified, gracious, chosen by God, and destined for History. Indeed he even willingly says this of another person in whose reflection he basks. This has been petrified and preserved in titles and forms of address such as Your Majesty, Your Eminence, Your Magnificence, and Your Grace, among others, which consciousness hardly animates anymore; but it shows up immediately again in full force today whenever man speaks in the mass. In particular a certain lower middle class of mind and soul is quite shameless toward the need for arrogance in this regard the moment it can strut within the shelter of the party, nation, sect, or art movement and say "we" instead of "I."

With one reservation, which is obvious and can be ignored, this arrogance may also be called vanity, and in fact today the soul of many peoples and nations is dominated by feelings among which vanity undeniably occupies a privileged position; but between stupidity and vanity an inner connection has existed for ages, and perhaps this connection offers us a clue. A stupid person usually has the effect of appearing vain because he is not clever enough to hide it; but such cleverness is not really necessary, for the relationship between stupidity and vanity is more straightforward: a vain person gives the impression of accomplishing less than he could; he resembles a machine that allows its steam to escape through a leak. This is what the old saying means, that stupidity and pride grow on the same tree, as does the expression that vanity "dazzles." What we really connect with the idea of vanity is the expectation of underachievement, for the word *vain*, in its primary sense, means almost the same as *in vain*. And we also expect this diminution of achievement where in truth there is achievement: vanity and talent are also found together fairly often, but in that case we have the impression that still more *could* be accomplished if the vain person were not getting in his own way. This notion of the diminution of achievement, which sticks like a burr, will later reveal itself to be the most universal notion of stupidity that we have.

But this vain attitude is clearly not avoided because it can be stupid, but principally because it disturbs propriety. "Praising oneself stinks," a pithy saying has it, and this means that boasting and praising and talking about oneself a lot is considered not only not clever, but also indecent. If I'm not mistaken, the demands of propriety that this offends belong to the many forms of those commandments of discretion and the maintaining of distance whose purpose is to spare one's self-conceit, which assumes that this self-conceit is no less in someone else than it is in oneself. Such precepts for maintaining distance are also directed against the use of words that are too frank, regulate forms of greeting and address, and do not permit people to contradict one another without apologizing, or a letter to begin with the word "I"; in short, they demand the observance of certain rules just so that people do not "get too close" to one another. It is the task of these rules to smooth communication, to alleviate loving one's neighbor and oneself and to maintain, as it were, a moderate climate in human intercourse; such precepts are found in every society, even more in primitive societies than in highly civilized ones, indeed even the wordless animal world knows them, as may easily be deduced from its many ceremonies. But according to the sense of these rules for maintaining distance, it is forbidden to praise not only oneself obtrusively, but others as well. To say to someone's face that he is a genius or a saint would be almost as monstrous as saying it about oneself; and to smear one's face and pull out one's hair would, by contemporary standards of feeling, be no better than cursing another person. As I have stated, one contents oneself with the observation that one is not particularly stupider or worse than others.

In stable circumstances it is obviously extravagant and licentious expressions to which the prohibition is applied. And as I spoke earlier about the vanity in which peoples and political parties today are arrogant about being enlightened, to complete the picture I must now say that the majority that lives life to the full—just like the individual megalomaniac in his daydreams—has not only commandeered wisdom, but virtue as well, and regards itself as courageous, noble, invincible, pious, and beautiful; and that there is a particular propensity in the world for people, wherever they appear in great numbers, to permit themselves collectively everything that would be forbidden them individually. These privileges of the "we" that has grown so powerful today frankly give the impression that the increasing civilizing and taming of the individual ought to be balanced by a proportionately increasing *de*civilization of nations, states, and alliances of the like-minded; what obviously emerges in this is an emotional disturbance, a disturbance of the emotional balance that fundamentally underlies both the opposition between "I" and "we" and all moral valuation as well. But is this—one will need to ask—still stupidity, indeed, is it still connected with stupidity at all?

Dear listeners! No one doubts that it is! But before proceeding with our response, let us catch our breath with an example that is not without its charm. All of us, we men in particular, and especially all well-known writers, know the lady who positively insists on confiding in us the novel of her life, and whose soul has, it appears, always found itself in interesting circumstances without this ever having led to success, which she rather expects from us. Is this lady stupid? Something arising from the profusion of our impressions is accustomed to whisper to us: She is! But politeness as well as justice demand the concession that she is not absolutely and not always stupid. She talks a lot about herself, and she talks a great deal. She judges in a most determined way, and judges everything. She is vain and immodest. She often lectures us. Usually there is something amiss with her love life, and in general life has not been kind to her. But aren't there other sorts of people of whom all or most of this would also be true? To talk a lot about oneself, for instance, is also a rudeness of egoists, of the restless, and even of a certain kind of melancholy person. This applies especially to young people, in whom it is one of the symptoms of the growing process to talk a lot about themselves, to be vain, to lecture others, and to have not quite got their lives

together; demonstrating, in a word, precisely the same deviations from as-
tuteness and propriety, without on that account being stupid, or more stupid
than is determined naturally by their—just not having become clever!

Ladies and gentlemen! The judgments and anthropology of everyday life
happen for the most part to hit the mark, but they usually miss it as well.
They did not arise for the sake of some correct doctrine; all they really represent are intellectual gestures of assent and self-defense. So even this example only teaches us that something can be stupid, but doesn't have to be;
that meaning changes with the context in which something appears, and
that stupidity is densely interwoven with other things, without a thread
sticking out anywhere that would allow the weave to be ripped apart with a
single pull. Even genius and stupidity are inextricably connected with each
other, and by means of the writer mankind has got around the prohibition
of being taken for stupid on pain of punishment by talking too much, and
talking too much about itself in a peculiar way. The writer may state in the
name of mankind that it tasted good, or that the sun stands in the sky; he
may bare his soul, babble secrets, make confessions, deliver ruthless personal accountings (at least, many writers insist on this!); and it all looks
exactly as if mankind were here permitting itself an exception to what it
otherwise forbids. In this way mankind speaks incessantly about itself, and
with the aid of the writer has recited the same stories and experiences millions of times, merely changing the circumstances, without producing for
itself any progress or intellectual advance: is not, ultimately, stupidity also
to be suspected in the use mankind makes of its literature? As far as I can see
it doesn't seem at all impossible!

Between the range of application of stupidity and that of immorality—
this last term is understood in the broader sense, uncommon today, that is
almost the same as lack of spirituality or intellectuality [*Ungeistigkeit*], but
not like imprudence or silliness [*Unverständigkeit*]—there is, at any rate, a
complex identity and differentiation. And this association is doubtless similar, as J. E. Erdmann has expressed it in an important passage in the lecture I
mentioned previously, to brutality's being "applied stupidity." Erdmann
says, "Words are . . . not the only manifestation of a state of mind. It can
reveal itself in action as well. So, too, can stupidity. Not only being stupid,
but acting stupidly, doing stupid things"—in other words, applied stupidity—"or stupidity in action, is what we call brutality." This winning assertion teaches nothing less than that stupidity is a mistake of feeling—for
brutality is a feeling! And this leads straight back to that "emotional disturbance" and "disturbance of emotional balance" that were touched upon earlier without our having been able to explain them. But the explanation
contained in Erdmann's words cannot entirely accord with the truth, for

aside from the fact that this explanation merely targets the crude, un-polished individual in contrast to "culture," and in no way embraces all the applicable forms of stupidity, brutality is also not just simply stupidity, and stupidity not just simply brutality; so there is still much to be explained in the relationship between affect and intelligence when they combine as "applied stupidity," and this can probably best be brought out, once again, through examples.

. .

In order for the outlines of the notion of stupidity to emerge properly, it is first of all necessary to soften the verdict that stupidity is merely, or particularly, a deficiency of understanding; as has already been stated, the most general notion we have of stupidity, that of failure in the most varied activities, seems to be the fundamental notion of physical and mental deficiency in general. In our Austrian dialects there is an expressive example of this in the characterization of a person as being hard of hearing, in other words referring to a bodily defect, by the word *derisch* or *terisch*, which is probably *törisch* [deaf—trans.], and so is close to stupidity. For in precisely the same way, the reproach of stupidity is also used in other situations among the common people. If an athlete fails at a decisive moment or makes a mistake, he says afterwards, "It was like being nailed to the spot!" or "I don't know where my head was!" although the degree of the head's participation in swimming or boxing may be regarded in any case as rather hazily defined. In the same way, among boys and sports buddies, someone whose actions are awkward will be called stupid even if he should be a Hölderlin. There are also business relationships in which a person who is not cunning and ruthless is considered stupid. All in all, these are the stupidities that go with older kinds of cleverness than the one that stands so high in public esteem today; and if I have been properly informed, in old Teutonic times it was not only moral ideas but also the notions of what was expert, experienced, and wise, in other words intellectual concepts, that were related to war and battle. Thus every cleverness has its stupidity, and even animal psychology has discovered in its testing of intelligence that a "type of stupidity" can be ascribed to every "type of achievement."

If one were therefore looking for the most general notion of stupidity, these comparisons would yield something like the notion of capability or soundness, and everything that is incapable or unsound might then, on occasion, also be called stupid; and in reality this is what happens, if the capability belonging to a particular stupidity is not literally given the name of cleverness. What kind of capacity occupies the foreground in this case, and imparts meaning to the concept of cleverness and stupidity, depends on the shape life has at a given time. In periods of personal insecurity, the concept of cleverness is stamped by cunning, violence, sagacity, and physical dexterity; in periods of spiritualized middle-class conventions—with the limitations that are unfortunately necessary, one would also have to say—it is replaced by mental work. More accurately, this should be the job of the higher intellectual powers, but in the course of things this has turned into a preponderance of rational achievements, which is written in the empty face of bustling mankind beneath its hard forehead; and so it has come about that today cleverness and stupidity, as if it could not be otherwise, are connected only with the intellect and its degree of capability, although that is pretty one-sided.

The general idea of incapability that has been associated with the word *stupid* from the beginning—in the sense of being incapable of anything, as well as in the sense of any particular incapacity—has a quite impressive consequence, which is that *stupid* and *stupidity*, because they signify general incapability, can occasionally serve for any word intended to characterize a particular incapacity. This is one of the reasons why people's reproaching each other with stupidity is so enormously widespread today. (In another connection, it is also the reason why the concept is so hard to pin down, as our examples have demonstrated.) Look at the notes written in the margins of pretentious novels that have been circulating for a while in the near-anonymous traffic of lending libraries: here, where the reader is alone with the writer, his favorite judgment is expressed in the word "stupid!" or its equivalents, such as "idiotic!" "unspeakable stupidity!" and the like. And when people at theatrical performances or art exhibits take offense and rise up en masse against the artist, these are likewise their first words of indignation. The word *kitsch* also comes to mind, a term of immediate reaction beloved of artists themselves like no other; without, however, at least so far as I am aware, its concept being defined or its applicability explained, except by means of the verb *verkitschen*, which in common parlance means something like "selling below value" or "dumping." *Kitsch*, therefore, has the meaning of wares that are too cheap or throwaway, and I believe that this sense, of course transposed to the intellectual level, lurks in the word every time it is unconsciously used correctly.

Since throwaway goods, junk, enter into the word *kitsch* principally through their associated meaning of unfit, useless wares, but incapability and uselessness also form the basis for our use of the term *stupid*, it is hardly an exaggeration to maintain that we tend to address everything we don't agree with—especially when, apart from that, we pretend to respect it as intellectual or aesthetic!—as "somehow stupid." And in determining what this "somehow" means, it is significant that the use of expressions for stupidity is shot through and through with a second usage, which embraces the equally imperfect expressions for what is vulgar and morally repellent and leads one's attention back to something it had already once noticed, the fateful conjoining of the notions "stupid" and "indecent." For not only "kitsch," which is the aesthetic expression of intellectual origin, but also the moral words "filth!" "repulsive!" "horrid!" "sick!" and "insolent!" are undeveloped kernels of art criticism and judgments about life. But perhaps these expressions still do contain some intellectual exertion, a discrimination of meaning, even if they are used indiscriminately; then the ultimate term that jumps into the breach for them is the *really* already half-speechless exclamation "how vulgar!" which replaces everything else and which, together with the exclamation "how stupid!" is able to share in dominating the world. For both these terms can manifestly, on occasion, jump in for all other terms, since *stupid* has taken on the meaning of general incapability and *vulgar* that of a general offense against morals; and if one eavesdrops on what people today say about one another, it appears that the self-portrait of mankind, as it arises unretouched from reciprocal group photographs, is simply no more than a mixture of the variations of these two outlandish expressions!

Perhaps this is worth thinking about. Without doubt, both terms represent the lowest level of a judgment that has not crystallized enough to be formulated, a criticism that is still completely undifferentiated, which feels that something is wrong but is not able to indicate what. Use of these terms is the plainest and worst self-protective expression there is; it is the beginning of a rejoinder, and already its end as well. There is something of a "short circuit" in this, and it is more understandable if we consider that *stupid* and *vulgar*, whatever they may mean, are also used as terms of abuse. For the meaning of these terms, as we are well aware, lies not so much in their content as in the way they are used; many among us might well love the donkey, but be insulted if we are called one. The insult does not stand for what it signifies, but for a mixture of ideas, feelings, and intentions which it can not even remotely express, but which it can signal. Incidentally, the term of invective shares this characteristic with the faddish word and foreign words, which is why these appear indispensable, even if there are perfectly good substitutes for them. For this reason abusive language also has about it something unimaginably exciting, which may well be connected with its intention but not its content: this is perhaps most clearly seen in the teasing and kidding words of children: a child can say "monster!" and on the basis of hidden associations throw another child into conniptions.

But what can be said in this fashion about terms of abuse and about teasing words, faddish words, and foreign words can also be said about witty words, catchwords, and amorous words: what they all have in common, however incomparable they may otherwise be, is that they are in the service of an affect, and it is precisely their lack of precision and absence of referent that enables them to suppress, when they are used, whole realms of words that are more accurate, more relevant, and more correct. Evidently life sometimes needs this, and we have to allow for it; but what happens in such cases is without doubt stupid; it wanders, so to speak, along the same path as stupidity. This connection can be shown most clearly in the biggest public spectacle of mindlessness, the case of panic. If something that affects a person is too overwhelming for him, whether sudden fright or an unremitting spiritual pressure, it can happen that this person suddenly "loses his head." He can begin to howl, basically no differently from the way a child howls; he can "blindly" rush away from a danger or just as blindly rush into it; he can be overcome by an explosive tendency to destroy, swear, or wail. Altogether, instead of purposive behavior that would be appropriate to his situation he will engage in a great many other kinds of behavior that always appear to be, and in reality all too often are, aimless, and indeed counterproductive. We are most familiar with this kind of contrariness as "panic fear"; but if the term is not taken in too narrow a sense, we could also speak of panics of rage, of greed, and even of tenderness; or indeed wherever a condition of excitation cannot give satisfaction in such vivid, blind, or senseless fashion. A man as intelligent as he was courageous noted long ago that there is a panic of courage, which is only distinguished from the panic of fear by its reversal of polarity.

Psychologically, what takes place when panic breaks out is regarded as a suspension of the itelligence, indeed of the entire higher intellectual faculty, in place of which a more primitive spiritual mechanism emerges; but it might well be added that with the paralyzing and ligature of reason in such cases, what happens is not so much a descent to acting instinctively as rather a descent leading straight through this area to a deeper instinct of ultimate necessity and an ultimate emergency form of action. This kind of action takes the form of total confusion: it has no plan, and is apparently bereft of reason and every other saving instinct; but its unconscious plan is to replace quality of action with quantity, and its not inconsiderable cunning rests on the probability that among a hundred blind attempts that are washouts there is one that will hit the target. A person who has lost his head, an insect that bumps against the closed half of a window until by accident it "plunges" through the open half to freedom: in their confusion they are doing nothing but what military strategy does with calculated deliberation when it "saturates" a target with a volley or with sweeping fire, or indeed when it uses shrapnel or a grenade.

What this means, in other words, is allowing a single intentional action to be represented by a great many, and nothing is more human than substituting the *quantity* of words and actions for their *character*. But using imprecise words is very similar to using lots of words, for the more imprecise a word is, the greater the area it covers; and the same is true of irrelevance. If these things are stupid, then through them stupidity is related to the panic condition; nor is excessive use of this reproach and others like it too far removed from attempting spiritual salvation through archaic-primitive methods—which are, as we may doubtless quite properly assert, pathological. And indeed we can recognize in the proper use of the reproach that something is truly stupid or vulgar not only a failure of intelligence, but also the blind inclination to mindless destruction or flight. These words are not only invective, they stand for a whole fit of invective. Where they still just barely manage to express something, assault is not far away. To return to examples brought up earlier, in such cases paintings are attacked with umbrellas (and moreover in place of the person who painted them), and books are flung to the ground as if their poison could in that way be neutralized. But also present is the devitalizing pressure that precedes this action and that the action is meant to relieve: a person "almost suffocates" on his anger; "there aren't enough words" aside from the most vulgar and senseless ones; one is "at a loss for words," one must "gain breathing space." This is the degree of speechlessness, indeed mindlessness, that precedes the explosion! It indicates an oppressive condition of insufficiency, and the explosion is then usually introduced with the profoundly transparent words that "something has finally become just *too* stupid" for one to take. But this something is oneself. In periods when energetic, sweeping action is highly esteemed, it is essential to also be reminded of what sometimes resembles action to the point of being mistaken for it.

. .

Ladies and gentlemen! Today there is a lot of talk about mankind's crisis of confidence, a crisis that up till now has been located in people's sense of humanity; it might also be called a panic that is on the point of replacing the assurance that we are able to conduct our affairs rationally and in freedom. And we should not deceive ourselves that both these moral, and also moral-artistic concepts, freedom and reason, which have come down to us as tokens of human dignity from the classical period of German cosmopolitanism, have since the middle of the nineteenth century, or slightly later, not been in the very best of health. They have gradually gone out of circulation, one no longer knows what to "do" with them; and that they have been allowed to atrophy has been due less to the success of their opponents than of their friends. So we should not deceive ourselves: it is most unlikely that we, or those who come after us, will go back to these unchanged ideas; our task, and the sense of the trials laid upon the spirit, will rather be—and this is the painful yet hopeful task, so rarely understood, of the people of every age—to complete the always necessary, indeed deeply desired, transition to the new with the least possible loss. The more so since, having failed to make at the proper time the transition that those conserving and yet changing ideas must undergo, in carrying out this activity we need help from ideas of what is true, reasonable, meaningful, and clever, and also, by inverse reflection, from ideas of what is stupid. But what notion or partial notion of stupidity can we form when the notions of reason and wisdom are shaky? I would just like to demonstrate by one small example how much views change with time. In a once quite well known psychiatric manual the question, "What is justice?" and its answer, "That the *other* person gets punished," are adduced as an instance of imbecility, whereas today they form the basis of a much-discussed concept of law. So I fear that even the most modest explanations cannot be ultimately settled without at least indicating a kernel independent of temporary variations. This leads to a few more questions and observations.

I have no right to stand before you as a psychologist, and no intention of doing so; but casting at least a brief glance at this science is probably the first thing we might do in looking for help, given our situation. Older psychology distinguished among sensation, will, feeling, and the ability to form ideas, or intelligence; for this psychology it was clear that stupidity was a lesser degree of intelligence. But contemporary psychology has robbed the basic discriminations among the soul's capacities of their importance and recognized the mutual dependence and interpenetration of the soul's various accomplishments, and in doing so has made much less simple the answer to the question of what stupidity signifies psychologically. There is of course, even in the contemporary view, a conditional independence of the rational ability, but according to this view even in the calmest situations attention, comprehension, memory, and other things, indeed just about everything that is part of reason, are apparently also dependent on the qualities of the emotions; and to this moreover is added, in the course of emotional as well as totally intellectualized experiencing, a second interpenetration of intelligence and affect that is absolutely unresolvable. This difficulty in keeping reason and feeling separate in the notion of intelligence is naturally also reflected in the notion of stupidity. If, for instance, medical psychology describes the thinking of feebleminded people with words such as "poor," "imprecise," "incapable of abstract deduction," "obscure," "slow," "easily diverted," "superficial," "one-sided," "stiff," "laborious," "overexcited," or "distracted," it can easily be seen that these qualities point partly to the understanding and partly to the emotions. So one might well say that stupidity and cleverness depend as much on the understanding as on the emotions, and it can be left to the experts whether there is more of one than of the other, or whether for example in the case of imbecility it is the weakness of the intelligence or the lameness of the emotions, as many rigorous moralists who are highly regarded would have it, that "stands in the foreground," while we lay people must resort to a somewhat more flexible attitude.

In life one usually means by a stupid person one who is "a little weak in the head." But beyond this there are the most varied kinds of intellectual and spiritual deviations, which can so hinder and frustrate and lead astray even an undamaged innate intelligence that it leads, by and large, to something for which the only word language has at its disposal is stupidity. Thus this word embraces two fundamentally quite different types: an honorable and straightforward stupidity, and a second that, somewhat paradoxically, is even a sign of intelligence. The first is based rather on a weakness of understanding, the second more on an understanding that is weak only with regard to some particular, and this latter kind is by far the more dangerous.

Honorable stupidity is a little dull of comprehension, and has what one calls a "dim wit." It is poor in ideas and words, and awkward in applying them. Honorable stupidity prefers the ordinary because the ordinary manages through constant repetition to imprint itself firmly on the slow mind, and once this mind has grasped something it is not in a hurry to let it be taken away again, to let it be analyzed, or to explain it away itself. Honorable stupidity has more than a little of life's rosy cheeks. It is, to be sure, often vague in its thinking, and its thoughts easily come to a standstill when faced with new experiences, but to make up for this it prefers to cling to what is graspable by those senses that it can, as it were, count off on its fingers. It is, in a word, that dear "bright stupidity," and if it were not sometimes also so credulous, obscure, and at the same time so uneducable that it can drive one to despair, it would be a thoroughly charming phenomenon.

I cannot resist the opportunity to furnish this phenomenon with a few more examples illustrating it from other sides, which I have taken from Bleuler's *Manual of Psychiatry*: An imbecile expresses what we would dispose of with the formula "doctor by the sickbed" with the words, "There's a man, he's holding another man's hand, the other man is lying in bed, then there's a nurse standing there." This is the way a savage who paints would put it! Or a housemaid who is not all there considers it a bad joke that she should be expected to put her savings in a bank where it would earn interest; her response is that no one would be stupid enough to pay her something for keeping her money for her. There is in this a chivalric frame of mind, a relationship to money that in my youth one could still find here and there among refined elderly people. Finally, it is put down as a bad symptom when a third imbecile maintains that a two-mark coin is worth less than a one-mark coin and two half marks, because—his reasoning runs—one has to get it changed, and you would get too little back! I hope I'm not the only imbecile in this hall who heartily endorses this theory of value for people who never pay attention to their change!

But to return once again to the relationship to art, plain, straightforward stupidity often acts like a woman artist. Instead of replying to a stimulus word with another word, as was once customary in many experiments, she immediately answers in whole sentences, and one may say what one will, these sentences contain something like poetry. I repeat a few such responses, first indicating the stimulus word:

> Ignite: The baker ignites the wood.
> Winter: Consists of snow.
> Father: Once threw me down the stairs.
> Wedding: Kind of entertainment.
> Garden: In the garden the weather is always fine.
> Religion: When you go to church.
> Who was Wilhelm Tell: He was played in the forest; there were dressed-up women and children in it.
> Who was Peter: He crowed three times.

The naiveté and great concreteness of such responses, which substitute the telling of a simple story for higher levels of conceptualization; the serious narrating of superfluous and accessory circumstances; and then too the abbreviating condensation, as in the example with Peter: these are ancient literary practices, and even though I believe that too much of this, such as is now very much in vogue, brings the poet close to the idiot, still one cannot mistake the poetic in the idiot, and it sheds light on the fact that the idiot can be represented in literature, with special pleasure being taken in representing his mind.

The higher, pretentious form of stupidity stands only too often in crass opposition to this honorable form. It is not so much lack of intelligence as failure of intelligence, for the reason that it presumes to accomplishments to which it has no right; and it can have all the bad characteristics of weakness of reason, and in addition all those characteristics brought about by every mind that is not in balance, that is misshapen and erratically active; in short, every mind that deviates from health. To put it more accurately: because there are no "normalized" minds, this deviation expresses an insufficient play of harmony between the one-sidedness of feeling and a reason that is not strong enough to hold it in check. This higher stupidity is the real disease of culture (but to forestall misunderstanding: it is a sign of nonculture, of misculture, of culture that has come about in the wrong way, of disproportion between the material and the energy of culture), and to describe it is an almost infinite task. It reaches into the highest intellectual sphere; for if genuine stupidity is a peaceful woman artist, then intelligent stupidity is what participates in the agitation of intellectual life, especially in its inconstancy and lack of results. Years ago I wrote about this form of stupidity that "there is absolutely no significant idea that stupidity would not know how to apply; stupidity is active in every direction, and can dress up in all the clothes of truth. Truth, on the other hand, has for every occasion only one dress and one path, and is always at a disadvantage." The stupidity this addresses is no mental illness, yet it is most lethal; a dangerous disease of the mind that endangers life itself.

Each of us should certainly pursue this in ourselves, and not recognize it only in its great historical outbursts. But recognize it by what? And with what unmistakable brand can it be stamped? Psychiatry today uses as a chief characteristic for those cases with which it is concerned the incapacity of a person to find himself in life, giving up in the face of all the tasks life poses, or suddenly when confronted with one that was not expected. Experimental psychology too, which is chiefly concerned with the healthy person, defines stupidity in a similar way. "We call 'stupid' behavior that does not carry out something for which all the conditions except the individual ones are given," a well-known representative of one of the newest schools of this discipline has written. This characteristic of the capacity for objective behavior, in other words soundness and efficiency, leaves nothing to be desired in the unequivocal "cases" of the clinic, or the experimental station where apes are observed; but those "cases" that run around freely call for some additional considerations, because in these cases it is not always so evident what the right or wrong way of "carrying something out" is. In the first place, all the higher ambivalence of cleverness and stupidity is already present in the capacity always to behave the way a person equipped for life actually does behave in given circumstances, for "appropriate," "competent" behavior can either use the affair for personal advantage or to further its aim, and whoever does the one customarily considers someone who does the other stupid. (But only that person is *clinically* stupid who can do neither the one nor the other.) And second, it cannot be denied that behavior that is undirected, indeed pointless, may often be necessary, for objectivity and impersonality, and subjectivity and pointlessness, are related to one another; and as ridiculous as unrestrained subjectivity is, completely objective behavior is of course unthinkable, in both life and thought: how to balance them is indeed one of the major difficulties facing our culture. And finally, the objection might also be raised that on occasion no one behaves as cleverly as is called for: that each of us therefore is, if not always, at least from time to time, stupid. So a distinction must also be made between failing and incapacity, between occasional, or functional, and permanent, or constitutional, stupidity, between error and unreason. This is most important because of the way the conditions of life are today: so unintelligible, so difficult, so confused, that the occasional stupidities of the individual can easily lead to a constitutional stupidity of the body politic. This also ultimately leads observation from the realm of personal qualities to the idea of a society burdened with mental defects. Of course, one cannot transpose to whole societies what happens psychologically in a real sense in the individual, and this includes mental illnesses and stupidity, but still one might speak repeatedly today of a "social imitation of mental defects"; the examples are pretty blatant.

. .

With these additions we have again, of course, left the realm of psychological explanation behind. Psychological explanation itself teaches us that a clever way of thinking has specific qualities, such as clarity, precision, profusion, solubility in spite of solidity, and many others, which can be enumerated; and that these qualities are in part innate, in part also acquired as a kind of dexterity in thinking, along with the knowledge one assimilates: good reasoning and a nimble mind do, after all, amount pretty much to the same thing. All that needs to be overcome is inertia and disposition, and these can be trained; the funny word "thoughtsports" would not be a bad expression for what is at stake here.

"Intelligent" stupidity, on the other hand, has as its adversary not so much the understanding as the spirit [*Geist*], and if one is willing to imagine as "spirit" not merely a little heap of emotions, the sensibility [*Gemüt*] as well. Because thoughts and feelings act together, but also because it is the same person who is expressing himself through them, such notions as breadth, narrowness, flexibility, straightforwardness, and fidelity can be applied to thinking as well as to feeling; and even if the connection arising from this may not be entirely clear, it at least suffices for one to be able to say that understanding too is part of the sensibility, and that our feelings are also not without connection to cleverness and stupidity. This stupidity is to be contested by means of example and criticism.

The point of view represented here deviates from the usual opinion, which is by no means false but extremely one-sided, according to which a profound, genuine sensibility does not need the understanding, indeed is only contaminated by it. The truth is that in simple people certain worthwhile qualities such as loyalty, constancy, purity of feeling, and others like them appear unalloyed, but only because competition from the other qualities is weak; we saw a borderline case of this earlier in the image of amicably assenting feeblemindedness. Nothing could be further from my purpose than wanting to humble the good, upstanding mind with these arguments—the absence of this kind of mind even has an appropriate share in the higher stupidity!—but today it is even more important to place the concept of what is significant ahead of the upstanding mind; I will mention this concept only in the most utopian way.

The significant unites the truth we are able to perceive in it with qualities of the feelings that give us confidence for something new: for an insight, but also a resolve, for fresh perseverance, for whatever has both intellectual *and* emotional content and "presumes" a certain kind of conduct in ourselves or in others; this is the way it could be put; and what is most important in connection with stupidity is that the significant is accessible to criticism's understanding aspect as well as to its feeling aspect. The significant is also the opposite of both stupidity and brutality, and the general disproportion in which, today, emotions crush reason instead of inspiring it also merges with the notion of the significant. Enough about this, indeed perhaps already more than one might be able to answer for! For if anything still needs to be added, it could only be one thing, that with all I have said I have not indicated any reliable sign by which what is significant could in any way be recognized and distinguished, and that it would probably not be at all easy to give a sign that would be quite adequate. Precisely that, however, leads us to the final and most important weapon against stupidity: modesty.

Occasionally we are all stupid; occasionally we must also act blindly or half blindly, or else the world would stand still; and if someone were to try to derive a rule from the dangers of stupidity that would run, "Withhold judgment and resolution in everything you don't know enough about," we would all be paralyzed. But this situation, which is creating quite a stir today, is similar to one long familiar to us in the domain of understanding. For because our knowledge and ability are incomplete, we are forced in every field to judge prematurely; but we make the effort, and have learned to keep this error within recognized limits and occasionally improve on it, and by this means put our activity back on the right track. There is really no reason why this exact and proudly humble judgment and activity could not be carried over into other areas as well, and I believe that the principle, "Act as well as you can and as badly as you must, but in doing so remain aware of the margin of error of your actions!" would already be halfway toward a promising arrangement of life.

But with these indications I have already some time ago come to the end of my explanations, which, as I set out by way of apology at the beginning, are intended only as a preliminary study. And with my foot on the borderline I declare myself in no position to go further; for one step beyond the point at which we are stopping and we would leave the realm of stupidity, which even theoretically has an extraordinary variety, and would arrive in the realm of wisdom, a desolate region that is generally shunned.

APPENDIX A

These are sketches for an introduction to a collection of his essays that Musil planned, presumably between 1921 and 1923, a project that never materialized. They are taken from his diaries (Tagebücher, ed. Adolf Frisé, Reinbek: Rowohlt, 1976, 663–68).

Whenever in this introduction—or in what follows—the term *I* is used, it does not mean the private person of the writer; nor is it an invented *I* as in a novel. What is important for me is not the interrelationships of ideas and feelings that present themselves for discussion as they occur in one person, and therefore not in my person either, but only their interrelationships among themselves.

But I am not in a position to make this into a philosophy. The materials I have before me are fragments. Perhaps one can feel the whole to which they *could* belong, and perhaps one piece might be taken in a suggestive way as continuing another; but I am forced to fill out what lies between them with "I believe," "I state," "I want." I can only speak imaginatively, not in realities: therefore it is I who speak and not the matter itself.

This would, of course, be easy to dismiss in a time like ours. What Hume wrote nearly two hundred years ago in the introduction to his *Treatise of Human Nature* sounds strangely contemporary:

Disputes are multiplied, as if everything was uncertain, and these disputes are managed with the greatest warmth, as if everything was certain. Amidst all this bustle, it is not reason which carries the prize, but eloquence; and no man needs ever despair of gaining proselytes to the most extravagant hypothesis, who has art enough to represent it in any favourable colors. The victory is not gained by the men at arms, who manage the pike and the sword, but by the trumpeters, drummers, and musicians of the army.[52]

So in a time like ours one could casually posit what one is ignorant of as objective truth, and if this were done with an elegant wave of the hand could count on greater success than someone who is hesitant. Since we have in Germany, on the other hand, the ideal of a professional philosophy written for professional philosophers, which holds itself aloof from contact with the gloriously gossipy joys and sorrows of life, one cannot even take it entirely amiss that alongside it a kind of newspaper and magazine philosophy has sprung up, a philosophy of "the most flattering light" in which, juggled by literary hands, pretty much everything flies around that can be shaken out of the volumes of an international library of philosophy if you cut open their spines. I will have occasion to speak of this later, but for now suffice it to say that it can be more modest to speak about oneself than about ideas.

But if the connections of ideas among themselves are not entirely satisfactory, and if the connection in the person of the author is rejected—that kind of personal trumpeting and indirect sketching of an interesting author—what remains is a connection that is neither subjective nor objective, but could well be both: a *possible* image of the world, a *possible* person, and it is both of these that I am seeking. The things I say become my mistakes and, so long as I am not a fool, have my good qualities; but it should depend on the objective connection, not on this personal variation. But where the connection within the object itself is not firm enough, the personal connection that has formed will peek out; but then it ought to expand in a utopian direction, and sketch a picture not of what the author is, but of what he loves. "I love something" contains as much of the self's subjectivity as of the something's objectivity! One can think in this manner, and it doesn't need to be either a personal thought that is part of my self, or an entirely impersonal thought to which is ascribed the impersonality of truth.

In my opinion these are the thoughts with which essays are written.

I have been asked to publish those of mine that have appeared in scattered fashion over a period of ten years in various liter[ary] periodicals. I have not been able to make up my mind to do so, because I feel entirely too much how some common denominator that is beneath their surface was shaped by the occasion that was foisted upon me when I really did not feel I was ready to write: what was really important to me was always contained in what was incidental to the subject.

Today I am attempting to place what is important to me in the context in which it belongs. I know that this will only succeed in a suggestive way, and my aim is to do no more than add up much that I have written and determine the "balance brought forward." I'm no philosopher, I'm not even an essayist, but a writer of serious literature; for years, however, I have been involved in the battle of minds, or whatever it should be called in Germany, and since I have attracted some notice I assume that the ideas I want to give an account of, and the compulsion to think them, are not mine alone.

I confess that however much I am convinced that personal accomplishment signifies a barely perceptible alteration in the intellectual capital one takes over from others, I also believe just as strongly that this is true not only of what one owes to the great traditions, but also of what one absorbs with every breath, so much have I felt myself all my life to be an outsider in contemporary Germany, and I know that within present-day literature I am also attacked as something alien, misunderstood, or underestimated. For that reason this book is also a polemic, although I am not attacking any names, but conditions.

The rule "Create, artist, don't talk" is not only an aesthetic but also a shrewd political admonition. The motto "Here I stand and could neither go further nor act differently" has in the last few years rather exposed many confessional writers, and I am convinced that I too will not be able to keep from showing some damage.

I hope that I will not lack for sympathy.

.   .

Another possibility: leave the essays as they are and comment on them.

I have often been asked to publish these essays, but I have consistently refused. I really don't like the man who wrote them. He gives the impression of being a man who always did and wrote something other than what he wanted. All his essays have something occasional and inopportune about them. It seems he has been given the assignment of writing about a tin bathing suit, and he, who could otherwise never make up his mind to write, does so because he has been invited to; but he uses the occasion to slip in something or other about the things he can never make up his mind to write about. Nor does it happen any differently if he is asked to write about such an important problem as the fate of his country. He starts off, and one feels: here is a person with something to say; but before long the matter is speaking. He gets into sociological or social-philosophical ideas. They are not without originality, but are the opposite of the "shorter writings" of scholars: beginnings, stubs. Many of these ideas might be worth developing, but then they would become a book, a work of several years, and altogether the work of a lifetime. One feels: that's not what he wanted; he only wrote it because no one else did. There is something unproven in this person's attitude, but a compulsion to reach again and again for the means of proof. What does this mean? Again and again he pulls back to himself with some force what is moving out into the objective sphere. The conclusion is inescapable: behind this game of struggling with the impersonal, behind this wanting to be expressed but not to express oneself, lies something personal. One might call it an intellectual imagination. But not only the initial stage of scientific activity, the dissemination of insights, but also the ultimate stage of artistic activity, the formal binding into a unity. These stand in a certain contradiction to one another but have a shadowy way of belonging together.

Finally, the determining factor for me was the interest in what would really emerge. So I have done what one does in preparing any immanent criticism: taken the individual studies apart and placed the subjects that belong together in the appropriate context. I seemed to have a very clear notion that certain connections run through the whole, but they are often subterranean, and it is not impossible that I have sometimes suppressed the more important things. Therefore I indicate the sources where the originals are to be found, in case anyone is interested in looking for them, which, frankly, I do not anticipate. I have made myself a picture of the person and his situation in his time, and I act accordingly; somewhat capriciously, to be sure, but with the aim of rousing interest in the imperfect person through rousing the interest that an age deeply stamped by its peculiarities deserves.

For the expressions of what I am publishing are indeed everywhere quite imperfect. But they—or I, or the time?—have the peculiarity of apparently not yet allowing themselves to achieve perfection. Thus forced to be modest, I have cited as much as possible according to the original text, and merely spun out the little that I, as an older person today, have added to my knowledge since. I have also cited the original texts so extensively because, as we know, ideas of this sort do not let themselves be torn from their contexts without undergoing change. As they are they form a whole; and the length of a nose depends on the face it belongs to. One cannot grasp such assertions with one's hands: one must look them in the face. Since it is not seldom a face that seems to me immature, especially in the youthful pieces, I have tried, along with the division by subject, to preserve a kind of biographical connection. My intention is to give a kind of biogram, the line of development of certain ideas through a young life, or perhaps only the line by which they were approached. Where I have been able I have also indicated the direction in which this would necessarily lead.

I need hardly say that I am publishing the work of a dead man. It will be evident that according to his own definition he was already dead when he wrote many of his ideas down.

. .

Outsider: explanation of the title.

Could really stand at the head of my collected works, so that what I am writing here is only a part of my efforts.

Feeling when I was young that the givens of life went far beyond the concepts of my elders.

This youthful feeling has stayed with me. What I have seen of more recent young people seems to me rather to vary the ways of thinking of the older folks than to correspond to the new facts. I have the feeling of living in an effete, eclectic, and uncreative time. (Better than cursing opponents!)

Think of those who also want a different kind of man, revolutionary man. In many respects grateful for their holy zeal, but they believe the new man is merely an old one who needs to be liberated.

APPENDIX B

Dates of First Publication

Volume and page numbers at the end of each entry refer to Robert Musil, *Gesammelte Werke in neun Bänden*, ed. Adolf Frisé (Reinbek: Rowohlt, 1978), on which the translation is based. Titles in square brackets are translations of titles furnished by the editor of the German edition.

Address at the Memorial Service for Rilke in Berlin (Rede zur Rilke-Feier in Berlin). Berlin: Rowohlt, 1927. 8 : 1229–42.
Anschluss with Germany (Der Anschluss an Deutschland). *Die neue Rundschau*, Mar. 1919. 8 : 1033–42.
Buridan's Austrian (Buridans Österreicher). *Der Friede*, Feb. 14, 1919. 8 : 1030–32.
Cinema or Theater (Kino oder Theater). *Magdeburgische Zeitung*, Dec. 25, 1926. 9 : 1717–19.
Commentary on a Metapsychics (Anmerkung zu einer Metapsychik). *Die neue Rundschau*, Apr. 1914. 8 : 1015–19.
The German as Symptom (Der deutsche Mensch als Symptom). Published in part by Elisabeth Albertsen and Karl Corino, under the same title. Reinbek: Rowohlt, 1967. Complete text, 8 : 1353–1400.
The Goals of Literature (Die Ziele der Dichtkunst). 8 : 1330–31.
Helpless Europe (Das hilflose Europa). *Ganymed*, Jahrbuch für die Kunst, ed. Julius Meier-Graefe, vol. 4. Munich, 1922. 8 : 1075–94.
[Lecture. Paris] (Vortrag in Paris). In *Tagebücher, Aphorismen, Essays, und Reden* (*Gesammelte Werke*, vol. 2). Reinbek: Rowohlt, 1955. 8 : 1259–65.

Literary Chronicle (Literarische Kronik). In Marie-Louise Roth, *Robert Musil: Ethik und Ästhetik*. Munich: Paul List, 1972. 8 : 1338–40.

Literati and Literature (Literat und Literatur). *Die neue Rundschau*, Sept. 1931. 8 : 1203–25.

The Mathematical Man (Der mathematische Mensch). *Der lose Vogel*, no. 10–12, Apr.–June 1913 (unsigned). 8 : 1004–8.

Mind and Experience (Geist und Erfahrung). *Der neue Merkur*, Mar. 1921. 8 : 1042–59.

Moral Fruitfulness (Moralische Fruchtbarkeit). *Der lose Vogel*, no. 8–9, Feb.–Mar. 1913 (unsigned). 8 : 1002–4.

"Nation" as Ideal and as Reality (Die Nation als Ideal und als Wirklichkeit). *Die neue Rundschau*, Dec. 1921. 8 : 1059–75.

Novellas (Novellen). In Karl Corino, *Robert Musils "Vereinigungen": Studien zu einer historisch-kritischen Ausgabe*. Munich: Fink, 1974. 8 : 1314–15.

The Obscene and Pathological in Art (Das Unanständige und Kranke in der Kunst). *Pan*, Mar. 1, 1911. 8 : 977–83.

[On Criticism] (Über Kritik). 8 : 1331–34.

On Robert Musil's Books (Über Robert Musils Bücher). *Der lose Vogel*, no. 7, Jan. 1913 (unsigned). 8 : 995–1001.

On Stupidity (Über die Dummheit). Monograph in "Ausblicke" series. Vienna: Bermann-Fischer, 1937. 8 : 1270–91.

[On the Essay] (Über den Essay). 8 : 1334–37.

Political Confessions of a Young Man (Politisches Bekenntnis eines jungen Mannes). *Die weissen Blätter*, Nov. 1913. 8 : 1009–15.

Politics in Austria (Politik in Österreich). *Der lose Vogel*, no. 6, Dec. 1912 (unsigned). 8 : 992–95.

Profile of a Program (Profil eines Programms). In Karl Corino, *Robert Musils "Vereinigungen": Studien zu einer historisch-kritischen Ausgabe*. Munich: Fink, 1974. 8 : 1315–22.

[Psychology and Literature] (Psychologie und Literatur). 8 : 1345–47.

The Religious Spirit, Modernism, and Metaphysics (Das Geistliche, der Modernismus, und die Metaphysik). *Der lose Vogel*, no. 2, Feb. 1912 (unsigned). 8 : 987–92.

Ruminations of a Slow-witted Mind (Bedenken eines Langsamen). Published partially in *Tagebücher, Aphorismen, Essays, und Reden* (*Gesammelte Werke*, vol. 2). Reinbek: Rowohlt, 1955. Complete text, 8 : 1413–35.

The Serious Writer in Our Time (Der Dichter in dieser Zeit). In *Tagebücher, Aphorismen, Essays, und Reden* (*Gesammelte Werke*, vol. 2). Reinbek: Rowohlt, 1955. 8 : 1243–58.

Sketch of What the Writer Knows (Skizze der Erkenntnis des Dichters). *Summa*, 1918. 8 : 1025–30.

Toward a New Aesthetic (Ansätze zu neuer Ästhetik). *Der neue Merkur*, Mar. 1925. 8 : 1137–54.

Woman Yesterday and Tomorrow (Die Frau gestern und morgen). In *Die Frau von Morgen wie wir sie wünschen*, ed. Friedrich M. Huebner. Leipzig: Seemann, 1929. Also published in the newspaper *Prager Presse*, July 12, 1931. 8 : 1193–99.

NOTES

1. Ernst Mach (1838–1916) was an Austrian physicist and philosopher of science whose critique of Newtonian physics prepared the way for Einstein's theory of relativity. Hendrik Antoon Lorentz (1853–1928), Dutch physicist and winner of the Nobel Prize in 1902, contributed to electron theory and relativity. Hermann Minkowski (1864–1909), German mathematician, helped develop the implications of the relativity principle formulated by Lorentz and Einstein. Louis Couturat (1868–1914) was a French logician, linguist, and Leibniz scholar. Giuseppe Peano (1858–1932), Italian mathematician and logician, was influential at the turn of the century.

2. *The Confusions of Young Törless* is Musil's first novel, published in 1906; *Unions* was his first collection of stories, published 1911.

3. Julius Robert von Mayer (1814–78) was a German physicist whom Musil regarded as a martyr and one of the finest minds of the nineteenth century. Although an outsider to the professional scientific community, Mayer was one of the early formulators of the principle of the conservation of energy.

4. *Die Aktion* was an Expressionist left-wing journal concerned with rallying intellectuals and with the cultural struggle throughout German-speaking central Europe. It was close to Musil's own political sentiments, though more radical; it resisted identification with any specific party or ideology and expressed a militant humanism that was critical of the pseudoliberal press. *Die neue Rundschau*, published by Samuel Fischer in Berlin, set the highest standards of intellectual life and debate; it was at the center of intellectual developments before 1914 and remained one of the most important literary journals during the 1920s. Musil wrote for both these German journals but not for *Die neue freie Presse* (1864–1939), a liberal Viennese daily oriented toward the German-speaking elites in the Dual Monarchy.

5. Franz Blei (1871–1942), Austrian writer and editor, helped establish Musil in the German literary world before 1914. He remained a good friend and a writer

Musil admired. Musil wrote a number of his prewar essays for Blei's journal *Der lose Vogel*. Karl Kraus (1874–1936) was a satirist and the editor and principal author of the journal *Die Fackel*, which criticized the Habsburg Monarchy and the liberal establishment.

6. Herbert Eulenberg (1876–1949) was an important Expressionist writer before the First World War.

7. Maurice Maeterlinck (1862–1949), Belgian symbolist writer, strongly influenced the change in German literature from naturalism to a more psychological and mystic orientation. Musil was particularly influenced by Maeterlinck's view of the limits of language in expressing inwardness.

8. The voice of German Protestantism to the Romantic and idealistic intellectuals of the early nineteenth century, Friedrich Schleiermacher (1768–1834) developed a theology for a more emotional style of religion quite different from that of the *Aufklärung*, the German Enlightenment. Friedrich Wilhelm Josef von Schelling (1775–1854) was an idealist philosopher and contemporary of Hegel. Ferdinand Lassalle (1825–64), German socialist and contemporary of Bismarck, founded the General German Workers' Union in 1863. His social monarchism was strongly influenced by Hegel's view of the state. (In 1875 Lassallians and Marxists united to found the Social Democratic Party.)

9. Walther Rathenau (1867–1922), the model for Paul Arnheim in *The Man without Qualities*, was a wealthy industrialist who was in charge of supplying raw materials for Germany during the First World War. After the war he helped found the German Democratic Party and served briefly as Foreign Minister of the Weimar Republic until his assassination by nationalists. Rathenau was also a writer concerned with synthesizing spiritual and cultural values.

10. Rudolf Eucken (1846–1926), German neo-idealist philosopher, won the Nobel Prize for Literature in 1908.

11. Hermann Bahr (1863–1934) was a leading figure of "Young Vienna," the Austrian literary avant-garde of the 1890s, and a writer and journalist of high intelligence and somewhat trendy susceptibilities.

12. "Ein-Falt," literally "one-fold," or "sim-plex." *Einfalt* is the German word for "simplicity."

13. Heinrich Zille (1858–1929) was a naturalist urban artist and social critic during the Second Reich. Elise was the pseudonym of the German writer Helene von Rüts (1833–68).

14. Kasimir Edschmid (1890–1966) was an Expressionist writer.

15. Musil is apparently referring here to Wilhelm von Scholz (1874–1969), president of the Writers' Academy from 1926 to 1928.

16. These right-wing intellectuals were prominent in the conservative cultural revolution in Germany after 1890 and helped make Hitler's Germanic ideology acceptable to many educated Germans. Houston Stewart Chamberlain (1855–1927), Richard Wagner's son-in-law, was an influential figure in Germany and Austria before the First World War; his conservative critique of culture gave respectability to anti-Semitism, racism, and Germanic ideology. Chamberlain was a friend of

Wilhelm II and an admirer of Hitler; his most important book was *Die Grundlagen des neunzehnten Jahrhunderts* (The foundations of the nineteenth century, 1899). "Rembrandt German" refers to Julius Langbehn's *Rembrandt als Erzieher* (Rembrandt as educator, 1890), which had a powerful influence on German cultural conservatives (see Fritz Stern's *The Politics of Cultural Despair*, Berkeley: University of California Press, 1961). Langbehn (1851–1907) represented an irrationalist idealism that sought to preserve traditional values in the face of modernization. His attack on science and modern culture in the name of art was anti-Semitic and antiliberal and advocated the creation of a new Germanic elite through a nationally-minded literature and art. Felix Dahn (1834–1912) was a scholar of German antiquity best known for historical novels idealizing the German past.

17. The *grossdeutsch* idea was a conception of German unification that included Austria as well as Prussia and the smaller German states. The *kleindeutsch* idea was a conception of unification with Austria excluded from Germany, along the lines of what Bismarck actually achieved in 1871.

18. *Protektion* is the distinctively Austrian term for "old-boy network," i.e., a system of personal patronage and connections. It played a decisive role in bureaucratic appointments in Austria.

19. Richard Kralik, Ritter von Meyrswalden (1852–1934), was an Austrian Catholic writer. Ottokar Kernstock (1848–1928) was a patriotic Austrian writer and author of the Austrian nationalist anthem used in the authoritarian Catholic-corporatist regime of Engelbert Dollfuss and Kurt von Schuschnigg during the 1930s.

20. Hjalmar Ekdal is the weak and hapless protagonist in Ibsen's *The Wild Duck*.

21. A leading figure of Germanic ideology in the nineteenth century, Paul de Lagarde (1827–91) was antiliberal, anti-Semitic, and critical of Bismarck's *kleindeutsch* solution.

22. Jakob Wassermann, *Mein Weg als Deutscher und Jude* (Berlin, 1921).

23. Walter Bloem (1868–1951) was an advocate of nationalist literature between the wars. Carl Hilty (1833–1909), Swiss philosopher, advocated a Christian humanism.

24. Anton Wildgans (1881–1932) was an Austrian playwright whom Musil considered mediocre; he found it especially offensive that Austrians regarded Wildgans as a great writer while largely ignoring Musil.

25. Friedrich Hebbel (1813–63) was a German writer of highly intellectual plays who settled in Vienna in the 1840s. He was often regarded as an Austrian writer.

26. Wolfgang Köhler (1887–1967) was cofounder of the Berlin school of Gestalt psychology. Musil is here referring to *Die physischen Gestalten in Ruhe und im stationären Zustand* (Erlangen: Philosophische Akademie, 1924).

27. Rudolf Steiner (1861–1925) was the founder of Anthroposophy.

28. Ernst Robert Curtius, *Syndikalismus der Geistesarbeiter in Frankreich* (Bonn: F. Cohen, 1921).

29. Walter Strich (1882–1963), author of an essay Musil admired, "Der Fluch

des objektiven Geistes" (The curse of the objective spirit), *Der neue Merkur*, 3. Jhrg., no. 7, 1919/20.

30. Caspar (or Kaspar) von Schwenckfeld von Ossig (1489–1561), Sebastian Franck (c. 1499–c. 1542), and Valentin Weigel (1533–88) were major figures in the tradition of German Lutheran mysticism and pietism.

31. Rudolf Kassner (1873–1959) was one of the great Austrian essayists of Musil's generation and one of the first important writers to draw attention to Kierkegaard.

32. "Sketch of What the Writer Knows."

33. Samuel Fischer (1859–1934) was the leading literary publisher of Weimar Germany; before the First World War he helped establish Musil as a writer and hired him as an editor of *Die neue Rundschau*.

34. The reference is to *Summa*, 1918, and "Sketch of What the Writer Knows."

35. The School of Chartres was the most important intellectual center of the twelfth-century revival of learning. This French cathedral school emphasized the union of Christian faith with classical literary culture.

36. Alexander von Humboldt (1769–1859), geographer and botanist, was known for his scientific work and the account of his expedition to South America, to which Musil is referring here.

37. Wilhelm von Humboldt (1767–1835), German humanist, founded the University of Berlin. Musil is here confusing him with his brother Alexander.

38. Leo Frobenius (1873–1938) was a German explorer and cultural anthropologist.

39. Paul Heyse (1830–1914) was a German writer highly regarded by the *Bürgertum* in the late nineteenth century but ridiculed by the writers of Musil's generation. He won the Nobel Prize in 1910.

40. Anselm of Canterbury was an eleventh-century theologian (d. 1109) whose attempt to balance the claims of reason and faith prepared the way for the accomplishments of Scholasticism.

41. Arne Garborg (1851–1924) was a Norwegian writer and social reformer. Jens Peter Jacobsen (1847–85) was an important Danish writer who had a strong influence on Rilke and Thomas Mann. Georg Brandes (1842–1927) was a Danish critic and the leading figure in the "modern breakthrough" in Scandinavian literature in the late nineteenth century. Brandes was also a major European critic, influenced by Mill and Taine as well as by Kierkegaard and Nietzsche.

42. An Italian economist whose work on value theory anticipated Marx, Ferdinando Galiani (1728–87) was one of the finest minds of the Italian Enlightenment.

43. Verlag der Marées Gesellschaft was the Marées Society Publishers in Munich.

44. Peter Altenberg (1859–1919) was a Viennese impressionist and aphorist and a representative figure of "Young Vienna" and of café intellectuals during the 1890s. Hermann Stehr (1864–1940) was a writer, mystic, and Silesian *Heimatdichter*. Jakob Wassermann (1873–1934), writer, was for a time on the staff of *Simplicissimus* in Munich and a regular contributor to *Die neue Rundschau*. Stefan

George (1868–1933) was one of the most important lyric poets of prewar Germany and was strongly influenced by Nietzsche. Joseph Roth (1894–1939) wrote *Radetzkymarsch* (Radetzky march) [Berlin: G. Kiepenhauer, 1932], a nostalgic novel portraying Habsburg Austria under Franz Joseph. Otto Flake (1880–1965) was a novelist influenced by Expressionism. Rudolf Borchardt (1877–1945) was a member of the George circle and a friend of Hugo von Hofmannsthal.

45. Ernst Jünger (1895–) was a right-wing intellectual and irrationalist author who idealized the soldier and the experience of war. Hans Blüher (1888–1955) was a member of the German Youth Movement in the 1890s and later its historian, and a leading figure in conservative intellectual circles during the 1920s. Like the Youth Movement as a whole, Blüher was strongly influenced by Langbehn and the idea of the Rembrandt-German.

46. "Literature of the soil." Musil uses the term for a clump or clod of dirt, *Scholle,* to refer derisively to the "literature of blood and soil" (*Blut- und Bodenliteratur*), an antiurban, anticosmopolitan movement in the German literature of the time, which advocated nationalist rural fiction and was often associated with anti-Semitism.

47. Ludwig Fulda (1862–1939) was the dramatist who, along with Thomas Mann and Hermann Stehr, founded the literary section of the Prussian Academy of the Arts. Musil's contemptuous opinion of him was widely shared.

48. Theodor Däubler (1876–1934) was a lyric poet, Expressionist, and Dadaist.

49. Richard Dehmel (1863–1920), lyric poet, became an enthusiastic patriot in the First World War; a thinker in the tradition of Schopenhauer and Nietzsche, Dehmel regarded will rather than intellect as the essence of human experience.

50. In 1837, when the new king of Hanover abrogated the constitution under which English kings had ruled Hanover for more than a century, seven professors at the University of Göttingen protested and were dismissed from their positions. They became a symbol of liberalism, civic courage, and academic freedom.

51. Robert Hamerling (1830–89) was an advocate of Austrian philosophy against German idealism and was strongly influenced by Herbart and Leibniz.

52. Cited from the English original; Musil used a German translation.